CRIME AND SCHIZOPHRENIA: CAUSES AND CURES

CRIME AND SCHIZOPHRENIA: CAUSES AND CURES

ADRIAN RAINE
EDITOR

Nova Science Publishers, Inc.
New York

For permission to use material from this book please contact us:
Telephone 631-231-7269; Fax 631-231-8175
Web Site: http://www.novapublishers.com

LIBRARY OF CONGRESS CATALOGING-IN-PUBLICATION DATA

Crime and Schizophrenia: Causes and Cures / Adrian Raine (Editor)
p. ; cm.
Includes bibliographical references and index.
ISBN 1-59454-609-6
1. Schizophrenia. I. Raine, Adrian
[DNLM: 1. Schizophrenic Psychology. 2. Schizophrenia--etiology.
3. Schizophrenia--classification. 4. Crime--psychology. 5. Crime
--prevention & control. WM 203 C929 2005]
RC514.C755 2005
616.89'8--dc22 2005023126

Published by Nova Science Publishers, Inc. ✢New York

DEDICATION

This book is dedicated to Sarnoff A. Mednick (left) and Peter H. Venables (right) for their lifelong distinguished scientific contributions to furthering our understanding of schizophrenia and criminal behavior.

CONTENTS

PREFACE

While the link between crime and schizophrenia has been noted for almost a century, it is only recently that research has provided convincing, broad-based evidence for this association. This advance in knowledge also brings with it the troublesome danger that schizophrenia patients could be doubly-stigmatized in society: they suffer from a serious mental illness and furthermore they are potentially dangerous. This understandable fear has lead to significant resistance in accepting that the crime – schizophrenia relationship truly exists.

While well-meaning, this resistance has resulted in three unfortunate consequences. First, by not recognizing that the relationship exists, the comorbid antisocial and violent behavior of schizophrenia patients has gone unchecked, and consequently the stigma associated with this comorbidity goes on unabated. Second, research in this area has become almost fixated on the simple establishment of a link between the two conditions, and has not moved on to more important research that could help develop new perspectives on the nature of the crime – schizophrenia relationship in a way which will significantly benefit our understanding and treatment of both conditions. Frustratingly, we actually know surprisingly little about the crime – schizophrenia relationship. The third and more indirect consequence is that the issue of schizophrenia-spectrum disorder in antisocial and criminal populations is almost entirely ignored. Such individuals literally fall between the cracks in both the mental health system and the criminal justice system. For these reasons, it is argued that ignoring or denying the crime – schizophrenia relationship ultimately does more harm than good.

The main goal of this book is to stimulate a new generation of research on the crime – schizophrenia relationship which could benefit not just individuals with these two conditions, but also society in general. Going beyond the fundamental issue of whether there is a relationship between crime and schizophrenia, contributors to this book both outline risk factors for crime and schizophrenia and also develop hypotheses on which factors may give rise to both conditions, and hence in part explain the comorbidity issue. Furthermore, contributors go on to outline intervention and prevention programs for not just crime and schizophrenia, but also for both conditions simultaneously.

Another goal of this book is to honor the work of two senior scientists who have contributed in major ways to crime and schizophrenia research. The first, Sarnoff Mednick, has conduct decades of innovative, creative research on the etiology of schizophrenia. He was instrumental in generating the high-risk design for schizophrenia whereby the offspring of schizophrenics are assessed longitudinally in order to investigate early processes that predict and explain breakdown for schizophrenia. This innovative design has yielded breakthrough scientific information on the etiology of schizophrenia. His landmark contributions to schizophrenia research in the areas of neurodevelopment and psychophysiology will be reflected in many of the following chapters. Yet a remarkable feature of Mednick's career is that in addition to his novel and innovative research work on schizophrenia, he has also conducted pioneering research on criminal behavior. In 1984 he published findings from an adoption study demonstrating beyond reasonable doubt that there was a clear genetic basis to criminal behavior. This landmark study set the research landscape for a plethoria of behavioral and molecular genetic studies on antisocial and aggressive behavior over the course of the next two decades which has irrevocably changed our perspective on the causes of crime. Indeed, the focus in this book on the link between crime and schizophrenia is stimulated in part by Mednick's seminal contributions to these two research areas.

The second scientist to be honored, Peter Venables, is somewhat fittingly a longstanding colleague of Mednick and has similarly conducted groundbreaking research on schizophrenia. One of the world's leading authorities on psychophysiology, perhaps Venables' most original, influential, and seminal work was his 1964 paper on input dysfunction in schizophrenia. This citation classic became critically important in shaping the field of schizophrenia research because it was the first to clearly articulate the view that schizophrenia can be viewed as a disorder of attention and arousal that manifests itself differently in different sub-types of schizophrenics. It set the stage for a whole new cognitive approach to understanding the causes of schizophrenia based on fundamental neurophysiological abnormalities, and went on to stimulated a formidable body of empirical work testing his theoretical formulations. Like Mednick, his research interests have expanded into the domain of antisocial behavior, and consequently the focus of this book on the interface between schizophrenia and crime is doubly relevant.

Together, in 1972 these two scientists, together with Fini Schulsinger, set up a longitudinal study of child health and development in Mauritius. This study of 1,795 three-year-old children represents one of the largest longitudinal examinations of carefully-collected psychophysiological data in the world. Mednick and Venables were visionary in that, more than 30 years ago, they deciding to conduct a prevention study of psychopathology. Stratified random sampling was used to allocate 100 children to an early environmental enrichment for two years. This early enrichment was found to increase psychophysiological arousal and orienting at age 11 years and to reduce both schizotypal personality and antisocial / criminal behavior at age 23 years. Their bold scientific venture was a tour-de-force in translational research that was years ahead of its time, and hinted at the possibility that schizotypy and antisocial behavior may to some extent share common origins if the same prevention program could affect both conditions.

Contributions to this volume are in part based on an international meeting held on this topic at Chateau de la Bretesche in Brittany, France in 2004, a meeting made possible by a generous grant from the Borchard Foundation. Presentations given by researchers from several different countries generated stimulating, lively, and intense discussion of a wide variety of issues pertaining to crime and schizophrenia. It is hoped that this energy will be in some way reflected in this volume, and will go some way towards stimulating a new, second generation of research on crime and schizophrenia that will go further than hitherto in delineating the causes and cures of crime and schizophrenia. From the perspective of the individuals who suffer from schizophrenia, their families, the victims of crime, and even the criminal offenders themselves, such advances are sorely needed and are long overdue.

PART 1. INTRODUCTION AND OVERVIEW

In: Crime and Schizophrenia: Causes and Cures
Editor: Adrian Raine, pp. 3-11
ISBN 1-59454-609-6

Chapter 1

PURSUING A SECOND GENERATION OF RESEARCH ON CRIME AND SCHIZOPHRENIA

Adrian Raine
Department of Psychology and Neuroscience Program,
University of Southern California

CRIME AND SCHIZOPHRENIA: A DEEP-SEATED COMMONALITY

The comorbidity between crime and schizophrenia may be surprising to some researchers and practitioners. These conditions present very differently and would appear to be very discrepant. Schizophrenics present to caregivers as clearly the victims of an illness which significantly impacts their cognitive, social, and occupational functioning and are in need of help. Criminals in contrast present to those who come into contact with them as psychologically near-normal and that it is society, not the individual, who is in need of protection. Put another way, schizophrenia patients with their reality distortion, social withdrawal, and anhedonia, are more likely viewed as having an "internalizing" disorder, while criminals with their disinhibited, rule-breaking behavior are more viewed as having an "externalizing" disorder. Furthermore, schizophrenia is viewed as a mental illness, while criminality has been viewed as a socio-legal concept.

It is argued here that these seeming wide conceptual differences at the superficial level mask a more deep-seated, fundamental commonality to these conditions. Recidivistic, criminal behavior has been construed as a clinical disorder which has its basis in relatively early genetic, biological, familial, and environmental processes (Raine, 1993). Diagnostically, criminality is almost synonymous with antisocial personality disorder in DSM-IV (American Psychiatric Association, 1994). It is also suspected that some of the early risk factors for crime are also risk factors for schizophrenia, but that the addition of other social, biological, and genetic risk factors may ultimately determine the clinical outcome path of either "schizophrenia" or "criminal".

Comorbidity between Crime and Schizophrenia

Kraepelin (1913) first noted a link between antisocial, psychopathic behavior and schizophrenia. Since then there is now recent, incontrovertible scientific evidence for a significant relationship between crime and schizophrenia. This relationship can be viewed from two perspectives. From the first perspective, if the study population consists of criminals or juvenile delinquents, they are found to have much higher rates of psychosis and schizophrenia than the general population (Eronen, Hakola, and Tiihonen, 1996; Gosden, Kramp, Gabrielsen, and Sestoft, 2003; Lewis, Yeager, Gidlow, and Lewis, 2001; Eronen et al., 1996; Arseneault, Cannon, et al. 2003). From the second perspective, flipping the direction of effects around, if the study group consists of patients with schizophrenia, multiple studies have shown that such patients are more criminal and violent than the general population (Tiihonen, Isohanni, Rasanen, Koiranen, and Moring, 1997; Brennan, Mednick, and Hodgins, 2000; Modestin and Ammann, 1996; Brekke, Prindle, Bae, and Long, 2001; Volavka, Laska, Baker, and Meisner, 1997; Wessely, 1997; Soyka and Ufer, 2002; Mullen, Burgess, Wallace, Palmer, and Ruschena, 2000; Hodgins, Mednick, Brennan, Schulsinger, and Engberg, 1996; Volavka et al., 1997; Rasanen et al., 1998).

This latter linkage has received substantive support from two different study designs. Follow-back studies of schizophrenics have found evidence of increased antisocial behavior in adolescence (Watt and Lubensky, 1976). Similarly, prospective longitudinal studies have similarly found increased antisocial and aggressive behavior during adolescence to be predictive of later breakdown for schizophrenia (Cannon, Mednick, and Parnas, 1990). The increased antisocial behavior in schizophrenics is neither confined to trivial antisocial behavior nor is the relationship weak; Eronen et al. (1996) found that male schizophrenia patients were eight times more likely to commit homicide, while female schizophrenics were 6.5 times more likely to commit homicide than controls. Schizophrenia patients are not just aggressive in the community, they are also more aggressive in hospitals; Steinert, Wiebe, and Gebhardt (1999) observed that 75% of male and 53% of female schizophrenics exhibit some form of aggressive behavior during hospitalization. Increased antisocial behavior is not an artifact of selective arrest of schizophrenia patients; Link, Andrews and Cullen (1992) found increased antisocial behavior on self-report as well as official conviction measures of crime which could not be accounted for by community confounds.

Clearly, the comorbidity between crime and schizophrenia cannot be easily dismissed. Large-scale epidemiological studies from many countries around the world now attest to the facts that schizophrenia patients are more likely than control groups to have a history of violent and criminal behavior, and furthermore that delinquent and criminal populations are more likely to show psychotic disorders including schizophrenia (see also Brennan and Alden, 2006). The fact that the large majority of findings have been reported in the past decade attests to the recent sea-change in opinion that has occurred in scientific opinion on this issue.

The Stigmatization Issue

Despite the links drawn between crime and schizophrenia early in the 20th century, historically an association between these disorders has been vigorously denied, particularly by practitioners and family members for understandable reasons. The stigma of having a serious mental disorder is hard enough for the patient and family members to bear, let alone having to deal with the additional significant stigma of criminality. The media also plays a significant role in exaggerating the link between schizophrenia and violence, with consequent negative social impact on all patients with schizophrenia. As but one example, following the violent attack on some German politicians in 1990 by two individuals with schizophrenia which was prominently featured in the media, population surveys documented a significant increase in social distancing of the general public from schizophrenia patients who were viewed as "dangerous" and "unpredictable" (Angermeyer and Matschinger, 1996). Clearly, the danger of stigma is both clear and important.

Despite the recent, strong scientific evidence for a significant link between crime / violence and schizophrenia, opponents to these data have argued that recognizing the schizophrenia – crime link will do more harm than good. In countering the view that schizophrenia patients are no more dangerous than the general public, Torrey (1994) argues persuasively that by denying the link, mental health advocates inadvertently do more harm than good. He argues that until the link with violence is acknowledged, serious attempts to tackle the problem will not be implemented, resulting in continuation of higher violence rates in schizophrenia patients with the consequent continued stigma. Torrey's argument is telling and persuasive. It is clear that to reduce the incidence of violence and crime in schizophrenia populations, we need to be much more proactive in both recognizing that the relationship exists, and developing a stronger knowledge-base on etiological processes that might be remediated. Such remediation attempts could then help significantly reduce the stigma associated with schizophrenia.

Advantages of Pursing the Crime-Schizophrenia Relationship

Despite a relative wealth of research establishing a relationship between crime and schizophrenia, we know surprisingly little about the nature of this relationship, and what implications it may have. Yet going beyond the empirical fact of this link could help develop new perspectives on the nature of the crime – schizophrenia relationship in a way which will significantly benefit our understanding and treatment of both conditions. Certainly, the fact that crime and schizophrenia are comorbid conditions has a number of implications.

At a theoretical level, it becomes clear that the conceptual frameworks we have developed for understanding the causes of both crime and schizophrenia are at the least incomplete, and at the worst misleading. Given that significant proportions of schizophrenia patients are also antisocial (and vice-versa), we need to develop new theoretical models to explain this linkage. Currently, to the author's knowledge, no theoretical models have been put forward for either disorder that incorporate the comorbidity issue. Without such new models, our explanations of crime and schizophrenia will inevitably remain incomplete and frustrate attempts to develop truly successful intervention and prevention programs.

At the empirical research level, another implication of the linkage between crime and schizophrenia is that it suggests that the two disorders may have risk factors in common. This in turn has a number of ramifications. One implication is that greater acknowledgement of this relationship would potentiate findings on both conditions. For example, there are conflicting findings on the neurobiological correlates of schizophrenia, and some of this inconsistency may be due to the fact that researchers are mixing together two quite separate groups of schizophrenia patients: those with comborbid antisocial behavior and a more "pure" group lacking this characteristic. Separating these groups may lead to stronger and more reliable effect sizes than are currently being obtained. Similarly, the correlates of antisocial behavior with concurrent schizophrenia-spectrum characteristics may be quite different to those who are "purely" antisocial, but this goes largely unrecognized. Developing a typology of both schizophrenia and crime based on the comorbid issue could significantly advance the empirical body of knowledge on both disorders.

At the inpatient treatment level, it is likely that the two subgroups of schizophrenia patients (those with and without criminal histories) are going to respond differently to treatment. Given the likelihood that there are etiological differences in their schizophrenia illness, differential responsivity of sub-groups of patients to anti-aggression medications may exist. Although some innovative studies have assessed the efficacy of different drugs in the treatment of the aggressive behavior shown by schizophrenia patients (e.g. Buckley et al., 1997; Volavka, 1999), these and other studies have not addressed the potentially important issue of differential responsivity to medication. Do those patients with a history of criminal behavior respond better or worse to such anti-aggressive treatment compared to schizophrenia patients without such a criminal history?

At a forensic level, the comorbidity of schizophrenia-spectrum disorders with criminal behavior is rarely if ever recognized with respect to the differential treatment of offenders in prison settings. With rare exceptions, it is only in more extreme cases of homicide with co-occurring schizophrenia that recognition is given to the fact that such offenders require different therapeutic intervention. In general, offenders with paranoid ideation, inappropriate / constricted affect, odd speech and behavior, and cognitive distortions are treated just the same as a psychiatrically normal offender. In essence, any comorbid schizotypal / schizoid / paranoid personality disorder is ignored in treatment terms. At the sentencing level, the role of schizophrenia-spectrum disorders in raising risk for offending is rarely if ever considered. As pointed out by Lamberti and Weisman (2004), those with schizophrenia-spectrum disorders are greatly at risk of "falling between the cracks" of on the one hand the mental health system, and on the other hand the criminal justice system. The loss lies in retarded development of programs which integrate health care and social services with the criminal justice system and which can be effective in improving community functioning and reducing recidivistic crime in mentally ill individuals with a criminal history (Lamberti et al., 2001).

In terms of respect and care for individuals with schizophrenia, loosing sight of the issue of violence can make society blind to the plight of those with this illness. Although it is true that schizophrenia patients are more likely to perpetrate criminal acts than the general population, one study of community schizophrenics found that they were 14 times more likely to be the *victims* of violence than to be arrested for committing violence (Brekke, Prindle, Bae, and Long, 2002). Greater understanding of factors which propel schizophrenia patients into a criminal career and which in turn make them vulnerable to victimization will help develop better treatment for antisocial / aggressive behavior and potentially reduce victimization. As outlined above, better understanding and remediation of aggressive behavior in schizophrenia patients is the key to reducing the stigma associated with this disorder (Torrey, 1994). In addition, one study of schizophrenia inpatients found that 17% of males and 26% of females attempted suicide within the first two years of hospitalization (Steinert et al., 1999); greater attention to aggressive behavior in schizophrenia patients may help reduce the rate of "aggression turned inwards" in these individuals.

A Second-Generation of Research on Crime and Schizophrenia

The work in the past decade in establishing an incontrovertible relationship between crime and schizophrenia has been of enormous importance. At the same time, there is a sense in which research in this field has become almost fixated on the simple establishment of this link. Crucially, it has not penetrated perhaps the more interesting questions that can be asked, questions which are critically important to answer if we are to make significant progress in reducing the burden and cost of these disorders in society. The field needs to move beyond the simple (albeit important) question of whether crime and schizophrenia are related and progress into a second generation of research which breaks into a new research territory.

It is important to emphasize that this goal is not easy. Psychiatrists and clinical psychologists alike are concerned that such a focus would increase, not decrease, stigmatization of schizophrenia patients. Perhaps more critically, there is no strong, substantive history of research in this field. Progress in this area will inevitably be slow, but the importance lies in beginning this second generation of research on crime and schizophrenia, no matter how initial. Three levels of such new research can be envisaged.

A modest beginning lies in attempting to document what the risk factors are for both crime and schizophrenia. This will lay the initial foundation for second-level attempts to identify the risk factors that are common to both disorders. This in turn will give rise to initial hypotheses as to the etiological processes that may predispose to both crime and schizophrenia which could be further tested in longitudinal studies where both clinical outcomes are assessed.

Relatedly, a second and much more ambitious level of research consists of the identification of risk factors that give rise to both disorders. To date, virtually nothing is known about this issue. Such research would be doubly invaluable if (a) it identified risk factors occurring relative early in life (b) these factors are not fixed and static, but are amenable to change.

A third level of this second-generation research on crime and schizophrenia lies in the even more ambitious task of attempting to develop intervention and prevention efforts based on findings from the prior two levels that can impact both crime and schizophrenia-spectrum disorders. This third level may be overly-ambitious at the present time, but a beginning can be made. Even documenting the current treatment and prevention attempts to ameliorate these disorders and comparing them would be a step forward. Ultimately, one could envisage targeting groups who are comorbid for both disorders for specialized intervention and treatment.

Introduction to the Current Contributions

With the above issues in mind, this book attempts to highlight the crime – schizophrenia relationship in order to at least draw further research attention to this important area. It begins with a detailed meta-analysis of the crime – schizophrenia relationship by Brennan and Alden which concludes that in adults there are medium to large effect sizes which cannot be attributed to confounds, and that the strength of the relationship may instead be significantly underestimated. McMillan and Walker extend this perspective developmentally and conceptually by assessing the links between schizotypal personality and antisocial/ aggressive behavior in adolescents, and argue for a relationship across both genders when one considers unmedicated participants.

The following section deals with documenting risk factors for crime. Moffitt and colleagues demonstrate that after controlling for genetic factors, there is still an influence of social factors on outcome for aggressive behavior in childhood; although the size of these environmental effects are substantially reduced after controlling for genetic influences, it is argued that there may be important gene x environment interactions that reinforce the importance of social factors. The focus of the contribution of Raine and colleagues similarly covers biosocial interactions, but focuses more on behavior genetics, molecular genetics, pregnancy and birth complications, neurotransmitters, environmental toxins, and neurocognition, with an emphasis on biosocial interactions. Liu and colleagues review the evidence for malnutrition as a risk factor for antisocial behavior, and provide evidence for a dose-response relationship between early postnatal malnutrition and externalizing behavior problems at ages 8, 11, and 17 years, with this relationship mediated by poor cognitive ability but not by social adversity.

The next section in turn focuses on risk factors for schizophrenia, with an emphasis on early developmental processes. Venables presents data to show that postnatal malnutrition at age 3 years is associated with schizotypy at age 17 years, a finding not mediated by either social disadvantage or cognitive ability. Krebs argues for a continuum between neurodevelopment and post-natal maturation, and emphasizes the interaction between the early environmental and early brain insults. She also presents findings suggesting that violence in schizophrenia patients may be in part due to a functional 5HTTLPR polymorphism in the serotonin transporter system.

The section on risk factors common to both crime and schizophrenia provides both new data and new theoretical models to stimulate further work on this important perspective on the crime - schizophrenia relationship. Gurion reviews the developmental processes that give rise to both schizophrenia and violence, and develops an integrative model based on the cognitive, neurobiological and neuroanatomical risk factors that are common to both conditions, with a focus on prefrontal dysfunction. Machon, Mednick and colleagues present new data showing that exposure to influenza during the sixth and seventh month of gestation results in a significant increase in convictions for violence in the offspring, whereas exposure in the sixth month is associated with an outcome for schizophrenia. They argue that the overlap in risk periods may in part account for the comorbidity between the two disorders. Neugebauer and colleagues reviews evidence indicating that prenatal malnutrition is associated with both schizophrenia and also antisocial personality disorder.

The next section deals with the treatment and prevention of crime and schizophrenia-spectrum disorders, and opens with a chapter by Raine and colleagues detailing a study which shows that early environmental enrichment from ages 3-5 years (which focuses on better nutrition, more physical exercise, and cognitive stimulation) reduces criminal behavior and schizotypal personality at ages 17 and 23 years, particularly in those with poor early nutrition. Tremblay argues that three lines of evidence (genetic, developmental, and experimental intervention) lead to the conclusion that the prevention of aggressive behavior should target early childhood. Thibaut reviews the literature on schizophrenia and deviant sexual behavior as well as the literature on testosterone and aggression, and discusses anti-androgen treatments for sex offenders and schizophrenic patients. Volavka then reviews the literature on the psychopharmacological treatment of aggression in schizophrenia patients and argues for a pharmacogenetic approach for better understanding the efficacy of some drugs in reducing aggression.

While these contributions will hopefully help advance our understanding of crime, schizophrenia, and the crime – schizophrenia relationship, they are inevitably only a beginning. It is nevertheless hoped that they will at least act as a stimulus for a new, second-generation of research on the crime – schizophrenia question that will make more significant advances in helping society better understand, and ultimately prevent, these conditions which are damaging at both individual and societal levels.

Acknowledgements

This paper was written with the support of an Independent Scientist Award from NIMH (K02 MH01114-01) and a grant from the Borchard Foundation.

References

American Psychiatric Association. (1994). *Diagnostic and statistical manual of mental disorders*. (4th ed.). Washington, D.C.: American Psychiatric Association.

Angermeyer, M. C., and Matschinger, H. (1996). The effect of violent attacks by schizophrenic persons on the attitude of the public towards the mentally ill. *Social Science and Medicine, 43*, 1721-1728.

Arseneault, L., Cannon, M, Murray, R, Poulton, R, Caspi, A, and Moffitt, T E. (2003). Childhood origins of violent behaviour in adults with schizophreniform disorders. *British Journal of Psychiatry, 183*, 520-525.

Brekke, J. S., Prindle, C, Bae, S W, and Long, J D. (2001). Risks for individuals with schizophrenia who are living in the community. *Psychiatric Services, 52*, 1358-1366.

Brekke, J. S., Prindle, C, Bae, S W, and Long, J D. (2002). Risk for individuals with schizophrenia who are living in the community - Reply. *Psychiatric Services, 53*, 485

Brennan, P. A., Mednick, S A, and Hodgins, S. (2000). Major mental disorders and criminal violence in a Danish birth cohort. *Archives of General Psychiatry, 57*, 494-500.

Brennan, P. A., Alden, A. (2006). Schizophrenia and violence: The overlap. In A. Raine (ed). *Crime and schizophrenia: Causes and cures*. Hauppauge, NY: Nova.

Buckley, P. F., Ibrahim, Z Y, Singer, B, Orr, B, Donenwirth, K, and Brar, P S. (1997). Aggression and schizophrenia: Efficacy of risperidone. *Journal of the American Academy of Psychiatry and the Law, 25*, 173-181.

Cannon, T. D., Mednick, S A, and Parnas, J. (1990). Antecedents of predominantly negative- and predominantly positive-symptom schizophrenia in a high-risk population. *Archives of General Psychiatry, 47*, 622-632.

Eronen, M., Hakola, P, and Tiihonen, J. (1996). Mental disorders and homicidal behavior in Finland. *Archives of General Psychiatry, 53*, 497-501.

Gosden, N. P., Kramp, P, Gabrielsen, G, and Sestoft, D. (2003). Prevalence of mental disorders among 15-17-year-old male adolescent remand prisoners in Denmark. *Acta Psychiatrica Scandinavica, 107*, 102-110.

Hodgins, S., Mednick, S A, Brennan, P A, Schulsinger, F, and Engberg, M. (1996). Mental disorder and crime - Evidence from a Danish birth cohort. *Archives of General Psychiatry, 53*, 489-496.

Kraepelin, E. (1913). *Psychiatrie*. (8th ed.). Leipzig: Barth.

Lamberti, J. S., and Weisman, R L. (2004). Persons with severe mental disorders in the criminal justice system: Challenges and opportunities. *Psychiatric Quarterly, 75*, 151-164.

Lamberti, J. S., Weisman, R L, Schwarzkopf, S B, Price, N, Ashton, R M, and Trompeter, J. (2001). The mentally ill in jails and prisons: Towards an integrated model of prevention. *Psychiatric Quarterly, 72*, 63-77.

Lewis, D. O., Yeager, C A, Gidlow, B, and Lewis, M. (2001). Six adoptees who murdered: Neuropsychiatric vulnerabilities and characteristics of biological and adoptive parents. *Journal of the American Academy of Psychiatry and the Law, 29*, 390-397.

Link, B. G., Andrews, H, and Cullen, F T. (1992). The violent and illegal behavior of mental patients reconsidered. *American Sociological Review, 57*, 275-292.

Modestin, J., and Ammann, R. (1996). Mental disorder and criminality: Male schizophrenia. *Schizophrenia Bulletin, 22*, 69-82.

Mullen, P. E., Burgess, P, Wallace, C, Palmer, S, and Ruschena, D. (2000). Community care and criminal offending in schizophrenia. *Lancet, 355*, 614-617.

Raine, A. (1993). *The psychopathology of crime: Criminal behavior as a clinical disorder*. San Diego: Academic Press.

Rasanen, P., Tuhonen, J, Isohanni, M, Rantakallio, P, Lehtonen, J, and Moring, J. (1998). Schizophrenia, alcohol abuse, and violent behavior: A 26-year follow-up study of an unselected birth cohort. *Schizophrenia Bulletin, 24*, 437-441.

Soyka, M., and Ufer, S. (2002). Aggressiveness in schizophrenia: Prevalence, psychopathological and sociodemographic correlates. *Fortschritte der Neurologie Psychiatrie, 70*, 171-177.

Steinert, T., Wiebe, C, and Gebhardt, R P. (1999). Aggressive behavior against self and others among first-admission patients with schizophrenia. *Psychiatric Services, 50*, 85-90.

Tiihonen, J., Isohanni, M, Rasanen, P, Koiranen, M, and Moring, J. (1997). Specific major mental disorders and criminality: A 26-year prospective study of the 1966 Northern Finland birth cohort. *American Journal of Psychiatry, 154*, 840-845.

Torrey, E. F. (1994). Violent behavior by individuals with serious mental illness. *Hospital and Community Psychiatry, 45*, 653-662.

Volavka, J. (1999). The effects of clozapine on aggression and substance abuse in schizophrenic patients. *Journal of Clinical Psychiatry, 60*, 43-46.

Volavka, J., Laska, E, Baker, S, and Meisner, M. (1997). History of violent behaviour and schizophrenia in different cultures. Analyses based on the WHO study on Determinants of Outcome of Severe Mental Disorders. *British Journal of Psychiatry, 171*, 9-14.

Watt, N. F., and Lubensky, A N. (1976). Childhood roots of schizophrenia. 44, 363-375. *Journal of Consulting and Clinical Psychology, 44*, 363-375.

Wessely, S. (1997). The epidemiology of crime, violence and schizophrenia. *British Journal of Psychiatry, 170*, 8-11.

Part 2. Comorbidity: The Relationship between Crime and Schizophrenia

In: Crime and Schizophrenia: Causes and Cures
Editor: Adrian Raine, pp. 15-27
ISBN 1-59454-609-6

Chapter 2

SCHIZOPHRENIA AND VIOLENCE: THE OVERLAP

Patricia A. Brennan and Amanda Alden
Emory University

Media accounts often sensationalize violent crimes committed by individuals with a history of mental illness. These stories suggest that a strong relationship exists between serious mental illnesses such a schizophrenia and serious violent crimes. But what does empirical research on schizophrenia and violence reveal about this relationship—is there truly an overlap, and if so what implications does this overlap have for policy and research? In this chapter, we attempt to answer these questions through a quantitative review of the literature and a series of empirical analyses using data from Danish birth cohorts. It is important to note that none of our work in this area would be possible without the guidance and mentorship of Professor Sarnoff Mednick, to whom this chapter is dedicated.

The past two decades have shown an influx of studies on the relationship between violent crime and mental illness, particularly at the level of large-scale, epidemiological samples (e.g., Link, Andrews and Cullen, 1992; Swanson, Holzer, Ganju and Jono, 1990). Results from these recent studies have prompted Monahan (1992) to conclude that "...there is a relationship between mental disorder and violent behavior, one that cannot be fobbed off as chance or explained away by third factors that caused them both...I now think the no-relationship [between violence and mental disorder] conclusion is at least premature and may well be wrong...new studies find a consistent, albeit modest relationship between mental disorder and violent behavior." This conclusion has policy implications for the treatment of the mentally ill and the prevention of criminal violence. In light of the research evidence, denying this relationship would do disservice to the public as well as to individuals with mental illness.

Our particular concern in this chapter, however, is more specific than examining the relationship between mental illness and crime—we are concerned with examining the overlap between the particular disorder of schizophrenia and the particular behavior of violent offending. Our first step in examining this overlap was to undertake a quantitative analysis of the literature on this topic.

Quantitative Review

Specifically, we conducted a meta-analysis to test the hypothesized relationship between schizophrenia and violent behavior. In interpreting the results of this analysis, it should be noted that there were a limited number of studies available for this review, and that there is considerable heterogeneity in the effects for the studies reviewed. Meta-analyses presented here should therefore be considered as suggestive, rather than conclusive, and attempts should be made to replicate and expand these findings as more studies are published in this area.

The studies that we included in our meta-analysis met the following criteria: (1) schizophrenia or schizophrenia spectrum diagnoses was utilized as the independent variable, (2) official or self-reported violence was utilized as the dependent variable, (3) a non-mentally ill control group was included or general population estimates of violence were provided for comparison, and (4) adequate data were provided for calculation of effect sizes. Only one effect size was calculated per study. For the New Zealand study (Arsenault, Moffitt, Caspi, Taylor and Silva, 2000), which included both official and self-reports of violence, the effect size for the overall meta-analysis was calculated based on the official data. According to these criteria, nine studies were included in our meta-analysis. A description of these studies is shown in Table 1. It should be noted that all of these studies have been completed in the last two decades. Therefore, the literature we review reflects the relationship between schizophrenia and violence during the current era of deinstitutionalization, and our conclusions may not generalize to other historical time periods.

Prior to 1988 there was only one study that met our criteria for inclusion in the meta-analysis, and unfortunately the results of that study may have been influenced by sampling bias. In this study, 42 schizophrenic patients were randomly selected from a psychiatric outpatient clinic of a Canadian hospital and compared to 42 non-psychiatric medical patients drawn from the same hospital (Chuang, Williams, and Dalby, 1987). Self-reports of criminal involvement were compared for these samples and no differences were found in the rate of crimes committed against persons--three of the 42 individuals in each of the samples reported such behavior. It is important to note, however, that the Chuang et al. sample was drawn from a population of schizophrenics who were in compliance with an outpatient regimen. It is conceivable that these schizophrenics are a uniquely compliant, non-aggressive, less seriously ill subsample of the schizophrenic population at large. If that is the case, then their rates of violence might be an underestimation of the rates of violence in the complete schizophrenic population.

A comparison of White House case subjects with schizophrenia and matched controls also failed to find a significant difference in future rates of violent crime commission (Shore, Filson and Rae, 1990). Upon more in-depth analyses of their data, these researchers found that the control group in this study had higher rates of *previous* violent offending than the subjects with schizophrenia. Importantly, once statistical controls were applied to account for this sampling bias, analyses revealed higher future violent crime arrest rates for the schizophrenic group.

Table 1. Description of Studies Included in Meta-Analysis

Study	Author	Year	N	Violence Measure
Australia	Mullen et al.	2000	552	Criminal conviction
Canada	Chuang et al	1987	84	Self-report crimes against persons
Denmark	Brennan et al	2000	358,180	Arrests for violent crime
Finland	Tiihonen et al.	1997	12.058	Violent crime in criminal register
New Zealand	Arsenault et al.	2000	961	Self-report and criminal convictions
Sweden	Lindqvist and Allebeck	1990	644	Official police register w/ 15 year follow-up
Switzerland	Modestin and Ammann	1996	564	Violent convictions
USA (ECA)	Swanson et al.	1990	10,059	Self-report violence
Washington DC	Shore et al.	1990	384	Arrests for violence w/ 10 year follow-up

Indeed in the last fifteen years, a growing number of studies have revealed a significant, positive relationship between schizophrenia and violence in the community. In one such study Lindqvist and Allebeck (1990) completed a longitudinal follow-up study of 644 schizophrenics in Stockholm. They compared the rates of violence and crime observed in their sample to the expected rates estimated from official statistics. Their results suggested that schizophrenia was associated with an increased rate of violence for both males and females. An association between schizophrenia and crime in general was found only for the females in the sample, and not the males. A patient community study in Switzerland also noted an increased risk for violent convictions, but not general crime convictions, for male patients with schizophrenia compared to controls (Modestin and Ammann, 1996). A more recent patient control study also noted an increase in lifetime rates of violent crime for individuals with a diagnosis of schizophrenia (Mullen, Burgess, Wallace, Palmer and Ruschena, 2000). This finding was consistent across two samples admitted to hospitals before and after deinstutionalization.

Three unselected birth cohort studies have also examined the relationship between schizophrenia and violence. First, a large-scale birth cohort study in Finland (Tiihonen, Isohanni, Rasanen, Koiranen and Moring, 1997) examined the official criminal records and psychiatric hospital records for 12,058 individuals through the age of 26. Similar to previous studies they found that male schizophrenics had a higher risk for violent crime, but not for other types of crime, when compared to controls. These researchers also noted that more than half of the schizophrenic offenders also had problems with alcohol, and that the rates of violence were especially high for schizophrenics with coexisting substance abuse.

We have also examined the relationship between schizophrenia and violence using data from the 1944-1947 Danish birth cohort study (n=358,180; Brennan, Mednick and Hodgins, 2000), and we expand on our initial findings later in this chapter. As we noted in our previous publication, hospitalization for schizophrenia was significantly related to arrest for criminal violence in both males and females. Similar to the results of the Tiihonen study, we found that a secondary diagnosis of substance abuse substantially increased the risk for violence within the schizophrenic patients in our sample.

In the only study to date that has included both self report and arrest data on violence, Arsenault and her colleagues (Arsenault et al., 2000) examined data from the Dunedin birth cohort in order to assess the schizophrenia and violence relationship. They found that individuals with schizophrenia spectrum disorders were more likely to have higher self reports and more arrests for violence than controls. In addition they found that increased perceptions of threat were associated with a stronger relationship between schizophrenia and violence, suggesting that particular symptoms of the disorder might play an important role in risk for violence.

The largest self-report study of major mental disorder and violence was completed in the context of the NIMH Epidemiologic Catchment Area (ECA) survey (Swanson et al., 1990). This study examined the self-reported commission of four types of violence (hitting a partner, hitting a child, physical fighting with others and weapon use during a fight) over the past year in a pooled sample of approximately 10,000 respondents. Diagnoses were determined from psychiatric interviews rather than hospitalization records. Results from this study indicated that individuals diagnosed with schizophrenia self-reported more violent behavior than individuals with no mental disorder (Swanson et al., 1990).

Individual effect sizes were computed for each study in our meta-analysis (see Figure 1). These effect sizes were weighted for sample size and combined to obtain a mean overall effect size for this sample of studies. According to Cohen (1992), effect sizes can be interpreted as follows: .20 is small, .50 is medium, and .80 and above is large. This overall effect size (d = .81) is therefore considered to be large, suggesting a strong positive relationship between schizophrenia and violence.

A test of homogeneity using weighted effect sizes produced significant results, indicating that there is also significant heterogeneity across studies (Q (8) = 181.79, $p < .001$). Two studies in particular, the Canadian and DC studies stand out with lower effect sizes. As we noted earlier, the Chuang et al. study focused on outpatients who were compliant with outpatient treatment. This focus may have produced a higher functioning and perhaps less violent sample of individuals. The effect size for the Shore et al. study would have been higher and reached significance if these authors had controlled for previous violent offenses in their analyses (an important control due to sampling bias). In order to identify other possible sources of heterogeneity across the studies, moderator analyses were conducted regarding the definition of schizophrenia, sample size, gender, sampling strategy, and measurement of violent offending.

Definition of Schizophrenia

Of the nine studies in the meta-analysis, six defined schizophrenia on the basis of inpatient status (d = .81) and three did not (d = .92). Moderator analyses suggested that this variable did not affect the overall effect size of the relationship between schizophrenia and violence (QB = 2.11, p = .15). This is an interesting finding given that the use of hospitalized samples was thought to be a potential bias in this area of research. Specifically, it has been suggested that schizophrenics who have been hospitalized might represent a more criminal or violent group than those who have never been hospitalized. Our moderator analyses do not support this contention.

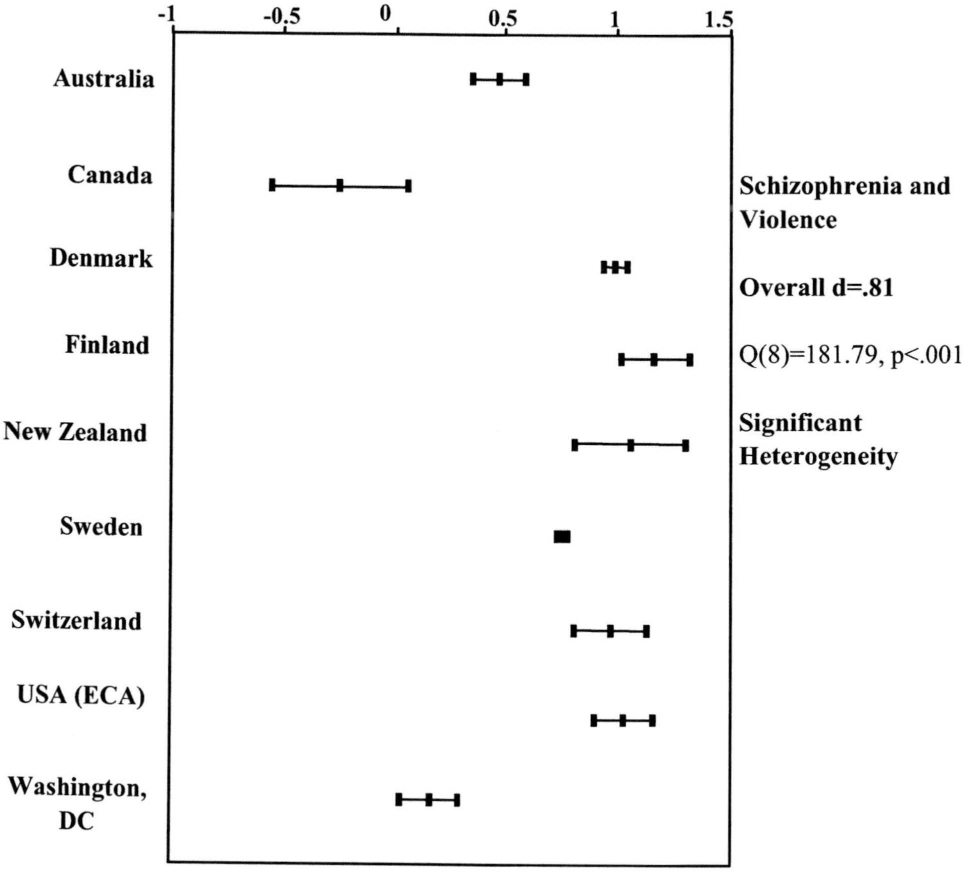

Figure 1. Meta-analytic review of the relationship between schizophrenia and violence: Weighted effect sizes across studies

Sample Size

Sample size was defined by those with a sample using less than 250 subjects (d = .81) and those using a sample composed of greater than 250 subjects (d = .83). This variable did not have a significant moderating effect on the relationship between schizophrenia and violence (QB = 7.96, p = .78). This finding suggests that samples do not have to be very large to detect an effect, and this makes sense given that the overall effect size is large.

Gender

Three of the samples included males only, whereas the other six included both males and females. Moderator analyses suggested that gender may change the effect size in the schizophrenia and violence relationship ($QB = 35.95$, $p < .001$). The effect size was higher in cases where females were included in the sample ($d = .83$) than when they were not ($d = .50$).

Sampling Strategy

We also examined whether sampling strategy in terms of using unselected cohorts might moderate the effect size of the relationship between schizophrenia and violence. According to our analysis, sampling strategy does act as a moderator ($QB = 104.54$, $p < .001$). Effect sizes for studies which employed the use of an unselected cohort were higher ($d = 1.00$) than those that did not ($d = .73$).

Measurement of Violence

Finally, the measurement of violence was examined as a possible moderator. As was stated at the outset, the use of official data was favored in the one case where a study provided both self-report and official categories of violence. For the purposes of this moderator analysis, the effect size based on self-report data in the New Zealand study was considered in addition to the effect size based on official data. Three studies using self-report were therefore compared to seven studies using official data. The method of measurement of violence did moderate the relationship between schizophrenia and violence ($QB = 6.79$, $p < .01$). Specifically, our analysis suggested that the effect size might be even greater for self-reports ($d = 1.01$) than for arrests and convictions ($d = .81$).

Caution should be taken in interpreting these moderator analyses. Due to the low number of studies that qualified, results of these moderator analyses may not be reliable. The results of the moderator analyses would clearly need to be replicated with a greater number of studies. However, the overall picture does suggest that there is good research evidence for a relationship between schizophrenia and violence, and that this relationship cannot be explained away by methodological biases.

Birth Cohort Analyses

Despite the information gained through our quantitative meta-analysis, we are left with many unanswered questions. Among these questions are some that we can attempt to answer using the empirical analysis of birth cohort data from Denmark. These questions include: Can the relationship between schizophrenia and violence be explained by demographics? What is the role of secondary substance abuse or personality disorder in the schizophrenia/violent crime relationship? Are certain symptoms or subtypes of schizophrenia particularly related to violence? What role does a previous criminal record play in the relationship between schizophrenia and violence? Is schizophrenia particularly related to certain types of violence? Finally, what generally comes first, the disorder or the violence?

Sample

The following analyses are based on psychiatric and criminal data obtained from a Danish birth cohort of 358,180 total individuals born between 1944 and 1947. The dead and emigrated were excluded from analyses. Schizophrenics had a higher rate of death, but death did not moderate the relationship between schizophrenia and violence. The final sample consisted of 173,509 (51.7%) males and 162,272 (48.3%) females. Subjects' marital status, as reported in 1991,was: 12.3% single, 71.8% married, 14.4% divorced, and 1.3% widowed. Socioeconomic status was indexed using occupational status and classified using a revision of Svalastoga's eight-point prestige scale developed for the Danish population (Svalastoga, 1959). Occupation was not available for 16.3% of the subjects. As per the recommendation of Cohen and Cohen (1975) these missing data were coded to the mean, and a dummy coded variable (1=socioeconomic data present) was included as a statistical control in the logistic regression analyses.

Criminal Register Data

Official arrest and conviction data through 1991 were obtained from the Danish National Police Register in Copenhagen. As Wolfgang noted, "the criminal registry office in Denmark is probably the most thorough, comprehensive, and accurate in the Western world" (1977; p. v.). Clearance rates (the proportion of reported crimes that result in arrest and conviction) for index (felony level) crimes in Denmark ranged from 10.2 percent for the theft of mopeds to 97.7 percent for homicide at the time these data were collected (Politiets aarsberetning 1989).

In Denmark, as opposed to common law countries, the police do not have the discretionary power of whether or not to arrest a person suspected of having committed a crime. Mentally-ill individuals who commit a crime are first arrested, and then transferred for treatment. Later, many of these individuals may not be prosecuted for their offenses. This differs from police practice in the U.S. where mentally disordered individuals might be taken by police to a hospital rather than charged with an offense. The Danish practice of arresting all offenders regardless of their mental status reduces any prejudice, positive or negative, based on a suspect's mental status at the time of arrest. Therefore, arrest data, rather than conviction data, were examined in this study.

Lifetime arrest data were available for all types of offenses (traffic, special business laws, and index offenses). However, only criminal index, violent offenses were considered in this study. The earliest age of arrest in the sample was nine years. The age of majority in Denmark is 15. If a person is arrested for a serious offense before the age of 15, however, that information is also included on his or her arrest record. Less than one percent of the violent arrests in the data were recorded before the age of majority.

Violent offenses included the following violations of the Danish Penal Code: murder (7.6% of total violent offenses), attempted murder (11.0% of total), rape (11.1% of total), violence against authority (e.g., assault on a police officer; 9.2% of total), assault (52.0% of total), domestic violence (.09% of total), and robbery (8.2% of total).

Psychiatric Register Data

Records of psychiatric hospitalizations through 1991 were obtained from the Danish Psychiatric Register at the Institute for Psychiatric Demography in Aarhus Denmark. This register contains information for Denmark on all dates of admission and discharge to psychiatric hospitals, and the codes for primary, secondary and tertiary diagnoses according to the International Classification of Diseases (ICD 8). Previous studies employing data from the Psychiatric Register have found an agreement rate of over 90% between the ICD-8 Register diagnoses and the diagnostic systems of DSM-III and DSMIII-R (Jorgensen, Teasdale, Parnas, Mednick, and Schulsinger 1987). In the current analyses, an individual was considered to be schizophrenic if they had ever received a hospital discharge diagnosis for schizophrenia (including all subtypes).

Secondary diagnoses of substance abuse (drug and/or alcohol) and personality disorder (schizoid, antisocial, paranoid, explosive, hysterical, and/or asthenic) (ICD-8) were also recorded.

Statistical Analyses

Logistic regression analyses were conducted to examine the associations between schizophrenia and arrests for violent crime while controlling for the potential confounds of marital status and socioeconomic status. All alpha levels were set at .05.

Results

The first question we examined was: Can the relationship between schizophrenia and violence be explained by demographics? When we controlled for socioeconomic status and marital status in our analyses, a significant relationship between schizophrenia and violence was still detected for the males (Table 2) and the females (Table 3) in this sample. Results for females showed higher effect sizes, but lower rates of violence overall. The rate of violence is particularly low in the female control group.

Our second question, was: What is the role of secondary substance abuse or personality disorder in the schizophrenia/violent crime relationship? We found that the relationship between schizophrenia and violence was still significant, but somewhat reduced when additional controls for substance abuse and personality disorder were included (see Tables 2 and 3). This is a conservative test, because we do not have accurate data on substance abuse and personality disorders for our non-hospitalized controls.

Next, the possible moderating role of substance abuse in the relationship between schizophrenia and violence was examined. There was a significant interaction effect for males such that in the group of individuals with no substance abuse diagnoses, schizophrenia predicted an increase in violence. In the case of individuals with substance abuse diagnoses, schizophrenia did not predict violence (see Table 2). It is important to note, however, that only hospitalized individuals are included in this second group, which means that the comparison is between schizophrenics and other inpatients. According to the larger literature, this comparison is often not significant. Results for females were similar, however schizophrenia predicted violence in both groups, with a lower effect size in the substance abuse group (see Table 3).

Table 2. Schizophrenia and Violence: Males

	N	Wald	p	OR
With Demographic Controls	173,509	47.19	<. 001	2.42*
Additional Controls for Substance Abuse and Personality Disorders	173,509	10.77	.001	1.52*
Paranoid v. Other Schizophrenia Types	1,148	6.93	<.01	1.68*
Interaction with Substance Abuse	173,509	4.67	<.05	No SA 2.22* SA 1.07
Interaction with Personality Disorder	173,509	21.95	<.001	No PD 2.67* PD 0.87
Interaction with Previous Arrest Record	173,509	6.24	<.05	No Record 5.05* Record 1.25

*Significant Odds Ratio. SA=Substance Abuse, PD=Personality Disorders

Table 3. Schizophrenia and Violence: Females

	N	Wald	p	OR
With Demographic Controls	162,272	44.23	<.001	7.79*
Additional Controls for Substance Abuse and Personality Disorders	162,272	16.67	<.001	3.38*
Paranoid v. Other Schizophrenia Types	680	6.08	<.05	3.32*
Interaction with Substance Abuse	162,272	8.03	<.01	No SA 7.49* SA 3.03*
Interaction with Personality Disorder Personality Disorder	162,272	13.11	<.001	No PD 12.12* PD 1.89
Interaction with Previous Arrest Record Arrest	162,272	10.25	<.01	No Record 14.37* Record 0.97

*Significant Odds Ratio. SA=Substance Abuse, PD=Personality Disorders

A similar pattern of findings was noted when the moderating effects of personality disorder were examined. Again, schizophrenia predicted violence only in the non-personality disorder group for males (see Table 2). Schizophrenia also predicted violence only in the absence of a diagnosis of a personality disorder and not in the presence of personality disorders in females (see Table 3).

Next, we examined this question: Are certain symptoms or subtypes of schizophrenia particularly related to violence? In these analyses only those individuals with a diagnosis of schizophrenia were included. They were divided into those diagnosed with the paranoid subtype as compared to those diagnosed with other subtypes. A small but significant difference in the rates of violence was detected in both males (see Table 2) and females (see Table 3), with those diagnosed with the paranoid subtype having a greater risk for violence. The results were slightly stronger for females (see Table 3). These results might suggest that paranoid symptoms play a role in the risk for violence; however, it is important to note that the literature to date is somewhat mixed on this topic.

Our next question was: What role does a previous criminal record play in the relationship between schizophrenia and violence? Analyses revealed that previous index arrest acts as a moderator in the relationship between schizophrenia and violent behavior. In the case of males with a record of an index offense, the additional knowledge that they have a diagnosis of schizophrenia would not help in predicting risk for violence. In the case where there is no previous record, a diagnosis of schizophrenia is predictive of a higher likelihood of violence (see Table 2). A similar result was noted for females (see Table 3).

An important question in this type of study is the timing of schizophrenia versus violence. If an individual commits violence before they are identified and diagnosed, then obviously, the diagnosis is of minimal predictive utility. So what comes first, hospitalization and diagnosis or arrest for violence? For the males in our sample, diagnosis preceded arrest for violence 50% percent of the time. The corresponding rate for females was 53%. In the males, diagnosis preceded arrest for murder in 60% of the cases. In females, the diagnosis preceded an arrest for murder 89% of the time. This suggests that our findings have relevance and utility in clinical prediction.

Finally, we examined whether type of violent crime made a difference in the schizophrenia/violent crime relationship. Odds ratios were significant for each category of violence for males, though the effect size was lower for assault, the least serious type of offense (see Table 4). For females the effect sizes were more varied and robbery was not linked to schizophrenia. Odds ratios for violence against authority and murder were very high, again partly due to the very low base rate of these crimes in the controls (see Table 4).

Table 4. Odds Ratios for Schizophrenia and Types of Violence

Type	Males	Females
Violence Against Authority	3.79	11.70
Assault	2.08	6.96
Robbery	3.30	3.02
Rape	2.87	No Cases
Murder	2.90	22.26

Adoption Cohort Review

Although the sample size for the Danish birth cohort is quite large and allowed for the examination of many descriptive questions, there are still many important questions remaining including: What is the process underlying the relationship between schizophrenia and violence? Are there two types of schizophrenic violent offenders? What is the role of medication compliance? Is there a common etiology between schizophrenia and violent behavior? What are the influences of brain functioning, attention deficits, perinatal factors, and genetics?

Although it will be up to future researchers to examine the bulk of these questions, we were able to examine a potential genetic connection between schizophrenia and violence in a Danish adoption cohort of 14,427 adoptions (Brennan, Mednick and Jacobsen, 1996). In Denmark, biological fathers are well identified and a national crime register exists. Data on adoptee schizophrenia enabled us to examine the relationship between father violence and child schizophrenia in the context of this adoption cohort. We found a significant relationship between biological father violence and adoptee schizophrenia for both males and females in this sample. It is important to note that we did not find a significant relationship between biological father violence and adoptee violence, so this potential confound cannot explain our results.

We also examined the possibility that this finding was potentially due to assortative mating. Although we did note the highest rates of schizophrenia in cases where the mother was mentally ill and the father was violent, we found that the relationship between biological father violence and adoptee schizophrenia existed even in those cases where the mother was not mentally ill.

Additional analyses were performed to control for a number of other potential confounds. These analyses included the removal of cases of parent schizophrenia, the removal of cases of parent mental illness, controlling for the amount of time spent with biological parents, controlling for the adoptive parents' socioeconomic status, and controlling for the adoptive parents' knowledge of father's criminal background. Our initial result was again confirmed—biological father violence was significantly related to adoptee schizophrenia. These findings may be indicative of a common inherited biological risk. As the field of genetics research is advancing very rapidly, this result might find some support in the area of molecular genetics in the near future.

Research and Policy Implications

Methodological Issues

The studies examined in our quantitative review have used a variety of methods—community-based samples and birth cohorts, inpatient samples and outpatient samples, self-reports and official measures of violence. The weight of the evidence suggests a significant and large effect of schizophrenia on risk for violence. Is this likely an overestimate or underestimate of the true effect? It has been suggested that psychotic individuals who are identified for research studies as a result of being treated (particularly in inpatient samples) may be more criminal or violent than the overall population of psychotic individuals. Therefore the results of studies focused on treatment-based samples are presumed to overestimate the relationship between major mental disorder and crime. However, our meta-analysis found that inpatient status did not moderate the overall effect size of the schizophrenia and violence relationship. It has also been argued that the schizophrenia and violence relationship may be overestimated if one relies on official measures of violent crime, in that individuals with schizophrenia might be more likely to be caught or arrested for crimes (Teplin, 1984). Our effect size analyses, however, reveal that the relationship between schizophrenia and violence is actually stronger in studies that utilize self-report rather than official measures of violence. This suggests that the overall effect noted between schizophrenia and violence might be an underestimate of the true effect, as most of the studies reviewed have used official measures of crime.

Several other methodological factors suggest that studies reviewed here may underestimate the true effect of the relationship between schizophrenia and violence. First, the relationship between major mental disorder and violence may be stronger at older ages, and most samples used in previous research have primarily included young adults. Second, a psychotic individual's refusal to participate in the study or its follow-up interviews might be related to his or her propensity for violence. If so, the rates of violence for those who are included in these samples may be an underestimate of the true rates of violence for individuals with schizophrenia. Finally, most studies of schizophrenia and violence do not control for the incapacitation effects of hospitalization, and most acts of violence in inpatient settings do not lead to arrest. Therefore, the true risk for violence in hospitalized, schizophrenic individuals may be underestimated in studies that rely only on official crime statistics.

Research and Policy Implications

The effect size for the relationship between schizophrenia and violence is medium to large. In contrast, the attributable risk within the population is small. We must be careful to balance the risks of stigmatization versus those of denial while remembering that continued violence increases stigmatization. Future research should examine the role of other possible moderators in the schizophrenia and violence relationship. Increased knowledge in this area will help improve the predictive utility of diagnoses of schizophrenia for violent behavior. The reviewed research also indicates that common etiological factors may exist for schizophrenia and violent behavior. Future research in this area may reveal avenues for the prevention of violent acts associated with mental illness.

Acknowledgements

This research was supported by grant R1MH50017A from the National Institute of Mental Health and grant CX0063 from the National Institute of Justice.

REFERENCES

Arseneault, L., Moffitt, T. E., Caspi, A., Taylor, P. J. and Silva, P. A. (2000). Mental disorders and violence in a total birth cohort: Results from the Dunedin Study. *Archives of General Psychiatry. 57,* 979-986.

Brennan, P. A., Mednick, S. A., and Hodgins, S. (2000). Major mental disorders and criminal violence in a Danish birth cohort. *Archives of General Psychiatry. 57(5)* 494-500.

Brennan, P., Mednick, S. A., and Jacobsen, B. (1996). Assessing the role of genetics and crime using adoption cohorts. In J. Goode (Ed.) ***Genetics of criminal and antisocial behavior*** (pp. 115-127). London: CIBA.

Chuang, H. T., Williams, R., and Dalby, J. T. (1987). Criminal behaviour among schizophrenics. *Canadian Journal of Psychiatry, 32*(4), 255-258.

Cohen, J. (1992). A power primer. *Psychological Bulletin, 112*, 155-159.

Cohen J, and Cohen P (1975). *Applied multiple regression/correlation analysis for the behavioral sciences*. Hillsdale NJ: Lawrence Erlbaum Associates.

Jorgensen, A. A., Teasdale, T. W., Parnas, J, Mednick, S. A., and Schulsinger F. (1987). The Copenhagen high-risk project: the diagnosis of maternal schizophrenia and its relation to offspring diagnosis. *British Journal of Psychiatry, 151,* 753-757.

Lindqvist, P., and Allebeck, P. (1990). Schizophrenia and crime: A longitudinal follow-up of 644 schizophrenics in Stockholm. *British Journal of Psychiatry, 157*, 345-350.

Link, B., Andrews, H., and Cullen, F. (1992). The violent and illegal behavior of mental patients reconsidered. *American Sociological Review, 57*, 275-292.

Modestin, J., and Ammann, R. (1996). Mental disorder and criminality: Male schizophrenia. *Schizophrenia Bulletin, 22*, 69-82.

Monahan, J. (1992). Mental disorder and violent behavior: Perceptions and evidence. *American Psychologist, 47,* 511-521.

Mullen, P. E., Burges, P., Wallace, C., Palmer, S. and Ruschena, D. (2000). Community care and criminal offending in schizophrenia. *Lancet, 355,* 614-617.

Politiets aarsberetning 1989. Copenhagen, Denmark: Rigspolitichefens Informationstjenesten; 1990.

Shore, D., Filson, C. R., and Rae, D. S. (1990). Violent crime arrest rates of White House case subjects and matched control subjects. *American Journal of Psychiatry, 147*, 746-750.

Svalastoga K. *Prestige, class and mobility*. Copenhagen: Glydendal; 1959.

Swanson, J. W., Holzer, C. E., Ganju, V. K., and Jono, R. T. (1990). Violence and psychiatric disorder in the community: Evidence from the epidemiologic catchment area surveys. *Hospital and Community Psychiatry, 41*, 761-770.

Teplin, L. A. (1984). Criminalizing mental disorder: The comparative arrest rate of the mentally ill. *American Psychologist, 39,* 794-803.

Tiihonen, J., Isohanni, M., Raesaenen, P., Koiranen, M., and Moring, J. (1997). Specific major mental disorders and criminality: A 26-year prospective study of the 1996 Northern Finland Birth Cohort. *American Journal of Psychiatry, 154*, 840-845.

Wolfgang ME. (1977). Foreward. In: Mednick SA, Christiansen KO, editors. *Biosocial bases of criminal behavior*. New York: Gardener Press.

In: Crime and Schizophrenia: Causes and Cures
Editor: Adrian Raine, pp. 29-41
ISBN 1-59454-609-6

Chapter 3

SEX DIFFERENCES IN AGGRESSIVE AND DELINQUENT BEHAVIOR IN SCHIZOTYPAL ADOLESCENTS[1]

Amanda McMillan and Elaine Walker
Department of Psychology, Emory University

There is a well-documented link between schizophrenia and antisocial behavior. For example, studies of violent offenders worldwide find a significantly elevated prevalence of schizophrenia and spectrum disorder diagnoses (Gosden, Kramp, Gabrielsen, and Sestoft, 2003; Arseneault, Moffitt, Caspi, Taylor, and Silva, 2000). Conversely, studies of patient populations reveal higher rates of antisocial behavior. In an investigation of a large Danish birth cohort in their forties, proportionately more of the men and women who developed schizophrenia were convicted of non-violent and violent crimes (Brennan, Mednick, and Hodgins, 2000). Similar results were obtained in investigations of population cohorts in Australia (Mullen, Burgess, Wallace, Palmer, and Ruschena, 2000), Israel (Stueve and Link, 1997), and New Zealand (Arseneault et al., 2000).

Investigations into the specific links between symptoms and antisocial behavior suggest that the severity of positive symptoms is the strongest predictor of aggressive and violent behavior. Further, some findings indicate that individuals at risk for developing schizophrenia and spectrum disorders are more likely to manifest antisocial behaviors. The link between premorbid antisocial behavior and psychosis has been examined in both retrospective and prospective longitudinal studies. In a retrospective study of childhood-onset schizophrenia, Schaeffer and Ross (2002) found a high proportion of parents reporting oppositional behavior, violence, aggression, temper tantrums, and rages as premorbid signs in their children. Similarly, Arsenault et al. (2000) found that individuals with schizophrenia-spectrum disorders were more likely to have a childhood history of conduct disorder.

The rate of premorbid antisocial behaviors appears to increase with age as the individual approaches late adolescence/early adulthood, the peak risk period for the onset of psychosis.

In examining the premorbid developmental course through childhood, Neumann, Grimes, Walker and Baum (1995), used the Child Behavior Checklist (CBCL) and found a significant increase in aggressive behaviors in preschizophrenic children between 8 and 12 years of age. Two empirically-derived clusters were observed; Cluster I manifested early onset and escalating behavioral abnormalities, whereas Cluster II did not begin to differ from controls until adolescence. By 8 to 12 years, Cluster I was not only exhibiting more aggressive behavior than control subjects but Cluster II individuals as well. Using a similar retrospective design, Rossi, Pollice, Daneluzzo, Marinangeli and Stratta (2000) collected maternal reports of behavioral abnormalities for five age periods from birth through adolescence and found that all behavioral abnormality dimensions, including delinquent and aggressive behavior, were higher in the patient group when compared to the normal controls, and increased consistently with age.

Prospective studies of children at high risk for psychotic disorders yield similar findings. Bearden et al. (2000) followed a population cohort from childhood into adulthood to identify behavioral problems that preceded schizophrenia. They assessed a range of behaviors, including emotional reactivity and hostility, when the subjects were aged 4 and 7 years. Their findings indicate that a progression from initial social deficits to more severe behavioral deviance precedes adult-onset schizophrenia. Bergman, Wolfson and Walker (1997) examined behavioral problems in the offspring (mean age 9.75 years) of parents with a diagnosis of schizophrenia. Compared to those whose parents had no mental illness, the high-risk children exhibited elevated levels of externalizing behaviors (aggression and delinquency) on the CBCL. Further, the rate of behavior problems increased from the initial assessment to the follow-up, one year later. In a subsequent report from the Edinburgh High Risk Study, Miller, Byrne, Hodges, Lawrie and Johnstone (2002) obtained reports on the CBCL at two time periods, prior to age 13 and from ages 13-16. The high-risk individuals who later developed schizophrenia displayed significantly more externalizing behaviors when compared to those who did not go on to develop the illness. Specifically, prior to age 13, high risk children who later developed schizophrenia were more aggressive, and the difference became stronger in the 13-16 age period, with a much higher incidence of aggressive and delinquent behaviors in those individuals who later developed schizophrenia.

There is evidence that premorbid externalizing behaviors are linked with more pronounced cognitive impairment and clinical symptoms in patients. Baum and Walker (1995) used retrospective CBCL data, and found that patients who showed more childhood aggression and delinquency between ages 8 and16 years also manifested greater cognitive disorganization in adulthood. Neumann, Baum, Walker and Lewine (1996) found that escalating childhood delinquency predicted deficits in adult motor functioning, whereas both childhood delinquency and aggression predicted cognitive impairment. Replicating this pattern of findings, in a study of adult-onset schizophrenia patients, the presence of premorbid disciplinary problems was associated with more pronounced adult neuropsychological deficits (Silverstein, Mavrolefteros, and Turnbull, 2003). Among the various disciplinary problems, physical violence showed the strongest relation with adult neuropsychological deficits. Additionally, there is evidence to suggest that the association between childhood behavior and adult cognitive function may reflect underlying brain dysfunction. Walker, Lewine and

[1] This research was supported by Grant # RO1 MH62066-01 awarded to Dr. Walker from the National Institute of Mental Health.

Neumann (1996) found that premorbid externalizing problems in childhood were related with greater brain abnormalities in adult schizophrenia patients. Specifically, increases in delinquent behaviors were associated with ventricular enlargement and smaller whole brain volume.

Schizotypal Personality and Antisocial Behavior

Schizotypal personality disorder (SPD) is a syndrome that involves deficits in interpersonal functioning, and perceptual and ideational abnormalities. There is an extensive body of literature showing that schizotypal signs are more prevalent in the biological relatives of patients with schizophrenia and other psychotic disorders. This has led to the assumption that there is a genetic link between schizophrenia and SPD. Further, schizotypal signs often predate the onset of schizophrenia, so the manifestation appears to represent a prodromal developmental phase of the disorder in some patients.

As is the case with schizophrenia, there is evidence that SPD is associated with an increase in antisocial behavior. A study of schizotypal symptoms and interpersonal behaviors in undergraduate students revealed that students who scored higher on measures of perceptual aberration and magical ideation were more likely to engage in hostile interactions, including expressions of irritation, belligerence and anger (Shean and Wais, 2000). Similarly, in a study aimed at differentiating between positive and negative schizotypy in an undergraduate population, those with more positive symptoms (perceptual distortions) also scored higher on measures of antisocial personality disorder (Dinn, Harris, Acyicegi, Greene, and Andover, 2002). Raine, Venables, Mednick and Mellingen (2002) looked at persistently schizotypal adults and found that they scored higher on measures of conduct disorder, including both physical and verbal aggression, than controls. In a retrospective study of adolescents with SPD, Walker, Baum and Diforio (1998) obtained parental reports of behavior problems throughout childhood. When compared to normal subjects, there was a significant developmental increase in externalizing behaviors in the schizotypal adolescents, especially in the early adolescent age period (12-15 years). In summary, research utilizing a variety of methodologies has revealed that schizophrenia-spectrum disorders are associated with an increase in the rate of antisocial behavior, ranging from interpersonal hostility to physical aggression to violence. Further, it appears that there is a developmental increase in the risk for these behaviors, with a marked rise in adolescence.

There is also evidence that gender moderates the relation between antisocial behavior and schizophrenia spectrum disorders. In a review of the literature, Walker, Walder, Lewine and Loewy (2002) found that, with increasing age, preschizophrenic males are characterized as exhibiting increased externalizing behaviors while females show a higher rate of internalizing behaviors. Summarizing the findings on violence and schizophrenia, Hodgins, Hiscoke and Freese (2003) conclude that, as is the case in the general population, the presence of violent behaviors prior to the onset of schizophrenia is much more common among men than women. But, along with other investigators, they also note evidence that schizophrenia more significantly increases the risk for violence in women than in men (Brennan et al., 2000; Hodgins and Janson, 2002). In other words, the presence of a schizophrenia-spectrum disorder raises the risk for antisocial behavior to a greater extent in women. Further, in the controlled environment of an inpatient ward, women with psychotic disorders are just as likely to behave violently as are their male counterparts (Newhill, Mulvey, and Lidz, 1995).

THE EMORY UNIVERSITY ADOLESCENT DEVELOPMENT PROJECT: A PROSPECTIVE STUDY OF SCHIZOTYPAL ADOLESCENTS

We have explored the relation between schizotypal symptoms and antisocial behavior in the Emory University Adolescent Development Project. Based on past findings, it was predicted that adolescents who meet diagnostic criteria for SPD will manifest a higher rate of externalizing behavior problems, including delinquency and aggression, than adolescents with no Axis II disorder. It was also predicted that ratings of the positive schizotypal symptoms, but not negative symptoms, will be significantly linked with delinquent and aggressive behavior. Finally, we examined the effect of sex on the nature and strength of the relation between antisocial behavior and schizotypy.

Currently enrolled participants in the Emory Study are 118 children, ranging in age from 12 to 18 years. Children with personality disorders were recruited through an announcement directed at parents of youth with adjustment problems. The announcement described the key diagnostic criteria for schizotypal personality disorder in lay terms. Telephone screening interviews were conducted, and prospective participants who seemed likely to meet criteria for SPD, or another personality disorder, were scheduled for the research assessment. Healthy participants were primarily recruited through a University based registry of children in the Atlanta area. Demographic characteristics of the sample are presented in Table 1. Exclusion criteria were neurological disorder, mental retardation, Axis I disorder, and substance abuse/addiction.

A battery of diagnostic measures was administered, including the Structured Interview for DSM-IV Personality disorders (SIDP-IV) (Pfohl, Blum, and Zimmerman, 1997) and the Structured Clinical Interview for Axis I DSM-IV Disorders (SCID) (First, Spitzer, Gibbon, and Williams, 1995). Interviews were administered by trained graduate-level examiners, and diagnoses were made by review of the videotaped interviews and other materials by research project staff, including a licensed psychologist and psychiatrist. As expected, the announcement elicited responses from parents whose children manifested a range of problems, and met criteria for SPD as well as other Axis II disorders. Consistent with previous reports, the rate of comorbid personality disorder was 51%.

Parents of the children completed the Child Behavior Checklist. This behavioral rating Scale contains 104 items (CBCL; Achenbach, 1991; Achenbach and Edelbrock, 1981). The CBCL was chosen because it contains items that measure a broad range of behavioral problems and yields scores for seven behavior problem dimensions, including two that index externalized behavior problems and are the focus of the present study, namely "delinquent behavior," and "aggressive behavior." As described above, previous studies have shown that scores on these scales predict subsequent diagnosis with SPD and schizophrenia. Also, the CBCL has been demonstrated to have good reliability. For example, in a study of parents' reports of normal and disturbed children (aged 4–16 years), the interclass correlations were .90 or greater for interparent agreement, 1-week test–retest reliability, and inter-interviewer reliability (Achenbach and Edelbrock, 1981). Composite scores for the CBCL behavior problem dimensions are derived by summing the items in the particular behavior dimension. The mother served as the informant about childhood behavior for most of the participants.

Table 1. Subject Demographic Information and Medication Status

	SPD (n=32)	OPD (n=37)	NoPD (n=49)
Age			
Mean	14.25	14.34	14.08
Standard Deviation	1.723	1.697	1.935
Sex			
Males	21	19	27
Females	11	18	22
PD Comorbidity (%)	72	32	0
Medication Status			
Stimulant	8	1	3
Antidepressant	5	3	3
Both	3	4	2

RESULTS OF DATA ANALYSES

Diagnostic group comparisons revealed no significant difference in mean age, however, the SPD group included a higher proportion of males than the other groups, $\chi^2 = 4.90$, p=.03.

An ANOVA was conducted on the CBCL externalizing behavior ratings, with diagnostic group and sex as the independent variables. Figure 1 displays the aggression scores by sex and diagnostic group. The analysis of aggression scores revealed a significant main effect for diagnostic group, F(2,110)= 4.82, p<.01, and a significant Diagnostic group X Sex interaction F(2,110)= 3.08, p<.05. T-test comparisons showed that the diagnostic group differences in aggression ratings for males did not reach statistical significance. But among females, the normal controls had significantly lower scores for aggression than the SPD, t(36)= 3.10, p<.01, and other personality disorder (OPD), t(36)= 2.88, p<.01, groups. Consistent with past reports, among normals, males showed significantly more aggression than females, t(45)= 2.35, p<.05. In contrast, there were no sex differences in ratings for aggression in the SPD or OPD groups. This is counter to some past reports which indicated that antisocial behavior is greater in preschizophrenic males.

The analysis of delinquency scores revealed a significant main effect for diagnostic group, F(2,110)= 7.07, p<.001, but the interaction did not reach significance. Figure 2 displays the delinquency scores by sex and diagnostic group. T-test comparisons showed that there was a significant group difference in delinquency, with the OPD group showing a higher mean score than the normal group, t(74)= 3.59, p<.001, and the SPD group t(74)= 2.19, p<.05. This is consistent with the fact that the OPD group contained a subgroup with antisocial personality/conduct disorder. The differences between the normal and SPD group approached significance, t(74)= 1.62, p<.10, with the SPD group showing more delinquency. Among normals, consistent with past reports, males showed a trend toward more delinquency than females, t(45)= 1.64, p<.10. There were no sex differences in ratings for delinquency in the SPD or OPD groups.

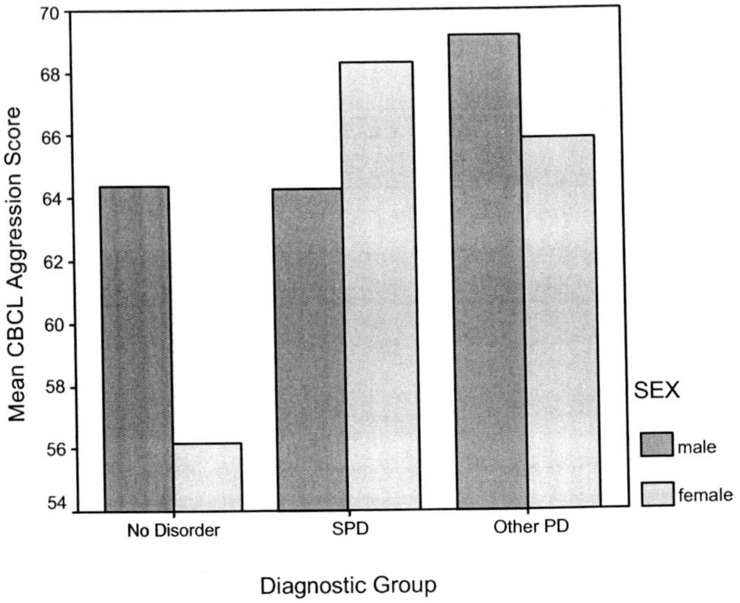

Figure 1. Mean aggression score by diagnostic group

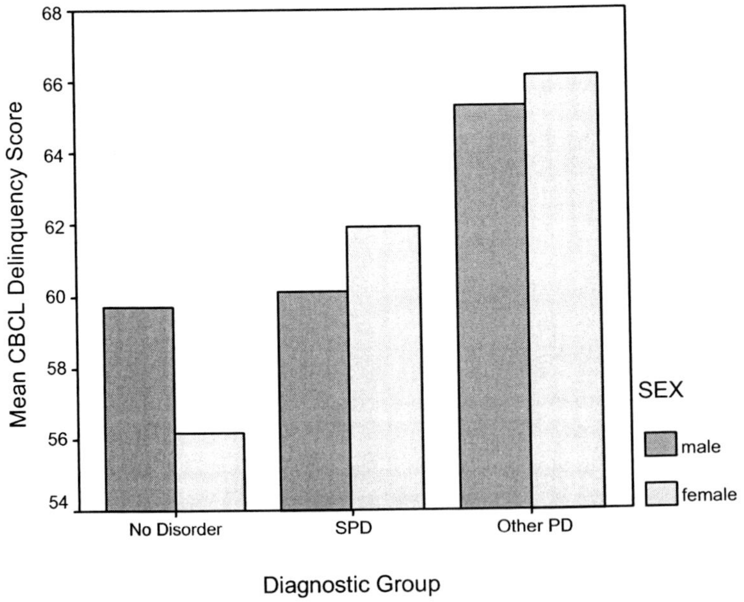

Figure 2. Mean delinquency score by diagnostic group

Correlational analyses were conducted to examine the relation of SPD symptoms with delinquent and aggressive behavior. Given the significant sex differences in the behavioral profiles of the diagnostic groups, analyses were conducted separately by sex. The results are listed in Table 2, for the three diagnostic groups combined. (Analyses were conducted with the combined groups because the separate diagnostic groupings are based on the symptom ratings.) As shown, for boys there were no significant relations between ratings of SPD symptoms and delinquent and aggressive behavior. In contrast, for girls, there were significant positive associations between aggression and almost all of the SPD symptoms: ideas of reference, odd beliefs/magical thinking, unusual perceptual experiences, odd thinking and speech, suspiciousness, inappropriate or constricted affect, and odd behavior or appearance. The only symptoms that were not associated with increased aggression were lack of friends and social anxiety. Thus for girls, but not boys, more severe positive schizotypal symptom ratings were associated with higher parent-rated aggression in the child. The only significant relation for delinquency was with ratings of suspiciousness in females.

As described, the sex differences revealed in our group comparisons ran counter to our predictions based on past reports. We therefore sought to determine whether psychotropic medication might be contributing to these effects. Specifically, a substantial number of the research participants, especially those meeting diagnostic criteria for SPD, were currently taking psychotropic medication. The most common were stimulant and antidepressant medication. For the total sample, 44% had a lifetime history of psychotropic medication, 33% were currently on medication, and 23% were receiving, or had received, two or more medications simultaneously. The classes of psychotropics and the number of participants taking each are listed in Table 1. For about one half of those on medication, the prescribing physician was a pediatrician. The breakdown for current medication was as follows: Antidepressant alone n=11; Stimulant alone n=12; Antipsychotic alone n=2; Antidepressant and Antipsychotic n=5; Antidepressant and Stimulant n=9; Antipsychotic and Stimulant n=1; All three medications n=4.

We first sought to determine whether medication status was linked with the behavior ratings. Regression analysis was conducted using current status on the three classes of psychotropics (stimulants, antidepressants and antipsychotics) as the predictor variables, and ratings on the aggression and delinquency factors as the dependent variables. The results showed that, taken together, the medication variables accounted for a significant proportion of the variance in aggression ratings, $F(3,112)= 4.93$, $p<.01$. As independent predictors, both stimulant and antidepressant use showed a trend toward significant association with higher aggression ratings. When the same analysis was conducted on the delinquency rating, the equation did not reach significance, $F(3,112)= 1.74$, $p=.13$. But, stimulant use was a significant independent predictor, $t=2.14$, $p<.05$. Again, medication was linked with higher ratings.

Table 2. Correlations (Pearson) between ratings of schizotypal symptoms and delinquent and aggressive behavior by sex

	Schizotypal Symptoms									
	Ideas of Reference	Magical Thinking	Perceptual Experiences	Odd Thinking	Paranoid Ideation	Inappropriate Affect	Odd Behavior	Lack of Friends	Social Anxiety	Total Symptoms
Males n=67										
Delinquency	-0.032	0.031	-0.152	-0.178	0.128	-0.013	-0.051	0.032	-0.058	-0.042
Aggression	-0.043	0.110	0.001	-0.119	0.035	0.107	-0.002	0.086	-0.089	0.027
Females n=51										
Delinquency	0.124	0.180	-0.024	0.158	0.287*	0.113	0.190	0.089	-0.020	0.183
Aggression	0.257	0.332**	0.247*	0.393**	0.263*	0.288*	0.471**	0.177	0.149	0.395**

n=66 for males in the Paranoid Ideation Symptom rating

* Correlation is significant at the 0.05 level (1-tailed)

** Correlation is significant at the 0.01 level (1-tailed)

When the diagnostic group X sex ANOVA of delinquency scores was conducted, excluding those on stimulants or antidepressants, the results were similar to those obtained with the entire sample. There was a significant main effect for diagnostic group, $F(2,79)= 8.75$, $p<.001$, but the interaction did not reach significance. T-test comparisons showed that there was a significant group difference in delinquency, with the OPD group showing a higher mean score than the normal group, $t(60)= 3.92$, $p<.01$, and the SPD group, $t(44)= 2.38$, $p<.02$. There was a trend toward higher delinquency ratings in the SPD group compared to the normal control subjects, $t(60)= 1.37$, $p<.10$. Consistent with past reports among normals, males showed a trend toward more delinquency than females, $t=2.12$, $p= .06$. There were no sex differences in ratings for delinquency in the SPD or OPD groups.

When the Diagnostic group X Sex ANOVA was conducted on the aggression scores, excluding those on antidepressants or stimulants, the results differed from those reported above. There was a significant main effect for diagnostic group, $F(2,90)= 4.91$, $p<.01$, but the sex X diagnostic group interaction did not reach significance. The OPD group scored higher on aggression than the normal group, $t(60)= 3.00$, $p<.01$. The SPD adolescents showed more aggression than the normal control group, $t(60)= 1.85$, $p<.05$. There was no difference between the SPD and OPD groups.

The change in the findings for aggression ratings that resulted from the exclusion of those on medication appears to be a consequence of the differential effect of medication on externalizing behavior in males and females. Figure 3 displays the aggression scores, by medication status (stimulant or antidepressant), sex and diagnostic group.

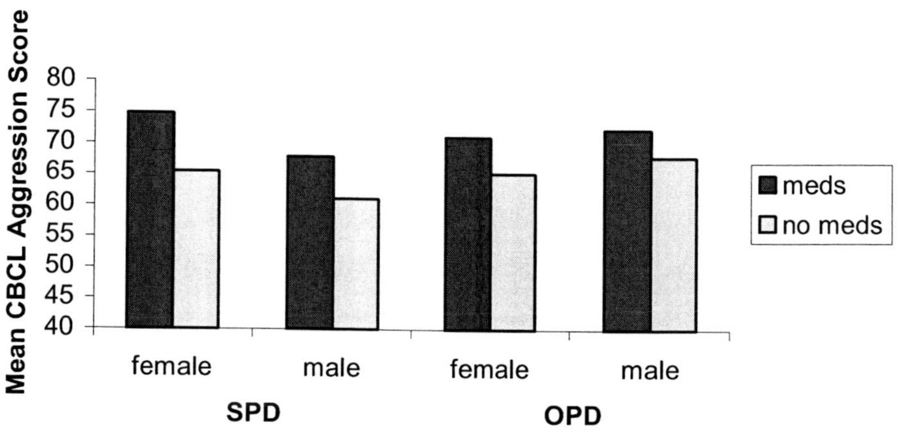

Figure 3. Mean aggression score by diagnostic group, gender and medication status

As illustrated in Figure 3, both males and females on medication score higher on aggression than those not on medication. We tested the relation of medication status with behavior ratings for males within diagnostic group. For normal control and SPD males, those on medication scored significantly higher on aggression than those off medication, $t(23)= 4.18$, $p<05$, and $t(23)= 2.06$, $p<05$. As shown, the number of female subjects in some groups was too small to permit statistical tests. We therefore combined the two personality disorder groups to test for the medication effect in females. In the combined SPD/OPD group, both females and males currently on medication had significantly higher aggression ratings than their same-sex counterparts, $t(27)= 1.87$, $p<05$, $t(38)= 1.71$, $p<05$, respectively.

DISCUSSION

Consistent with previous reports, we find elevations in aggressive and delinquent behavior in adolescents with SPD. But the pattern differed by sex, and appeared to be influenced by medication status. These findings suggest that the association between SPD and antisocial behavior is complex.

Our analyses revealed that aggression ratings were elevated in participants who were receiving antidepressant or stimulant medication. When the participants who were on these drugs were excluded, the analyses revealed a pattern of diagnostic group differences in aggression and delinquency that did not vary by sex. Namely, the SPD adolescents manifested more aggression and a trend toward more delinquency than the healthy adolescents. These findings converge with past studies that have found a link between SPD and elevations in antisocial behaviors.

It is important to note that although the CBCL aggression and delinquency dimensions include items that pertain to criminal activity and physical aggression, adolescents can score high on these scales because they manifest noncriminal delinquent activity (e.g., noncompliance with adult authority figures) and verbal aggression. Thus the antisocial behaviors manifested by these SPD adolescents do not necessarily include the violent or criminal behaviors that have been the subject of much of the research on schizophrenia and antisocial behavior.

The findings of the present investigation diverge from past reports with respect to sex differences. Past research on schizophrenia has typically shown that male patients manifest more aggressive and criminal behavior than females (Steinert, Wiebe, and Gebhardt, 1999). Similarly, studies of the childhood precursors of schizophrenia-spectrum disorders have consistently revealed more aggressive and delinquent behavior in preschizophrenic males. We do not find this sex difference in the present study; among SPD youth, males and females displayed comparable levels of antisocial behavior.

There are several possible explanations for the discrepancy between the present results and those of previous investigations. First, it may be that the sex difference in premorbid antisocial behavior does not extend into the adolescent period, after the onset of the SPD syndrome. In other words, once the severity of schizotypal signs exceeds the threshold for SPD criteria, females may show a more dramatic developmental rise in antisocial behavior. This could, therefore, eliminate the premorbid sex difference. Such an interpretation is consistent with the notion that schizophrenia-spectrum disorders are linked with a more dramatic increase in antisocial behavior in females than in males.

Alternatively, the present findings may indicate a cohort shift in the rate of antisocial behavior among females. Thus, the previously reported sex difference in antisocial behavior among those with spectrum disorders may not hold for current cohorts. One trend that could produce cohort changes is the increase in the administration of psychotropics, especially antidepressants and stimulants, to youth. This increase has been documented over the past two decades, and is especially pronounced in the United States. It has been shown that these two medications are being prescribed, often by pediatricians, to children who manifest a variety of adjustment problems. It is therefore not surprising that many of the youth in our samples who meet diagnostic criteria for Axis II disorders have taken psychotropic medications.

There is suggestive evidence that these medications increase some externalizing behaviors in children. Barkley (1977) in a review analysis of relevant clinical trials reported increased irritability in children receiving stimulant medications. This medication-induced agitation could contribute to increases in aggression and delinquency. Recent reviews also cite irritability as an adverse side effect to stimulant usage (Greenhill, 2001). Additionally, Mann and Kapur (1991) cite reports of multiple and pharmacologically diverse antidepressants associated with the appearance of suicidal and aggressive behavior. Specifically, the SSRI fluvoxamine has been indicated for triggering aggression and violence, particularly in children and adolescents (Breggin, 2001). Vitiello and Swedo (2004) report increased agitation, particularly in children receiving SSRIs when compared to those receiving a placebo. Of course, it may also be that elevations in antisocial behaviors precede and/or precipitate the administration of medication. In future studies, we will explore this question by examining the relation between developmental changes in behavior and changes in medication status.

Our hypothesis, that antisocial behaviors would be linked with more pronounced positive schizotypal symptoms, received partial support. In this sample, the relation was only observed among females. Specifically, females with higher ratings on positive symptoms were also rated by their parents as showing greater aggressive behavior. This may parallel the findings on sex differences in violence in adult schizophrenia patients. Again, the link between antisocial tendencies and schizophrenia-spectrum signs may be stronger in females. In summary, the present findings lend further support to the notion that SPD, like schizophrenia, is associated with higher rates of antisocial behavior.

Finally, the relationship between antisocial behavior and vulnerability to schizophrenia may provide yet another opportunity for early identification and intervention. Interestingly, an environmental enrichment program aimed at reducing both schizotypal personality and antisocial behavior produced a lower incidence of schizotypal and criminal outcomes in participants, suggesting a possible interaction between the two distinct sets of problematic behaviors (Raine, Mellingen, Liu, Venables, and Mednick, 2003).

References

Achenbach, T. (1991). *Child Behavior Checklist.* Department of Psychiatry, University of Vermont, Burlington, VT.

Achenbach, T., and Edelbrock, C. (1981). Behavioral problems and competencies reported by parents of normal and disturbed children aged four through sixteen. *Monographs of the Society for Research in Child Development, 46*(1), 82.

Arseneault, L., Moffitt, T., Caspi, A., Taylor, P., and Silva, P. (2000). Mental disorders and violence in a total birth cohort: Results from the Dunedin study. *Archives of General Psychiatry, 57*(10), 979-986.

Barkley, R. (1977). A review of stimulant drug research with hyperactive children. *Journal of Child Psychology and Psychiatry, 18*, 137-165.

Baum, K., and Walker, E. (1995). Childhood behavioral precursors of adult symptom dimensions in schizophrenia. *Schizophrenia Research, 16*, 111-120.

Bearden, C., Rosso, I., Hollister, J., Sanchez, L., Hadley, T., and Cannon, T. (2000). A prospective cohort study of childhood behavioral deviance and language abnormalities as predictors of adult schizophrenia. *Schizophrenia Bulletin, 26*(2), 395-410.

Bergman, A., Wolfson, M., and Walker, E. (1997). Neuromotor functioning and behavior problems in children at risk for psychopathology. *Journal of Abnormal Child Psychology, 25*(3), 229-237.

Breggin, P. (2001). Fluvoxamine as a cause of stimulation, mania and aggression with a critical analysis of the FDA-approved label. *International Journal of Risk and Safety in Medicine, 14*, 71-86.

Brennan, P., Mednick, S., and Hodgins, S. (2000). Major mental disorders and criminal violence in a Danish birth cohort. *Archives of General Psychiatry, 57*(5), 494-500.

Dinn, W., Harris, C., Acyicegi, A., Greene, P., and Andover, M. (2002). Positive and negative schizotypy in a student sample: Neurocognitive and clinical correlates. *Schizophrenia Research, 56*, 171-185.

First, M., Spitzer, R., Gibbon, M., and Williams, J. (1995). *Structured Clinical Interview for the DSM-IV Axis I Disorders* (SCID-I), Patient Edition. American Psychiatric Press, Washington, DC.

Gosden, N., Kramp, P., Gabrielsen, G., and Sestoft, D. (2003). Prevalence of mental disorders among 15-17 year-old male adolescent remand prisoners in Denmark. *Acta Psychiatrica Scandinavica, 107*, 102-110.

Greenhill, L. (2001). Clinical effects of stimulant medication in ADHD. In M. Solanto and A. Arnsten (Eds.), *Stimulant drugs and ADHD: Basic and clinical neuroscience* (Vol. xii, pp. 31-71). London: Oxford University Press.

Hodgins, S., Hiscoke, U., and Freese, R. (2003). The antecedents of aggressive behavior among men with schizophrenia: A prospective investigation of patients in community treatment. *Behavioral Sciences and the Law, 21*, 523-546.

Hodgins, S., and Janson, C. (2002). *Criminality and violence among the mentally disordered: The Stockholm Project Metropolitan* (Vol. xi). New York: Cambridge University Press.

Mann, J., and Kapur, S. (1991). The emergence of suicidal ideation and behavior during antidepressant pharmacology. *Archives of General Psychiatry, 48*(11), 1027-1033.

Miller, P., Byrne, M., Hodges, A., Lawrie, S., and Johnstone, E. (2002). Childhood behaviour, psychotic symptoms and psychosis onset in young people at high risk of schizophrenia: early findings from the Edinburgh High Risk Study. *Psychological Medicine, 32*, 173-179.

Mullen, P., Burgess, P., Wallace, C., Palmer, S., and Ruschena, D. (2000). Community care and criminal offending in schizophrenia. *Lancet, 355*(9204), 614-617.

Neumann, C., Baum, K., Walker, E., and Lewine, R. (1996). Childhood behavioral precursors of adult neuropsychological functioning in schizophrenia. *Neuropsychiatry, Neuropsychology, and Behavioral Neurology, 9*(4), 221-229.

Neumann, C., Grimes, K., Walker, E., and Baum, K. (1995). Developmental Pathways to Schizophrenia: Behavioral Subtypes. *Journal of Abnormal Psychology, 104*(4), 558-566.

Newhill, C., Mulvey, E., and Lidz, C. (1995). Characteristics of violence in the community by female patients seen in a psychiatric emergency service. *Psychiatric Services, 46*(8), 785-789.

Pfohl, B., Blum, N., and Zimmerman, M. (1997). *Structured Interview for DSM-IV Personality* (SIDP-IV). American Psychiatric Press, Washington, DC.

Raine, A., Mellingen, K., Liu, J., Venables, P., and Mednick, S. (2003). Effects of environmental enrichment at ages 3-5 years on schizotypal personality and antisocial behavior at ages 17 and 23 years. *The American Journal of Psychiatry, 160*(9), 1627-1635.

Raine, A., Venables, P., Mednick, S., and Mellingen, K. (2002). Increased psychophysiological arousal and orienting at ages 3 and 11 years in persistently schizotypal adults. *Schizophrenia Research, 54*, 77-85.

Rossi, A., Pollice, R., Daneluzzo, E., Marinangeli, M., and Stratta, P. (2000). Behavioral neurodevelopment abnormalities and schizophrenic disorder: A retrospective evaluation with the Childhood Behavior Checklist (CBCL). *Schizophrenia Research, 44*, 121-128.

Schaeffer, J., and Ross, R. (2002). Childhood-onset schizophrenia: Premorbid and prodromal diagnostic and treatment histories. *Journal of the American Academy of Childhood and Adolescent Psychiatry, 41*(5), 538-545.

Shean, G., and Wais, A. (2000). Interpersonal behavior and schizotypy. *The Journal of Nervous and Mental Diseases, 188*(12), 842-846.

Silverstein, M., Mavrolefteros, G., and Turnbull, A. (2003). Premorbid factors in relation to motor, memory, and executive functions deficits in adult schizophrenia. *Schizophrenia Research, 61*, 271-280.

Steinert, T., Wiebe, C., and Gebhardt, R. (1999). Aggressive behavior against self and others among first-admission patients with schizophrenia. *Psychiatric Services, 50*(1), 85-90.

Stueve, A., and Link, B. (1997). Violence and psychiatric disorders: Results from an epidemiological study of young adults in Israel. *Psychiatric Quarterly, 68*(4), 327-342.

Vitiello, B., and Swedo, S. (2004). Antidepressant medications in children. *The New England Journal of Medicine, 350*(15), 1489-1491.

Walker, E., Baum, K., and Diforio, D. (1998). Developmental changes in the behavioral expression of vulnerability for schizophrenia. In M. Lenzenweger and R. Dworkin (Eds.), *Origins and development of schizophrenia: Advances in experimental psychopathology* (pp. 469-491). Washington, DC: American Psychological Association.

Walker, E., Lewine, R., and Neumann, C. (1996). Childhood behavioral characteristics and adult brain morphology in schizophrenia. *Schizophrenia Research, 22*, 93-101.

Walker, E., Walder, D., Lewine, R., and Loewy, R. (2002). Sex differences in the origins and premorbid development of schizophrenia. In F. Lewis-Hall and T. Williams (Eds.), *Psychiatric illness in women: Emerging treatments and research* (Vol. xxii, pp. 193-214). Washington, DC: American Psychiatric Publishing, Inc.

PART 3. RISK FACTORS FOR ANTISOCIAL BEHAVIOR

In: Crime and Schizophrenia: Causes and Cures
Editor: Adrian Raine, pp. 45-81
ISBN 1-59454-609-6

Chapter 4

EVIDENCE FROM BEHAVIORAL GENETICS FOR ENVIRONMENTAL CONTRIBUTIONS TO ANTISOCIAL CONDUCT

Terrie E. Moffitt and Avshalom Caspi
Institute of Psychiatry, King's College London, and
University of Wisconsin, Madison

This chapter reviews recent behavioral-genetic research that is helping to address questions about the non-genetic, environmental causes of antisocial conduct. We illustrate how behavioral-genetic methods are being newly applied to detect the genuine environmental influences among the many risk factors for antisocial behavior. We further examine interactions between genes and environments, in which environmental effects may be stronger than previously assumed, within genetically vulnerable children.

Despite assiduous efforts to eliminate it, antisocial behavior is still a problem. Approximately 20% of people in the developed world experience victimization by perpetrators of violent and non-violent illegal behavior each year (U.S. Bureau of Justice Statistics, 2002). The *World Report on Violence and Health* (WHO, 2002) tallies the staggering burden of mortality, disease, disability, and compromised well-being brought about by perpetrators of family violence and other violent crimes. Behavioral science needs to achieve a more complete understanding of the causes of antisocial behavior to provide an evidence base for effectively controlling and preventing antisocial behavior. A new wave of intervention research in the last decade has demonstrated clear success for a number of programs designed to prevent antisocial behavior (http://www.preventingcrime.org; Heinrich, Brown and Aber, 1999; Sherman et al., 1999; Weissberg, Kumpfer and Seligman, 2003). Nevertheless, the reduction in antisocial behavior brought about by even the best prevention programs is, on average, modest (Dodge, 2003; Wasserman and Miller, 1998; Olds et al., 1998; Heinrich, Brown and Aber, 1999; Wandersman and Florin, 2003; Wilson, Gottfredson and Najaka, 2001). The best-designed intervention programs reduce serious juvenile offenders' recidivism only by about 12% (Lipsey and Wilson, 1998). This modest success of interventions that were theory-driven, well-designed and amply-funded sends a clear message that we do not yet understand the causes of antisocial behavior well enough to prevent it.

Why Look for Causes of Antisocial Behavior in the Family?

Simultaneous with the new wave of research evaluating interventions is a wave of research pointing to the concentration of antisocial behavior in families. In the 1970's, the astounding discovery that fewer than 10% of individuals perpetrate more than 50% of crimes (Wolfgang, Figlio and Sellin, 1972) prompted researchers to investigate individual career criminals (Blumstein and Cohen, 1987) and examine the childhood origins of such persistent re-offenders (Moffitt, 1993). This research constructed the evidence base supporting the new wave of preventive intervention trials (Yoshikawa, 1994). Recently journalists have drawn public attention to certain families who across several generations seem to contain far more than their share of criminal family members (Butterfield, 1996; 2002). This familial concentration of crime has been confirmed as a characteristic of the general population (Farrington, Barnes, and Lambert, 1996; Farrington, Jolliffe, Loeber, Stouthamer-Loeber, and Kalb, 2001; Rowe, and Farrington, 1997). In general, fewer than 10% of the families in any community account for more than 50% of that community's criminal offenses. The family concentration of antisocial behavior could be explained by a genetic influence on antisocial behavior, but it could just as easily be explained by non-genetic social transmission of antisocial behavior within families. Again, causation is not well understood. Studies that cannot disentangle genetic and environmental influences cannot help.

Antisocial Behavior Research Is Stuck in the Risk-Factor Stage

Influential reviewers have concluded that the study of antisocial behavior has been stuck in the 'risk factor' stage (Farrington, 1988; 2003; Hinshaw, 2002; Rutter, 2003a; 2003b) because so few studies have used designs that are able to document causality (Rutter, Pickles, Murray and Eaves, 2001). A variable is called a 'risk factor' if it has a documented predictive relation with antisocial outcomes, whether or not the association is causal. The causal status of most risk factors is unknown; we know what statistically predicts psychopathology outcomes, but not how or why (Kraemer, 2003; Kraemer et al. 1997). There are consequences to the field's failure to push beyond the risk factor stage to achieve an understanding of causal processes. Valuable resources have been wasted because intervention programs have proceeded on the basis of risk factors, without sufficient research to understand causal processes. Mentoring programs are based on evidence that poor adult-child bonding is a risk factor for antisocial outcomes. Family preservation programs are based on evidence that family dissolution is a risk factor. Peer-group skills programs are based on evidence that peer delinquency is a risk factor. Mentoring progams and family preservation have not worked

(Wasserman, and Miller, 1998), and peer-group programs have been shown to exacerbate adolescent offending (Dishion, McCord, and Poulin, 1999; Klein, 1995).

Similarly, Drug Abuse Resistance Education (DARE), gun buybacks, boot camps, outward-bound-type programs, after-school leisure-time programs, youth job programs, and neighborhood watch programs were all originally designed to correct known risk factors for delinquent offending, but formal evaluation has revealed that none of these interventions work to reduce antisocial behavior, and some of them have marked iatrogenic effects (Sherman et al., 1999). Simply put, the cost of getting causation wrong is not trivial.

A central barrier to interpreting an association between an alleged environmental risk factor and antisocial outcome as a cause-effect association is, of course, the old bugbear that correlation is not causation. Some unknown third variable may account for the association, and that third variable may well be heritable. For example, does the cycle of violence from abusive parent to aggressive child arise from environmental transmission, or genetic transmission? (DiLalla and Gottesman, 1991). More than 100 studies have addressed the question of genetic influence on antisocial behavior, and reviews and meta-analyses of this literature conclude that genes influence 40% to 50% of its variation in the population (Miles and Carey, 1997; Rhee and Waldman, 2002). Perhaps the most pragmatic implication from this evidence of genetic influence for antisocial behavior is that we can no longer blithely assume environmental causation, but rather we must re-examine each putative environmental risk factor for antisocial behavior, one by one, while using research methods that are capable of applying explicit controls for genetic effects (Rutter et al., 2001). Because much research on intergenerational transmission continues without genetic controls (Serbin and Karp, 2003), this point cannot be made too often. Without control for genetic variation, further risk-factor research remains ambiguous if not uninformative.

During the 1990s, the assumption that 'nurture' influences behavior came under fire. Traditional socialization studies of antisocial behavior, which could not separate environmental influences from their correlated genes, were challenged by four important empirical discoveries: (a) ostensible environmental measures are influenced by genetic factors (Plomin and Bergeman, 1991); (b) parents' heritable traits influence the environments they provide for their children (Kendler, 1996; Plomin, 1994); (c) people's genes influence the environments they encounter (Kendler, 1996; Plomin, DeFries, and Loehlin, 1977); and (d) environmental influences did not seem to account for the similarity among persons growing up in the same family (Rowe, 1994). It was said that although non-behavioral-genetic studies might show that certain rearing experiences predict young people's antisocial outcomes, theories of causation based on findings from such designs were guilty of a fundamental logical error: mistaking correlation for causation (Scarr, 1992). These challenges culminated in admonishments that so far the evidence for genetic influences outweighed the evidence for environmental influences within the family (Harris, 1998; Rowe, 1994). Many social scientists responded to this claim, re-asserting evidence for environmental influences (Collins, Maccoby, Steinberg, Hetherington, and Bornstein, 2000; Reid, Patterson, and Snyder, 2002; Vandell, 2000). However, the reason there is all this controversy about the importance of the family environment in the first place is that the evidence base was not decisive enough to compel both camps. The best way forward to resolve the debate is to use research designs that can provide leverage to test environmental causation.

Ordinary studies cannot test whether a risk factor is causal, and it would be unethical to assign children to experimental conditions expected to induce aggression. Fortunately, researchers can use three other methods for testing causation: natural-experiment studies of within-individual change (Cicchetti, 2003; Costello, Compton, Keeler and Angold, 2003), treatment experiments (Howe, Reiss, and Yuh, 2002), and the focus of this review: behavioral genetic designs. None of the three alone can provide decisive proof of causation, but if all supply corroborative evidence by ruling out alternative non-causal explanations about a risk factor, then a strong case for causation can be made.

How Can Behavioral-Genetic Research Help?

Behavioral-genetic designs are a useful addition to a toolkit for testing environmental causation. It is somewhat counterintuitive to think about using behavioral-genetic designs to control for and rule out genetic influences while highlighting environmental influences in bas relief, but paradoxically, this is one of their strongest applications. Behavioral genetics disentangles genetic from non-genetic aspects of familial transmission, and thereby can rule out one of the most serious challenges to environmental causation: a heritable third variable that accounts for the correlation between a putative environmental risk factor and antisocial outcome. Behavioral genetics also has methods to put genetic and non-genetic influences back together again in a systematic and controlled way, to work out how they jointly cause behavior. Behavioral genetics has been rapidly moving beyond the initial question of heritability (Dick and Rose, 2002; Kendler, 2001), to apply its methods to a broad array of causal questions (Moffitt, 2005). Concurring evidence from behavioral-genetic methods, natural experiments of within-individual change, and treatment experiments will move the study of antisocial behavior beyond the risk-factor stage where it has been stuck, to inform strong causal theory about how antisocial behavior develops.

Testing Hypotheses about Environmental Causation

Before reviewing studies that have applied behavioral-genetic designs to testing environmental causation, we address two often-voiced reservations about behavioral-genetic studies. One reservation is about whether effect sizes from studies of twins and adoptees can be generalized to the general population. The other reservation is about whether assumptions limit inference from twin studies or adoption studies.

How Well Do Twins and Adoptees Represent the Population?

An important issue is whether the prevalence rates and distributions of antisocial behaviors among twins and adoptees represent antisocial behaviors among ordinary people (Rutter, 2002). This issue is relevant to the question of whether estimates of environmental influence from behavioral-genetic samples apply to the general population. Although this has been assumed more than it has been examined, the assumption is probably defensible for twin studies because twin-versus-singleton comparisons have not found differences in the prevalence rates of antisocial behavior or antisocial personality traits (Gjone and Novik,

1995; Johnson, Krueger, Bouchard, and McGue, 2002; Levy, Hay, McLaughlin, Wood, and Waldman, 1996; Moilanen et al., 1999; Simonoff et al., 1997; van den Oord, Koot, Boomsma, Verhulst and Orlebeke, 1995; van der Valk, Verhulst, Stroet and Boomsma, 1998). Adoptees, on the other hand, tend to show elevated rates of antisocial outcomes, although the skewed distribution of these outcomes has the same shape within adoptee samples as in the general population (Hutchings and Mednick, 1973; Sharma, McGue and Benson, 1998). Importantly, the effect sizes for *associations between* risk factors and psychopathology outcomes have been found to be similar across behavioral-genetic and non-genetic studies. For instance, in our own Environmental Risk Longitudinal Twin Study (The E-risk Study; Moffitt et al., 2002), associations between children's behavior and maternal depression, exposure to domestic violence, maternal warmth and negativity, maternal smoking during pregnancy, socio-economic status, and neighborhood deprivation are all comparable to these associations in the wider literature.

Inference from Different Types of Behavior-Genetic Designs

Antisocial behavior has been studied in twins reared together, adoptees, and twins reared apart. Behavior genetics research is not limited to exotic samples; researchers also examine ordinary families whose members vary in genetic relatedness (e.g., full siblings, half-siblings, step-siblings, cousins, and unrelated children reared in the same family) (Rowe, Almeida, and Jacobson, 1999). This variety of research designs offers a special advantage for inference, because comparing their estimates tells us that the environmental effect sizes for antisocial behavior are robust across different designs; they are not biased by the limitations and flaws peculiar to one design.

A number of potential flaws are unique to adoption studies. First, adoption agencies may attempt to maximize similarity between the adoptee's biological and adoptive families to increase the child's chance of fitting in with the new family (this is called 'selective placement'). Relatedly, biological mothers who intend to give their baby away may neglect prenatal care and continue to abuse substances during pregnancy, and many unwanted babies experience institutionalization before they are adopted. If adoptive homes, prenatal care and institutional care are selectively worse for the babies given up by antisocial biological mothers, this could bias estimates of heritability upward and estimates of environment effects downward, by misattributing the criminogenic influences of these three unmeasured non-genetic factors to any criminogenic influence of genes (Mednick, Moffitt, Gabrielli and Hutchings, 1986). Second, both adoptees and twins reared apart are likely to be reared in home environments that are unusually good for children because adoptive parents are carefully screened. Adoption breaks up the association between genetic risk and environmental risk naturally occurring in ordinary families by removing genetically at-risk children from damaging homes and placing them in salutary homes. As a result, interactions between environmental adversity and genetic vulnerability that exacerbate behavior problems in ordinary children (and twins) are uncommon among adoptees (Stoolmiller, 1999). The restricted range of rearing environments resulting from screening of adoptive parents could suppress estimates of environmental effects and thus bias heritability estimates upward (Fergusson, Lynskey and Horwood, 1995; Stoolmiller, 1999). However, this flaw of adoption studies is offset by studies of national twin registers (e.g., Cloninger and Gottesman, 1987) or stratified high-risk twin samples (e.g., Moffitt et al., 2002), because such sampling frames represent the complete population range of environmental and genetic backgrounds.

Studies of twins avoid the potential flaws of adoption studies, but they suffer several potential flaws of their own. First, the logic of the twin design assumes that all of the greater similarity between MZ than DZ twins can safely be ascribed to MZ twins' greater genetic similarity. This 'equal environments assumption' requires that MZ twins are not treated more alike than DZ twins on the causes of antisocial behavior (Kendler, Neale, Kessler, Heath, and Eaves, 1994). Because MZ twins look identical they might be treated more similarly than DZ twins in some way that promotes antisocial behavior, and as a result, estimates of heritability from studies of twins reared together could be biased upward, and estimates of environmental effects could be biased donward, relative to the correct population value (DiLalla, 2002). In fact, we found that young MZ twins receive somewhat more similar discipline than DZ twins (Jaffee, Caspi, Moffitt, Polo-Tomas, Price and Taylor, 2004). However, studies of adoptees do not suffer this flaw, and neither do studies of twins reared apart, because MZ twins reared apart do not share environments (unless their genetically influenced behaviors evoke similar reactions from care-givers in their separate rearing environments, which is a genetic effect). Second, in studies of twins, MZ twins differ more than DZ twins in prenatal factors affecting intrauterine growth; for example, MZ twins sharing the same chorion appear to suffer more fetal competition for nutrients. These intrauterine factors also violate the assumption that environments are equal for MZ and DZ twins, but intrauterine differences tend to make MZ twins less alike than their genotypes and thus would bias heritability estimates downward and environmental effects upward (Rutter, 2002). Third, genomic factors that make some MZ twin pairs' genotypes less than perfectly identical (such as random inactivation of genes on one of each girl's two X chromosomes; Jorgensen et al., 1992) could in theory affect twin-study estimates, but so far no evidence shows that these processes influence behavior. Fourth, parental assortative mating can bias heritability estimates. Coupled partners are known to share similarly high or low levels of antisocial behaviors (Galbaud du Fort, Boothroyd, Bland, Newman, and Kakuma, 2002; Krueger, Moffitt, Caspi, Bleske, and Silva, 1998). When parents of twins mate for similarity this should increase the genetic similarity of DZ twins, but MZ twins' genetic similarity cannot increase beyond its original 100%, and as a result heritability estimates will be biased downward and environmental estimates upward, relative to the correct population value. The implication of biological-parent assortative mating for adoption studies is the opposite; biological-parent similarity for antisocial behaviors would bias adoptees' heritability upward relative to the correct population value (because adoptee/biological-parent correlations would represent a double-dose of parental genes). Fifth, twin studies using adult reports to measure behavior sometimes suffer from rater artifacts; for example, adults may mix up or conflate the behavior of MZ twins and they may exaggerate differences between DZ twins. Such a rater artefact does not afflict adoption studies (nor twin studies using the twins' self-reports, as twins do not confuse themselves).

In any case, comparisons between designs have revealed that studies of twins reared together yield estimates that are more similar than different to the estimates from studies of twins reared apart or of adoptees (Rhee and Waldman, 2002). On the one hand, this is because any bias arising from factors such as selective adoptee placement, violations of the equal-environment assumption, intrauterine twin differences, or assortative mating, is only very small (Miles and Carey, 1997; Rutter, 2002). On the other hand, these factors bias estimates upward as often as they bias them downward, cancelling each other out. The bottom line is that it is important for tests of environmental risk to exploit a variety of behavioral-genetic designs, as well as experimental designs and studies of within-individual change.

Behavioral Genetic Studies of Parenting Effects on Children's Aggression

To illustrate how behavior-genetic designs are helping to move the study of antisocial behaviors from the risk factor stage to causal understanding, we next review research investigating one risk factor, parents' "bad parenting" of their children, and one antisocial outcome, "children's aggression". We have construed bad parenting broadly; this review includes risk factors from mothers' smoking heavily during pregnancy, to inconsistent or unskilled discipline, to frank child neglect and abuse. The outcome, "children's physical aggression" includes hitting, fighting, bullying, cruelty, and so forth. It is already known that "bad parenting" statistically predicts children's aggression, and bad parenting plays a central causal role in leading theories of antisocial behavior (Lahey, Moffitt and Caspi, 2003; Thornberry, 1996). The aim of the research reviewed here is to determine whether the relation between bad parenting and children's aggression is a true cause-effect relation, such that interventions that stop bad parenting can reasonably be expected to prevent aggression from emerging. This aim is fundamental because studies of adoptions have documented the dispiriting fact that aggression emerges in adopted children despite the fact that they were separated from their at-risk biological parents at birth and reared by skilled and loving adoptive parents.

Our research review systematically tackles six questions in turn. (1) Is there evidence that children's aggression cannot be wholly explained by genetic factors, and must have non-genetic environmental causes as well? (2) Do parents' genes influence bad parenting? (3) Does a genetic effect on parents' bad parenting confound a cause-effect interpretation of the association between bad parenting and children's aggression? (4) Does a genetic "child effect" evoke bad parenting to further confound a cause-effect interpretation of the association between bad parenting and children's aggression? (5) After all genetic confounds are controlled, does bad parenting have an environmentally mediated causal effect on children's aggression? (6) Does bad parenting interact with genetic risk, such that the effects of bad parenting are even stronger among genetically vulnerable children? Each question is presented in a separate section below, first describing research designs that can answer each question, and then reviewing findings so far. The research designs covered here are not intended to be exhaustive, but are intended to illustrate what kinds of studies could be done, using the logic of behavioral-genetic methods.

Question 1: Is Children's Aggression Wholly Accounted for by Genetic Factors, or Does it Have Non-Genetic Causes as Well?

More than 100 twin, adoption, and sibling studies have been carried out to answer this question. This work has revealed that genetic causal processes account for only about half of the population variation in antisocial behavior, thereby unequivocally proving that environmental influences account for the other half. This fact constitutes a remarkable contribution to the understanding of causation (Plomin, 1994). In addition, it is now recognized that the heritability coefficient indexes not only the direct effects of genes, but also the effects of interactions between genes and family-wide environments (Purcell 2002; Rutter and Silberg, 2002). In such interactions the effect of an environmental risk may be even larger than previously reported, among the subgroup of individuals having a vulnerable genotype. This is likely to be the case for antisocial behaviors.

One useful feature of behavioral-genetic research designs is that they offer two powerful methods for documenting the importance of environmental effects (Plomin, DeFries, McClearn and McGuffin, 2001). One of these methods of detecting environmental influence tests whether any of the family members in a study sample are more similar than can be explained by the proportion of genes they share. For instance, MZ twins' genetic similarity is twice that of DZ twins, and therefore, if nothing but genes influenced antisocial behavior MZ twins' behavior ought to be at least twice as similar as DZ twins'. If not, then something environmental has influenced the twins and enhanced their similarity. For almost all human behavioral traits studied so far, environmental factors shared by family members (variously labeled the "family-wide," "common," or "shared" environment) have not been found to make family members similar. In other words, the estimated influence of shared environment has been found to be almost nil for most human behavioral traits (Rowe, 1994). Antisocial behavior is a marked exception. A comparison of shared-environment effects across 10 psychiatric disorders revealed that such effects were stronger for antisocial personality and conduct disorder than for affective, anxiety, or substance disorders (Kendler, Prescott, Myers, and Neale, 2003). Estimates of shared-environment effects on population variation in antisocial behavior are about 15% to 20% as reported by meta-analyses and reviews (Miles and Carey, 1997; Rhee and Waldman, 2002). The small size of this shared-environment estimate should not be too surprising, because the twin-study coefficient indexing the shared environment does not include environmental effects involved in gene-environment interactions. We can think of the shared-environment coefficient as the residual effects of shared environments that remain, after controlling for gene-environment interactions. As most human behavior involves nature-nurture interplay, it is remarkable that as much as 20% of the population variation in antisocial behavior can be attributed to direct environmental effects not conditional on genetic vulnerability.

The second method of detecting the presence of environmental influence is to test whether any family members are less similar than expected from the proportion of genes they share (Plomin and Daniels, 1987). For instance, if a pair of MZ twins, despite sharing all their genes, are not perfectly identical in antisocial behavior, this indicates that experience has reduced their behavioral similarity. After estimates of the influences of heritability (50%) and shared family environment (20%) on antisocial behavior are calculated, the remainder of population variation, 30%, is assumed to reflect environmental influences not shared by family members (variously labelled "unique," "person-specific" or "non-shared," experiences). These experiences might include criminogenic experiences unique to the individual and not shared with his sibling, such as a head injury, being the unique target of sexual abuse, living with an antisocial spouse, or serving a prison sentence. There are two caveats about estimates of the effect of non-shared environments. First, measurement error inflates these estimates because random mistakes in measuring behavior will result in scores that look different for twins in an MZ pair, and it is not easy to differentiate such faux MZ differences from true MZ differences caused by the twins' non-shared experiences. The second caveat is that the coefficient for non-shared environmental effects indexes not only the direct effects of non-shared experiences, but also the effects of interactions between non-shared environments and genes (Purcell, 2002; Rutter and Silberg, 2002). Thus, some portion of the non-shared environment effect may be attributable to error or genes, and the size of this portion is unknown.

It would be highly unlikely that any behavior disorder is wholly determined by genes, but it is important to begin any program of research into causal processes by ascertaining what effect sizes we can expect for both genetic and environmental influences under natural conditions, in the absence of intervention. For overall population variation in antisocial behavior, these effects are 50:50. Therefore, behavioral-genetic studies have shown that the answer to question 1, "does children's aggression have any non-genetic causes?" is a definite yes, there is strong evidence that environmental causes must exist.

Question 2: Do Parents' Genes Influence Bad Parenting?

It is important to know the size of the contribution of parents' genotypes to their bad parenting, because if parenting is substantially influenced by parents' genotype, then its correlation with children's aggression cannot be confidently interpreted as a cause-effect relation. But how much do people's genes influence their parenting? Answering this question requires researchers to treat parenting as a phenotype in behavioral-genetic research.

What Research Designs Can Be Used to Answer this Question?

We can study *adoptions* to test if biological parents' bad parenting (of the children they did not give up for adoption) predicts that their adopted-away child will also engage in bad parenting when she becomes a parent. This study would show that bad parenting is genetically transmitted, in the absence of social transmission. However, this study has not been conducted, because of the difficulty of obtaining parenting data from two generations of adults separated by adoption.

We can study *adult MZ twins reared apart* to test whether they are similar in using bad parenting on their children. The Swedish Adoption Twin Study of Aging carried out this design, by asking 50 pairs of adult MZ twins reared apart to report their own parenting styles using the Moos Family Environment Scale (Plomin, McClearn, Pederson, Nesselroade and

Bergeman, 1989). Results indicated that 25% of the variation in parenting was genetically influenced.

We can study *adult twin parents* to ascertain how much variation in their bad parenting is attributable to genetic versus environmental sources. The aforementioned Swedish twin study carried out this design, studying 386 adult twin pairs, and again results indicated that 25% of the variation in the Family Environment Scale was genetically influenced (Plomin et al., 1989). In another study, 1117 pairs of mid-life twin volunteers who had on average reared 3 children reported their own parenting styles. The heritability estimate for an overall measure of parenting, called "care", was 34% (Perusse, Neale, Heath, and Eaves, 1994). A Virginia sample of 262 pairs of adult twin mothers reported their own parenting styles, and the heritability estimates were 21% for "physical discipline", 27% for "limit-setting", and 38% for "warmth" (Kendler, 1996; Wade and Kendler, 2000). An Oregon sample of 186 pairs of adult twin mothers and adoptee mothers reported their own parenting styles, and the heritability estimates ranged from 60% for "positive support" to 24% for "control" (Losoya, Callor, Rowe, and Goldsmith, 1997). These findings were echoed by a study of 236 pairs of adult twin mothers reporting their own parenting, in which genetic effects were found for "positivity" and "monitoring" (Towers, Spotts, and Neiderhiser, 2001; Neiderhiser et al., 2004). Finally, a study of 1034 adult twin mothers found a heritability estimate of more than 50% for self-reported smoking during pregnancy, which is a known prenatal parenting risk factor for children's aggression (D'Onofrio, et al. 2003).

What Research Is Needed?

This very small literature is a good beginning, but a number of limitations need to be overcome. First, the studies have relied on the twin design, and twin-design weaknesses ought to be complemented by the strengths of the adoption design (see Deater-Deckard, Fulker, and Plomin, 1999). Second, measurement has relied on parents' self reports, and thus the findings are a mix between genetic influences on actual parenting behavior and genetic influences on self-perception and self-presentation (Kendler, 1996; Plomin, 1994). As a third limitation, studies have tended to focus on mothers and excluded fathers, for the obvious reason that fathers' non-participation in research disproportionately characterizes families of aggressive children. However, fathers' antisocial behavior in the home is a central aspect of bad parenting that predicts children's aggression (Jaffee, Moffitt, Caspi, and Taylor, 2003). Fourth, and most serious for our purposes of investigating antisocial behavior, the samples under-represent families at serious risk, and the parenting measures do not address the most powerful bad-parenting risk factors for children's aggression, such as exposure to domestic violence, child neglect, maternal rejection, and child abuse. These serious forms of bad parenting themselves constitute antisocial acts, and as a result we should anticipate that the influence of parents' genes on them is much stronger than the genetic influences found for parenting styles within the normative range, such as spanking, monitoring, or limit-setting. Because serious bad parenting is antisocial, it is not un-reasonable to expect genetic influence on serious bad parenting to resemble genetic influence on other antisocial behaviors (50%).

The answer to question 2, "Do parent's genes influence bad parenting?", seems to be "probably". It may surprise that so little research has been done into the question of a genetic contribution to bad parenting. The question has been neglected because parenting has not often been viewed by behavioral-genetic researchers as a phenotypic outcome variable. Moreover, developmental researchers who are interested in parenting as an outcome almost never adopt behavior-genetic research methods. It is quite likely that bad parenting is under some amount of genetic influence because parenting styles are known to be associated with parents' personality traits (Belsky and Barends, 2002; Spinath and O'Connor, 2003) and personality traits are known to be under genetic influence (Plomin and Caspi, 1999). Bad parenting should be treated as a phenotype in future behavioral-genetic research (McGuire, 2003).

Question 3: Does an Effect of Parents' Genes on Bad Parenting Confound a Cause-Effect Interpretation of the Association between Bad Parenting and Children's Aggression?

The technical term for this question is "passive" correlation between genotype and an environmental measure, often abbreviated as "rGE" (Plomin, DeFries, and Loehlin, 1977). A passive rGE confound occurs when a child's behavior and the environment his parents provide are correlated because they have the same origins in his parents' genotype (i.e., not because bad parenting itself causes children's aggression). Parents may transmit to their child a genetic liability for aggression, and simultaneously provide an environment of violent, abusive maltreatment that is symptomatic of the parent's genetic liability for aggression. To the extent that such parenting is under genetic influence, then the observed association between bad parenting and child aggression could be a spurious artefact of a third variable that causes both: genetic transmission. This is why it is important to study passive rGE.

It is important to note that the mere evidence that bad parenting is under influence of parents' genes (question 2) is not sufficient to conclude that this genetic influence goes on to mediate the connection between bad parenting and children's aggression. Rutter and Silberg (2002) make this point, explaining that genes influence which mothers have low birth weight babies but babies' birth weights are wholly determined by environmental conditions, not by any genes inherited from their mothers. To take this point to an extreme, genes influence which breeds of dog bite readily, but once a dog bites, injury to the unfortunate victim is wholly environmentally mediated. Therefore, despite the fact that antisocial behavior is concentrated in families and this concentration is known to be under the influence of parental genes, it remains possible that the pathway from bad parenting to children's aggression is wholly environmentally mediated. For this reason it is important to disentangle (a) the genetic origins of bad parenting from (b) the genetic and environmental mechanisms by which bad parenting produces children's aggression.

Nonetheless, the pairing of bad parenting with children's aggression as risk-factor-and-outcome intuitively raises the question of genetic mediation. The reason behind this intuition is that bad parenting and children's aggression both bear a relation to the antisocial trait. Bad parenting and juveniles' aggression both violate the rights and safety of victims, and both are criteria for antisocial personality disorder (American Psychiatric Association, 1994). Moreover, aggressive children followed up to adulthood are found to be bad parents (Fagot,

Pears, Capaldi, Crosby and Leve, 1998; Jaffee, Caspi, Moffitt, Taylor and Dickson, 2001; Serbin and Karp, 2003). If bad parenting and children's aggression are age-heterotypic expressions of the same genetically influenced trait, this could constitute a rGE that rules out any causal status for bad parenting.

What Research Designs Can Be Used to Answer this Question?

There are at least four appropriate research designs, but to our knowledge none of them has been carried out. We can study *adoptions* to test if the biological parents' bad parenting predicts the adopted-away children's aggression, even if parent and child never have contact. This study has not been conducted, because of the difficulty of obtaining parenting data from adopted children's biological parents. We can compare correlations between bad parenting and children'aggression in *natural families versus adoptive families*. If the correlation is stronger in natural families (which have both genetic and environmental processes of transmission) than in adoptive families (which have only environmental transmission), then genetic transmission is taking place (Plomin, 1994). However, this design is biased toward finding evidence of an rGE confound, because there is more variation in bad parenting among natural than adoptive families, which could produce larger correlations with children's aggression in natural families (Stoolmiller, 1999). To avoid such bias, we can conduct a study *within adoptive families* to test if rearing parents' bad parenting is more strongly correlated with their natural children's aggression than with their adoptive child's aggression (Rutter and Silberg, 2002). The within-family design holds constant the variation in bad parenting across natural versus adoptive parent-child pairs, but requires a sample of families having both an adopted and a natural child, not too far apart in age. We are not aware of a study that has compared the correlations between bad parenting and natural children's aggression versus adoptive children's aggression. However, a study was conducted of 667 adoptive families, which found adoptive parents' reports of "family functioning" were more strongly correlated with self-reported antisocial behavior in their natural child than their adopted child (McGue, Sharma, and Benson, 1996).

A particularly promising method studies *the families of adult MZ twins who are mothers* to test if MZ aunts' bad parenting predicts their nephews' aggression. In this twin-mothers design, both MZ sisters are genetic mothers to each others' birth children. However, the MZ aunt does not provide the rearing environment for her nieces and nephews; only the children's birth mother is an environmental mother to them. If the MZ aunts' and the MZ mothers' parenting predicts the children's aggression to the same extent, this would be strong evidence of a complete rGE confound. But, if the MZ mother's parenting predicts the children's aggression better than does the MZ aunt's parenting, this would show that bad parenting has an environmental effect. This elegant design offers unprecedented capacity to disentangle sources of bad parenting from mechanisms of risk for the children of bad parents, particularly when DZ twin mothers as well as MZ twin mothers are sampled (D'Onofrio et al., 2003; Silberg and Eaves, 2004). This children-of-twins design is newly being applied to the question of causes of children's aggression by Silberg and colleagues (2002), but findings were not available at the time of this writing.

The aforementioned methods test the hypothesis that genetic transmission explains the observed association between bad parenting and child aggression by looking for an effect of parenting on behavior over and above genetic influence on behavior. Another method is to *compare the effect size of the association between bad parenting and children's aggression before versus after genetic influences are controlled.* Any shrinkage estimates the extent to which the association is mediated by genetic transmission. This method is an instance of the familiar test for mediation (Baron and Kenny, 1986). In their meta-analysis of studies of differential treatment of siblings, Turkheimer and Waldron (2000, see their Table 3) showed that the effect sizes for associations between risk factors and behavior outcomes tended to shrink by at least half when genetic confounds were controlled. However, this meta-analysis compared effect sizes across two groups of studies, those with versus without genetic designs, and the groups of studies differed on design features such as sample composition or sample size. Comparisons of the effect sizes for bad parenting predicting children's aggression before and after genetic controls within the same sample would be more informative.

What Research Is Needed?

A close reading of the literature reveals that researchers have neglected the questions of whether genes contribute to bad parenting and whether genetic transmission confounds environmental interpretations of the link between bad parenting and children's aggression. The field seems to have presupposed affirmative answers to these questions but not built a conclusive evidence base. As such, research applying any of the designs described here to parenting is needed. However, a comparison of effect sizes in studies with versus without genetic controls suggests genetic transmission might explain as much as half the connection. The answer to question 3, "Are cause-effect interpretations of the connection between bad parenting and children's aggression confounded by genetic transmission?", seems to be "probably".

Question 4: Does a Genetic "Child Effect" Evoke Bad Parenting to Confound a Cause-Effect Interpretation of the Association between Bad Parenting and Children's Aggression?

The technical term for this question is "evocative" correlation between genotype and an environmental measure, and it is also abbreviated as "rGE" (Plomin, DeFries, and Loehlin, 1977). Evocative rGE occurs when a child's behavior and the parenting he receives are correlated because they have the same origins in his own genotype (i.e., not because bad parenting itself causes children's aggression). The evocative rGE is a conceptual extension of the "child effect" discussed by Bell (1968), who pointed out that children influence their parents' behavior. The child-effect hypothesis has been shown to apply to the question at hand here; namely, children's aggression can elicit bad parenting (e.g., Lytton, 1990). Behavioral geneticists add the hypothesis that the child's parent-provoking behaviors may be under genetic influence. Like passive rGE, evocative rGE confounds interpretation of the association between parenting and children's aggression. To the extent that bad parenting is elicited by a child's genetically influenced behavior, then the observed association between bad parenting and child aggression could be a spurious artefact of a third variable that causes both: the child's genotype.

What Research Designs Can Be Used to Answer this Question?

A large number of studies has ascertained *twins' recollections of how they were treated by their parents* during childhood, and found that MZ twins' ratings of their parents' child-rearing are more similar than DZ twins' ratings, suggesting an influence of childrens' genotype on parents' parenting (Hur and Bouchard, 1995; Rowe, 1983; Kendler, 1996). This literature has been reviewed elsewhere (e.g., Plomin and Bergeman, 1991; Plomin, 1994). There is a basic difficulty with this literature, however. Although it seems reasonable to interpret the findings as evidence for a child effect on bad parenting, studies of twins' self-reports about their parents' treatment of them do not rule out the alternate interpretation of a genetic effect on perceptual bias, according to which MZ twins are more alike than DZ twins in how they interpret their parents' treatment or how they revise their childhood memories (Krueger, Markon and Bouchard, 2003). Nonetheless, the body of studies is generally interpreted as evidence for genetic child effects on parenting because several other studies have shown genetic child effects using adoption and sibling family designs instead of twins, and by using observational or multi-informant measures of parenting instead of twins' self-reports (Braungart, Plomin, and Fulker, 1992; Deater-Deckard, et al., 1999; Neiderhiser et al., 2004; O'Connor, Hetherington, Reiss and Plomin, 1995, Reiss, Neiderhiser, Hetherington, and Plomin, 2000; Rende, Slomkowski, Stocker, Fulker, and Plomin, 1992). These numerous studies decidedly demonstrated that a genetic child effect on parenting exists, but they did not demonstrate what it is that children do to provoke bad parenting. In other words, these studies did not include children's aggression as a measured variable.

Another research design is to study *adoptions*, to test if adoptees' aggression predicts their adoptive parents' bad parenting, while establishing that the adoptees' aggression has a genetic basis (i.e., that it is predicted by their biological parents' antisocial behavior). Three studies have used this compelling design (Ge et al., 1996; O'Connor, Deater-Deckard, Fulker, Rutter and Plomin, 1998; Riggins-Caspers, Cadoret, Knutson, and Langbehn, 2003). The first study examined 41 adolescent adoptees, defined genetic risk as the biological parent's official diagnosis, measured adoptee antisocial behaviors via multiple sources, and measured adoptive parents' hostility, warmth, nurturant involvement, and harsh-inconsistent parenting via multiple sources, including observations (Ge et al., 1996). The second study examined 56 to 80 child adoptees (depending on the analysis), defined genetic risk via biological mother's self-report, and measured adoptee antisocial behaviors and adoptive parents' negative control via adoptive parent self-report (O'Connor et al., 1998). The third study examined 150 adult adoptees, defined genetic risk as biological parent's diagnosis, measured adoptee conduct problems via adoptees' retrospective self-reports, and measured adoptive parents' harsh discipline via adoptee's retrospective reports (Riggins-Caspers et al., 2003). All three studies reported that adoptees who are at high genetic risk for psychopathology receive more discipline and control from their adoptive parents than adoptees who are at low genetic risk. Furthermore, unlike prior research, the three studies demonstrated that the link from a child's genetic risk to adoptive parent's parenting is mediated by the child's genetically influenced aggressive behavior problems. Individual studies in this threesome were limited by a small sample, or by single-source retrospective data, but as a set the three studies provide robust evidence for a genetically mediated child effect in which the causal arrow runs from children's aggression to parenting. However, adoption samples are not well-suited to ascertaining whether the child effect applies to parenting outside the normal range. As a result of self-selection by older, better-educated, higher-income applicants and subsequent screening by adoption agencies, adoptive parents are better prepared than ordinary parents, and moreover they tend to have unusually high motivation for parenting, and responsibility for few children (Stoolmiller, 1999). Designs other than adoption designs are needed to test whether the evocative genetic child-effect extends to the sorts of bad parenting (e.g., child neglect, psychological abuse, physical maltreatment) found in families whose members exhibit serious, persistent antisocial outcomes.

A third design for testing genetic child effects is to study *twin children*, asking whether twin A's aggression predicts the bad parenting received by twin B, and vice versa. This is an application of bi-variate twin modeling. Its basic logic is that if the correlation between Twin A's aggression and Twin B's experience of bad parenting is higher among MZ pairs than DZ pairs, this would indicate that the same set of genetic influences causes children's aggression and provokes bad parenting. Bad parenting must be measured separately for each twin, so that it can be used as a phenotype, like each twin's aggression. Two studies of several hundred sibling pairs taking part in the study of Nonshared Environment in Adolescent Development (NEAD), have applied variations of this bi-variate approach, using multi-source measures of adolescents' and parents' behavior. A genetic child effect accounted for most of the correlation between adolescents' antisocial behavior and parents' negativity assessed cross-sectionally (Pike, McGuire, Hetherington, Reiss, and Plomin, 1996), and longitudinally after accounting for the continuity of adolescent antisocial behavior (Niederhiser, Reiss, Hetherington, and Plomin, 1999).

As noted earlier, it is important to know whether the genetic child effect for ordinary parenting (as indicated by previous adoption studies and the NEAD study) also applies to extreme forms of bad parenting associated with serious, persistent antisocial behavior. We applied the bi-variate modelling approach to this question in our "E-risk" longitudinal study of 1116 British families with young twins (Jaffee, Caspi, Moffitt, Polo-Tomas, Price, and Taylor, 2004 a). To do this, the E-risk study incorporated two innovations (Moffitt et al., 2002). First, it assessed a birth cohort in which 1/3 of families were selected to over-sample families who were at high risk (findings are weighted back to represent the population of British families having babies in the 1990's). Second, the study interviewed mothers about parenting that was beyond normal limits (physical maltreatment: neglectful or abusive care resulting in injury, sexual abuse, registry with child protection services) as well as about parenting in the normative range (frequency of corporal punishment: grabbing, shaking, spanking). Children's genes influenced which children received corporal punishment, explaining 24% of the variation in the cohort, but children's genes were unrelated to becoming a victim of maltreatment. Bi-variate twin modelling of the cross-twin, cross phenotype correlations revealed that children's genes accounted for almost all of the correlation between corporal punishment and children's aggression, indicating that most of the observed association between this form of parenting and children's aggression is a genetic child effect. However, children's genes did not account for the correlation between physical maltreatment and children's aggression, indicating that extreme, serious bad parenting causes children's aggression for reasons that are not genetic. Although difficult children can and do provoke their parents to use frequent corporal punishment in the normal range, factors leading to injurious maltreatment lie not within the child, but within the family environment or the adult abuser. There are limits to child effects.

What Research Is Needed?

Taken together, the adoption and twin studies reviewed in this section provide evidence to answer question 4: Yes, the observed association between normative parenting and child aggression is in large part a spurious artefact of a third variable that causes both: the child's genotype. The child-to-parent effect strongly outweighed any parent-to-child effect in five of the six studies (Ge et al., 1996; Jaffee et al., 2004 a; Niederhiser et al., 1999; Pike et al., 1996; Riggins-Caspers et al., 2003). A provocative deduction from this group of studies is that Scarr (1991) may have been correct when she argued that improving parenting in the normal range of environments will not produce significant changes in children's outcomes because the associations between ordinary parenting and child outcome are not causal. "There is no evidence that family environments, except the worst, have any significant effect on the development of conduct disorders, psychopathy, or other common behavior disorders" (Scarr, 1991, p. 403). Scarr (1992) further argued that damaging environmental conditions outside the expected range will have causal influences on children quite apart from genetic influences, and in keeping with this notion, one study showed maltreatment makes children aggressive apart from any influence of their genotypes. This distinction between normative versus extreme forms of parenting has implications for future research. Most of the genetically informative studies to date have assessed parenting using omnibus measures (e.g., 'family functioning', 'negativism', 'control') because the goal was to ascertain whether or not genetic child effects existed at all. However, parenting intervention programs try to change specific well-defined forms of parental behavior. To inform these interventions, research is needed to query genetic versus environmental mediation of specific features of parenting. Furthermore, the aspects of parenting that correlate with children's aggression are probably quite different in early childhood, later childhood, and adolescence. Genetically informative studies of samples at different ages are needed to inform parenting interventions tailored to developmental stages.

We have looked here at the specific question of whether children's genotype evokes bad parenting, but it is useful to note that the evocative type of rGE is a subset of a larger class referred to as active rGE. Active rGE encompasses at least three different processes, when people's genetically influenced behavior leads them to "(1) create, (2) seek, or (3) otherwise end up in environments that match their genotypes" (Rutter and Silberg, 2002, p. 473). Restated, environments are provoked by a person's genetically influenced behavior, or a person chooses environments consonant with her genotype, or a person's genotype results in him selectively finding himself in certain environments. Antisocial behavior can bring about each of these three processes at any point in the life course (Scarr and McCartney, 1983). Antisocial behavior creates social reactions from others when aggressive toddlers evoke harsh discipline, when child bullies are rejected by peers, when teenagers who fight are expelled from schools, when young shoplifters are convicted by courts, or when abusive husbands are divorced by their wives. Antisocial individuals seek environmental settings consonant with their proclivities when antisocial children gravitate toward a delinquent peer group, when antisocial men and women mate assortatively, when people who like to fight frequent certain bars or attend soccer games, when pedophiles seek volunteer work with children, or when psychopaths infilter retirement communities for easy access to fraud victims. People who have behaved antisocially selectively find themselves in criminogenic environments when troubled children are tracked into special classes for disturbed pupils, when troubled teenagers are recruited by gangs, when violent young men are incarcerated in prisons, or when parolees find nothing but unsavory, unskilled jobs available to them. These active rGE processes are of enormous importance in understanding the continuity of antisocial behavior across the entire life-course (Caspi and Moffitt, 1995; Laub and Sampson, 2003). Once genetically influenced behavior has brought a person into contact with an environment, the environment may have unique causal effects of its own, cutting off opportunities to develop alternative prosocial behaviors, promoting the persistence of antisocial behavior, and exacerbating its seriousness (Moffitt, 1993). Research is needed to test for active rGE processes involved in antisocial behavior at developmental stages across the life course.

Question 5: After All Genetic Confounds Are Controlled, Does Bad Parenting Have Any Environmentally Mediated Effect on Children's Aggression?

The new generation of research designs that can evaluate whether a risk factor has an environmentally mediated effect on children's aggression has three key features. First, the studies must employ a genetically sensitive design to control for the confounding effects of parents' genes or children's genes on putative environmental measures. As we have seen, these confounding effects are at least small to moderate, and in the case of child effects they may be large, so they must be controlled.

The second key feature is that designs must employ an observed measure of the construct alleged to have environmental effects on children; in the case here, bad parenting. Traditional behavioral-genetic studies have reported latent environmental variance components, but not observed measures. This has been problematic because even very large twin studies are underpowered to detect environmental influence on twin similarity as a latent variance component, whereas statistical power to detect such influence is increased if a putative environmental variable is measured so its effects can be estimated empirically (Kendler, 1993). In keeping with this, significant effects for a measured variable have been found even despite the presence of a nonsignificant shared-environment variance component (Kendler, Neale, Kessler, Heath, and Eaves, 1992). In this section we abandon the distinction between 'shared' and 'non-shared' environmental variance components because shared and non-shared effects are not features of a measured environmental risk; one form of bad parenting, such as maltreatment, can exert either shared or non-shared effects, or both (Rutter and Silberg, 2002; Turkheimer and Waldron, 2000).

The third key feature is that genetically informative samples must accurately represent the full range of families' environmental circumstances. Many behavioral-genetic samples suffer substantial biases in recruitment and attrition, inadvertently restricting their range of participating families to primarily the middle class. Contemporary theories of psychopathology implicate experiences outside the normal range such as exposure to domestic violence or child maltreatment, which are generally concentrated in the poorest segment of the population, the segment not sampled by most behavioral-genetic studies. (Scandinavian national twin registers of psychiatric hospital and court records accurately represent variation in the population, but such register studies have been unable to measure children's environments directly.) Newer studies are striving to provide a strong and fair test of the hypothesis that rearing environments influence behavior disorders in a causal manner.

What Research Designs Can Be Used to Answer This Question?

Four basic behavioral-genetic methods can be used to rule out gene-environment correlation confounds while testing causation by putative environmental risk factors. As mentioned before, natural experiments and intervention experiments can also assess environmental causation but here we focus on genetically sensitive designs.

We can study *adoptions* to test if the adoptive parents' bad parenting increases adoptees' aggression, over and above the genetic influence from the biological parents' aggression. The large adoption studies of antisocial behavior that emerged from Scandinavia and the United States in the 1970's and 1980's were primarily cited for their innovation of demonstrating genetic influences; they showed that adoptees' criminal offending was significantly associated with the antisocial behavior of their biological parents, although these parents did not rear the adoptees. However, some of these same studies asked whether adoptees' criminal offending was also associated with the antisocial behavior of the adoptive parents who did rear them (Bohman, Cloninger, Sigverdsson and von Knorring, 1982; Cadoret, Cain, and Crowe, 1983; Mednick and Christiansen, 1977). Rates of antisocial behavior in adoptive parents were extremely low (because of adoption agency screening), and the adoptive-parent effects were very small and often non-significant, but these studies constituted the first real empirical attempts to test if bad parental behavior exerts a non-genetic effect on children's aggression.

To our knowledge, an adoption study of antisocial behavior was the first ever in the behavioral sciences to apply behavioral-genetic methods to control for genetic confounds while testing an environmental hypothesis (VanDusen, Mednick, Gabrielli and Hutchings, 1983). It was well established that low socio-economic status is a risk factor for offending, but Mednick and colleagues were concerned that some dysfunctional genetic susceptibilities transmitted within families might account for the coincidence of fathers' low-status occupations with sons' antisocial activities. As such, they used the Danish Adoption Study data to disentangle the socio-economic status that adoptees were conceived in (their biological father's occupational status) from the socio-economic status in which they were reared (adoptive father's status). Results demonstrated that biological inheritance could not explain the majority of the class-crime connection; the social class in which people grow up had a direct causal environmental effect on their probability of criminal offending (VanDusen et al., 1983).

A recent update of this approach measured marital problems, legal problems, and psychopathology in adoptive parents (Cadoret, Yates, Troughton, Woodworth, and Stewart, 1995). Although these problems initially appeared to be correlated with adoptees' antisocial outcomes, the study detected an interaction between genetic and environmental risk, which indicated that adoptive parents' problems had no effect of their own, in the absence of genetic risk. This finding that adoptive parenting has no effect of its own apart from in interaction with pre-existing genetic risk has been reported by other adoption studies (Mednick, Gabrielli, and Hutchings, 1984). However, it may be difficult to detect parenting effects using adoptive parents, because their parenting tends to be restricted to the normal range (Stoolmiller, 1999). It is possible that mildly bad parenting in the normal range has such weak effects that it only makes a difference if the child is already at genetic risk.

We can study the *children of adult MZ twin mothers*. As described earlier in this article, in this children-of-twin mothers design, the MZ aunt constitutes a genetic mother to the child, but not an environmental mother (Silberg and Eaves, 2004). Thus, if a MZ mother-son correlation is larger than its companion MZ aunt-nephew correlation, this provides evidence that environmental mothering influences children, over and above genes. Such research is underway (D'Onofrio et al., 2003; Silberg, 2002).

We can study *twin children* to test if the shared experience of bad parenting makes children more similar on aggression than could be predicted based on their degree of genetic relationship. A basic approach is to conduct ordinary behavior-genetic modelling that apportions genetic versus environmental effects on child behavior (denoted ACE), and then add a measured putative environmental risk factor (denoted M-ACE) to test if the children's shared experience of that risk factor can account for any of the shared environmental variation in their behavioral phenotype. The first twin study to apply this approach to problem behavior reported that living in a deprived neighborhood explained a significant 5% of the shared environmental variation in two-year-olds' behavior problems (Caspi, Taylor, Moffitt, and Plomin, 2000). Another study applied this approach to examine 5-year-old's exposure to their mothers' experience of domestic violence (Jaffee, Moffitt, Caspi, Taylor, and Arseneault, 2002). Exposure to domestic violence over the first five years of their lives was particularly relevant for children who developed both externalizing and internalizing problems simultaneously; such co-occurring problems are associated with poor prognosis. Domestic violence exposure explained a significant 13.5% of the shared environment variance in children's comorbid outcome. A third, unpublished study reports that measured parental monitoring accounted for 15% of the shared environment variance in behavior problems in a large sample of 11-12 year old Finnish twins (described in Dick and Rose, 2002). A caveat about this approach is in order. Inference of environmental causation is compromised if parent and child share genes that simultaneously influence both the measure of parenting and the measure of child aggression.

The basic twin design can be improved upon by adding indicators of mothers' and fathers' behavioral phenotype to the usual indicators of twin behavior. This approach, called the "extended twin-family design" (Kendler, 1993) estimates the effect of the putative environmental risk factor on child behavior while controlling for genetic effects on both parents and children. An assumption of the design is that the parental phenotype measures carry genetic information parallel to that in the child phenotype measures. (Although this assumption is seldom fulfilled perfectly it seems not unreasonable for antisocial behavior, which has strong child-to-adult continuity.) The first twin study to apply this approach to parenting was reported from the Virginia Twin Study of Adolescent Behavioral Development (Meyer et al., 2000). Antisocial conduct problems were assessed for adolescent twins and their parents in 1350 families. The measured parenting variables were called 'marital discord' and 'family adaptability'. No effect was found for marital discord, but measured family adaptability accounted for 4% of the variance in adolescents' conduct problems.

A complementary approach to testing whether a risk factor has a causal (vs. non-causal) role in the origins of antisocial behavior has been used by studies that rule out passive rGE through statistical controls for parental antisocial behavior. This approach does not differentiate whether the risk factor is influenced at the genotype versus phenotype level of parental antisocial behavior. However, it does offer the advantage that it can be employed in non-twin samples, if phenotypic data are collected for all family members. In the above-mentioned E-Risk longitudinal twin study of 1116 families, we examined the effects of fathers' bad parenting on young children's aggression (Jaffee et al., 2003). Mothers' antisocial behavior was statistically controlled, to make clear that the findings applied specifically to fathers' behavior. As expected from the literature on single mothers, a prosocial father's absence predicted more aggression by his children. But the study revealed a new finding: an antisocial father's *presence* predicted more aggression by his children, and this harmful effect was exacerbated the more years a father lived with the family and the more time each week he spent taking care of the children. Inference of environmental causation was supported because the finding for conventional fathers (less involvement predicts more child aggression) was opposite that for antisocial fathers (more involvement predicts more child aggression), and the latter association held after ruling out passive rGE by statistically controlling for both parents' antisocial histories. Obtaining data from fathers is challenging (Caspi et al., 2001), but because fathers are often a target of social policies, a better evidence base about their parenting is needed.

In another report, the E-risk study evaluated the hypothesis that maternal depression promotes children's aggression (Kim-Cohen, Moffitt, Pawlby, Taylor and Caspi, 2005). Research has shown that the children of depressed mothers are likely to develop conduct problems. However, it has not been clear that this correlation represents environmental transmission, because women's depression is under genetic influence (Kendler et al., 1992), it often co-occurs with a girlhood history of antisocial conduct, which is also under genetic influence (Moffitt, Caspi, Rutter and Silva, 2001), and depressed women often mate assortatively with antisocial men (Moffitt et al., 2001). We controlled for antisocial behavior in the twins' biological father, and for the mothers' own antisocial history. Although the connection between mothers' depression and children's conduct problems decreased after this stringent control for familial liability, it remained statistically significant. It concerned us that depressed women might exaggerate ratings of their children's problem behaviors, but the pattern of findings remained the same when teachers' ratings of child behavior were substituted as the outcome measure. A temporal analysis showed that the effect of maternal depression on children's aggression depended on the timing of the depression episodes (a type of natural experiment design). If E-risk mothers experienced depression, but only before their children's birth and not after, the children were not unusually aggressive. In contrast, only if mothers suffered depression while rearing their children were the children likely to develop aggression. Finally, the possibility that a child effect (in which children's aggression provoked mothers' depression) explained the association was ruled out by documenting within-individual change. After controlling for each child's aggression up to age 5, the children exposed to an episode of maternal depression between ages 5 and 7 became more aggressive by the age 7 assessment. Taken together, these four results are not consistent with a genetic account of the association between maternal depression and children's aggression.

The E-risk study also examined the effects of physical maltreatment on young children's aggression (Jaffee, Caspi, Moffitt, and Taylor, 2004b), using twin-specific reports of maltreatment. This study satisfied six conditions that together supported the hypothesis that physical maltreatment has an environmentally mediated causal influence on children's aggression. (1) Children's maltreatment history prospectively predicted aggression, (2) the severity of maltreatment bore a dose-response relation to aggression, (3) the experience of maltreatment was followed by increases in aggression from prior levels, within individual children, (4) there was no child effect provoking maltreatment, (5) maltreatment predicted aggression while mothers' and fathers' antisocial behavior were statistically controlled, and (6) modest but significant effects of maltreatment on aggression remained present after controlling for genetic transmission of liability to aggression in the family. A similar analytic approach using twin-specific measures of risk was taken by the Minnesota Twin Family Study (Burt, Krueger, McGue, and Iacono, 2003), which studied 808 11-year-old twin pairs. Models revealed that measured parent-child conflict accounted for 12% of the variance in the externalizing syndrome of oppositional, conduct, and attention-deficit-hyperactivity disorders (23% of the common environment variation in this syndrome).

A potential challenge to the findings from the aforementioned studies of parenting effects on twin children is that some of the findings may arise from child effects provoking bad parenting. The finding about parental monitoring is susceptible to this challenge because parental monitoring is known to be subject to strong child effects (Kerr and Stattin, 2000). However, it seems less plausible that children provoke their mothers' domestic violence experience, or their fathers' antisocial history. Ill-behaved children might provoke maternal depression but the study took this into account by showing that children exposed to maternal depression subsequently developed new antisocial behavior. Finally, the possibility that an environmental child effect accounted for the observed influence of maltreatment or parent-child conflict on children's aggression was ruled out by modeling twin-specific measures.

As a final design, we can study *MZ twin children*, to test if differences between siblings in their exposure to bad parenting makes them different on aggression. The fact that MZ twins are not perfectly concordant for aggression opens a window of opportunity to uncover if a non-genetic cause specific to one twin has produced the behavioral difference. A number of studies have tested if differential parental treatment can account for antisocial-behavior differences between siblings and cousins within a family (e.g., Conger and Conger, 1994; Reiss, 2000; Rodgers, Rowe and Li, 1994). Most of these studies have already been reviewed by Turkheimer and Waldron (2000). However, comparing the parenting experiences of discordant MZ twins allows the least ambiguous interpretation of results. Three studies have reported that MZ-twin differences in bad parenting are correlated with MZ-twin differences in antisocial behavior (Asbury, Dunn, Pike and Plomin, 2003; Caspi et al., 2004; Pike, Reiss, Hetherington and Plomin, 1996).

The E-Risk Study reported that within 600 MZ twin pairs, the twin who received relatively more maternal negativity and less maternal warmth developed more antisocial behavior problems (Caspi et al., 2004). Negativity and warmth were measured by coding voice tone and speech content in mothers' audiotaped speech about each of their twins separately, according to the well-known "expressed emotion" paradigm. This study provided the strongest evidence to date that the effect of mothers' emotional treatment of children causes aggression, by ruling out five alternative explanations of the finding. (1) Using MZ twin pairs ruled out the possibility that a genetically transmitted liability explained both the mother's emotion and her child's antisocial behavior. (2) Using MZ twins also ruled out the possibility that a genetic child effect provoking maternal emotion accounted for the finding. (3) The study used the longitudinal natural experiment approach to rule out that any non-genetic child effect provoking maternal emotion accounted for the finding, by controlling for prior behavior that could have provoked maternal negative emotion and showing that individual children whose mothers were negative toward them at age 5 evidenced a subsequent increase of antisocial behavior between age 5 and age 7. (4) The study controlled for twin differences in birth weight in an effort to rule out the possibility that twins with neuro-developmental difficulties had more behavior problems and elicited more negative emotion from mothers. (5) The study measured the children's behavior using teacher reports to rule out the possibility that a mother's negativity toward a child led her to exaggerate her report of the child's behavior problems. Effect sizes for the influence of maternal emotion on children's aggression ranged from large ($r = .53$) to small ($r = .10$), depending on how many controls were applied.

Not All Tests of Putative Environmental Risk Factors Confirm Environmental Effects

Lest readers assume that application of behavioral-genetic methods to a putative environmental risk factor will necessarily affirm that its effects are environmentally mediated, it is useful to mention that some known risk factors do not appear to be causal. First, as noted above, we found that children's genes accounted for virtually all of the association between their corporal punishment (i.e., spanking) and their conduct problems. This indicated a "child effect", in which children's bad conduct provokes their parents to use more corporal punishment, rather than the reverse (Jaffee et al., 2004 a).

Second, studies have reported that mothers' smoking during pregnancy is correlated with children's conduct problems, but pregnancy smoking is known to be concentrated among mothers who are antisocial, have mental health problems, mate with antisocial men, and rear children in conditions of social deprivation. When the family liability for transmission of psychopathology from parents to children was controlled through statistical controls for the parents' antisocial behavior, mental health, and social deprivation, the effect of even heavy smoking during pregnancy disappeared. This study suggests that although pregnancy smoking undoubtedly has undesirable effects on outcomes such as infant birth weight, it is probably not a cause of conduct problems (Maughan, Taylor, Caspi, and Moffitt, 2004).

A third finding of nil environmental influence concerned father absence. In families having absent fathers, the children are known to have more conduct problems. However, absent fathers are more antisocial on average than fathers who stay with their children, and antisocial behavior can be genetically transmitted. We controlled for mother's and father's antisocial history, and found that the association between father absence/presence and children's conduct problems disappeared. This suggests that father absence is not a direct cause of conduct problems, but rather is a proxy indicator for familial liability to antisocial behavior (Jaffee et al., 2003).

What Research Is Needed?

To date, question 5, "Does bad parenting have an environmentally mediated causal effect on children's aggression?" has been answered in the affirmative by behavioral-genetic reports from several twin samples, finding such effects for family adaptability, parent-child conflict, parental monitoring, bad fathering, maternal depression, physical maltreatment, and mothers' negative expressed emotions. These studies share an Achilles' heel; because different forms of parenting risk are concentrated in the same families, the particular parenting measure targeted in a study may be a proxy for some other, correlated risk factor. Research is needed that isolates the effects of one risk factor from its correlates. Nevertheless, whatever the most influential parenting behaviors are, the studies attest that parents can have environmentally mediated effects.

All of the studies testing measured environmental variables were conducted very recently, illustrating that such testing is a new direction in behavior-genetic research (Dick and Rose, 2002; Kendler, 2001). In keeping with this article's example program of research into bad parenting and children's aggression, we reviewed only studies measuring "bad parenting". It wasn't necessary to use bad parenting to illustrate how behavioral-genetic methods can be used to study environmental causation; the methods can and should be applied to any known risk factor for antisocial behavior, from lead toxicity to unemployment. However, our choice of bad parenting allowed us to cover the majority of studies published to date that have looked at measured risk factors for antisocial behavior using genetically sensitive designs. So far, behavior-genetic designs have been applied to test causation for only a handful of other risk factors for antisocial behavior: neighborhood deprivation (Caspi et al., 2000; Cleveland, 2003), school classmates' behavior (Rose, Viken, Dick, Bates, Pulkkinen, and Kaprio, 2003), and child sexual abuse (Dinwiddie, et al. 2000). This small set of studies signals the beginning of a major research initiative. We expect the list of risk factors studied with behavioral-genetic controls to grow to encompass environmental factors ranging from prenatal teratogens to prison sanctioning of adult offenders.

The Environmental Effects Reported in Studies that Controlled for Genetic Influences Were Uniformly Small

It may surprise some developmentalists to learn that when familial liability and child effects are controlled, parenting influences on children drop to small effect sizes. However, small effects ought to be expected, for three reasons. First, it must be remembered that these small effects reflect true environmental associations after they have been purged of the confounding influences that inflate effect sizes in non-genetic studies. Associations between risk factors and behavior outcomes tend to shrink by at least half when genetic confounds are controlled (Turkheimer and Waldron, 2000). This shrinkage suggests that the risk-outcome correlations that social scientists are accustomed to seeing are inflated to about double their true size. Second, small effects for any particular risk factor make sense, in view of evidence that clear risk for antisocial behavior accrues only when a person accumulates a large number of risks (Rutter, Giller and Hagell, 1998), each of which may individually have only a small effect (Daniels and Plomin, 1985).

A third reason why small effects should not be too surprising is that they represent the main effects of measured environments, apart from any environmental effects involved in gene-environment interactions. Recall that adoption studies found no effects of bad adoptive parenting in the absence of genetic liability, but bad adoptive parenting was associated with elevated antisocial outcomes for adoptees at genetic risk (Cadoret et al., 1995; Mednick et al., 1984). In twin designs, when testing whether the shared experience of bad parenting enhances twin similarity in aggression over and above genetic influences on similarity, gene x environment interactions are controlled along with other genetic influences. In twin designs testing whether differential experiences of bad parenting are associated with MZ-twin differences in aggression, differential outcomes arising from gene x environment interactions are ruled out by the twins' identical genotypes. In contrast, genetic risk and bad parenting are not usually disentangled in real life as they are in behavioral-genetic studies. In ordinary lives, genetic and environmental risks often coincide. It is possible in theory that environmental effects conditional on genetic vulnerability could be quite large. We next turn to the question of gene x environment interactions influencing antisocial behavior.

QUESTION 6: TESTING THE HYPOTHESIS OF INTERACTION BETWEEN GENES AND ENVIRONMENTS

The study of gene-environment interaction entails substantial methodological challenges. It requires measured environments that are truly environmental, measured genetic influence, some means of separating them from each other, and enough statistical power for a sensitive test of interaction (Rutter and Silberg, 2002). Despite the challenges, theory-driven hypotheses of GxE interaction are well worth testing, because where measured GxE are found to influence behavior disorders, both specific genes and specific environmental risks can conceivably have moderate-to-large effects, as opposed to the very small effects expected from prior quantitative genetic research. Specific genes revealed to be stronger in the presence of environmental risk would guide strategic research into those genes' expression, possibly leading to genetic diagnostics and improved pharmacological interventions (Evans and Relling, 1999). Specific environmental effects revealed to be stronger in the presence of genetic risk would prompt a new impetus for specific environmental prevention efforts, and would help to identify who needs the prevention programs most. The study of GxE is especially exciting in antisocial behavior research, where investigations have pioneered the way for all behavioral disorders. Studies of antisocial behavior were first to report evidence of interaction between latent genetic and latent environmental risks ascertained in adoption studies, and also first to report evidence of an interaction between a measured genetic polymorphism and a measured environmental risk. Four research designs have been used.

Adoption Studies of Latent GxE

The first evidence that genetic and environmental risks influence antisocial behavior together in a synergistic way came from adoption studies. Among the 6,000 families of male adoptees in the Danish Adoption Study, 14% of adoptees were convicted of crime though neither their biological nor adoptive parents had been convicted, whereas 15% were convicted if their adoptive parent alone was convicted, 20% were convicted if their biological parent alone was convicted, and 25% were convicted if both biological and adoptive parents were convicted, although there were only 143 such cases (Mednick and Christiansen, 1977). This pattern of percentages did not represent a statistically significant cross-over interaction term, but it did illustrate clearly that the effects of genetic and environmental risk acting together were greater than the effects of either factor acting alone. The finding was buttressed by two studies from American and Swedish adoption registers completed about the same time (Cadoret, Cain and Crowe, 1983; Cloninger, et al.,1982).

Adoption Studies of Latent G x Measured E

In a pool of 500 adoptees from the Iowa and Missouri adoption studies, adoptees had the most elevated antisocial behaviors when they experienced "adverse circumstances" in their adoptive homes as well as having birth mothers with antisocial personality problems or alcoholism (Cadoret, et al.1983). This landmark study documented that the interaction was statistically significant, and replicated across two independent samples. This finding was replicated and extended in another Iowa adoption cohort of 200 families (Cadoret, et al., 1995). Adoptive parents' adversity was defined according to the presence of marital problems, legal problems, substance abuse, or mental disorder and it interacted significantly with biological parents' antisocial personality disorder to predict elevated rates of childhood aggression, adolescent aggression, and diagnosed conduct disorder in the adoptees. This same Iowa adoption study was creatively analyzed to demonstrate that adversity in the adoptive home can moderate the genetic child-effect in which children's aggression provokes bad parenting (Riggins-Caspers et al., 2003). Adoptees' genetic liability for antisocial behavior (defined as biological parents' psychopathology) provoked more harsh discipline from the adoptive parents in homes where the adoptive parents suffered adversity (marital, legal, substance or psychopathology problems). There is one problem with studying GxE in adoption designs, and that is that adoption itself breaks up the naturally occurring processes of rGE that characterize the non-adopted majority population, thereby precluding the possibility of GxE. This separation allows the empirical study of GxE, but paradoxically, it probably results in an underestimate of the influence of GxE on antisocial outcomes in the general population. For this reason, adoption GxE studies should be complemented with twin studies.

A Twin Study of Latent G x Measured E

Our E-risk twin study also yielded evidence that genetic and environmental risks interact (Jaffee, Caspi, Moffitt, Dodge, Rutter, Taylor, and Tully, 2005). Because we already knew that conduct problems were highly heritable in the E-risk twin sample at age 5 years (Arseneault et al., 2003), we were able to estimate each child's personal genetic risk for conduct problems by considering whether his or her co-twin had already been diagnosed with conduct disorder, and whether he or she shared 100% versus 50% of genes with that diagnosed co-twin. This method's usefulness had been demonstrated previously in a landmark GxE study showing that the risk of depression following life-event stress depends on genetic vulnerability (Kendler, et al.,1995). For example, an individual's genetic risk is highest if his or her co-twin sibling already has a diagnosis of disorder and the pair is monozygotic. Likewise, an individual's genetic risk is lowest if his or her co-twin has been free from disorder and the pair is monozygotic. Individuals in dizygotic twin pairs fall between the high and low genetic risk groups. In our study an interaction was obtained such that the effect of maltreatment on conduct problem symptoms was significantly stronger among children at high genetic risk than among children at low genetic risk. (Because there was no genetic child effect provoking maltreatment, the genetic risk groups did not differ on concordance for maltreatment or the severity of maltreatment). In addition, the experience of maltreatment was associated with an increase of 24% in the probability of diagnosable conduct disorder among children at high genetic risk, but an increase of only 2% among children at low risk.

Studies of Measured G x Measured E; Testing a Measured Gene

The aforementioned adoption and twin studies established that genotype does interact with bad parenting in the etiological processes leading to antisocial behavior. However, the studies did not implicate any particular genes. We conducted one study to test the hypothesis of gene x environment interaction using a measured environmental risk, child maltreatment, and an identified gene, the MAOA polymorphism (Caspi, et al., 2002). We selected the MAOA gene as the candidate gene for our study for four reasons (supporting research is cited in Caspi et al., 2002). First, the gene encodes the MAOA enzyme, which metabolizes the neurotransmitters linked to maltreatment victimization and aggressive behavior by previous research. Second, drugs inhibiting the action of the MAO enzyme have been shown to prevent animals from habituating to chronic stressors analogous to maltreatment, and to dispose animals toward hyper-reactivity to threat. Third, in studies of mice having the MAOA gene deleted, increased levels of neurotransmitters and aggressive behavior were observed, and aggression was normalized by restoring MAOA gene expression. Fourth, an extremely rare mutation causing a null allele at the MAOA locus was associated with aggressive psychopathology among some men in a Dutch family pedigree, although no relation between MAOA genotype and aggression had been detected for people in the general population.

We selected maltreatment for this study for four reasons (supporting research is cited in Caspi et al., 2002). First, childhood maltreatment is a known predictor of antisocial outcomes. Second, not all maltreated children become antisocial, suggesting that vulnerability to maltreatment is influenced by heretofore unstudied individual characteristics. Third, our abovementioned twin research had established that maltreatment's effect on children's aggression is environmentally mediated, i.e., the association is not an artefact of a genetic child-effect provoking maltreatment nor of transmission of aggression-prone genes from parents. As such, maltreatment can serve as the environmental variable in a test of gene x environment interaction. Fourth, animal and human studies suggest that maltreatment in early life alters neurotransmitter systems in ways that can persist into adulthood and can influence aggressive behavior.

Based on this logic to support our hypothesis of GxE, we measured childhood maltreatment history (8% severe, 28% probable, 64% not maltreated) and MAOA genotype (37% low-activity risk allele, 63% high-activity allele) in the 442 caucasian males of the longitudinal Dunedin Multidisciplinary Health and Development Study. We found that maltreatment history and genotype interacted to predict four different measures of antisocial outcome: an adolescent diagnosis of conduct disorder, an age-26 personality assessment of aggression, symptoms of adult antisocial personality disorder reported by informants who knew the study members well, and court conviction for violent crime up to age 26, the latest age of follow-up. Among boys having the combination of the low-MAOA-activity allele and severe maltreatment, 85% developed some form of antisocial outcome. Males having the combination of the low-activity allele and severe-to-probable maltreatment were only 12% of the male birth cohort, but they accounted for 44% of the cohort's violent convictions, because they offended at a higher rate on average than other violent offenders in the cohort.

Replication of this study was of utmost importance, because the study reported the first instance of interaction between a measured gene and a measured environment in the behavioral sciences, and because reports of connections between measured genes and disorders are notorious for their poor replication record (Hamer, 2002). One initial positive replication, and extension, has emerged from the Virginia Twin Study for Adolescent Behavioral Development (Foley, et al., 2004). This team studied 514 caucasian male twins and measured environmental risk using an adversity index comprised of parental neglect, inter-parental violence, and inconsistent discipline. MAOA genotype and adversity interacted significantly such that 15% of boys having adversity but the high-MAOA-activity allele developed conduct disorder, in comparison to 35% of boys having adversity plus the low-activity allele. This study went a step further, controlling for maternal antisocial personality disorder to rule out the possibility that passive rGE might have resulted in the co-occurrence of environmental and genetic risk. This study thus replicated the original GxE between the MAOA polymorphism and maltreatment, extended it to other forms of parental treatment, and showed that it is not an artefact of passive rGE.

Genes as Protective Factors Promoting Resilience

An intriguing finding from the two MAOA GxE studies was that, in contrast to the GxE interaction's marked effects on antisocial outcomes, the unique effects of maltreatment apart from its role in the GxE interaction were very modest. Maltreatment initially predicted antisocial outcomes in the full cohorts, but within the high-MAOA-activity genotype group its effects were reduced by more than half (Caspi et al., 2002; Foley et al., 2004). This pattern is in keeping with the findings from adoption and twin studies cited earlier in this section, all of which found that measured bad parenting had relatively little effect on children who were at low genetic risk (Cadoret et al., 1983; Cadoret et al., 1995; Cloninger et al., 1982; Jaffee et al., 2005; Mednick et al., 1984). Taken together, these findings suggest the novel notion that genotype can be a protective factor against adversity. Some people respond poorly to adversity while others are resilient to it, and the reason for this variation has been a holy grail in developmental research. The search for sources of resilience has tended to focus on social experiences thought to protect children, overlooking a potential protective role of genes (but see Kim-Cohen, Moffitt, Caspi, and Taylor, 2004). The potential protective effect of genes deserves more attention (Insel and Collins, 2003).

In this chapter we reviewed the first studies in a new generation of research that exploits behavioral-genetic designs to address the interplay between measured environmental risks and genetic risks in the origins of antisocial behavior. This work has only recently accelerated, and more of it is needed before drawing conclusions. However, even the few studies so far counteract prior claims that associations between family risk factors and child antisocial outcome might be nothing more than a spurious artifact of familial genetic transmission. This argument can be subjected to empirical test, and such tests need to address both child effects on environments (involving children's genes) and gene-environment correlations (involving parents' genes). Further, although the "residual main effects" of environmental risk factors may appear small after controlling for genetic transmission, that is not the whole story. Emerging evidence about gene-environment interactions suggests that environmental risks can affect people more strongly than previously appreciated, in genetically vulnerable segments of the population. Although this chapter has argued that twin and adoption studies together can provide a good evidence base, the most compelling information about gene-environment interplay will come from converging findings from behavioral-genetic designs, treatment experiments, and longitudinal natural experiments showing within-individual change.

ACKNOWLEDGEMENTS

Work on this review was supported by grants from the US National Institute of Mental Health (MH45070 and MH49414), the UK Medical Research Council (G9806489 and G0100527), and a Royal Society-Wolfson Research Merit Award.

REFERENCES

American Psychiatric Association (1994). *Diagnostic and statistical manual of mental disorders,* (4th ed.). Washington, DC: Author.

Arseneault, L., Moffitt, T.E., Caspi, A., Taylor, A., Rijsdijk, F.V., Jaffee, S., Ablow, J.C., and Measelle, J.R. (2003). Strong genetic effects on cross-situational antisocial behaviour among 5-year-old children according to mothers, teachers, examiner-observers, and twins' self-reports. *Journal of Child Psychology and Psychiatry, 44,* 832-848.

Asbury, K., Dunn, J., Pike, A., and Plomin, R. (2003). Nonshared environmental influences on individual differences in early behavioral development: A monozygotic twin differences study. *Child Development, 74,* 933-943.

Baron, R.M., and Kenny, D.A. (1986). The moderator-mediator distinction in social psychological research: Conceptual, strategic, and statistical considerations. *Journal of Personality and Social Psychology, 511*, 1173-1182.

Belsky, J., and Barends, N. (2002). Personality and parenting. In M.H. Bornstein (Ed.), *Handbook of parenting: Vol. 3: Being and becoming a parent (2nd ed.)* (pp. 415-438). Mahwah, NJ: Lawrence Erlbaum Associates.

Bell, R.Q. (1968). A reinterpretation of the direction of effects in socialization. *Psychological Review, 75*, 81-95.

Blumstein, A., and Cohen, J. (1987). Characterizing criminal careers. *Science, 237,* 985-991.

Bohman, M., Cloninger, R., Sigvardsson, S., and von Knorring, A.L. (1982). Predisposition to petty criminality in Swedish adpotees. I. Genetic and environmental heterogeneity. *Archives of General Psychiatry, 39,* 1233-1241.

Braungart, J.M., Plomin, R., and Fulker, D.W. (1992). Genetic mediation of the home environment during infancy: A sibling adoption study of the HOME. *Developmental Psychology, 28*, 1048-1055.

Burt, A.S., Krueger, R.F., McGue, M., and Iacono, W. (2003). Parent-child conflict and the comorbidity among childhood externalizing disorders. *Archives of General Psychiatry, 60*, 505-513.

Butterfield, F. (1996). *All God's children: the Bosket family and the American tradition of violence.* NY: Avon.

Butterfield, F. (2002, August 21). Father steals best: Crime in an American family. *The New York Times*, from http://www.nytimes.com/2002/08/21/national/21FAMI.html

Cadoret, R.J., Cain, C.A., and Crowe, R.R. (1983). Evidence for gene-environment interaction in the development of adolescent antisocial behavior. *Behavior Genetics, 13*, 301-310.

Cadoret, R.J., Yates, W.R., Troughton, E., Woodworth, G, and Stewart, M.A.S. (1995). Genetic-environmental interaction in the genesis of aggressivity and conduct disorders. *Archives of General Psychiatry, 52,* 916-24.

Caspi, A., McClay, J, Moffitt, T.E., Mill, J., Martin, J., Craig, I., Taylor, A., and Poulton, R. (2002). Role of genotype in the cycle of violence in maltreated children. *Science, 297*, 851-854.

Caspi, A., and Moffitt, T.E. (1995). The continuity of maladaptive behavior. In D. Cicchetti and D. Cohen (Eds.), *Manual of developmental psychopathology* (Vol. 2; pp. 472-511). New York: Wiley.

Caspi, A., Moffitt, T., Morgan, J., Rutter, M., Taylor, A., Arseneault, L., Tully, L., Jacobs, C. Kim-Cohen, J, and Polo-Tomas, M. (2004). Maternal expressed emotion predicts children's antisocial behavior problems: Using MZ-twin differences to identify environmental effects on behavioral development. *Developmental Psychology, 40(2)* 149-161.

Caspi, A, Taylor, A, Moffitt, T.E., and Plomin, R. (2000). Neighborhood deprivation affects children's mental health: Environmental risks identified using a genetic design. *Psychological Science, 11*, 338-342.

Caspi, A., Taylor, A., Smart, M.A., Jackson, J., Tagami, S., and Moffitt, T.E. (2001). Can women provide reliable information about their children's fathers? Cross-informant agreement about men's antisocial behaviour. *Journal of Child Psychology and Psychiatry, 42*, 915-920.

Cichetti, D. (2003). Experiments of nature: Contributions to developmental theory. *Development and Psychopathology, 15,* 833-835.

Cleveland, H.H. (2003). Disadvantaged neighborhoods and adolescent aggression: Behavioral genetic evidence of contextual effects. *Journal of Research on Adolescence, 13,* 211-238.

Cloninger, C.R., and Gottesman I.I. (1987). Genetic and environmental factors in antisocial behavior disorders. In S.A. Mednick, T.E. Moffitt, and S.A. Stack (Eds.), *The causes of crime: New biological approaches* (pp. 92-109). New York: Cambridge University Press.

Cloninger, C.R., Sigvardsson, S., Bohman, M., and von Knorring, A.L. (1982). Predisposition to petty criminality in Swedish adoptees. II. Cross-fostering analysis of gene-environment interaction. *Archives of General Psychiatry, 39*, 1242-1247.

Collins, W.A., Maccoby, E.E., Steinberg, L., Hetherington, E.M., and Bornstein, M.H. (2000). Contemporary research on parenting. *American Psychologist, 55,* 218-232.

Conger, K.J., and Conger, R.D. (1994). Differential parenting and change in sibling differences in delinquency. *Journal of Family Psychology, 8*, 287-302.

Costello, E.J., Compton, S.N., Keeler, G., and Angold, A. (2003). Relationships between poverty and psychopathology: A natural experiment. *Journal of the American Medical Association, 290,* 2023-2029.

Daniels, D., and Plomin, R. (1985). Differential experience of siblings in the same family. *Developmental Psychology, 21,* 747-760.

Deater-Deckard, K., Fulker, D.W., and Plomin, R. (1999). A genetic study of the family environment in the transition to early adolescence. *Journal of Child Psychology and Psychiatry, 40,* 769-775.

Dick, D.M., and Rose, R.J. (2002). Behavior genetics: What's new? What's next? *Current Directions in Psychological Science, 11,* 70-74.

DiLalla, L.F. (2002). Behavior genetics of aggression in children: Review and future directions. *Developmental Review, 22,* 593-622.

DiLalla, L.F., and Gottesman, I.I. (1991). Biological and genetic contributions to violence: Widom's untold tale. *Psychological Bulletin, 109,* 125-129.

Dinwiddie, S., Heath, A.C., Dunne, M.P., Bucholz, K.K., Madden, P.A.F., Slutske, W.S., Bierut, L.J., Statham, D.B., and Martin, N.G. (2000). Early sexual abuse and lifetime psychopathology: A co-twin control study. *Psychological Medicine, 30,* 41-52.

Dishion, T.J., McCord, J., and Poulin, F. (1999). Iatrogenic effects in interventions that aggregate high-risk youth. *American Psychologist, 54,* 1-10.

Dodge, K.A. (2003). Investing in the prevention of youth violence. *International Society for the Study of Behavioral Development Newsletter, 2,* 8-10.

D'Onofrio, B.M., Turkheimer, E.N., Eaves, L.J., Corey, L.A., Berg, K., Solaas, M.H., and Emery, R.E. (2003). The role of the children of twins design in elucidating causal relations between parent characteristics and child outcomes. *Journal of Child Psychiatry and Psychology, 44,* 1130 – 1144.

Evans, W.E., and Relling, M.V. (1999). Pharmacogenetics: Translating functional genomics into rational therapeutics. *Science, 286,* 487-491.

Fagot, B.I., Pears, K.C., Capaldi, D.M., Crosby, L., and Leve, C.S. (1998). Becoming an adolescent father: Precursors and parenting. *Developmental Psychology, 34,* 1209-1219.

Farrington, D.P. (1988). Studying changes within individuals: The causes of offending. In M. Rutter (Ed.) *Studies of psychosocial risk: The power of longitudinal data* (pp.158-183). Cambridge: Cambridge University Press.

Farrington, D.P., Barnes, G.C., and Lambert, S. (1996). The concentration of offending in families. *Legal and Criminological Psychology, 1,* 47-63.

Farrington, D.P., Jolliffe, D., Loeber, R., Stouthamer-Loeber, M., and Kalb, L. (2001). The concentration of offenders in families, and family criminality in the prediction of boys' delinquency. *Journal of Adolescence, 24,* 579-596.

Farrington, D.M. (2003) Developmental and life-course criminology. *Criminology, 41,* 201-235.

Fergusson, D.M., Lynskey, M., and Horwood, L.J. (1995). The adolescent outcomes of adoption: A 16-year longitudinal study. *Journal of Child Psychology and Psychiatry, 36,* 597-615.

Foley, D, Eaves, L., Wormley, B., Silberg, J., Maes, H., Hewitt, J., Kuhn, J., and Riley, B. (2004). Childhood adversity, MAOA genotype, and risk for conduct disorder. *Archives of General Psychiatry, 61,* 738-744.

Galbaud du Fort, G., Boothroyd, L.J., Bland, R.C., Newman, S.C., and Kakuma, R. (2002). Spouse similarity for antisocial behaviour in the general population. *Psychological Medicine, 32,* 1407-1416.

Ge, X., Conger, R.D., Cadoret, R.J., Neiderhiser, J.M., Yates, W., Troughton, E., and Steward, M.A. (1996). The developmental interface between nature and nurture: A mutual influence model of childhood antisocial behavior and parent behavior. *Developmental Psychology, 32*, 574-589.

Gjone, H., and Novik, T.S. (1995). Parental ratings of behaviour problems: A twin and general population comparison. *Journal of Child Psychology and Psychiatry, 36*, 1213-1224.

Hamer, D. (2002). Rethinking behavior genetics. *Science, 298*, 71-72.

Harris, J.R. (1998). *The nurture assumption.* New York: Free Press.

Heinrich, C.C., Brown, J.L., and Aber, J.L. (1999). *Evaluating the effectiveness of school-based violence prevention: Developmental approaches* (Society for Research in Child Development Social Policy Report, XIII, No. 3, pp. 1-18). Ann Arbor, MI: SRCD Executive Office.

Hinshaw, S. P. (2002). Intervention research, theoretical mechanisms, and causal processes related to externalizing behavior patterns. *Development and Psychopathology, 14,* 789 – 818.

Howe, G.W., Reiss, D., and Yuh, J. (2002). Can prevention trials test theories of etiology? *Development and Psychopathology, 14,* 673-694.

Hur, Y., and Bouchard, T.J. Jr. (1995). Genetic influences on perceptions of childhood family environment: A reared-apart twin study. *Child Development, 66,* 330-345.

Hutchings, B., and Mednick, S.A. (1973). Genetic and environmental influences on criminality in Denmark. In B.S. Brown, and E.F. Torrey (Eds.), *International collaboration in mental health* (pp. 113-123). Rockville. MD: National Institute of Mental Health.

Insel, T.R., and Collins, F.S. (2003). Psychiatry in the genomics era. *American Journal of Psychiatry, 160,* 616-620.

Jaffee, S.R., Caspi, A., Moffitt, T.E., Taylor, A., and Dickson, N. (2001). Predicting early fatherhood and whether young fathers live with their children: Prospective findings and policy recommendations. *Journal of Child Psychology and Psychiatry, 42,* 803-815.

Jaffee, S. R., Caspi, A., Moffitt, T. E., and Taylor, A. (2004 b*).* Physical maltreatment victim to antisocial child: Evidence of an environmentally-mediated process. *Journal of Abnormal Psychology, 113(1),* 44-55.

Jaffee, S.R, Caspi, A., Moffitt, T.E., Polo-Tomas, M., Price, T., and Taylor, A. (2004 a). The limits of child effects: Evidence for genetically-mediated child effects on corporal punishment, but not on maltreatment. *Developmental Psychology, 40,* 1047-1058.

Jaffee, S.R., Caspi, A., Moffitt, T.E., Dodge, K., Rutter, M., and Taylor, A., Tully, L. (2005). Nature x Nurture: Genetic vulnerabilities interact with physical maltreatment to promote behavior problems. *Development and Psychopathology, 17*, 67-84.

Jaffee, S.R., Moffitt, T.E., Caspi, A, and Taylor, A. (2003). Life with (or without) father: The benefits of living with two biological parents depend on the father's antisocial behavior. *Child Development, 74,* 109-126.

Jaffee, S. R., Moffitt, T.E., Caspi, A., Taylor, A., and Arseneault, L. (2002). The influence of adult domestic violence on children's internalizing and externalizing problems: An environmentally-informative twin study. *Journal of the American Academy of Child and Adolescent Psychiatry, 41*, 1095-1103.

Johnson, W., Krueger, RF, Bouchard, T.J, and McGue, M. (2002). The personalities of twins: Just ordinary folks. *Twin Research, 5,* 125-131.

Jorgensen, A.L., Phillip, J., Raskind, W.H., Matsushita, M., Christensen, B., Dreyer, V., and Motulsky, A.A. (1992). Different patterns of X inactivation in MZ twins discordant for red-green color vision deficiency. *American Journal of Human Genetics, 51,* 291-298.

Kendler, K.S. (1993). Twin studies of psychiatric illness. *Archives of General Psychiatry, 50,* 905-915.

Kendler, K.S. (1996). Parenting: A genetic epidemiologic perspective. *American Journal of Psychiatry, 153,* 11-20.

Kendler, K.S. (2001). Twin studies of psychiatric illness: An update. *Archives of General Psychiatry, 58,* 1005-1014.

Kendler, K.S., Kessler, R.C., Walters, E.E., MacLean, C., Neale, M.C., Heath, A.C., and Eaves, L.J. (1995). Stressful life events, genetic liability and onset of an episode of major depression in women. *American Journal of Psychiatry, 152,* 833-842.

Kendler, K.S., Neale, M.C., Kessler, R.C., Heath, A.C., and Eaves, L.J. (1992). Childhood parental loss and adult psychopathology in women: A twin study perspective. *Archives of General Psychiatry, 49*, 109-116.

Kendler, K.S., Neale, M.C., Kessler, R.C., Heath, A.C., and Eaves, L.J. (1994). Parental treatment and the equal environments assumption in twin studies of psychiatric illness. *Psychological Medicine, 24,* 579-590.

Kendler, K.S., Prescott, C.A., Myers, J., and Neale, M.C. (2003). The structure of genetic and environmental risk factors for common psychiatric and substance use disorders in men and women. *Archives of General Psychiatry, 60*, 929-937.

Kerr, M., and Stattin, H. (2000). What parents know, how they know it, and several forms of adolescent adjustment: Further support for a reinterpretation of monitoring. *Developmental Psychology, 36*, 366-380.

Kim-Cohen, J., Moffitt, T.E., Caspi, A. and Taylor, A. (2004). Genetic and environmental processes in young children's resilience and vulnerability to socio-economic deprivation. *Child Development*, *75(3),* 651-668.

Kim-Cohen, J., Moffitt, T.E., Taylor, A., Pawlby, S.J., Caspi, A. (2005). Maternal Depression and children's antisocial behavior: Nature and nurture effects. *Archives of General Psychiatry, 62,* 173-181.

Klein, M.W. (1995). *The American street gang*. New York: Oxford University Press.

Kraemer, H.C. (2003). Current concepts of risk in psychiatric disorders. *Current Opinion in Psychiatry, 16*, 421-430.

Kraemer, H.C, Kazdin, A.E., Offord, D.R., Kessler, R.C., Jensen, P.S., and Kupfer, D.J. (1997). Coming to terms with the terms of risk. *Archives of General Psychiatry, 54,* 337-343.

Krueger R.F., Markon K.E., Bouchard T.J. (2003). The extended genotype: The heritability of personality accounts for the heritability of recalled family environments in twins reared apart. *Journal of Personality, 71*, 809-833.

Krueger, R.F., Moffitt, T.E., Caspi, A., Bleske, A., and Silva, P.A. (1998). Assortative mating for antisocial behavior: Developmental and methodological implications. *Behavior Genetics, 28,* 173-186.

Lahey, B., Moffitt, T.E., and Caspi, A. (Eds.) (2003). *The causes of conduct disorder and serious juvenile delinquency.* NY: Guilford.

Laub, J.H., and Sampson, R.J. (2003). *Shared Beginnings, Divergent Lives: Delinquent Boys to age 70.* Cambridge, MA: Harvard University Press.

Levy, F., Hay, D., McLaughlin, M., Wood, C., and Waldman, I. (1996). Twin-sibling differences in parental reports of ADHD, speech, reading, and behavioural problems. *Journal of Child Psychology and Psychiatry, 37*, 569-578.

Lipsey, M.W., and Wilson, D.B. (1998). Effective intervention for serious and violent juvenile offenders: Synthesis of research. In R. Loeber, and D.P. Farrington (Eds.), *Serious and violent juvenile offenders* (pp. 313-345) Thousand Oaks, CA: Sage Publications, Inc.

Losoya, S.H., Callor, S., Rowe, D.C., and Goldsmith, H.H. (1997). Origins of familial similarity in parenting: A study of twins and adoptive siblings. Developmental Psychology, 33, 1012-1023.

Lytton, H. (1990). Child and parent effects in boys' conduct disorder: A reinterpretation. *Developmental Psychology, 26*, 683-697.

Maughan, B., Taylor, A., Caspi, A., and Moffitt, T.E. (2004). Prenatal smoking and child conduct problems: testing genetic and environmental explanation of the association. *Archives of General Psychiatry, 61,* 836 – 843.

McGue, M., Sharma, A., and Benson, P. (1996). The effect of common rearing on adolescent adjustment: Evidence from a U.S. adoption cohort. *Developmental Psychology, 32*, 604-613.

McGuire, S. (2003). The heritability of parenting. *Parenting: Science and Practice, 3,* 73-94.

Mednick, S.A., and Christiansen, K.O. (1977). *Biosocial bases of criminal behavior.* New York: Gardner Press.

Mednick, S.A., Gabrielli, W.F., and Hutchings, B. (1984). Genetic factors in criminal behavior: Evidence from an adoption cohort. *Science, 224*, 891-893.

Mednick, S.A., Moffitt, T.E., Gabrielli, W.F., and Hutchings, B. (1986). Genetic factors in criminal behavior: A review. In J. Block, D. Olweus, and M.R. Yarrow (Eds.), *The development of antisocial and prosocial behavior* (pp. 33-50). New York, NY: Academic Press Inc.

Meyer, J.M., Rutter, M., Silberg, J.L., Maes, H., Simonoff, E., Shillady, L.L., Pickles, A., Hewitt, J.K., and Eaves, L.J. (2000). Familial aggregation for conduct disorder symptomatology: The role of genes, marital discord, and family adaptability. *Psychological Medicine, 30*, 759-774.

Miles, D.R., and Carey, G. (1997). Genetic and environmental architecture of human aggression. *Journal of Personality and Social Psychology, 72,* 207-217.

Moffitt, T.E. (1993). "Life-course-persistent" and "adolescence-limited" antisocial behavior: A developmental taxonomy. *Psychological Review, 100*, 674-701.

Moffitt, T.E. (2005). The new look of behavioural genetics in developmental psychopathology: Gene – environment interplay in antisocial behaviors. *Psychological Bulletin, 131,* 533-554.

Moffitt, T.E., Caspi, A., Rutter, M., and Silva, P.A. (2001). *Sex differences in antisocial behaviour: Conduct disorder, delinquency, and violence in the Dunedin longitudinal study.* Cambridge, UK: Cambridge University Press.

Moffitt, T.E., and the E-risk Study Team (2002). Teen-aged mothers in contemporary Britain. *Journal of Child Psychology and Psychiatry, 43,* 1-16.

Moilanen, I., Linna, S.L., Ebeling, H., Kampulainen, K., Tamminen, T., Piha, J., and Almqvist, F. (1999). Are twins' behavioural/emotional problems different from singletons'? *European Child and Adolescent Psychiatry, 8,* 62-67.

Niederhiser, J.M., Reiss, D., Hetherington, E.M., and Plomin, R. (1999). Relationships between parenting and adolescent adjustment over time: Genetic and environmental contributions. *Developmental Psychology, 35*, 680-692.

Niederhiser, J.M., Reiss, D., Pederson, N., Lichtenstein, P., Spotts, E.L., Hansson, K., Cederblad, M., and Elthammer, O. (2004). Genetic and environmental influences on mothering of adolescents: A comparison of two samples. *Developmental Psychology, 40,* 335-351.

O'Connor, T.G., Deater-Deckard, K., Fulker, D., Rutter, M., and Plomin, R. (1998). Genotype-environment correlations in late childhood and early adolescence: Antisocial behavioral problems in coercive parenting. *Developmental Psychology, 34*, 970-981.

O'Connor, T.G., Heatherington, E.M., Reiss, D., and Plomin, R. (1995). A twin-sibling study of observed parent-adolescent relations. *Child Development, 66*, 812-829.

Olds, D., Henderson, C.R. Jr., Cole, R., Eckenrode, J., Kitzman, H., Luckey, D., Pettitt, L., Sidora, K., Morris, P., and Powers, J. (1998). Long-term effects of nurse home visitation on children's criminal and antisocial behavior: 15-year follow-up of a randomized trial. *Journal of the American Medical Association, 280,* 1238-1244.

Pike, A., McGuire, S., Hetherington, E.M., Reiss, D., and Plomin, R. (1996). Family environment and adolescent depressive symptoms and antisocial behavior: a multivariate genetic analysis. *Developmental Psychology, 32*, 590-603.

Pike, A., Reiss, D., Hetherington, E.M., and Plomin, R. (1996). Using MZ differences in the search for nonshared environmental effects. *Journal of Child Psychology and Psychiatry, 37*, 695-704.

Plomin, R. (1994). *Genetics and experience: The interplay between nature and nurture.* Thousand Oaks, CA: Sage.

Plomin, R., and Bergeman, C.S. (1991). The nature of nurture: Genetic influences on 'environmental' measures. *Behavioral and Brain Sciences, 14*, 373-427.

Plomin, R., and Caspi, A. (1999). Behavior genetics and personality. In L.A. Pervin, and O.P. John (Eds.), *Handbook of personality* (pp. 251-276). New York: Guilford Press.

Plomin, R., and Daniels, D. (1987). Why are children in the same family so different from each other? *Behavioral and Brain Sciences, 10*, 1-16.

Plomin, R., DeFries, J.C., and Loehlin, J.C. (1977). Genotype-environment interaction and correlation in the analysis of human behavior. *Psychological Bulletin, 84*, 309-322.

Plomin, R., DeFries, J.C., McClearn, G.E., and McGuffin, P. (2001). *Behavioral Genetics, 4th edition.* New York: W.H. Freeman.

Plomin, R., McClearn, G.E., Pederson, N.L., Nesselroade, J.R., and Bergeman, C.S. (1989). Genetic influence on adults' ratings of their current family environment. *Journal of Marriage and the Family, 51*, 791-803.

Purcell, S. (2002). Variance components models for gene-environment interaction in twin analysis. *Twin Research, 5,* 554-571.

Reid, J., Patterson G.R., and Snyder J. (2002). *Antisocial behavior in children and adolescents.* Washington DC: American Psychological Association.

Reiss, D., Neiderhiser, J.M., Hetherington, E.M., and Plomin, R. (2000). *The relationship code: Deciphering genetic and social influences on adolescent development.* Cambridge, MA: Harvard University Press.

Rende, R.D., Slomkowski, C.L., Stocker, C., Fulker, D.W., and Plomin, R. (1992). Genetic and environmental influences on maternal and sibling interaction in middle childhood: A sibling adoption study. *Developmental Psychology, 28*, 484-490.

Rhee, S.H., and Waldman, I.D. (2002). Genetic and environmental influences on antisocial behavior: A meta-analysis of twin and adoption studies. *Psychological Bulletin, 128,* 490-529.

Riggins-Caspers, K.M., Cadoret, R.J., Knutson, J.F., and Langbehn, D. (2003). Biology-environment interaction and evocative biology-environment correlation: Contributions of harsh discipline and parental psychopathology to problem adolescent behaviors. *Behavior Genetics, 33*, 205-220.

Rodgers, J.L., Rowe, D.C., and Li, C. (1994). Beyond nature versus nurture: DF analysis of nonshared influences on problem behaviors. *Developmental Psychology, 30*, 374-384.

Rose, R.J., Viken, R.J., Dick, D.M., Bates, J.E., Pulkinnen, L., and Kaprio, J. (2003). It does take a village: Nonfamilial environments and children's behavior. *Psychological Science, 14*, 273-277.

Rowe, D.C. (1983). A biometric analysis of perceptions of family environment. *Child Development, 54,* 416-423.

Rowe, D.C. (1994). *The limits of family influence: Genes, experience, and behavior.* NY: Guilford Press.

Rowe, D.C., Almeida, D.M., and Jacobson, K.C. (1999). School context and genetic influences on aggression in adolescence. *Psychological Science, 10,* 277-280.

Rowe, D.C., and Farrington, D.P. (1997). The familial transmission of criminal convictions. *Criminology, 35,* 177-201.

Rutter, M. (2002). Nature, nurture, and development: From evangelism through science toward policy and practice. *Child Development, 73*, 1-21.

Rutter, M. (2003a). Commentary: Causal processes leading to antisocial behavior. *Developmental Psychology (special issue on violent children), 39*, 372-378.

Rutter, M. (2003b). Crucial paths from risk indicator to causal mechanism. In B. Lahey, T.E. Moffitt, and A. Caspi (Eds.), *The causes of conduct disorder and serious juvenile delinquency* (pp. 3-24). NY: Guilford Press.

Rutter, M., Giller, H., and Hagell, A. (1998). *Antisocial behaviour by young people.* Cambridge, UK: Cambridge University Press.

Rutter, M., Pickles, A., Murray, R., and Eaves, L. (2001). Testing hypotheses on specific environmental causal effects on behavior. *Psychological Bulletin, 127,* 291-324.

Rutter, M., and Silberg, J. (2002). Gene-environment interplay in relation to emotional and behavioral disturbance._ *Annual Review of Psychology, 53*, 463-490.

Scarr, S. (1991). The construction of the family reality. *Behavioral and Brain Sciences, 14,* 403-404.

Scarr, S. (1992). Developmental theories for the 1990's: Development and individual differences. *Child Development, 63,* 1-19.

Scarr, S., and McCartney, K. (1983). How people make their own environments. *Child Development, 54*, 424-435.

Serbin, L., and Karp, J. (2003). Intergenerational studies of parenting and the transfer of risk from parent to child. *Current Directions in Psychological Science, 12,* 138-142.

Sharma, A.R., McGue, M.K., and Benson, P.L. (1998). The psychological adjustment of United States adopted adolescents and their nonadopted siblings. *Child Development, 69,* 791-802.

Sherman, L.W., Gottfredson, D.C., MacKenzie, D.L, Eck, J., Reuter, P., and Bushway, S.D. (1999). *Preventing crime: What works, what doesn't, what's promising.* NY: Russell Sage Foundation. Also available from the U.S. Department of Justice, *http://www.ojp.usdoj.gov/nij.*

Silberg, J.L., (2002*). Parental effects on depression and disruptive behavior in the children of twins: A proposal to the US National Institute of Mental Health.* Richmond, VA: Medical College of Virginia.

Silberg, J.L. and Eaves, L.J. (2004). Analysing the contributions of genes and parent-child interaction to childhood behavioural and emotional problems: A model for the children of twins. *Psychological Medicine, 34,* 1-10.

Simonoff, E., Pickles, A., Meyer, J.M., Silberg, J., Maes, H., Loeber, R., Rutter M., Hewitt J.K., and Eaves L.J. (1997). The Virginia Twin Study of adolescent behavioral development, *Archives of General Psychiatry, 54,* 801-808.

Spinath, F.M., and O'Connor, T.G. (2003). A behavioral genetic study of the overlap between personality and parenting. *Journal of Personality, 71,* 785-808.

Stoolmiller, M. (1999). Implications of the restricted range of family environments for estimates of heritability and nonshared environment in behavior-genetic adoption studies. *Psychological Bulletin, 125,* 392-409.

Thornberry, T.P. (Ed.) (1996*). Advances in criminological theory: Developmental theories of crime and delinquency.* London: Transactions Publishers.

Towers, H., Spotts, E.L., and Neiderhiser, J. (2001). Genetic and environmental influences on parenting and marital relationships: Current findings and future directions. *Marriage and Family Review, 33,* 11-29.

Turkheimer, E., and Waldron, M. (2000). Nonshared environment: A theoretical, methodological, and quantitative review. *Psychological Bulletin, 126,* 78-108.

U.S. Bureau of Justice Statistics. (2002). *Criminal Victimization 2001.* (NCJ Report 194610). Washington, DC: U.S. Department of Justice. Available at http://www.ojp.usdof.gov/bjs

Vandell, D.L. (2000). Parents, peer groups, and other socializing influences. *Developmental Psychology, 36,* 699-710.

van den Oord, E.J.C.G., Koot, H.M., Boomsma, D.I., Verhulst, F.C., and Orlebeke, J.F. (1995). A twin-singleton comparison of problem behaviour in 2-3 year olds. *Journal of Child Psychology and Psychiatry, 36,* 449-458.

van der Valk, J.C., Verhulst, F.C., Stroet, T.M., and Boomsma, D.I. (1998). Quantitative genetic analysis of internalising and externalising problems in a large sample of 3-year-old twins. *Twin Research, 1,* 25-33.

VanDusen, K., Mednick, S.A., Gabrielli, W.F., and Hutchings, B. (1983). Social class and crime in an adoption cohort. *Journal of Criminal Law and Criminology, 74,* 249-269.

Wade, T.D., and Kendler, K.S. (2000). The genetic epidemiology of parental discipline, *Psychological Medicine, 30,* 1303-1313.

Wandersman, A., and Florin, P. (2003). Community interventions and effective prevention. *American Psychologist, 58,* 441-448.

Wasserman, G.A. and Miller, L.S. (1998). The prevention of serious and violent juvenile offending. In R. Loeber and D.P. Farrington (Eds.), *Serious and violent juvenile offenders* (pp.197-247). Thousand Oaks, CA: Sage.

Weissberg, R.P., Kumpfer, K.L., and Seligman, M.E.P. (2003). Prevention that works for children and youth. *American Psychologist, 58,* 425-432.

Wilson, D.B., Gottfredson, D.C., and Najaka, S. S. (2001). School-based prevention of problem behaviors: A meta-analysis. *Journal of Quantitative Criminology, 17,* 247-272.

Wolfgang, M.E., Figlio, R.M., and Sellin, T. (1972). *Delinquency in a birth cohort.* Chicago: University of Chicago Press.

World Health Organization (2002). *World report on violence and health.* Geneva: Author.

Yoshikawa, H. (1994). Prevention as cumulative protection. *Psychological Bulletin, 115,* 28-54.

In: Crime and Schizophrenia: Causes and Cures
Editor: Adrian Raine, pp. 83-107 ISBN 1-59454-609-6

Chapter 5

BIOLOGICAL RISK FACTORS FOR ANTISOCIAL AND CRIMINAL BEHAVIOR

***Adrian Raine*[1]*, Laura Baker*[1] *and Jianghong Liu*[2]**
[1]Department of Psychology, University of Southern California
[2]Social Science Research Institute, University of Southern California

INTRODUCTION

There is increasing recognition that biological processes are at some level implicated in the development of criminal behavior. There is certainly debate about the precise contribution of such factors to crime outcome, and there is considerable debate about the precise mechanisms that these biological factors reflect. The disciplines of criminology and sociology have been reluctant to embrace this new body of knowledge. Yet few serious scientists in psychology and psychiatry would deny that biological factors are relevant to understanding crime, and there is increasing public interest and understanding of this perspective.

There are certainly many reasons to take this body of knowledge seriously. Biology is not destiny, and we *can* benignly change many of the biological predispositions that shape the violent offender. One of the reasons why we have been so unsuccessful in preventing adult crime is because interventions to date have systematically ignored the biological side of the biosocial equation that produces crime. If we are to be truly serious about tackling crime and violence in society, we need to give more attention to the biological factors that cause crime.

The main aim of this chapter is to provide readers who have more familiarity with schizophrenia a basic overview of what we know about main genetic and biological predispositions to criminal behavior. This in turn will help lay the foundations for understanding the mechanisms and processes that crime and schizophrenia have in common – and ways in which they differ. In addition, attention will be given to interactions between biological and social factors because while have been relatively neglected, they are probably of critical importance to a deeper and more complete understanding of the cause of crime.

First, we will outline the evidence for behavioral and molecular genetic predispositions to crime. If genetic factors are indeed involved, then there has to be some biological basis to crime (although it should also be made clear that environmental factors in addition give rise to biological risk factors for crime). We then turn to a discussion of obstetric factors, including pregnancy complications, birth complications, and minor physical anomalies. Hormonal and neurotransmitter predispositions are then elaborated upon, followed by environmental pollutants and toxins (e.g. lead and manganese exposure) and neurocognitive correlates of antisocial and criminal behavior. Some processes (e.g. malnutrition, brain imaging) together with prevention and intervention implications of biological research will not be covered here as they are dealt with in other chapters. Similarly, a recent review of the psychophysiology of antisocial behavior may be found in Scarpa and Raine (2003).

GENETICS

Overview

There are numerous reviews of behavioral genetic studies of antisocial behavior, which include phenotypes ranging from mild forms of aggression, to other more deviant forms such as law-breaking (criminal) behavior (e.g., Cloninger and Gottesman, 1987; Venables and Raine, 1987; Raine and Venables, 1989; Plomin, Nitz and Rowe,1990; Rutter et al., 1990; DiLalla and Gottesman, 1991; Mason and Frick, 1994; Raine, 1993; Carey, 1994; Carey and Goldman, 1997; DiLalla 2002; Rhee and Waldman 2002; Baker 2002). Studies of twins, nuclear families, and adoptive families all suggest that genetic influences are important to antisocial behavior. These effects vary, however, by the age and gender of subjects, as well as the type of antisocial behavior and the method of assessment used. An overview of the major findings from these studies is provided here, with an emphasis on criminal offending. The most recent reviews by Rhee and Waldman (2002), Baker (2002), and DiLalla (2002) may be consulted for a more detailed presentation of these studies.

The primary approach in behavioral genetic studies involves the study of resemblance among relatives of varying degrees of genetic and environmental relatedness. Phenotypes may be quantitative (e.g., trait aggression) or qualitative (e.g., criminal convictions, psychiatric diagnoses such as antisocial personality disorder in adults or conduct disorder in children). Even when qualitative measures of antisocial behavior are studied, their underlying predispositions (or liabilities) are almost always presumed to be quantitative. Twin, family, and adoption studies all examine familial resemblance for antisocial behavior in various forms, attempting to quantify the relative importance of genes and environment in quantitative traits or the underlying quantitative predisposition. These studies examine the genetic and environmental effects at a global level, without specification of which genes or environmental influences are important, or what their underlying mechanisms may be.

While the majority of studies investigating the genetic basis of antisocial behavior involve such global, quantitative genetic approaches, several studies have begun to examine genes at a molecular level. Linkage and association studies provide a more fine-grained approach, as they attempt to identify specific chromosomal regions or candidate genes that play a role in risk of engaging in ASB. This approach is relatively new and only a few studies have begun to examine specific genes in this area.

Behavioral Genetics

Several large-scale twin and adoption studies of criminal offending have provided some of the most convincing evidence of genetic influences in antisocial behavior. These studies have been conducted in several countries, including the United States and three Scandinavian countries (Sweden, Denmark, and Norway). Concordance between twins for property crimes such as thievery and vandalism is generally greater for monozygotic (MZ) pairs, who share 100% of their genes, compared to dizygotic (DZ) pairs, who share 50% of their genes, on average. Property crime convictions among adopted individuals are significantly increased when a biological parent (especially the mother) has been convicted. In comparison, conviction rates show little or no increase in adopted children raised by adoptive parents with property crime convictions. Thus, environmental influences in criminal offending do appear largely non-familial and specific to the individual rather than shared by relatives living together.

Although large sex differences in criminal offending are evident—males are convicted far more often than females—the genetic effects in criminal behavior are of the same magnitude across the two sexes. For example, greater MZ than DZ concordance for criminal convictions has been found in both male and female same-sex pairs. Opposite-sex (male-female) DZ twins are often less similar than same-sex pairs, however, suggesting "sex limitation" effects, i.e., that different genes and or environments may be important within each sex (Cloninger and Gottesman, 1987). These same patterns of genetic influence for non-violent criminal offending hold true for other measures of antisocial behavior, including aggression (see Rhee and Waldman, 2002)—that is, there is little or no sex difference in magnitude of genetic effect, but some sex-limitation may be evident.

Genetic and environmental effects in antisocial behavior depend to some extent on the method of assessment employed in a given study. In general, studies relying on assessments by others (parents and teachers) demonstrate greater effects of both shared family environment and genetics compared to self-report measures, while studies employing official record data (e.g., criminal convictions) show no effect of family environment. Studies of official records also tend to show greater effects of non-additive genetic influences, which may be due to genetic dominance (interactions of alleles at a given locus) and epistasis (interactions of genes at different loci) (Rhee and Waldman 2002). Method of assessment, however, is confounded with operationalization of antisocial behavior (e.g., studies of crime rely more heavily on official records) as well as age of subjects (e.g., studies of children rely upon parent and teacher reports).

Developmental factors may also be important to genetic influences in antisocial behavior in at least two ways. First, heritability of antisocial behavior, including criminal offending, appears to vary across the lifespan, although the direction of difference varies across studies and reviews. Some studies show larger genetic effects during adulthood compared to childhood and adolescence (e.g., Miles and Carey, 1997), while others suggest greater heritability of antisocial behavior during childhood compared to adolescence and adulthood (e.g., DiLalla and Gottesman, 1989). To some extent this discrepancy of results may be due to the fact that methods of measurement of antisocial behavior are confounded with age of subjects—studies of children tend to rely on parent and teacher reports, while studies of adults utilize official records (e.g., convictions) and self-reported antisocial behavior more often. Thus, the patterns of genetic and environmental influences across the lifespan are not yet clearly established. The second way that developmental factors may be important to antisocial behavior is that there may be different genetic and environmental influences for various subtypes of individuals with different life-course patterns of offending. It has been suggested that life-course persistent offenders may be at greater genetic risk compared to adolescence-limited offenders, who may in turn be more influenced by social factors (e.g., peer influences) (Moffitt 1989). The longitudinal twin or adoption studies required to establish the different genetic influences in developmental subtypes of antisocial individuals have yet to be done.

Interestingly, the consistent finding of genetic influences in property crimes does not hold true for crimes of a violent nature. None of the major adoption studies reported any increased risk for violent conviction as a function of either biological or adoptive parent criminal background, although one twin study did find greater MZ than DZ concordance for violent convictions (Cloninger and Gottesman, 1987). The combination of findings of twin but not parent-offspring similarity for violent criminal behavior suggests the possibility of non-additive genetic effects, which would result in increased resemblance for siblings but not parents and offspring.

Studies of younger subjects have typically not distinguished between violent and non-violent offending. Nor have self-report methods of assessment been frequently used in studies of delinquent behavior in children. One exception is the USC twin study of risk factors for antisocial behavior (Baker, Raine, and Lozano, 2004), in which 605 pairs of 9-10 year old twins were administered a self-report Delinquency Interview (Baker and Raine 2004). Figure 1 shows the effects additive genetic (A), common environment (C) and individual environment (E) for four scales of non-violent delinquent behavior: MINOR rule-breaking (e.g., watching TV without permission), THEFT (e.g., shoplifting or stealing money from a family member or peer), PROPERTY damage (e.g., street graffiti or breaking things on purpose), and TRUANCY (e.g., leaving school or home without permission); as well as two scales of violent behaviors, which involve hitting, shoving, or biting one's TWIN or OTHER person outside of one's family. In contrast to the large genetic influence for criminal offending in adults, these childhood behaviors appear to be explained primarily by environmental (both C and E) and not genetic factors. There are small genetic influences in MINOR rule-breaking (.20) and THEFT (.12), however, suggesting that these effects may begin to emerge for propensity to engage in non-violent delinquent behavior prior to adolescence. Consistent with research on adult offending, as well as the Rhee and Waldman (2002) meta-analysis of antisocial behavior, the magnitudes of genetic and environmental influences are not significantly different in boys and girls. For both violent scales, however, the best fitting models estimated the correlation between common environmental influences in boys and girls to be less than unity ($r_{Cmf} = 0.19$ for TWIN and 0.39 for OTHER violence). It may be expected that genetic influences will increase for non-violent behaviors in these children as they move into the high-risk period of adolescence.

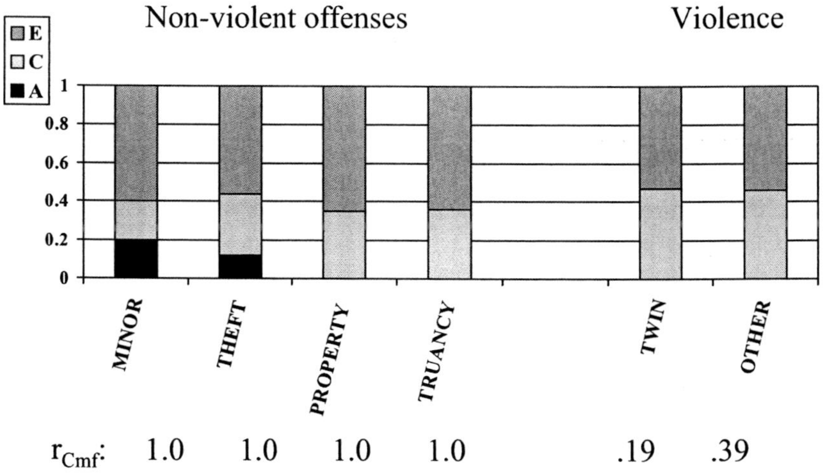

Figure 1. Genetic and environmental influences in self-reported delinquent behavior in children

Gene x Environment Interactions

Perhaps most importantly, genetic influences in criminal offending appear to be moderated by environmental factors themselves. A gene X environment (GxE) interaction has been consistently found in all major adoption studies of criminal convictions, such that the genetic predispositions (indicated by biological parent antisocial behavior) present the greatest risk to the adopted offspring in the presence of adverse environmental conditions (indicated by adoptive parent antisocial behavior). Viewed conversely, negative environmental factors stemming from being raised by antisocial parents may exert their greatest effects on individuals who are genetically predisposed towards antisocial behavior. This finding in particular has profound implications for our understanding the role of parents and other environmental aspects in producing aggressive and other antisocial outcomes of children.

Molecular Genetics

The consistent findings of heritable influences in certain forms of antisocial behavior have led several investigators to search further for specific genes that may explain some of these global genetic influences. Most of these studies do not investigate criminal or antisocial behavior as a primary variable, however, but instead focus on personality dimensions relevant to criminal and other antisocial behavior (e.g., impulsivity, harm avoidance, novelty seeking), or personality disorders for which antisocial behavior is but one diagnostic criterion (e.g., antisocial personality disorder or Type 2 alcoholism). Several specific genes do appear relevant to these traits and disorders, including serotonin-related genes. A functional polymorphism in the serotonin transporter gene (5-HTTLPR) involves a repeating section, with “short” and “long” variations of the allele. Higher levels of neuroticism, or harm avoidance, as well as depression have been found in individuals carrying the "short" allele in some (e.g., Lesch, et al. 1996) but not all studies (for a review see Ebstein, Benjamin and Belmaker, 2003). Somewhat greater consistency of results has been found in studies of impulsivity, which has also demonstrated relationships to serotonin function. The short serotonin transporter allele has also been found to be associated with increased risk of Type 2 alcoholism, which includes antisocial, impulsive, and violent behavior (Hallikainen et al. 1999).

Only a few studies to date has focused on aggressive and criminal behavior, one of which linked adult aggression and violent behavior to a gene resulting in monoamine oxidase (MAO) deficiency (Brunner, Nelen, Breakefield, Ropers, and van Oost, 1993). Another study of the same MAO gene demonstrated that these effects may be most deleterious under adverse rearing conditions in which children at genetic risk have experienced harsh discipline or child abuse (Caspi, McClay, Moffitt, Mill, Martin, Craig, Taylor, and Poulton, 2002). This finding is especially intriguing, since it involves a genetic link to violence, which has shown to be less heritable in twin and adoption studies as discussed. However, the Caspi et al. results are consistent with the notion of GxE interactions known to be important in the risk for criminal behavior in general. Animal studies have also demonstrated a link between an MAO polymorphism and aggression, whereby knockout mice bred with a gene leading to MAO deficiency display extremely high levels of violence (Shih et al., 1999).

Summary of Genetic Research

The major findings of twin and adoption studies of criminal behavior can be summarized as follows: (1) genetic influences are important; (2) environmental factors are largely non-familial, i.e., are specific to each individual within a family; (3) environmental factors may act as a buffer, moderating the effects of genes (GxE interaction); (4) genetic influences vary by type of crime, with effects being greater for property offending compared to violence; (5) the relative effects of genes and environment are approximately equal for males and females; and (6) the relative importance of genes and environment on criminal offending may vary over the life span, with genetic effects probably emerging during adolescence and appearing greatest in adulthood. The underlying biological mechanisms and environmental interface for the expression of antisocial behavior are largely unknown, although many areas of biological risk factors including neurotransmitters appear promising avenues for future research.

Obstetric Factors

Biological risk factors for crime and violence start early. Indeed, there is growing evidence that obstetric factors can predispose to later antisocial and violent behavior. Obstetric influences can be divided into those that occur during pregnancy, and those that occur during the birth of the child.

Pregnancy

(a) Minor Physical Anomalies (MPAs)

Minor physical anomalies have been associated with disorders of pregnancy and are thought to be a marker for fetal neural maldevelopment towards the end of the first three months of pregnancy. As such, they may be viewed as an indirect marker of abnormal brain development. MPAs are relatively minor physical abnormalities consisting of such features as low-seated ears, adherent ear lobes, and a furrowed tongue. While MPAs may have a genetic basis, they may also be caused by environmental factors acting on the fetus such as anoxia, bleeding, and infection (Guy, Majorski, Wallace, and Guy, 1983).

At least six studies have found an association between increased MPAs and increased antisocial behavior in children (Raine, 1993). At least three of these studies have found that MPAs interact with social factors in predicting antisocial and violent behavior. Mednick and Kandel (1988) assessed MPAs in a sample of 129 12-year-old boys seen by an experienced pediatrician. MPAs were found to be related to violent offending as assessed nine years later when subjects were aged 21 years, although not to property offenses. However, as illustrated in Figure 2, when subjects were divided into those from unstable, non-intact homes and those from stable homes, a biosocial interaction was observed. MPAs only predicted violence in those individuals raised in unstable home environments. Similarly, Brennan, Mednick, and Raine, (1997) found that those with both MPAs and family adversity had especially high rates of adult violent offending within a sample of 72 male offspring of psychiatrically ill parents.

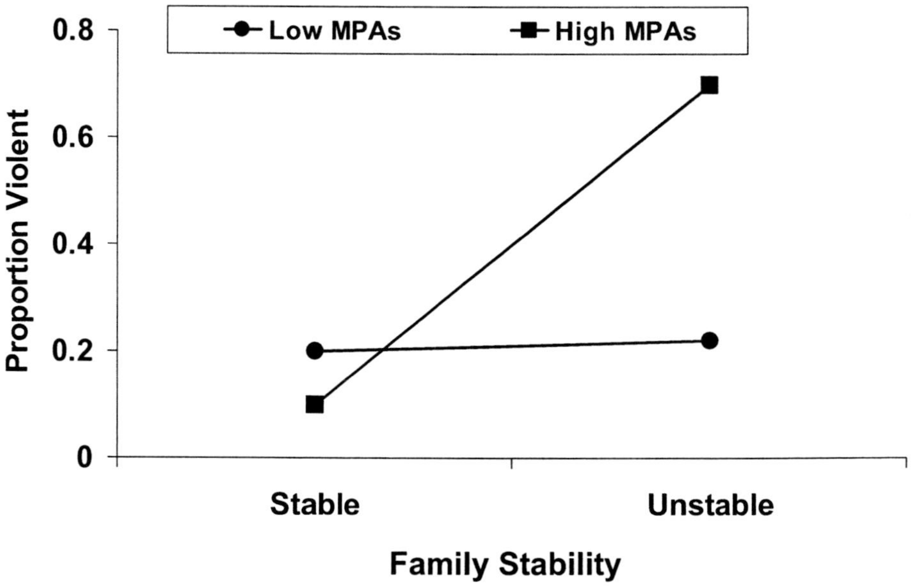

Figure 2. Interaction between family instability and high minor physical anomalies in the prediction of adult violence (Mednick and Kandel, 1988)

This interaction was again confirmed by Pine, Shaffer, Schonfeld, and Davies (1997) who found that MPAs in 7 year olds combined with environmental risk in predisposing to conduct disorder at age 17. These findings are similar to those on birth complications reported above; in both cases the presence of a negative psychosocial factor is required to "trigger" the biological risk factor, and in both cases the effects are specific to violent offending. In a study confirming specificity of MPAs to violence, Arseneault, Tremblay, Boulerice, Seguin, and Saucier (2000) found that MPAs assessed at age 14 predicted to violent delinquency at age 17 in 170 males, but not to nonviolent delinquency. In this study, effects were independent of family adversity.

(b) Nicotine Exposure

The effect of fetal exposure to alcohol in increasing risk for conduct disorders is well-known (e.g., Fast, Conry, and Loock, 1999; Olson et al., 1997; Streissguth, Barr, Bookstein, Sampson, and Olson, 1999), but recently a spate of studies has established beyond reasonable doubt a significant link between smoking during pregnancy and later conduct disorder and violent offending (see Raine, 2002b, for a review). Three of these studies have also observed interactions between nicotine exposure and psychosocial variables in the prediction of later violent offending, and are impressive in terms of their size, the prospective nature of data collection, long-term outcome, and control for third factors such as antisocial behavior in the parents, other drug use, and low social class. Brennan, Grekin, and Mednick, (1999), using a birth cohort of 4,169 males found a two-fold increase in adult violent offending in the offspring of mothers who smoked 20 cigarettes a day, and also found a dose-response relationship between increased number of cigarettes smoked and increased violence. However, a *five-fold* increase in adult violence was found when nicotine exposure was combined with exposure to delivery complications – there was no increase in violence in those who were nicotine-exposed but lacking delivery complications. Brennan et al. (1999) observed that effects were specific to persistent offending and did not apply to adolescent-limited offending. Similarly, Rasanen et al., (1999) found a twofold increase in violent criminal offending at age 26 in the offspring of women who smoked during pregnancy. In addition, nicotine exposure lead to an 11.9-fold increase in recidivistic violence when combined with single-parent family, and a 14.2-fold increase when combined with teenage pregnancy, single-parent family, unwanted pregnancy, and developmental motor lags. Again, odds-ratios were stronger for recidivistic violence than for non-recidivistic violence and property offending. Gibson and Tibbetts (2000) also found that maternal smoking interacted with parental absence in predicting early onset of offending in a U.S. sample.

Maternal smoking during pregnancy may be an important contributory factor to the brain deficits that have been found in adult offenders. Animal research has clearly demonstrated the neurotoxic effects of two constituents of cigarette smoke - carbon monoxide (CO) and nicotine (see Olds, 1997) for a detailed review). Prenatal nicotine exposure even at relatively low levels disrupts the development of the noradrenergic neurotransmitter system and disrupts cognitive functions (Levin, Wilkerson, Jones, Christopher, and Briggs 1996). Reduction of noradrenergic functioning caused by smoking would be expected to disrupt sympathetic nervous system activity, consistent with evidence for reduced sympathetic arousal in antisocial individuals (Raine, 1996). Pregnant rats exposed to nicotine have offspring with an enhancement of cardiac M2-muscarinic cholinergic receptors which *inhibit* autonomic functions (Slotkin, Epps T.A., Stenger, Sawyer, and Seidler, 1999). This would help to explain the well-replicated finding of *low* resting heart rate in antisocial individuals outlined above (Raine, 1993).

Birth Complications

Several studies have shown that babies who suffer birth complications are more likely to develop conduct disorder, delinquency, and commit impulsive crime and violence in adulthood when other psychosocial risk factors are present. Specifically, obstetric factors *interact* with psychosocial risk factors in relation to adult violence. Werner (1987) found that birth complications interacted with a disruptive family environment (maternal separation, illegitimate child, marital discord, parental mental health problems, paternal absence) in predisposing to delinquency. Similarly, Raine, Brennan, and Mednick (1994)) prospectively assessed birth complications and maternal rejection at age 1 year in 4,269 live male births in Copenhagen, Denmark. Birth complications significantly interacted with maternal rejection of the child in predicting to violent offending at age 18 years (see Figure 3, upper half). Only 4% of the sample had both birth complications and maternal rejection, but this small group accounted for 18% of all the violent crimes committed by the entire sample.

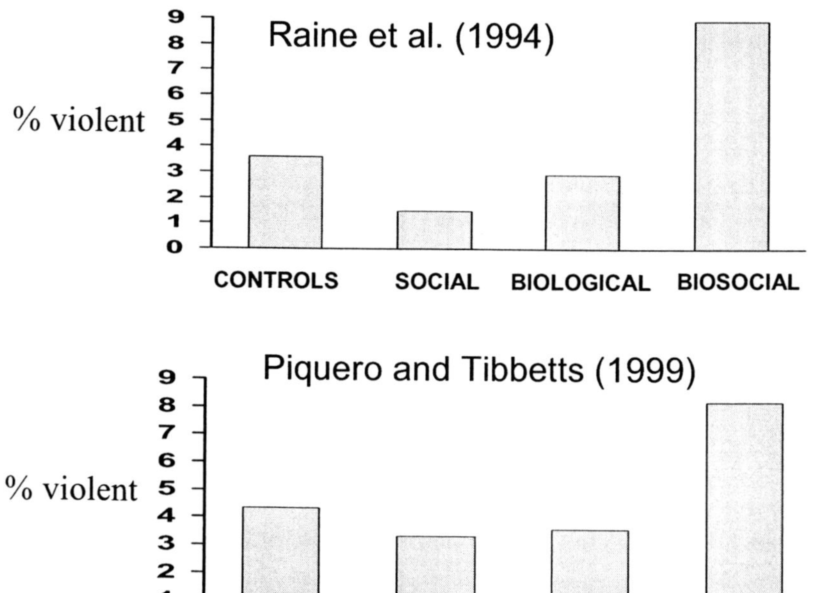

Figure 3. Interaction between birth complications and negative family outcome in the prediction of adult violence in both Danish (Raine et al. 1994) and U.S. (Piquero and Tibbetts, 1999) samples

In this latter study, the 4,269 babies were followed up to age 34 when outcome for violent crime was reassessed (Raine, Brennan, and Mednick, 1997). It was found that the biosocial interaction previously observed holds for violent but not non-violent criminal offending. Furthermore, the interaction was found to be specific to more serious forms of violence and not threats of violence. The interaction held for early onset but not late onset violence, and was not accounted for by psychiatric illness in the mothers. Rearing in a public care institution in the first year of life and attempt to abort the fetus were the key aspects of maternal rejection found to interact with birth complications in predisposing to violence.

This finding from Denmark has recently been replicated in four other countries (Sweden, Finland, Canada, U.S.A.) in the context of a variety of psychosocial risk factors. Piquero and Tibbetts (1999) in a prospective longitudinal study of 867 males and females from the Philadelphia Collaborative Perinatal Project found that those with both pre/perinatal disturbances and a disadvantaged familial environment were much more likely to become adult violent offenders (see Figure 2, lower half). Similarly, pregnancy complications interacted with poor parenting in predicting adult violence in a large Swedish sample of 7,101 men (Hodgins, Kratzer, and McNeil, 2001). In a Canadian sample of 849 boys, Arsenault, Tremblay, Boulerice, and Saucier (2002) found an interaction between increased serious obstetric complications and family adversity in raising the likelihood of violent offending at age 17 years. In a Finnish sample perinatal risk interacted with being an only child in raising the odds of adult violent offending by a factor of 4.4 in a sample of 5,587 males (Kemppainen, Jokelainen, Jaervelin, Isohanni, and Raesaenen, 2001). On the other hand, being an only child is not obviously linked to psychosocial adversity, and the meaning of this interaction required further elucidation.

A further study reported by Brennan, Mednick, and Mednick (1993)) and also from Denmark showed that birth complications interacted with parental mental illness in predicting violent crime in the male offspring (see Figure 4). On the other hand, no interaction between perinatal insult and family adversity was found for a smaller sample of German children (N = 322) where outcome was restricted to follow-up at age 8 years (Laucht et al., 2000). Similarly, no interaction effect was found between birth complications and psychosocial adversity in predisposing to externalizing behavior at age 11 years in a study reported in Liu et al., (2004). This latter effect could be due to the fact that the psychosocial processes assessed in this study did not include the key psychosocial processes which have been reported by other studies, such as parenting (Hodgins, et al. 2001) and maternal rejection (Raine et al. 1994).

More broadly, these latter two failures may be due to the fact that neurological deficits stemming from birth complications may particularly influence the more severe outcome of life-course persistent antisocial behavior rather than the more common outcome of child antisocial behavior (Moffitt, 1993; Moffitt and Caspi, 2001). Indeed, several of the above studies find that interaction effects involving birth complications and family factors show evidence of linkage to what may be broadly termed life-course persistent violent behavior rather than adolescent-limited antisocial behavior. In addition to these interactions with psychosocial variables, low Apgar scores at birth have been found to interact with maternal smoking in the prediction of adult violent offending (Gibson and Tibbetts, 1998).

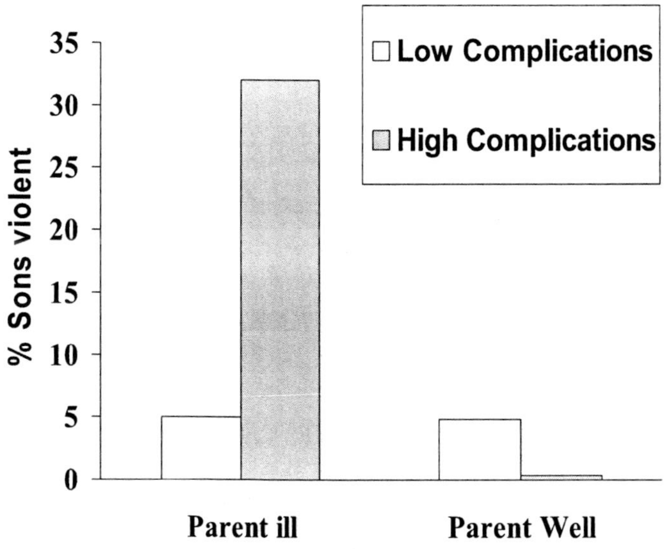

Figure 4. Interaction between birth complications and parental mental illness in the prediction of violent crime in the offspring (Brennan et. al. 1993)

Birth complications such as anoxia (lack of oxygen), forceps delivery, and pre-eclampsia (hypertension leading to anoxia) are thought to contribute to brain damage, and they may be just one of a number of early sources of brain dysfunction observed in child and adult antisocial groups. On the other hand, as indicated above, birth complications may not by themselves predispose to crime, but instead may require the presence of negative environmental circumstance to trigger later adult crime and violence. While they are likely to contribute to prefrontal damage, their effects would not be specific to this brain area but would impact multiple brain sites. For example, it is known that hypoxia selectively damages the hippocampus, one component of the limbic system that brain imaging research involved in aggression regulation (Carlson, 1998; Raine, Buchsbaum, and LaCasse, 1997; Raine et al. 2004). Recent brain imaging studies have shown that the hippocampus shows abnormal functioning in murderers (Raine, Buchsbaum, and LaCasse, 1997), and shows structural abnormalities in psychopaths (Laakso et al., 2001). Hypoxia or anoxia can result from maternal illness or stress, or from toxicity (Pillitteri, 2002). Furthermore, the brain could suffer mechanical damage during the birth process (e.g. forceps delivery) and be partly responsible for the neuropsychological impairments frequently found in delinquent and criminal offenders.

HORMONES

Research on links between hormones and antisocial, aggressive behavior illustrates the complexities of biology-behavior relationships, and clearly demonstrates the influence of the social context on biological functioning. Detailed reviews of the bi-directional relationship between hormones and behavior and of the influence of social context on hormones may be found in Dabbs, (1992), Mazur and Booth, (1999), Susman, (1993), Susman and Ponirakis,

(1997), and Tremblay et al., (1997). Emphasis here will be placed on two key hormones that feature in the crime and antisocial behavior literature: testosterone and cortisol.

Testosterone

While links between high testosterone and self-report measures of aggression are relatively weak (Archer, 1991), there is now convincing evidence from a wide number of *behavioral* studies for a link between high testosterone and increased aggressive and violent behavior (see reviews by Archer, 1991; Dabbs, 1992; Harris, 1999; Mazur and Booth, 1999; and Raine, 2002a). Testosterone levels are in part heritable (Turner et al. 1986) and it is conceivable that the genetic predisposition to crime may in part be expressed through the hormonal system. Nevertheless, it also appears that while aggression – testosterone links are well-established with respect to adult aggressive and violent behavior, this relationship may be absent, or even reversed, with respect to aggression during childhood (Tremblay et al., 1997).

An understanding of why the aggression-testosterone relationship washes out in childhood may be gained from consideration of social influences on testosterone. It is well-established that high testosterone is associated with both high dominance and high socio-economic status, and while experience of success increases testosterone, failure reduces it (Dabbs, 1992; Mazur and Booth, 1999). Aggressive children are more likely to be rejected by their peers in school (Dodge, Lochman, Harnish, and Bates, 1997), and it may be this social ostracization and failure in academia that artificially reduces their otherwise high testosterone levels. This interpretation is supported by two pieces of evidence. First, Tremblay et al. (1997) report that 13-year-old boys who are both physically tough *and* who are well-liked have high testosterone levels. Second, while Tremblay et al. (1997) found that aggressive boys have low testosterone at ages 13 and 14, follow-up at age 16 after 30% had dropped out of school show them to have substantially higher testosterone than non-aggressive boys. It may be that aggression-testosterone links are found in violent offenders during adulthood because they are better able to use their aggression proactively to raise their dominance status within their antisocial subcultures and achieve some degree of social success.

Is the testosterone – aggression link causal? Animal research suggests that the steroid hormone testosterone plays an important role in the genesis and maintenance of some forms of aggressive behavior in rodents, and early exposure to testosterone has been found to increase aggression in a wide range of animal species (Brain, 1990). In humans, one study which comes close to an ideal experimental manipulation is that of Wille and Beier (1989) who showed that 99 castrated German sex offenders had a significantly lower recidivism rate 11 years post-release (3%) compared to 35 non-castrated sex offenders (46%). There is in addition some limited evidence that less drastic methods of reducing testosterone levels such as administration of anti-androgens and progesterone derivatives have some effect in lowering violence and sexual aggression (Rubin, 1987; Brain, 1990; Archer, 1991). Particularly persuasive are experimental randomized, placebo-controlled, cross-over trials in normal men that show that testosterone administration increases aggression (Pope et al. 2000). Furthermore, with respect to adolescents, one double-blind, crossover hormone replacement study administered testosterone to male adolescents with delayed puberty and found that medium doses increased aggressive behavior 21 months later (Finkelstein et al.,

1997; Susman et al., 1998). It could be argued that extreme alterations in testosterone are not a good model for less severe variability found in the general population, and that moderate changes of this hormone do not significantly influence aggression. On the other hand, Loosen et al. (1994) found that mild reductions in testosterone in men were associated with reductions in outwardly-directed anger, thus suggesting that mild changes in testosterone can modulate aggression.

Cortisol

Cortisol (also called a glucocorticoid) is a hormone that is produced by a corticotropin-releasing factor (CRF), a peptide which is in turn produced by the hypothalamus in the brain and which regulates autonomic functions (e.g., heart rate, skin conductance) and emotional responses. Individuals who are aroused or stressed show an increase in cortisol. As such, one might expect reduced cortisol levels in antisocials who are thought to be relatively underaroused and fearless.

A number of studies in a wide variety of contexts have now shown that there is indeed a link between low resting cortisol and antisocial, aggressive behavior. McBurnett et al. (1991) found that boys with CD without comorbid anxiety disorder showed significantly lower concentrations of cortisol than did boys with CD and comorbid anxiety disorder. Cortisol has similarly been reported to be low in habitually violent incarcerated offenders (Virkkunen, 1985), in aggressive schoolchildren (Tennes and Kreye, 1985), in adolescents with conduct problems (Susman et al. 1992), boys with disruptive behavior (McBurnett et al. 2000), disinhibited children (Kagan et al. 1987), and boys with oppositional defiant disorder (van Goozen et al., 1998).

Taken together, these studies suggest that resting cortisol may play a non-trivial role in mediating antisocial, violent, and criminal behavior. In this context it supports and extends the findings described earlier for resting heart rate, confirming the finding of an autonomic arousal deficit in antisocial populations. On the other hand, the link between antisocial behavior and cortisol *reactivity* to a stressor (i.e. the change in cortisol before and after a stressful event) is less clear, with some studies finding decreased reactivity in antisocial children (e.g. van Goozen et al. 1998) while other studies find increased reactivity (e.g. Susman et al., 1997). Even accepting that there are differences in antisocial children in basal cortisol levels, it must be remembered that, as with many other biological measures, cortisol is part of a dynamic system which is responsive to environmental changes and demands (Susman et al. 1991; Susman and Ponirakis, 1997). As such, integration with social and environmental factors must be a primary aim of future studies in this area.

Biosocial Interactions for Testosterone and Cortisol

Despite the clear evidence that contextual and environmental influences alter both testosterone and cortisol, few researchers have tested for biosocial interactions in the way that interactions have been tested for psychophysiological and obstetric factors. That is, do social variables moderate the relationship between hormones and antisocial behavior? Dabbs and Morris (1990) found that in low SES subjects, those with high testosterone had higher levels of childhood and adulthood antisocial behavior, whereas these effects were not found for high SES subjects. On the other hand, risk ratios for some measures of antisocial behavior (military AWOL, marijuana use, many sex partners) were equally high in both SES groups, and consequently these initial findings should be viewed with caution. Nevertheless, Scarpa and Ollendick (2003) found that children who both gave large cortisol responses to a provocation task and who also had been physically abused had the highest aggression scores. Both of these hormonal studies are therefore similar in that biology – antisocial relationships were more marked in those from negative environments (low SES, abuse), and lie in contrast to studies measuring psychophysiological and brain imaging risk factors (low heart rate, low skin conductance, increased vagal tone, low prefrontal activity) which find antisocial – psychophysiology relationships strongest in those from *benign* home backgrounds. It remains to be seen whether further hormone studies find stronger hormone – antisocial links in those from negative rather than positive home backgrounds.

NEUROTRANSMITTERS

Basic neurotransmitters such as dopamine, norepinephrine, and serotonin form the basis to information processing and communication within the brain, and in this sense underlie all types of behavior, including sensation, perception, learning and memory, eating, drinking - and more controversially, antisocial behavior. Neurotransmitters are chemicals stored in the synaptic vesicles (small globules) of a communicating cell's axon; this axon carries the nerve impulse of the cell body to other cells. During cellular communication, these chemicals are discharged into the synaptic cleft (the space between two neurons), and are taken up by special receptors in the post-synaptic membrane of the other recipient cell, initiating what is termed a post-synaptic potential. On this basis, neurotransmitters form the basis to the transmission of information throughout the brain.

Paradoxically, the well-known and best studied neurotransmitters (serotonin, dopamine, norepinephrine) account for only a small proportion of cell firing in the brain. For example, serotonin is thought to be the transmitter substance in less than 0.1% of brain synapses. Nevertheless, they are thought to be highly important in the context of brain and behavior; for example, serotonin, norepinephrine, and dopamine have been implicated in the etiology of major disorders such as schizophrenia and depression.

A meta-analysis of 29 studies examined the relationship between norepinephrine, dopamine, and serotonin, and antisocial behavior (Raine, 1993). Results indicated a relatively large effect size (-0.75) between reduced central serotonin and antisocial behavior, and a medium effect size of -0.41 between reduced norepinephrine and antisocial behavior, with no effect for dopamine. Sub-analyses were conducted in an attempt to specify which sub-groups of antisocials these findings pertain to. These analyses indicated that serotonin was lowest in antisocials with a history of alcohol abuse, borderline personality disorder, and violence, while CSF norepinephrine was lowest in those with alcohol abuse, borderline personality, and depression.

Increased impulsivity has been associated with lower serotonin, and there is some evidence that aggressive individuals who are impulsive have particularly lower serotonin. Humans low in social class have also been found to have reduced serotonin, and it is possible that reductions in serotonin produced by a fall in dominance triggers impulsive aggression as a way of raising the individual in the dominance hierarchy. In evolutionary terms this would be adaptive as increased dominance gives greater access to food and sex, thus increasing the individual's ability to reproduce and pass on their genes. Yet again, poor diet may play a role. Diets low in, or otherwise blocking, the uptake of tryptophan or tyrosine (the precursors of serotonin and norepinephrine respectively) have been found to lower the levels of these transmitters in the brain (see Weisman, 1986). In addition, even when returned to a normal diet, brain serotonin levels are never fully compensated (Timiras et al. 1984). Poor nutrition possibly occurring in individuals of lower socio-economic status (including poor dietary care during pregnancy) could conceivably influence neurotransmitter levels throughout life.

Neurotransmitter research provides limited evidence of interactions with social and environmental processes. Moffitt et al., (1997) found that while violent offenders had higher blood serotonin levels than controls, those with both high blood serotonin and a conflicted family background were over three times more likely to become violent by age 21 compared to men with only high serotonin or only conflicted family background.

Environmental Pollutants and Neurotoxicity

It has long been suspected that exposure to pollutants, particularly heavy metals that have neurotoxic effects, can lead to mild degrees of brain impairment which in turn predisposes to antisocial and aggressive behavior. While research is limited in this field, to date, lead and manganese have been particularly implicated in predisposing to antisocial and aggressive behavior.

Lead

One of the best studies to date is that of Needleman et al. (1996) who assessed lead levels in the bones of 301 11-year-old schoolboys. Boys with higher lead levels were found to have significantly higher teacher ratings of delinquent and aggressive behavior, higher parent ratings of delinquent and aggressive behavior, and higher self-report delinquency scores. These findings do not occur in isolation: similar links between lead levels and antisocial, aggressive, and delinquent behavior and aggression have been found in at least six other studies in several different countries (see Needleman et al. 1996 for a review).

A further study is worthy of discussion. Burns et al. (1999) found that school children from a lead smelting community had increased externalizing behavior problems. This effect remained after controlling for a number of confounding variables, including the quality of the child's home environment, maternal psychopathology, and the child's IQ. Nevertheless, studies on child antisocial behavior and lead exposure are to date few and need further replication. The fact that experimental exposure to lead during development increases aggressive behavior in hamsters (Delville, 1999) is nevertheless intriguing in that it suggests a causal link between lead exposure and aggression.

Manganese, Zinc, Copper, and Cadmium

Less strong to date, but nevertheless provocative, are findings with respect to manganese. At high levels, manganese has toxic effects on the brain and can damage the brain so much that it can even lead to Parkinson-like symptoms. Furthermore, it reduces levels of serotonin and dopamine, neurotransmitters which play a key role in brain communication (see below). In addition, research on rats has found that microinjections of manganese chloride (McC12) can cause neurodegenerative processes that further alter the animal's emotional behavior (Ponzoni et al., 2000). One study by Gottschalk et al. (1991) found that three different samples of violent criminals compared to controls had higher levels of manganese in their hair. On the other hand, not all studies have found this association (Schauss, 1981). It may be that low levels of calcium intake interact with high manganese in predisposing to violent behavior because animal research indicates that the neurotoxic effect of manganese is particularly strong when the animal is deficient in calcium.

Regarding other toxins, in humans, individuals prone to aggression and violence have been found to show abnormal trace metal concentrations both in blood and hair (in particular elevated serum copper and depressed plasma zinc), while hair analysis has also revealed an elevated copper-to-sodium ratio (Walsh et al., 1997). Furthermore, some studies of prison inmates have argued for higher cadmium hair levels (in addition to manganese and lead) in violent offenders than in non-violent offenders or controls (Gottschalk et al., 1991; Masters et al., 1998; Masters and Coplan, 1999).

Biosocial Interactions and Mechanisms

Regarding biosocial interaction effects, one intriguing study is worthy of note. Masters, Hone, and Doshi (1998) in an analysis of violent crime rates in 1,242 counties in the U.S. found a three-way interaction between environmental lead or manganese exposure, high population density, and alcoholism rates, with highest rates of violence in counties with high densities, exposure to toxins, and alcoholism. As with research on hormones, there is a dearth of empirical data to support or refute a biosocial interaction hypothesis of antisocial and violent behavior with respect to toxins and further tests of this proposition are required.

An important question concerns how pollutants and toxins could predispose to antisocial behavior. In humans, low-level exposure to manganese has been implicated in neurological changes, decreased learning ability in school-aged children, and increased propensity for violence in adults (Finley, et al 2004). Experiment studies in rats have shown that manganese exposure could lead to behavioral, neurobiochemical and cytoimmunochemical toxicity of the brain in postnatal development (Zhang, et al 2002). Such adverse effects were especially true when the rats were concurrently exposure to both lead and manganese (Chandra, et al 1981). These animal studies have suggest that the toxic effects of lead and/or manganese on the brain are produced by reducing the levels of brain dopamine and 5-hydroxytryptamine which in turn induce manifest impairments in learning ability and increased aggressive behavior (Chandra, et al. 1981).

NEUROCOGNITIVE RISK FACTORS

Frontal Deficits in Antisocial Children

Brain imaging and neurological studies, combined with the substantial neuropsychological and EEG literature on antisocial and criminal behavior (Volavka, 1995; Raine, 1993; Raine and Yang, 2006) place beyond reasonable doubt the fact that there is a link between prefrontal deficits and antisocial, violent behavior in adults. But are these same links found in children? And is there evidence that damage to the prefrontal region of the brain actually causes antisocial, aggressive behavior in children?

The question of whether there are links between prefrontal structural / functional deficits and antisocial behavior in children would be most directly answered by imaging research. Although there is a growing literature on other externalizing disorders such as hyperactivity, which inconsistently implicates frontostriatal systems (Filipek, 1999), there appears to have been no studies conducted on conduct disorder, aggression, or antisocial behavior in children (although see Amen and Carmichael, 1997, for a report of increased anterior medial frontal blood flow as assessed by SPECT in 64 6-17 year olds with oppositional defiant disorder but lacking in conduct disorder). Instead, one must turn to traditional neuropsychological studies to answer the question of functional deficits in antisocial children.

Reviews of this evidence in child and adolescent samples indicate that antisocial behavior is characterized by neuropsychological impairments (Moffitt, 1993; Raine, 1993). More specifically, Moffitt (1990, 1993) has argued that antisocial children and delinquents specifically have a deficit with respect to executive functions, i.e. self-regulation and inhibitory control, concept-formation, abstract reasoning, problem-solving behavior, flexible behavior responsive to external contingencies, sustained attention, planning, and organization. The frontal cortex is the brain structure that has been most consistently implicated in executive function deficits, although it should be noted that executive function deficits do not always go hand-in-hand with frontal structural deficits. While Teicher and Golden (2000) argue that evidence for executive function deficits in antisocial children is variable, a recent meta-analysis of executive dysfunction and antisocial behavior by Morgan and Lilienfeld (2000) shows significant effect sizes (Cohen's d) of 0.40 for conduct disorder and 0.86 for juvenile delinquency, thus supporting Moffitt's position. There is debate, however, as to whether these effects are carried entirely by comorbid attention-deficit disorder in antisocial children (e.g. see Clark et al. 2000), or whether executive function deficits exist in aggressive children after controlling for hyperactivity (see e.g. Seguin et al., 1999). On balance, it seems likely that (a) conduct disordered children comorbid for attention-deficit disorder have the severest executive functional deficits; (b) conduct disordered children without attention-deficit have a less strong, but significant form of executive function deficits; (c) evidence for executive function deficits supports the notion of frontal lobe deficits in antisocial children.

While structural brain imaging studies of conduct disordered children are lacking, there are studies of the behavioral sequelae that follow head injuries in children. Overwhelmingly, these studies find that conduct disorder and externalizing behavior problems are common after head trauma (Hux et al., 1998; Max et al., 1998; Butler et al., 1997, Mittenberg et al., 1997). It is also clear that some children develop internalizing rather than externalizing behavior problems after head injury (e.g. Max et al. 1998), while others remain relatively unaffected. When the problem is approached from the other direction, by looking at base rates of head injury in delinquents and non-delinquents, rates are not too dissimilar, but parents of delinquent children are much more likely to report that behavior problems began to develop after head trauma compared to parents of non-delinquents (Hux et al. 1998).

Studies of children with lesions to the prefrontal cortex early in life lend further evidence to the view that head (and therefore brain) trauma can directly lead to antisocial and aggressive behavior. Anderson et al. (1999) reported on two cases (one female, one male) who suffered selective lesions to the prefrontal cortex in the first 16 months of life (bilateral polar and ventromedial in the female, and right polar-medial-dorsal in the male). Both showed early antisocial behavior that progressed into delinquency in adolescence and criminal behavior in adulthood, and included impulsive aggressive and nonaggressive forms of antisocial behavior. Both had autonomic deficits, poor decision-making skills, and deficits on learning from feedback. Pennington and Bennetto (1993) report on nine other cases of children suffering frontal lesions in the first 10 years of life. They noted that all nine suffered behavioral problems after the injuries, with 7 of the 9 being conduct disordered, and the remaining two exhibited either impulsive, labile, behavior or uncontrollable behavior. These cases when taken together strongly suggest that damage to the prefrontal cortex can directly lead to antisocial, aggressive, and criminal behavior.

Developmental Processes, Frontal Functions, and Antisocial Behavior

Brain imaging, neuropsychological, and neurological studies all suggest that damage or dysfunction to the prefrontal cortex is a significant predisposition to antisocial behavior. These findings are based predominantly on studies focusing on children and adolescents, or adults up to the mid-30s, but there is also recent evidence that aggression and antisocial behavior in elderly demented patients is particularly associated with deficits to the anterior and frontal regions of the brain (Hirono et al., 2000; Miller et al., 1997; Mega et al., 2000). Combined with studies showing that damage to the prefrontal cortex in the beginning of life produce antisocial and aggressive behavior, and imaging studies showing correlations between violent offending and reduced prefrontal structure/function in early to mid-adulthood, they together make a compelling case for the notion that prefrontal deficits can cause antisocial and aggressive behavior throughout the lifespan.

Adequate theories of antisocial and violent behavior need to explain why criminal offending peaks in the late teens, a phenomenon that has been called "at once the most robust and least understood empirical observation in the field of criminology" (Moffitt, 1993, p. 675). The adolescent-limited perspective of Moffitt (1993) in which social norms make antisocial, rebellious behavior during adolescence a normative but transient phenomenon is one persuasive account. It is argued here that a prefrontal dysfunction theory of crime can also contribute in part to understanding this crime-age relationship. Prior to adolescence, children live in a relatively structured environment where complex, life-changing planning and decision-making is not the norm. In contrast, late adolescence is a stage in life where enormous social demands are being placed on the rapidly growing teenager, a load that calls on resources of the frontal cortex and its associated executive functions. Such adolescents need to regulate, control, and inhibit a growing sex drive, deal with threats and challenges to their social status that arise within their peer groups, and plan and organize for a future career.

They need to sustain increasing attention to school performance in order to maximize career prospects. Those leaving school at 18 for a job in the real world lose the social structure and support systems that they have grown used to, and must adapt their behavior to the more variable contingencies, incentives, and disincentives that drive economic life. In addition, they must plan and develop strategies for attracting a partner (or choosing between possible partners), and they may need to make early parenting decisions. Throughout this period, they must evaluate and assess competing life-course strategies and engage in complex decision-making. At the same time the normative rebellious spirit and antisocial behavior that has characterized most adolescence (Moffitt, 1993) must be inhibited and suppressed in order to succeed in life and make way for new, more adaptive behavioral strategies.

The prefrontal cortex bears the burden of this magnified cognitive load that requires multiple executive functions – sustained attention, behavioral flexibility to changing contingencies, working memory, self-regulation and inhibition, abstract decision-making, planning and organization. Yet the prefrontal cortex is relatively late to mature and this processing load occurs at a time when this structure is still developing, with myelination of the frontal cortex continuing into the early 20s and even 30's. A minority of individuals with early damage or dysfunction of the prefrontal cortex would be particularly likely to suffer an information overload during this time period, resulting in further dysfunction of the prefrontal cortex, less regulatory control, and further, life-long, antisocial behavior. Others with an intact but particularly late-maturing prefrontal cortex may be antisocial during childhood and adolescence, but with further maturation of the frontal lobes in early adulthood may eventually discontinue their antisocial behavior. Others may have frontal dysfunction, but may be protected from antisocial behavior by having more social support or fewer social-transitional demands placed on them. Yet another group of late-onset offenders (Hamalainen and Pulkkinen, 1996; Ishikawa and Raine, 2001) may not evidence antisocial behavior until early adulthood when life stressors at this time overload a prefrontal cortex with latent functional impairments.

In summary, the fact that children, adolescents, adults, and elderly patients with prefrontal deficits are characterized by antisocial, aggressive behavior makes a compelling lifespan case for a prefrontal dysfunction theory of antisocial, aggressive behavior. It is hypothesized that the social and executive function demands of late adolescence place an overload on the late-developing prefrontal cortex, giving rise to prefrontal dysfunction and a lack of inhibitory control over antisocial, aggressive behavior at this age. This prefrontal overload is hypothesized to be particularly likely in individuals with developmental delays in prefrontal maturation or in hyperactive children with pre-existing prefrontal deficits. Furthermore, persistence into adulthood of antisocial behavior is thought to be especially likely in those who have suffered head trauma and which may prevent a maturational catch-up of the prefrontal cortex in adulthood.

Summary and Conclusions

This review of genetic and biological risk factors is by necessity non-comprehensive and selective in its perspective. In particular, we have not covered the increasing literature on brain imaging and psychophysiology (see respectively Raine and Yang, 2006, and Scarpa and

Raine, 2003). Nevertheless, we believe that we have highlighted some of the key genetic, biological, and biosocial influences on antisocial and criminal behavior in children, adolescents, and adults. Behavioral genetic studies indicate at a global level that genes play a role in the risk for criminal offending, and that environmental factors may serve to enhance or limit the genetic risk (GxE interactions). Initial molecular genetic studies have to date implicated the possible importance of neurotransmitter-related genes, including 5-HTTLPR and MAO-A, in increasing risk for criminal behavior or its associated personality traits. Several studies in different countries have replicated the finding that birth complications interact with early psychosocial adversity in predisposing to later violent offending. Similarly, maternal cigarette smoking during pregnancy is a replicable correlate of later violent and criminal offending. Similarly, fetal neural maldevelopment as indicated by minor physical anomalies appears to predispose to later antisocial behavior, especially when combined with a negative psychosocial environment. Links have been found between low cortisol and antisocial behavior, while experimental studies suggest a causal link between increased testosterone and increased aggressivity. Low serotonin is a well-replicated correlate of impulsive aggressive behavior, and there is some support for the notion of increased lead and manganese levels in predisposing to antisocial, aggressive behavior. Dysfunction to the prefrontal cortex is a well-documented predisposition to antisocial behavior in child, adolescent, and adult population and the social demands of adolescence may place an overload on the relatively late-developing prefrontal cortex, giving rise to prefrontal dysfunction and antisocial, aggressive behavior.

Acknowledgements

This paper was written with the support of an Independent Scientist Award from NIMH (K02 MH01114-01) to the first author and a research grant to the first and second authors from NIMH (R01 MH58354).

References

Archer, J. (1991). The influence of testosterone on human aggression. *British Journal of Clinical Psychology, 82*, 1-28.

Arsenault, L., Tremblay, R. E., Boulerice, B., and Saucier, J. F. (2002). Obstetrical complications and violent delinquency: Testing two developmental pathways. *Child Development, 73*, 496-508.

Arseneault, L., Tremblay, R. E., Boulerice, B., Seguin, J. R., and Saucier, J. F. (2000). Minor physical anomalies and family adversity as risk factors for violent delinquency in adolescence. *American Journal of Psychiatry, 157*, 917-923.

Baker, L.A. (2002). The nature-nurture problem in violence. In Heitmeyer, W. and Hagan, J. (Eds.) *International Handbook of Violence* (pp 735-762). Westdeutscher: Verlag.

Baker, L.A. and Raine, A. (2004). *The Delinquency Interview for Children (DI-C): A self-report measure of antisocial behavior*. Unpublished manuscript.

Baker, L. A. (2002), Raine, A., and Lozano, D. I. (2004). *Risk factors for antisocial behavior in childhood: Genetic and environmental influences.* Unpublished manuscript.

Brennan, P. A., Grekin, E. R., and Mednick, S.A. (1999). Maternal smoking during pregnancy and adult male criminal outcomes. *Archives of General Psychiatry, 56*, 215-219.

Brennan, P. A., Mednick, B.R., and Mednick, S.A. (1993). Parental psychopathology, congenital factors, and violence. In S. Hodgins (Ed.), *Mental disorder and crime* (pp. 244-261). Thousand Oaks, CA: Sage.

Brennan, P. A., Mednick, S. A., and Raine, A. (1997). Biosocial interactions and violence: A focus on perinatal factors. *Biosocial bases of violence* 163-174.

Brunner, H.G., Nelen, M., Breakefield, X.O., Ropers, H.H., and van Oost, B.A. (1993). Abnormal behavior associated with a point mutation in the structural gene for monoamine oxidase A. *Science, 262,* 578-580.

Burns, J.M., Baghurst, P.A., Sawyer, M.G., McMichael, A.J., Tong, S.L., (1999). Lifetime low-level exposure to environmental lead and children's emotional and behavioral development at ages 11–13 years. The Port Pirie Cohort Study. *American Journal of Epidemiology 149, 740–749.*

Carlson, N. (1998). *Physiology of Behavior* (6th ed.). Needham Heights, MA: Allyn and Bacon.

Carey, G. (1994). Genetics and violence. In A. J. Reiss and J. Roth (Eds.): *Understanding and preventing violence. Vol 2. Biobehavioral influences on violence,* pp. 21-58.

Carey, G., and Goldman, D. (1997). The genetics of antisocial behavior. In D. Stoff, J. Breiling, and J. Maser (Eds): *Handbook of antisocial behavior* (pp. 243-254). New York: John Wiley and Sons, Inc.,

Caspi, A., McClay, J., Moffitt, T., Mill, J., Martin, J., Craig, I.W., Taylor, A. and Poulton, R. (2002). Role of genotype in the cycle of violence in maltreated children. *Science, 297,* 851-854.

Chandra, A. V., Ali, M. M., Saxena, D. K., and Murthy, R. C. (1981). Behavioral and neurochemical changes in rats simultaneously exposed to manganese and lead. *Arch Toxicol., 49,* 49-56.

Cloninger, C. R., and Gottesman, I. I. (1987). Genetic and environmental factors in antisocial behavior disorders. In S.A. Mednick and T.E, Moffitt, and S.A. Stack (Eds). *The causes of crime: New biological approaches* (pp 92-109). Cambridge: Cambridge University Press.

Dabbs ,J. M. (1992). Testosterone measurements in social and clinical psychology. *Journal of Social and Clinical Psychology, 11*, 302-321.

Dabbs, J. M., and Morris, R. (1990). Testosterone, social class, and antisocial behavior in a sample of 4,462 men. *Psychological Science, 1*, 209-211.

Delville, Y., (1999). Exposure to lead during development alters aggressive behavior in golden hamsters. *Neurotoxicology and Teratology 21, 445–449.*

DiLalla, L.F. (2002). Behavior genetics of aggression in children: Review and future directions. *Developmental Review, 22* 593-622.

DiLalla, L. F. and Gottesman, I. I. (1989). Heterogeneity of causes for delinquency and criminality: Lifespan perspectives. *Development and Psychopathology, 1,* 339-349.

DiLalla, L. F. and Gottesman, I. I. (1991). Does violence beget violence? Widom's untold tale. *Psychological Bulletin, 109,* 125-129.

Dodge, K.A., Lochman, J. E., Harnish, J. D., and Bates, J. E. (1997). Reactive and proactive aggression in school children and psychiatrically impaired chronically assaultive youth. *Journal of Abnormal Psychology, 106*, 37-51.

Ebstein, R.P., Benjamin, J., and Belmaker, R.H. (2003). Behavioral Genetics, genomics, and personality. In R. Plomin and J. C. DeFries, I. W. Craig, and P. McGuffin (Eds.) *Behavioral Genetics in the Postgenomic Era,* Washington, DC: American Psychological Association.

Fast, D. K., Conry, J., and Loock ,C. A. (1999). Identifying Fetal Alcohol Syndrome among youth in the criminal justice system. *Journal of Developmental and Behavioral Pediatrics, 20*, 370-372.

Finley, J. W. (2004). Does environmental exposure to manganese pose a health risk to healthy adults? *Nutr Rev., 62,* 148-153.

Gibson, C. L., and Tibbetts, S. G. (1998). Interaction between maternal cigarette smoking and Apgar scores in predicting offending behavior. *Psychological Reports, 83*, 579-586.

Gibson, C. L., and Tibbetts, S. G. (2000). A biosocial interaction in predicting early onset of offending. *Psychological Reports, 86*, 509-518.

Gottschalk, L.A., Rebello, T., Buchsbaum, M., Tucker, H.G.,(1991). Abnormalities in hair trace elements as indicators of aberrant behavior. *Comprehensive Psychiatry 32,* 229–237.

Guy, J. D., Majorski, L. V., Wallace, C. J., and Guy, M. P. (1983). The incidence of minor physical anomalies in adult male schizophrenics. *Schizophrenia Bulletin, 9,* 571-582.

Hallikainen, T., Saito, T., Lachman, H. M., Volavka, J., Pohjalainen, T., and Ryynanen, O. P. et al. (1999). Association between low activity serotonin transporter promoter genotype and early onset alcoholism with habitual impulsive violent behavior. *Molecular Psychiatry, 4*, 385-388.

Harris, J.A. (1999). Review and methodological considerations in research on testosterone and aggression. *Aggression and Violent Behavior, 4*, 273-291.

Hodgins, S., Kratzer, L., and McNeil, T. F. (2001). Obstetric complications, parenting, and risk of criminal behavior. *Archives of General Psychiatry, 58*, 746-752.

Kemppainen, L., Jokelainen, J., Jaervelin, M. R., Isohanni, M., and Raesaenen, P. (2001). The one-child family and violent criminality: A 31-year follow-up study of the Northern Finland 1966 birth cohort. *American Journal of Psychiatry, 158*, 960-962.

Laakso, M. P., Vaurio, O., Koivisto, E., Savolainen, L., Eronen, M., Aronen, H.J., Hakola, P., Repo, E., Soininen, H., and Tiihonen, J. (2001). Psychopathy and the posterior hippocampus. *Behavioural Brain Research, 118*, 187-193.

Laucht, M., Esser, G., Baving, L., Gerhold, M., Hoesch, I., Ihle, W., Steigleider, P., Stock, B., Stoehr ,R. M., Weindrich, D., and Schmidt, M. H. (2000). Behavioral sequelae of perinatal insults and early family adversity at 8 years of age. *Journal of the American Academy of Child and Adolescent Psychiatry, 39*, 1229-1237.

Lesch, K. P., Bengel, D., Heils, A., and Sabol, S. Z., (1996). Association of anxiety-related traits with a polymorphism in the serotonin transporter gene regulatory region. *Science, 274* 1527-1531.

Liu, J., Raine, A., Wuerker, A. Venables, P. H., and Mednick S. A. (2004). *The impact of birth complications on externalizing behavior for early adolescents: Direct and mediational effects.* Manuscript submitted for publication.

Liu, J. (2004). Prenatal and perinatal complications as predispositions to externalizing behavior *Journal of Prenatal and Perinatal Psychology and Health, 18,* 301-311.

Mason, D.A., and Frick, P.J. (1994) The heritability of antisocial behavior: A meta-analysis of twin and adoption studies. *Journal of Psychology and Behavioral Assessment, 16*: 301-323.

Masters ,R. D., Hone, B., and Doshi, A. (1998). Environmental pollution, neurotoxicity, and criminal violence. In J. Rose (Ed.), *Environmental toxicology: Current developments.* (pp. 13-48). New York: Gordon and Breach.

Masters, R. D., Coplan, M., (1999). A dynamic, multifactorial model of alcohol, drug abuse, and crime: linking neuroscience and behavior to toxicology. *Social Science Information* (pp. 591–624). Sage, London.

Mazur, A., and Booth, A. (1999). The biosociology of testosterone in men. *Mind, brain, and society: Toward a neurosociology of emotion.* (Vol. 5) (pp. 311-338).

Mednick, S. A., and Kandel, E. S. (1988). Congenital determinants of violence. *Bulletin of the American Academy of Psychiatry and the Law, 16*, 101-109.

Miles, D. R. and Carey, G. (1997). Genetic and environmental architecture of human aggression. *Journal of Personality and Social Psychology, 72*, 207-217.

Moffitt, T.E., Caspi, A., Fawcett, P., Brammer, G. L., Raleigh, M., Yuwiler, A., and Silva, P. (1997). Whole blood serotonin and family background relate to male violence. In A. Raine, P. A. Brennan, D. P. Farrington, and S. A. Mednick (Eds.), *Biosocial bases of violence.* (pp. 231-249). New York: Plenum.

Moffitt, T. E. (1993). Adolescence-limited and life-course-persistent antisocial behavior: A developmental taxonomy. *Psychological Review, 100*, 674-701.

Moffitt, T. E., and Caspi, A. (2001). Childhood predictors differentiate life-course persistent and adolescence-limited antisocial pathways among males and females. *Development and Psychopathology, 13*, 355-375.

Olds, D. (1997). Tobacco exposure and impaired development: A review of the evidence. *Mental Retardation and Developmental Disabilities Research Reviews, 3*, 257-269.

Olson, H.C., Streissguth, A.P., Sampson, P.D., Barr, H.M., Bookstein, F.L., and Thiede ,K. (1997). Association of prenatal alcohol exposure with behavioral and learning problems in early adolescence. *Journal of the American Academy of Child and Adolescent Psychiatry, 36*, 1187-1194.

Pine, D.S., Shaffer, D., Schonfeld, I. S., and Davies, M. (1997). Minor physical anomalies: Modifiers of environmental risks for psychiatric impairment? *Journal of the American Academy of Child and Adolescent Psychiatry, 36*, 395-403.

Piquero, A., and Tibbetts, S. (1999). The impact of pre/perinatal disturbances and disadvantaged familial environment in predicting criminal offending. *Studies on Crime and Crime Prevention, 8*, 52-70.

Plomin, R. Nitz, K. and Rowe, D.C. (1990). Behavioral genetics and aggressive behavior in childhood. In M. Lewis and S.M. Miller, (Eds.) *Handbook of developmental psychopathology: Perspectives in developmental psychology.* (pp. 119-133). New York: Plenum Press.

Raine, A. (2002). The biological basis of crime. In J. Q. Wilson and J. Petersilia (Eds.), *Crime: Public Policies For Crime Control* (pp. 43-74). San Francisco: ICS Press.

Raine, A. (1993). *The psychopathology of crime: Criminal behavior as a clinical disorder.* San Diego: Academic Press.

Raine, A. (1996). Autonomic nervous system activity and violence. In D. M. Stoff and R. B. Cairns (Eds.), *Neurobiological approaches to clinical aggression research.* (pp. 145-168). Mahwah, N.J.: Lawrence Erlbaum.

Raine, A., Brennan, P., and Mednick, S. A. (1994). Birth complications combined with early maternal rejection at age 1 year predispose to violent crime at age 18 years. *Archives of General Psychiatry, 51*, 984-988.

Raine, A., Brennan, P., and Mednick, S. A. (1997). Interaction between birth complications and early maternal rejection in predisposing individuals to adult violence: Specificity to serious, early-onset violence. *American Journal of Psychiatry, 154*, 1265-1271.

Raine, A., Buchsbaum, M., and LaCasse, L. (1997). Brain abnormalities in murderers indicated by positron emission tomography. *Biological Psychiatry, 42*, 495-508.

Raine, A., and Venables, P. H. (1989). Antisocial behaviour: Evolution, genetics, neuropsychology, and psychophysiology. In A. Gale and M. Eysenck (Eds.), *Handbook of Individual Differences: Biological Perspectives.* Chichester: Wiley.

Raine, A. and Yang, Y. (2006). The neuroanatomical bases of psychopathy: a review of brain imaging findings. In C.J. Patrick (ed.) *Handbook of psychopathy.* (pp. 278-296) Guilford.

Rasanen, P., Hakko, H., Isohanni, M., Hodgins, S., Jarvelin, M.R., and Tiihonen, J. (1999). Maternal smoking during pregnancy and risk of criminal behavior among adult male offspring in the northern Finland 1996 birth cohort. *American Journal of Psychiatry, 156,* 857-862.

Rhee, S. H. and Waldman, I. (2002). Genetic and environmental influences on antisocial behavior: A meta-analysis of twin and adoption studies. *Psychological Bulletin, 128*: 490-529.

Rutter, M., Bolton, P., Harrington, R., le Couteur, A., McDonald, H.; and Simonoff, E.. (1990). Genetic factors in child psychiatric disorders: I. A review of research strategies. *Journal of Child Psychology and Psychiatry and Allied Disciplines, 31*, 3-37.

Scarpa, A., and Ollendick, T.H. (2003). Community violence exposure in a young adult sample: III. Psychophysiology and victimization interact to affect risk for aggression. *Journal of Community Psychology, 31*, 321-338.

Scarpa, A. and Raine, A. (2003). The psychophysiology of antisocial behavior: Interactions with environmental experiences. In A. Walsh and L. Ellis (Eds.) *Biosocial criminology: Challenging environmentalism's supremacy* (pp. 209-226). New York: Nova Science.

Shih, J., et al. (1999). Monoamine oxidase: From genes to behavior. *Annual Review in Neuroscience, 22* 197-217.

Slotkin, T .A., Epps T. A., Stenger, M. L., Sawyer, K. J., and Seidler, F. J. (1999). Cholinergic receptors in heart and brainstem of rats exposed to nicotine during development: implications for hypoxia tolerance and perinatal mortality. *Brain Research, 113*, 1-12.

Streissguth, A. P., Barr, H. M., Bookstein, F. L., Sampson, P. D., and Olson, H. C. (1999). The long-term neurocognitive consequences of prenatal alcohol exposure: A 14-year study. *Psychological Science, 10*, 186-190.

Susman, E. J. (1993). Psychological, contextual, and psychobiological interactions: A developmental perspective on conduct disorder. *Development and Psychopathology, 5*, 181-189.

Susman, E. J., and Ponirakis, A. (1997). Hormones--context interaction and antisocial behavior in youth. In A. Raine, P. A. Brennan, D. Farrington, and S. A. Mednick (Eds.), *Biosocial bases of violence.* (pp. 251-269). New York: Plenum.

Tremblay, R. E., School, B., Boulerice, B., Arseneault, L., Soussignan, R., and Perusse ,D. (1997). Male physical aggression, social dominance, and testosterone levels at puberty: A developmental perspective. In A. Raine, P. A. Brennan, D. P. Farrington, and S. A. Mednick (Eds.), *Biosocial bases of violence.* (pp. 271-291). New York: Plenum.

Venables, P.H. and Raine, A. (1987). Biological theory. In McGurk, Barry J.; Thornton, David M.; et-al. (Eds) *Applying psychology to imprisonment: Theory and practice.* (pp. 3-27). London, England UK: Her Majesty's Stationery Office Books.

Walsh, W. J., Isaacson, H. R., Rehman, F., Hall, A., (1997). Elevated blood copper/zinc ratios in assaultive young males. *Physiology and Behavior 62,* 327–329.

Werner, E. E. (1987). Vulnerability and resiliency in children at risk for delinquency: A longitudinal study from birth to young adulthood. In J. D. Burchard and S. N. Burchard (Eds.), *Primary prevention of psychopathology.* (pp. 16-43). Newbury Park, CA: Sage.

Zhang, D., He, X., Huang, S., and Li, Y. (2002). Toxicity of manganese exposure on the postnatal development of brain in mice. *Wei Sheng Yan Jiu., 31,* 73-75.

In: Crime and Schizophrenia: Causes and Cures
Editor: Adrian Raine, pp. 109-128
ISBN 1-59454-609-6

Chapter 6

MALNUTRITION, BRAIN DYSFUNCTION AND ANTISOCIAL CRIMINAL BEHAVIOR

Jianghong Liu[1], Adrian Raine[2], Peter Venables[1,3], and Sarnoff A. Mednick[1]

[1] Social Science Research Institute, University of Southern California, Los Angeles, CA 90089-0375
[2] Department of Psychology, University of Southern California, Los Angeles, CA 90089-1061
[3] Department of Psychology, University of York, Heslington, York, England

INTRODUCTION

For decades, research intended to reduce the incidence of criminal violence has been largely unsuccessful. Such efforts include psychoanalytic approaches, behavior modification techniques, and experimental drug therapies. One of the possible reasons for the failure is that designs do not consider biological factors such as malnutrition in the development of antisocial, violent and criminal behavior (Raine, 2002a). Although the role of malnutrition in the development of antisocial behavior has gained some attention, research has still placed little weight on this topic (Fishbein, 2001, Rutter et al, 1998). This is despite decades of the dictum "you are what you eat" which emphasized the importance of nutritional factors impacting on human being behavior. The purpose of this chapter is to provide an overview of malnutrition as a risk factor for antisocial behavior, and to identify possible brain mechanisms which may account for the malnutrition – antisocial behavior link. To better illustrate the interplay among risk factors, mechanisms and behavioral outcome, a hypothetical malnutrition–psychopathology model will be outlined to provide a conceptual framework. Using this framework, we will first review empirical research on nutrition and antisocial behavior. Three key areas of brain dysfunction due to malnutrition will then be explored. Following this, our recent findings from Mauritius on malnutrition and externalizing behavior will be briefly presented. Finally, the current limitations of nutritional research on antisocial behavior and future research direction are outlined.

OVERVIEW OF THE MODEL

Figure 1 outlines the conceptual model for understanding psychopathy – nutrition relationships. This heuristic yet complex model indicates the relationships among risk factors (left), mechanisms (middle) and outcomes (right). Malnutrition caused either by environmental or genetic risk factors during the prenatal and postnatal periods are viewed in this model as risk factors of the outcome, i.e., psychopathology. Insufficient food supply or malabsorption of nutritients are fundamental risk factors for malnutrition. The types of malnutrition, macro-malnutrition or micro-malnutrition, rely on the individual bioavailability of utilizing nutrients. Such malnutrition can predispose to psychopathology through the possible mechanism of brain dysfunction / impairment caused by three independent yet related routes: reducing brain cell development, alteration of biochemical processes, and increasing neurotoxicity. Brain damage/dysfunction is ultimately viewed as being responsible for predisposing to psychopathology. The behavioral outcomes in this model include both antisocial behavior and schizophrenia-spectrum disorders, and we suggest that they both share the common risk factor of malnutrition and the similar mechanism of brain dysfunction. However, this chapter focuses on antisocial behavior as schizophrenia is covered elsewhere (Venables et al., 2006).

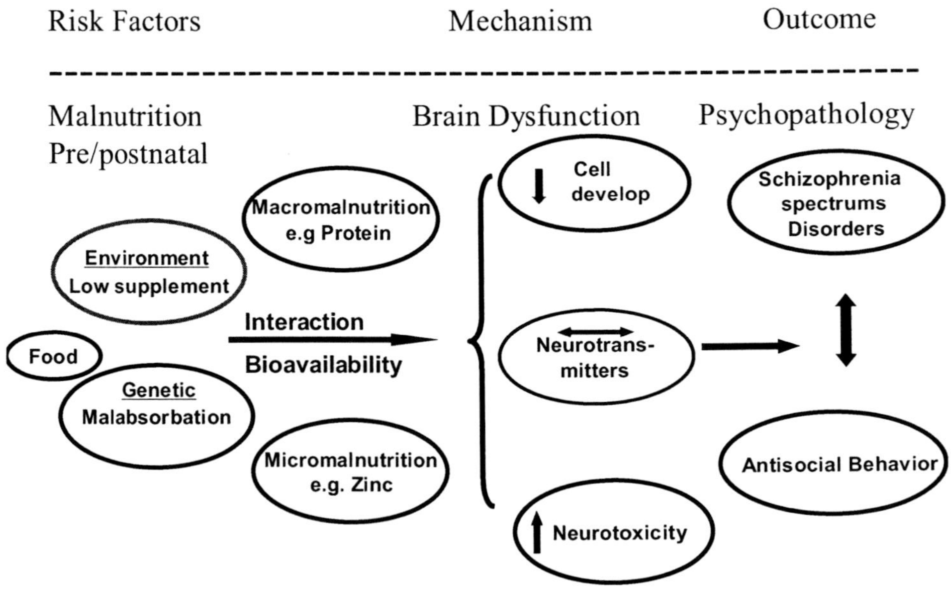

Figure 1. Malnutrition as risk factors for both schizophrenia spectrum disorder and antisocial behavior

Malnutrition as a Risk Factor for Antisocial Behavior

Although diet and nutrition have theoretical and clinical implications for understanding antisocial behavior (Raine et al 2003, Rutter et al., 1998), research in this area is only beginning to receive attention. While most studies on diet, nutrition, and behavior have focused on hyperactivity, deficiency in nutrition has itself been rarely studied in relation to aggression, violence, and criminal behavior. Several studies have, however, demonstrated the general effects of related processes on human aggressive behavior, including food additives, hypoglycemia, and more recently cholesterol (Breakey, 1997; Fishbein et al., 1994; Fishbein, 2001; Raine, 1993). Epidemiological studies have shown associations between over-aggressive behaviors and deficiencies of several essential nutrients (Breakey, 1997; Werbach, 1992). However, findings are conflicting and controversial (Rutter et al., 1998). This section will outline recent empirical findings that support the view that malnutrition is a risk factor for the development of aggressive, violent, and criminal behavior. For the purpose of discussion, this section is divided into the following four topics to elucidate the four lines of research supporting the view of malnutrition as a risk factor for antisocial behavior.

Macro-Malnutrition vs. Micro-Malnutrition

Nutrients are normally divided into two categories, macronutrients, and micronutrients (Beers, and Berkow, 1999). While macro-nutrients often refer to protein, carbohydrates, fats, macro minerals, and water, micro-nutrients include vitamins and trace minerals. The amounts needed are small - micrograms or milligrams a day – so they are called "micro" nutrients. They are necessary for regulatory systems in the body, for efficient energy metabolism, and for other functions. Malnutrition can be either at the macro level or the micro level, and most cases may involve a mixture of both. The World Health Organization (WHO) defines malnutrition as "the cellular imbalance between the supply of nutrients and energy and the body's demand for them to ensure growth, maintenance, and specific functions" (WHO, 2000). Although either type of nutritional deficiency may take place alone, it is more common for several nutrition deficiencies to coexist. It is estimated that up to half of all of the children in the world are deficient in iron and/or zinc (WHO, 2001). Studies have indicated that both types of malnutrition are associated with increased behavioral problems (Liu et al., 2004a). Finally, bioavailability is viewed as the proportion of an ingested nutrient or drug that is truly absorbed into the bloodstream (Shargel and Yu, 1999). Bioavailability of nutritients is greatly influenced by both genetics factors (e.g. poor absorption from the gastrointestinal tract) and environmental factors (e.g. food inhibitors and enhancers (Hallberg et al, 1989).

Macro-Malnutrition

Protein-energy malnutrition (PEM), or protein-calorie malnutrition, is a deficiency syndrome caused by the inadequate intake of macronutrients and is characterized by an energy deficit due to a reduction in all macronutrients. Protein malnutrition is a global problem, affecting many young children in developing countries. In animals, male rats fed a low-protein diet in early postnatal life have been reported to show increased aggressive behavior in pair interactions (Tikal et al., 1976). Recent studies of humans support these findings. The male offspring of pregnant women starved during the German blockade of food to Holland at the end of World War II had 2.5 times the rates of antisocial personality disorder in adulthood compared to controls. Effects were found for severe malnutrition during the first and second trimesters of pregnancy, but not the third trimester (Neugerbauer et al., 1999), suggesting that good nutrition is particularly crucial when the fetal brain is developing rapidly in the second trimester.

Amino acids, the biochemical building blocks of protein, have been also implicated in aggressive and violent behavior. Both monkeys and rats fed diets depleted in the amino acid tryptophan become more aggressive than controls, while high-tryptophan food reduces aggressive behavior (Bjork et al., 1999). Because tryptophan is the dietary building block of serotonin, diets low in tryptophan could contribute to the low levels of serotonin found in impulsive violent offenders (Volavka, et al 1990; Virkkunen et al., 1995; Werbach, 1995).

Micro-Malnutrition

The influence of micronutrition such as zinc or iron, or of vitamins on brain function and behavior problems has been evidenced only recently (Rosen et al., 1985; Tu, 1994; Sever et al., 1997). Several studies reported iron deficiency in aggressive and conduct disordered children (Rosen et al., 1985; Werbach, 1995). Rosen et al. (1985) found iron deficiency in a third of juvenile delinquents. Furthermore, in a clinical trail, Sever et al. (1997) found that non-iron deficient children with attention deficit hyperactivity disorder showed both cognitive and behavioral improvement after iron supplementation treatment.

Researches have also implicated zinc deficiency in aggression and violence (Watts, 1990). In animals, the offspring of rats zinc-deprived during pregnancy have been found to be significantly more aggressive than controls (Halas et al., 1977). In humans, zinc deficiency in pregnancy was found to be associated with hyperactivity in the offspring (Brophy, 1986).

In addition to mineral deficiency, research is beginning to implicate micronutrition deficiency in interacting with heavy metals in predisposing to antisocial behavior. Importantly, studies indicate that mineral deficits alone may not produce behavior problems, but that instead low mineral levels exacerbate the effects of toxic metals (Walsh et al., 1997). For example, adding calcium to the diet can decrease the toxic effects produced by lead exposure (Bogden et al., 1997).

More recently, research has implicated docosahexaenoic acid (DHA) in relation to human behavior. It has been reported that behavior problems in boys such as temper tantrums occur more often in subjects with lower total fatty acid concentrations in the plasma phospholipids fraction (Stevens et al, 1996). Fish oil supplements have also been found to reduce impulsivity in girls compared with a control group (Itomura et al, 2005). Some studies have also failed to demonstrate the effectiveness of DHA supplement on reducing externalizing behavior. Voigt et al. (2001) reported that although a 4-month period of DHA supplementation (345 mg/day) increased plasma phospholipid DHA concentrations 2.6-fold compared with a placebo group, it did not improve any objective or subjective measure of symptoms related to attention deficit hyperactivity disorder (ADHD). Although research in this area is mixed, the potential implications of DHA on behavior problems is worth further investigation.

Environmental Influence vs. Genetic Predisposition

If nutrition factors are possible risk factors for antisocial and criminal behavior, an important question concerns whether individual malnutrition is the result of a genetic predisposition or is alternatively caused by the environment. At a general level, malnutrition may be due to inadequate food intake (deficiency in food consumption), or alternatively due to inadequate food utilization (malabsorption of food). While there is no clear understanding of the fundamental causes of malnutrition, it could be caused by the interaction of both environmental and genetic factors.

More specifically, from an environmental perspective, if food supply fails to provide adequate amounts of nutrients to meet human needs, malnutrition will occur. From a genetic perspective, if an individual genetically lacks internal biochemical elements such as the enzymes to absorb, metabolize, and utilize nutrients, malnutrition can develop. This later view of genetic influences on antisocial behavior is supported by twin studies (Rowe, 1983) and adoption / cross fostering studies (Hutchings and Mednick, 1975) which have shown that antisocial and criminal behavior are partly genetically determined. In their adoptee study, Mednick et al. (1984) assessed court convictions of 14,427 adoptees whose biological and adoptive parents were themselves either criminal or noncriminal. Results showed a significant relationship between biological parents' criminal convictions and criminal convictions in their adopted-away children. That is, those whose biological parents were criminal were more likely to commit crime themselves as adults. In addition, the more crimes the biological parent had committed, the higher the rate of criminality in the adopted-away offspring. In the context of a genetic predisposition to malnutrition, it could be that there are genetically-determined individual differences in metabolism that in turn alters brain biochemistry which in turn impacts on antisocial behavior. Furthermore, a genetic predisposition for malnutrition could also be explained by the fact that antisocial parents are not good care-givers and consequently have children who are under-nourished. Nevertheless, gene-environment interactions perhaps may best explain the development of antisocial behavior. One of the fundamental causes of violent crime could be a biochemical predisposition triggered by environmental stress.

Prenatal Period vs. Postnatal Stage

Both animal and human studies have illustrated that prenatal as well as postnatal malnutrition can impact both aggressive behavior and brain development (Neugebauer et al., 1999, Liu et al., 2004a). Malnutrition limited to the prenatal period is not only sufficient to produce permanent alterations in brain structure, but can also cause enduring changes in behavior that are at least as powerful as those produced by postnatal malnutrition (Smart, 1986). Furthermore, animal intervention studies have showed that prenatal vitamin B supplementation in rats advances their hippocampal development (Mellott et al, 2004). A reduction in the area of the hippocampus has been found to be linked to aggression in male mice (Sluyter et al., 1994). On the other hand, Granados-Rojas et al. (2004) found that the mossy fiber system of the hippocampal formation in rats is decreased by chronic postnatal but not prenatal protein malnutrition. Although data on the effects of prenatal vs. postnatal malnutrition on brain development and its impact on behavior remain conflicting, it is generally believed that the brain is most vulnerable and sensitive to insults when it is growing most rapidly. This argument receives some support by Neugebauer et al. (1999), who showed that the male offspring of nutritionally deprived pregnant women were found to have 2.5 times the normal rate of antisocial personality disorder in adulthood when severe malnutrition occurred during the first and second trimesters of pregnancy (when the brain is developing rapidly), but not during the third trimester.

Permanent Consequences vs. Temporary Effects

There continues to be ambiguity in the field of nutrition research as to whether the effect of malnutrition on brain and behavior is permanent or revisable. In the past, it was generally accepted that early malnutrition permanently decreases brain size and cell numbers, resulting in irreversible cognitive impairment. Reductions in cognitive ability have been observed to account for the relationship between malnutrition and antisocial behavior in children (Liu et al, 2004a).

However, more recent views suggest that while some parts of brain (such as the cerebellum) are indeed impacted by malnutrition, such effects appear to be reversible with nutritional rehabilitation. We recently demonstrated that a multi-modal postnatal enrichment that included better nutrition significantly reduced conduct disorder at age 17 and criminal behavior at age 23, and furthermore that these beneficial effects on conduct disorder were potentiated in children with signs of malnutrition at entry into the prevention program (Raine et al, 2003). This finding and recent work on the effects of nutritional supplements in reducing antisocial / aggressive behavior in prisoners are not consistent with the traditional view that the negative effects of early malnutrition are permanent (Gesch et al, 2002). Instead, it is suggested that whether prenatal or postnatal, the deleterious effects of early malnutrition can be addressed.

Brain Dysfunction as a Mediator

From the above section, it is clear that malnutrition, either due to macro or micro malnutrition, may play a role in the development of antisocial and violent behavior. The causes of malnutrition could be both genetic and environmental. The effect of malnutrition on behavior could be both prenatal and postnatal. Long term effects of malnutrition on behavior could be reversible.

The important question that follows concerns the mechanism by which the risk factor of malnutrition predisposes to psychopathology. This section suggests that brain dysfunction may be a key consequence of malnutrition, and it explores the possibility that alterations in brain functioning account for the relationship between malnutrition and antisocial, criminal behavior. Although the precise mechanisms by which food and nutrients influence different aspects of brain functioning are not fully known, there is increasing understanding of how specific nutrients can operate both on brain and behavior. For example, while there is speculation that proteins and minerals play a direct role in brain cell growth and development, they may affect brain functioning by regulating neurotransmitters or hormones, or else by exacerbating neurotoxins, and in doing so predispose to aggressive and violent behavior (Coccaro, 1996, Liu, 2004b).

Decreasing Brain Cell Growth / Development

Investigations in animals have provided evidence that malnutrition during early life not only reduces the growth of the brain but also makes it permanently smaller in size and cellular content (Sara et al., 1976). Early in the study of malnutrition and the brain, the cerebellum was recognized as an area that is particularly sensitive to the effects of early malnutrition. Various cognitive-behavioral consequences are related to the effects of malnutrition on the brain, such as memory disturbance, learning impairments, and behavioral impairment. Studies have shown that following dietary protein restriction during pregnancy, the offspring of rats exhibit significantly smaller fetal body weight and alteration of brain cortical areas compared to controls (Gressens, 1997). The protein content of the diet is believed to play an important role on antioxidant mechanisms. Recent animal experimental studies have observed the effects of protein malnutrition on oxidation-reduction in the rat hippocampus. It has also been found that a deficiency in both the content of protein in the diet and in the essential amino acid methionine alters the antioxidant system and the oxidation-reduction state of the brain of rat (Bonatto, 2005).

It is increasingly recognized that micronutrients such as zinc and iron are essential elements in maintaining normal structure and function of the central nervous system (Liu et al., 2003). Thus, deficiency in iron or zinc can lead to alterations in brain growth and development. Recent studies on rats have indicated that supplementation of both zinc and iron help accelerate recovery of hippocampal functioning following iron deficiency (Shoham, and Youdim, 2002).

We now know from biochemical evidence that docosahexaenoic acid (DHA) deficiency and omega-3 long chain essential fatty acid (EFA) deficiency may exist in protein-energy malnutrition (PEM), and micronutrient deficiencies may contribute to impaired EFA bioavailability and metabolism (Smit et al, 2004). It is known that the brain is 60% fat, and DHA is the most rich fatty acid in the brain. DHA serves as the primary building block for the gray matter of the brain and the retina of the eye (Innis, 2004). Thus, DHA has a critical role in the brain development of the fetus, especially during the first few months of life when there is rapid cerebral cell membrane synthesis. In addition, EFA's are important components of nerve cell walls and are involved in the regulation of neurotransmitter release (Alessandri et al, 2004). There is increasing data to show that low levels of polyunsaturated fatty acids play a role in the pathophysiology of aggressive disorders. Buydens-Branchey et al (2003) in a sample of cocaine addict patients found that aggressive patients had significantly lower levels of DHA than patients without aggressive histories.

Furthermore, studies in human show that violent offenders display reduced glucose metabolism in the prefrontal region of the brain even after controlling for handedness, sex, ethnicity, and the presence/absence of head injury (Raine et al, 1997; Soderstrom et al., 2000). More recently, one study has shown that even slight, visually imperceptible reductions in prefrontal gray matter are significantly associated with antisocial personality disorder (Raine et al., 2000). Brain-imaging research is confirming that there are both structural and functional brain deficits in relation to violence. Malnutrition may directly cause this brain dysfunction by reducing brain cell growth and development and thus producing brain deficits that predispose to violent and criminal behavior (Liu, 2004b). Nevertheless, research in this area is limited.

Alternation in Neurochemistry

It is generally reported that neurochemical functioning in the brain is fundamentally related to the metabolism of nutrients (Wurtman et al, 1990). More specifically, neurotransmitter metabolism involves a chain of biochemical reactions that largely rely on vitamins and minerals which function as co-enzymes. Specific nutrients plays a role in neurotransmission functions such as production, release, inhibition, transmission, and receptor formation. Consequently, when the bioavailability of food / nutrients is impaired due to either environmental or genetic factors, alteration in neurotransmitters may occur. The neurotransmitter impairments implicated in impulsive and aggressive behavior include serotonin and dopamine.

For example, tryptophan is an essential amino acid. It is the precursor of the neurotransmitter serotonin. Its administration increases brain levels of tryptophan and may increase brain serotonin levels (Morand et al, 1983; Volavka, 1990). Considerable evidence from both animal and human studies indicate that alterations in brain tryptophan levels cause changes in brain neurotransmitters such as serotonin synthesis (Young, 2002). Serotonin (5-hydroxytryptamine; 5-HT) has been implicated in impulsiveness and aggression (Volavka et al, 1990). A recent study has shown that subjects who experience acute tryptophan depletion (by ingestion of a mixture of amino acids devoid of tryptophan) experience a decline in brain serotonin (Young, 2002). Furthermore, one new functional MRI study in humans reveals that tryptophan depletion produced by a dietary challenge reduces right inferior prefrontal activation during a response inhibition task (Rubia, et al. 2005).

Similarly, the bioavailability of iron in the brain has been shown to affect neurotransmitter production and function, mainly in the dopamine-opiate systems. Iron is an essential element in maintaining normal structure and function of the central nervous system. In the brain, zinc is with iron the most concentrated metal. The highest levels of zinc are found in the hippocampus in synaptic vesicles, and mossy fibers (Pfeiffer and Braverman, 1982). Furthermore, animal studies indicate that iron deficiency may alter behavior by reducing dopamine transmission (Weiser, 1994). It is also believed that zinc is a key co-factor for building up neurotransmitters and fatty acids, and indirectly involves metabolism of dopamine and fatty acids, which consequently effects on behavior (Arnold et al., 2000).

Moreover, animal studies have indicated that protein deficiency during pregnancy can induce a significant decrease in the activity of brain monoamine oxidase compare to controls. Low MAO-B activity has been reported to be linked to some personality traits, such as aggressiveness, impulsiveness and sensation-seeking behavior (Schalling et al., 1987; Stalenheim et al., 1997). Furthermore, recent animal studies have shown that there is a relationship between aggressiveness and MAO-A activity (Shih and Chen, 1999). MAO-A gene knock-out mice showed elevated brain levels of serotonin, norepinephrine and dopamine, and manifested aggressive behavior (Shih and Chen, 1999). Similarly, although the mechanisms linking cholesterol and antisocial/violent behavior are unknown, it has been suggested that low cholesterol influences 5-HT (serotonin) function. Monkeys fed a low-cholesterol diet have lower CSF serotonin than monkeys fed a high-cholesterol diet (Kaplan et al., 1997).

The relationship between neurotransmitters and aggressive behavior is reasonably well-known. Aggressive offenders have repeatedly been found to have lower levels of the neurotransmitter serotonin (Virkkunen et al., 1995; Halperin et al., 1994). Similarly, aggressive monkeys have also been found to have low levels of serotonin (Kyes et al., 1995). Both animal and human research suggests that increasing serotonin can significantly reduce aggressive behavior (Moskowitz et al, 2003). Drug research also suggests that the relationship may be causal. Prozac, which increases serotonin, has been found to reduce aggression in humans (Coccaro et al., 1997). Therefore, low serotonin could well predispose subjects to mood and impulse control disorders. Higher levels of serotonin may help to promote more constructive social interactions by decreasing aggression and increasing dominance (Young, 2002), and such effects apply to women as well as to men (Bond, 2001). Consequently, nutritional deficiency may directly and indirectly cause brain dysfunction by alterations in brain neurochemistry which in turn predispose to the likelihood of disruptive behavior. On the other hand, the exact mechanisms involve in this neurochemical process is a complex issue and further research needs to be conducted both in animals and human.

Increase in Neurotoxic Effects

Research in the effects of nutrition and environmental toxicity on children's behavior is beginning to recognize the significant effect of malnutrition in facilitating neurobehavioral toxicity in animals and humans. Although exactly how malnutrition is involved in this process is not fully understood, studies and clinical observations are beginning to provide initial empirical evidence to support this effect.

Research on the effects of metal toxicity on behavior has gained increasing attention in recent years. For example, lead exposure has long been known to negatively impact cognitive functions (Needleman et al., 1996). More recently, both animal studies (Delville, 1999) and human studies (Needleman et al., 1996) have found that higher lead exposure measured in bone and blood is significantly related to aggressive and delinquent behavior. Recently, research has found that postnatal lead exposure can have significant deleterious effects on progenitor cell proliferation and consequently affect the structure and function of the hippocampus (Schneider, 2005). In addition, research on rats has found that microinjections of manganese chloride (McCl2) can cause neurodegenerative processes that further alter the animal's emotional behavior (Ponzoni et al., 2000). Excessive copper in the neonatal brain is associated with abnormal development of the hippocampus, a brain structure that plays a critical role in learning and which functions abnormally in murderers (Masters et al., 1999; Raine et al., 1997b).

Notably, studies have shown that the individual effects of some neurotoxins do not directly cause behavior problems, but instead involve the occurrence of nutritional deficits such as protein or calcium deficiency. Animal research has found that protein deficiency during early life makes animals more susceptible to the neurobehavioral toxicity of styrene during both gestation and the early infancy period (Khanna et al, 1991). Masters et al. (1998) have reported that feeding animals a diet high in manganese does not lead to high levels of blood manganese when diets contained normal levels of calcium. In contrast, manganese uptake became significantly higher when the diet was deficient in calcium.

Although the mechanisms by which the neurotoxic effects on aggressive and violent behavior takes place are not fully understood, research has revealed that neurotoxins involve neurotransmitters processes. Murphy et al. (1991) found that levels of dopamine, norepinephrine, and serotonin were lowered in manganese-intoxicated animals. Thus, excessive manganese is thought to reduce brain levels of neurotransmitters such as serotonin while increasing serotonin concentrations elsewhere in the body (Masters et al., 1999). Interestingly, Moffitt et al. (1998) found antisocial individuals in a community sample had higher blood serotonin levels, a view opposite to the usual findings for CSF serotonin, but consistent with the notion that manganese exposure produces low CSF serotonin but high blood serotonin. As outlines earlier, the effects of manganese may be potentiated by low calcium. Just as manganese inhibits neurotransmitters, a recent molecular study on lead-exposed rats indicates that lead inhibits the NMDA receptor, which in turn plays a critical role in learning and conditioning (Nihei et al., 2000). Nevertheless, despite these findings, the research literature on the interaction effect of malnutrition and neurotoxins on externalizing behavior problems remains both limited and controversial.

It is concluded from this section that the effects of malnutrition on the brain can be the basis for the development of adverse behavior. Both animal and human studies provide evidence that malnutrition has a profound effect on the central nervous system and affects not only gross brain weight and cell structure and function, but also neurobiochemical constitution and processes. Consequently, malnutrition can cause brain dysfunction, which in turn can predispose to psychopathological behavior such as aggression and crime.

Malnutrition, IQ and Externalizing Behavior: The Mauritius Study

From the above discussion, there is reason to believe that malnutrition in the early years is linked to later psychopathological behavior, and that this link is mediated by brain dysfunction. However to date there appear to have been few prospective longitudinal studies testing this hypothesis. In this section, we will briefly present recent findings from the Mauritius longitudinal study indicating that malnutrition in the first few years of life predisposes to antisocial and aggressive behavior throughout childhood and late adolescence (see Liu et al 2004a for details). This analysis is of particular relevant to the theme of this book as Mednick and Venables initiated this study more than 30 years ago.

The Study Design

Participants consisted of a birth cohort of 1,795 children from Mauritius and are described in detail by Venables (1978). Subjects included both males (51.4%) and females (48.6%) with ethnic distribution consisting of Indian 68.7%, Creoles (African origin) 25.7%, and others (Chinese, English, and French) 5.6%. Verbal informed consent was obtained from the mothers of the participants in the early phases, and from participants themselves in the age

17 phase. The following three hypotheses were tested in this study: 1) poor nutrition at age 3 years predisposes to antisocial behavior at ages 8, 11, and 17 years, 2) such relationships are independent of early psychosocial adversity, and 3) IQ mediates the nutrition-antisocial relationship.

We tested the first hypothesis that poor nutrition at age 3 years predisposes to antisocial behavior at ages 8, 11, and 17 years. Participants were defined as suffering from nutritional deficits if at least one of the following four indicators was present at age three (22.6%): angular stomatitis (7.0 %.), hair dyspigmentation: (6.8%), sparse, thin hair (5.8%), and anemia (17%). Participants with no indicator present were defined as having relatively normative nutrition (77.4%) (Liu et al, 2003). We were also interested in a possible dose response relationship, i.e., that that the more indicators of malnutrition that the child has, the greater the level of later externalizing behavior. Subjects on whom behavior data were available were categorized into one of four groups: no malnutrition (N = 766 at age 8, N= 807 at age 11, N = 422 at age 17), one indicator of malnutrition (N = 160 at age 8, N = 172 at age 11, N = 90 at age 17), two indicators (N = 45 at age 3, N = 50 at age 11, N= 25 at age 17), three indicators (N = 10 at age 3, N = 13 at age 11, N = 4 at age 17). Because only two individuals had all four nutrition indicators, this category could not be included in dose-response analyses.

Externalizing behavior was assessed at three points of time among the subjects. The Childrens' Behavior Questionnaire (CBQ – Rutter, 1967) was used at age 8 years, with complete data of 1,130 on the aggression measure, and 1,128 on the hyperactivity measure. The three externalizing subscales (aggression, delinquency, hyperactivity) of the Child Behavior Checklist (CBCL- Achenbach and Edelbrock, 1983) were used at age of 11 years old with completed data on 1,206. The Revised Behavior Problem Checklist (RBPC - Quay and Peterson, 1987) was used at age of 17 years, with completed data on 608.

The Effects of Cognitive Ability and Psychosocial Adversity

We tested the second hypothesis that the malnutrition – externalizing behavior relationship is independent of psychosocial adversity. Psychosocial adversity was assessed at two points in time. The age 3 index of psychosocial adversity (Raine et al, 2002b, Raine et al, 1998) was based on nine psychosocial variables collected by social workers who visited the homes of the children at age 3 years (see Raine et al, 1997 for full details). Complete data for this construct were available on 1,795. The age 11 psychosocial adversity index (Raine et al., 2002b, Liu et al., 2003) was based on 14 variables collected by social workers who visited the homes of the children at age 11 years. Complete data were available on 1,272.

We also tested the third hypothesis that IQ mediates the relationship between nutrition and externalizing behavior problems. Cognitive ability was tested at two points of time. At age 3, measures of cognitive ability were derived from six sub-tests of the Boehm Test of Basic Concepts-Preschool Version (Boehm, 1986, Raine et al, 2002b), which assesses basic verbal and visual-spatial concepts that are fundamental for early school achievement. Data were available on 1,260 subjects. At age 11 years, estimates of full-scale IQ were assessed by using 7 subtests of the WISC (Wechsler, 1967), with Similarities and Digit Span forming an estimate of verbal IQ, while Block Design, Object Assembly, Coding, Mazes, and Picture

Completion formed an estimate of performance IQ. Data were available on 1,260 subjects for the above three measure.

MALNUTRITION - LOW IQ – EXTERNALIZING BEHAVIOR PROBLEMS

The three hypotheses proposed above were confirmed in this study. First, malnutrition at age three years was founded to be associated with increase scores on externalizing behavior problems at ages 8, 11 and 17 (see Figure 2). Second, the malnutrition-externalizing relationship was not found to be confounded by psychosocial adversity. Third, the relationship of malnutrition – externalizing behavior was founded to be mediated by cognitive ability, indicating that malnutrition predisposes to lower IQ which in turn predisposes to externalizing behavior problems. These results are also supported by the finding of dose-response relationships between degree of malnutrition and degree of externalizing behavior problems at ages 8 and 17 (see Figure 3), relationships that were again found to be mediated by low IQ. We believe these are the first findings to show prospectively that malnutrition assessed in the early postnatal years is associated with externalizing behavior problems from childhood to late adolescence, and also to show the mediating effects of cognitive ability. These findings in turn have potential implications for public health attempts to prevent the occurrence of child and adolescent externalizing behavior problems.

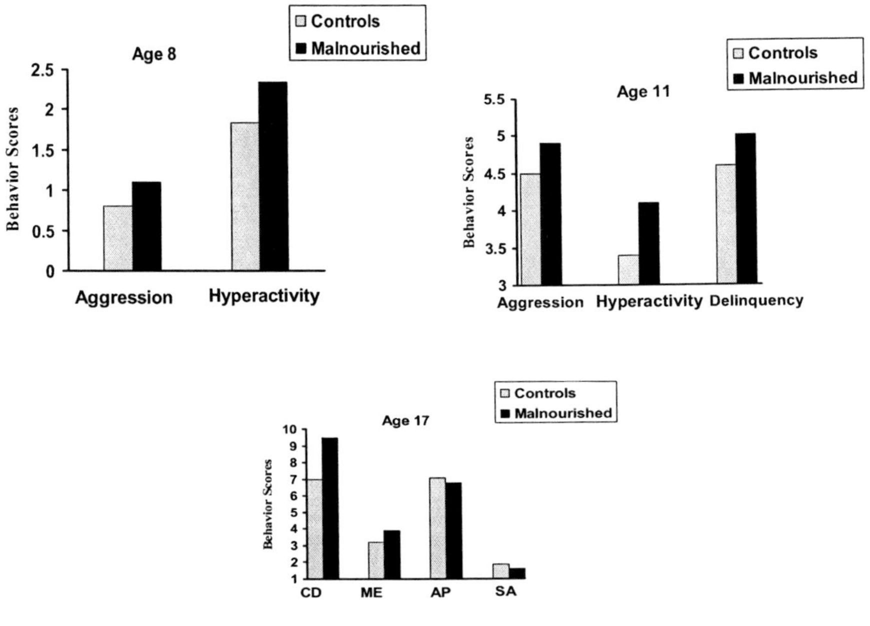

Figure 2. Scores for Externalizing Behaviors at Ages 8, 11, and 17 among Children in Mauritius Who Were or Were Not Malnourished at Age 3. CD: conduct disorder, SA: socialized aggression, ME: motor excess, and AP: attention problems.

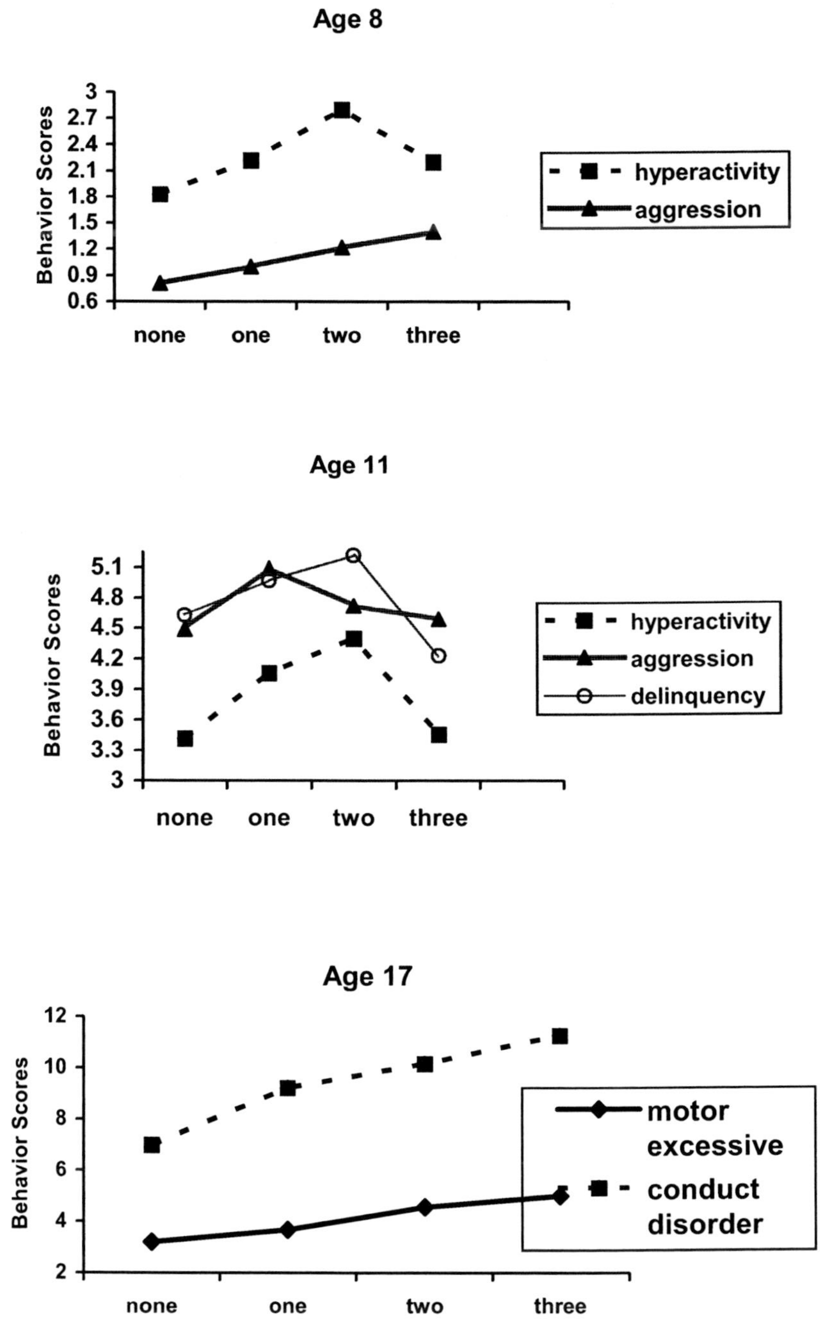

Figure 3. Dose-Response Relationships Between Number of Malnutrition Indicators at Age 3 and Externalizing Behaviors at Ages 8, 11, and 17 Among Children in Mauritius[a]

[a] Four indicators of malnutrition were assessed: angular stomatitis, hair dyspigmentation, sparse/thin hair, and anemia

Findings from the present study provide empirical support for the conceptual framework outlined at the beginning of this chapter. Findings suggest that early malnutrition could predispose to externalizing behavior problems by impairing brain mechanisms (such as the prefrontal cortex) which are thought to regulate emotion and inhibit impulsive aggressive behavior (e.g. Raine et al., 2000). Malnutrition could also predispose to externalizing behavior problems more indirectly by impacting cognitive functioning which in turn predisposes to externalizing behavior problems. Indicators of malnutrition in this study reflect deficits in protein (red hair, sparse/thin hair), iron (low hemoglobin), and zinc (red hair, sparse/thin hair). As we discussed above, there is extensive experimental evidence in animals both that zinc and protein deficiency impairs brain development (Bennis-Taleb, 1999, Halas, 1977, Oteiza et al., 1990), and also that protein, iron and zinc deficiency predisposes to aggression (Halas, 1977, Munro, 1987, and Tikal, 1976). Poor cognitive functioning (indirectly reflecting brain dysfunction) was recognized as a mediator for the malnutrition – externalizing relationship at ages 8 and 11 years in that controlling for the effect of IQ on externalizing behavior abolished the malnutrition – externalizing relationship. Poor cognitive ability has been found to be a consistent predisposition to externalizing behavior problems (Donnellan, 2000). Consequently, this study supports the conceptual framework outlined above which suggests that poor nutrition affects brain dysfunction which in turn predisposes to externalizing behavior.

Findings may have public health implications. Findings from Mauritius may provide a good model for understanding cognitive deficits in underserved sub-populations of U.S. society, particularly because up to 25% of adolescent girls in the U.S. are iron deficient (Bruner, 1996), because food insufficiency is relatively common in poor rural areas of the U.S. such as the Mississippi delta region (Smith et al, 1999), and because malnutrition is associated with poor behavioral functioning in low-income children in American inner-cities (Murphy et al 1998, Smith et al 1999). Consequently, findings suggest that better attention to nutrition could have significant implications for brain development in children and adolescents and further decreased the likelihood of behavior problems (Liu, 2004a).

Limitations of Research in this Field and Future Research Directions

Despite the potential significance of malnutrition in predisposing to violence, this research area has four important limitations. First, there are simply very few studies of this potential relationship. Second, little research has investigated prospectively the effects of early malnutrition on later violent behavior. Third, findings have not always been consistent. Fourth, few if any studies have tested for interactions with other risk factors.

Future research needs to place emphasis on investigating specific macro/micro-nutrition deficiency in relationship to the development of antisocial behavior, and experiments with animals can also establish *causal* relationships between early malnutrition, alterations in brain structures/function, and resulting psychopathology. Furthermore, the importance of early nutritional intervention on behavioral problems cannot be over-emphasized, although practical implications must be treated with caution.

Acknowledgements

This paper was written with the support of a NRSA fellowship (F32 NR-08661-2) from the National Institute of Health to the first author.

References

Alessandri, JM., Guesnet, P., Vancassel, S, Astorg, P., Deni, I., Langelier, B., Aid, S., Poumes-Ballihaut, C., Champeil-Potokar, G., and Lavialle, M (2004). Polyunsaturated fatty acids in the central nervous system: evolution of concepts and nutritional implications throughout life. *Reprod Nutr 44*, 509-538.

Achenbach, TM., and Edelbrock, CS. (1983). *Manual for the Child Behavior Checklist and Revised Child Behavior Profile.* Burlington: University of Vermont Department of Psychiatry

Arnold, L.E., Pinkham, S.M., and Votolato, N. (2000). Does zinc moderate essential fatty acid and amphetamine treatment of attention-deficit/hyperactivity disorder? *Journal of Child and Adolescent Psycho pharmacology 10*, 111–117.

Beers, MH., and Berkow, R (1999). *The Merck Manual of Diagnosis and Therapy.* 17th Edition, Merck Research Laboratories.

Bennis-Taleb, N., Remacle, C., Hoet, JJ. and Reusens, B. (1999). A low-protein isocaloric diet during gestation affects brain development and alters permanently cerebral cortex blood vessels in rat offspring. *Journal of Nutrition.129*, 1613-1619

Breakey, J. (1997). Journal of Pediatric Child Health. *The role of diet and behavior in childhood. 33*:190-194

Bjork, J. M., Dougherty, D. M., Moeller, F. G., Cherek, D. R., and Swann, A. C. (1999). The effects of tryptophan depletion and loading on laboratory aggression in men: Time course and a food-restricted control. *Psychopharmacology, 142,* 24-30.

Bogden, JD., Oleske, JM., and Louria, DB. (1997). Lead poisoning--one approach to a problem that won't go away. *Environ Health Perspect.105 (12):*1284-1287.

Bonatto, F., Polydoro, M., Andrades, ME., Frota, ML., Dal-Pizzol, F., Rotta, LN., Souza, DO., Perry, ML., and Moreira, JC. (2005). Effect of protein malnutrition on redox state of the hippocampus of rat. *Brain Res. 25*, 17-22.

Boehm, A. (1986). *Boehm Test of Basic Concepts - Preschool Version.* Psychological Corporation.

Bond, AJ., Wingrove, J., and Critchlow, DG. (2001). Tryptophan depletion increases aggression in women during the premenstrual phase. *Psychopharmacology. 156*, 477-480.

Brophy, M. H. (1986). Zinc and childhood hyperactivity. *Biological Psychiatry, 21,* 704-705.

Bruner, AB, Joffe, A., Duggan, AK., Casella, JF., Brandt, J (1996). Randomised study of cognitive effects of iron supplementation in non-anaemic iron-deficient adolescent girls. *Lancet. 348*, 992-996.

Buydens-Branchey, L., Branchey, M., McMakin, D., and Hibbeln, JR. (2003), Polyunsaturated fatty acid status and aggression in cocaine addicts *Drug and Alcohol Dependence 71*: 319-323

Coccaro, E. F., Kavoussi, R. J., and Hauger, R. L. (1997). Serotonin function and antiaggressive response to fluoxetine: a pilot study. *Biological Psychiatry, 42,* 546-552.

Delville, Y (1999). Exposure to lead during development alters aggressive behavior in golden hamsters. *Neurotoxicology and Teratology, 21,* 445-449.

Donnellan, MB., Ge, X., and Wenk, E. (2000). Cognitive abilities in adolescent-limited and life-course-persistent criminal offenders. *J Abnorm Psychol, 109,* 396-402

Fishbein, DH., Pease, SE. (1994). Diet, nutrition, and aggression. *Journal of Offender Rehabilitation 21,* 117-144

Fishbein, D., (2001). *Biobehavioral Perspectives in Criminology.* Wadsworth/Thomson Learning, Belmont, CA.

Gesch, C. B., Hammond, S M, Hampson, S E, Eves, A, and Crowder, M J. (2002). Influence of supplementary vitamins, minerals and essential fatty acids on the antisocial behaviour of young adult prisoners: Randomised, placebo- controlled trial. *British Journal of Psychiatry, 181,* 22-28.

Granados-Rojas, L., Aguilar, A., and Diaz-Cintra, S. (2004).The mossy fiber system of the hippocampal formation is decreased by chronic and postnatal but not by prenatal protein malnutrition in rats. *Nutr Neurosci. 7,* 301-308.

Gressens, P., Muaku, SM., Besse, L., Nsegbe, E., Gallego, J., Delpech, B., Gaultier, C., Evrard P, Ketelslegers, JM., and Maiter, D. (1997). Maternal protein restriction early in rat pregnancy alters brain development in the progeny. *Brain Res Dev Brain Res. 103,* 21-35.

Halas, E. S., Reynolds, G. M., and Sandstead, H. H. (1977). Intra-uterine nutrition and its effects on aggression. *Physiology and Behavior, 19,* 653-661.

Hallberg, L., Brune, M., Rossander, L (1989). Iron absorption in man: ascorbic acid and dose-dependent inhibition by phytate. *Am J Clin Nutr. 49,* 140-144

Halperin, JM., Sharma, V., Siever, L. J., Schwartz, S. T., Matier, K., Wornell, G. and others. (1994). Serotonergic function in aggressive and nonaggressive boys with ADHD. *American Journal of Psychiatry, 151,* 243-248.

Hutchings, B., and Mednick, S.A. (1975). Registered criminality in the adoptive and biological parents of registered male criminal adoptees. In S.A. Mednick, F. Schulsinger, J. Higgins, and B. Bell (Eds.), *Genetics, environment, and psychopathology* (pp. 215.227). Amsterdam: New Holland.

Innis, SM. (2004). Polyunsaturated fatty acids in human milk: an essential role in infant development. *Adv Exp Med Biol. 554,* 27-43.

Itomura, M., Hamazaki, K., Sawazaki S, Kobayashi, M., Terasawa, K., Watanabe, S, Hamazaki, T. (2005). The effect of fish oil on physical aggression in schoolchildren--a randomized, double-blind, placebo-controlled trial. *J NutrBiochem. 16,* 163-171. Khanna, VK., Husain, R, Hanig, JP., and Seth, PK. (1991). Increased neurobehavioral toxicity of styrene in protein-malnourished rats. *Neurotoxicol Teratol. 13,*153-159.

Kyes, R. C., Botchin, M. B., Kaplan, J. R., Manuck, S. B., and others. (1995). Aggression and brain serotonergic responsivity: response to slides in male macaques. *Physiol.and Beha. 5,* 205-208.

Lister, JP., Blatt, GJ., Debassio, WA., Kemper, TL., Tonkiss, J, Galler, JR., and Rosene, DL.(2005). Effect of prenatal protein malnutrition on numbers of neurons in the principal cell layers of the adult rat hippocampal formation. *Hippocampus.15,* 393-403.

Liu, J, Raine, A., Venables, P., and Mednick, S.A (2004a). Malnutrition at age 3 years predisposes to externalizing behavior problems at ages 8, 11 and 17 years. *American Journal of Psychiatry, 161, 2005-2013*

Liu, J (2004b). Concept Analysis: Aggression. *Issue in Mental Health Nursing 25, 693-714*

Liu, J, Raine, A, Venable, P, Dalais, C, and Mednick SA (2003) Malnutrition at age 3 years and lower cognitive ability at age 11 years: independence from psychosocial adversity. *Arch Pediatr Adolesc Med, 157,* 593-600

Masters, R.D, Hone, B., and Doshi. (1998). Environmental pollution, neurotoxicity, and criminal violence in J. Rose (Ed). *Environmental Toxicology* (pp. 13-48). London: Gordon and Breach. Masters, R. D., Coplan, M. (1999). A dynamic, multifactorial model of alcohol, drug abuse, and crime: linking neuroscience and behavior to toxicology. *Social Science Information*, 591-624. London: Sage.

Mednick, S. A., W. F. Gabrielli Jr., and B. Hutchings (1984) Genetic influences in criminal convictions: Evidence from an adoption cohort *Science 224*, 891-94

Mellott, TJ., Williams, CL., Meck, WH., Blusztajn, JK (2004). Prenatal choline supplementation advances hippocampal development and enhances MAPK and CREB activation. *FASEB J.* 18, 545-547.

Moffitt, T. E., Brammer, G. L., Caspi, A., Fawcett, J. P., Raleigh, M., Yuwiler, A. et al. (1998). Whole blood serotonin relates to violence in an epidemiological study. *Biological Psychiatry, 43,* 446-457

Morand, C., Young, SN., and Ervin FR (1983). Clinical response of aggressive schizophrenics to oral tryptophan. *Biol Psychiatry. 18*, 575-8.

Moskowitz, DS., Pinard, G., Zuroff, DC., Annable, L., and Young, SN.(2003) Tryptophan, serotonin and human social behavior. *Adv Exp Med Biol.527*:215-224.

Munro, N. (1987). A three year study of iron deficiency and behavior in rhesus monkeys. *International Journal of Biosocial Research, 9*, 35-62

Murphy, V., Rosenberg, J., Smith, Q., and Stanley, R. (1991). Elevation of brain manganese in calcium-deficient rats. *Neurotoxicology, 12,* 255-263.

Murphy JM, Wehler CA, Pagano ME, Little M, Kleinman RE, Jellinek MS (1998). Relationship between hunger and psychosocial functioning in low-income American children. *Journal of the American Academy of Child and Adolescent Psychiatry. 37*, 163-170.

Needleman, H. L., Riess, J. A., Tobin, M. J., Biesecker, G. E., and Greenhouse, J. B.(1996), Bone Lead Levels and Delinquent Behavior; *JAMA, 275* 363-369

Neugebauer, R., Hoek, HW., and Susser, E. (1999). Prenatal exposure to wartime famine and development of antisocial personality disorder in early adulthood. *JAMA 4*, 479–481

Nihei, MK., Desmond, NL., McGlothan, JL., Kuhlmann, AC., and Guilarte, TR. (2000). N-methyl-D-aspartate receptor subunit changes are associated with lead-induced deficits of long-term potentiation and spatial learning. *Neuroscience. 99(2)*:233-42.

Oteiza, PI. Hurley, L., Lonnerdal, B., Keen, C. (1990). Effects of marginal zinc deficiency on microtubule polymerization in the developing rat brain. *Biological Trace Element Research. 123*,13-23

Pfeiffer, C. C. and Braverman, E. R. (1982). Zinc, the brain and behavior. *Biol Psychiatry, 17*, 513-532.

Ponzoni, S., Guimaraes, F. S., Del Bel, E. A., and Garcia-Cairasco, N. (2000). Behavioral effects of intra-nigral microinjections of manganese chloride: Interaction with nitric oxide. *Progress in Neuro-Psychopharmacology and Biological Psychiatry, 24,* 307-325.

Quay, HC, Peterson, D. (1987). *Manual for the Revised Behavior Problem Checklist.* Coral Gables, FL, Department of Psychology, University of Miami.

Raine, A., Lencz, T., Bihrle, S., LaCasse, L., and Colletti, P. (2000). Reduced prefrontal gray matter volume and reduced autonomic activity in antisocial personality disorder. *Archives of General Psychiatry, 57,* 119-127.

Raine, A., (2002a). Biosocial studies of antisocial and violent behavior in children and adults: a review. *Journal of Abnormal Child Psychology, 30*, 311–326.

Raine, A., Yaralian, P., Reynolds, C., Venables, PH., and Mednick, SA (2002b). Spatial but not verbal cognitive deficits at age 3 years in persistently antisocial individuals. *Development and Psychopathology, 14*:25-44

Raine, A., Mellingen, K, Liu, J H, Venables, P H, and Mednick, S A. (2003). Effects of environmental enrichment at 3-5 years on schizotypal personality and antisocial behavior at ages 17 and 23 years. *American Journal of Psychiatry, 160*, 1627-1635.

Raine, A, Reynolds, C, Venables, PH, Mednick, SA, Farrington, DP. (1998). Fearlessness, stimulation-seeking, and large body size at age 3 years as early predispositions to childhood aggression at age 11 years . *Arch Gen Psychiatry, 55*, 745-751

Raine, A., Venables, PH., Mednick, SA. (1997). Low resting heart rate at age 3 years predisposes to aggression at age 11 years: Evidence from the Mauritius Child Health Project. *Journal of the American Academy of Child and Adolescent Psychiatry, 36*,1457-1464

Raine, A., Buchsbaum, M., and LaCasse, L. (1997a). Brain abnormalities in murderers indicated by positron emission tomography. *Biological Psychiatry, 42,* 495-508.

Raine, A., Brennan, P., Farrington D., and Mednick, S. A. (1997b). *Biosocial basis of violence*. New York: Plenum Press.

Rosen, GM, Deinard, AS, Schwartz, S, Smith, C, Stephenson, B, and Grabenstein, B. (1985): Iron deficiency among incarcerated juvenile delinquents *.J.of Adol. Health Care, 6*, 419-423

Rowe, D.C. (1983). Biometrical genetic models of self-reported delinquent behavior: A twin study. *Behavior Genetics, 13*, 473.489.

Rubia, K., Lee, F., Cleare, AJ., Tunstall, N., Fu, CH., Brammer, M., McGuire, P. (2005) Tryptophan depletion reduces right inferior prefrontal activation during response inhibition in fast, event-related fMRI. *Psychopharmacology (Berl). 26*

Rutter, M., Giller, H., Hagell, A. (1998). *Antisocial behavior by young people.* New York, NY, Cambridge University Press

Rutter, M (1967). A children's behaviour questionnaire for completion by teachers: Preliminary findings. *J.Child Psychology and Psychiatry. 8*, 1-11

Sara, V R; King, T L; and Lazarus, L, (1976). The influence of early nutrition and environmental rearing on brain growth and behaviour *Experientia. 32*, 1538- 1540

Schalling, D., Asberg, M., Edman, G. and Oreland, L. (1987). Markers for vulnerability to psychopathology: temperament traits associated with platelet MAO activity. *Acta Psychiatrica Scandinavica 76*, 172–182.

Schneider, JS., Anderson, DW., Wade, TV., Smith, MG., Leibrandt, P., Zuck, L., Lidsky, TI. (2005). Inhibition of progenitor cell proliferation in the dentate gyrus of rats following post-weaning lead exposure.*Neurotoxicology. 26*, 141-145.

Sever, Y., Ashkenazi, A., Tyano, S., Weizman, A.(1997). Iron treatment in children with attention deficit hyperactivity disorder. A preliminary report. *Neuropsychobiology 35*,178–180.

Shih, JC., Chen, K. (1999) MAO-A and -B gene knock-out mice exhibit distinctly different behavior. *Neurobiology 2*, 235-246.

Shoham, S., Youdim, MB (2002). The effects of iron deficiency and iron and zinc supplementation on rat hippocampus ferritin.: *J Neural Transm.109*, 1241-1256.

Sluyter, F., Jamot, L., van Oortmerssen, GA., and Crusio, WE. (1994). Hippocampal mossy fiber distributions in mice selected for aggression. *Brain Res.16, (64)*:145-148.

Smart, J. L. (1986) Undernutrition, learning and memory: review of experimental studies. In: *Proceedings of the 13th Congress of Nutrition* (Taylor, T. G. and Jenkins, N. K., eds.), pp. 74-78. Libbey, London, UK.

Smit, EN., Muskiet, FA., and Boersma, ER.(2004). The possible role of essential fatty acids in the pathophysiology of malnutrition: a review. *Prostaglandins Leukot Essent Fatty Acids. 71*, 241-250.

Smith, J., Lensing, S. Horton, JA., Lovejoy, J., Zaghloul, S., Forrester, I., McGee, BB., and Bogle, ML (1999). Prevalence of self-reported nutrition-related health problems in the Lower Mississippi Delta. *Am J Public Health 89*, 1418-1421.

Soderstrom, H., Tullberg, M., Wikkelsoe, C., Ekholm, S., Forsman, A. (2000). Reduced regional cerebral blood flow in non-psychotic violent offenders. *Psychiatry Research: Neuroimaging 98,* 29–41.

Stalenheim, E. G., von Knorring, L. and Oreland, L. (1997) Platelet monoamine oxidase activity as a biological marker in a Swedish forensic psychiatric population. *Psychiatry Research 69*, 79–87.

Stevens, L.J. Zentall, S.S. M.L. Abate, T. Kuczek and J.R. Burgess (1996). Omega-3 fatty acids in boys with behavior, learning, and health problems. *Physiol. Behav. 59*, 915–920.

Tikal, K., Benesova, O., and Frankova, S. (1976). The effect of pyrithioxine and pyridoxine on individual behavior, social interactions, and learning in rats malnourished in early postnatal life. *Psychopharmacologia, 46,* 325-332.

Tu, J. B., Shafey, H., and VanDewetering, C. (1994). Iron deficiency in two adolescents with conduct, dysthymic and movement disorders. *Canadian Journal of Psychiatry, 39,* 371-375.

Venables, P. H. (1978). Psychophysiology and psychometrics. *Psychophysiology, 15*, 302-315.

Venables, P. Raine, A. Dalais, C. Liu, J. and Mednick, SA (2006) Malnutrition, cognitive ability , and Schizotypy. In A. Raine (ed). *Crime and schizophrenia: Causes and cures.* New York: Nova Science Publishers.

Virkkunen, M., Goldman, D., Nielsen, D. A., and Linnoila, M. (1995). Low brain serotonin turnover rate (low CSF 5-HIAA) and impulsive violence. *Journal of Psychiatry and Neuroscience, 20,* 271-275.

Volavka, J., Crowner, M., Brizer, D., Convit, A., Van Praag, H., and Suckow, RF.(1990). Tryptophan treatment of aggressive psychiatric inpatients. *Biol Psychiatry. 15*, 728-732.

Voigt, R.G., Llorente, A.M., Jensen, C. L., Fraley, J. K., Berretta, M. C., and Heird, WC. (2001). A randomized, double-blind, placebo-controlled trial of docosahexaenoic acid supplementation in children with attention-deficit/hyperactivity disorder, *J. Pediatr. 139,* 189–196.

Walsh, W. J., Isaacson, H. R., Rehman, F., and Hall, A. (1997). Elevated blood copper/zinc ratios in assaultive young males. *Physiology and Behavior, 6,* 327-329.

Watts, D.L., (1990). Trace elements and neuropsychological problems as reflected in tissue mineral analysis (TMA) patterns. *Journal of Orthomolecular Medicine 5,* 159–166.

Werbach, MR. (1992). Nutritional influences on aggressive behavior. *J Orthomolecular Med.7,* 45–51

Wechsler, D. (1967). *Wechsler Preschool and Primary Scale of Intelligence* San Antonio: The Psychological Corporation.

Weiser, M., Levkowitch, Y., Neuman, M., and Yehuda, S. (1994). Decrease of serum iron in acutely psychotic schizophrenic patients. *Int J Neurosci., 78*, 49-52.

Wienk, KJ., Marx, JJ., and Beynen, AC. (1999). The concept of iron bioavailability and its assessment. *Eur J Nutr. 38*:51-75.

Wurtman, RJ. (1990). Ways that foods can affect the brain (pp. 106-113) in Ornstein, Robert Evan (ED) and Swencionis, Charles (ED).*The healing brain: A scientific reader New York, NY, US:* Guilford Press.

World Health Organization (WHO) (2001), Iron deficiency anaemia: assessment, prevention and control. *A Guide for Program Managers.* World Health Organization, Geneva.

World Health Organization (WHO) (2000) World Health Organization Dept. of Nutrition for Health and Development: *Nutrition for Health and Development: a Global Agenda for Combating Malnutrition* . Geneva World Health Organization

Young, S. N. (1996). Behavioral effects of dietary *neurotransmitter* precursors: Basic and clinical aspects *Neuroscience and Biobehavioral Reviews. 20*, 313-323

Young, S. N, and Leyton, M. (2002). The role of serotonin in human mood and social interaction. insight from altered tryptophan levels. *Pharmacol Biochem Behav. 71,* 857-865.

PART 4. RISK FACTORS FOR SCHIZOPHRENIA-SPECTRUM DISORDERS

In: Crime and Schizophrenia: Causes and Cures
Editor: Adrian Raine, pp. 131-150
ISBN 1-59454-609-6

Chapter 7

Malnutrition, Cognitive Ability and Schizotypy

Peter H. Venables[1], Adrian Raine[2], Cyril Dalais[3], Jianghong Liu[4] and Sarnoff A. Mednick[4]
[1]Department of Psychology, University of York, Heslington, York YO10 5DD, UK
[2]Department of Psychology, University of Southern California, Los Angeles USA
[3]Joint Child Health Project, Mauritius
[4]Social Science Research Institute, University of Southern California, Los Angeles USA

This chapter examines the interrelationships between three groups of variables. The first, aspects of poverty/disadvantage/malnutrition; the second, intellectual development; and the third, schizotypy/schizophrenia. Underlying the work to be reviewed and the new analyses to be presented is the contention that malnutrition impairs neurodevelopment in the developing foetus and in early childhood. There are instances in which factors may act at specific times during foetal development, as for example in the case of the effect of influenza on the development of schizophrenia where the critical point in foetal life appears to be the second trimester (Mednick, Machon, Huttenen, and Bonett, 1988, Mednick, Huttunen, and Machon, 1994). However, except when considering the effects of discrete teratogenic effects such as the Dutch hunger winter, ((Susser and Lin, 1992; Brown et al., 1996) it is probable that conditions producing malnutrition of the mother will also continue during the early years of her offspring. Nevertheless, care must be taken when theorising from those studies which clearly identify *in utero* exposure to a particular period insofar as findings may not generalize to studies which are concerned with more extended factors creating malnutrition.

Malnutrition and Cognitive Impairment

There is a wide literature relating malnutrition to cognitive impairment which will not be reviewed in detail here. Nevertheless, insofar as this study uses data from a developing country (Mauritius), some recent examples from other countries with similar economic conditions may serve to exemplify the area. Across different cultures, malnutrition is associated with reduced cognitive ability. Choudhary et al. (2002) studied the intelligence of children living in slum conditions in Delhi. They showed that the most significant factors affecting IQ were malnutrition and pre-school attendance. They also showed that those children living in shanty housing had significantly lower IQ than those from permanent housing. Pollitt (1994) reported that in low income families in developing countries it is concurrent illnesses and poor nutrition which lead to poor cognitive performance. Berkman et al. (2002) followed a cohort of Peruvian children and showed that even when adjusting for socio-economic status and schooling, those malnourished in the second year of life had lower WISC-R scores at age 9. Rivera and Sepulveda-Amor (2003) in summarizing the results from the Mexican National Nutrition Survey reported that under-nutrition (stunting and micronutrient deficiencies) was generally more prevalent in lower socio-economic groups.

The general position held by these studies had previously been summarized by Christiansen et al. (1974) who proposed a "social structural model". They suggested that low and unstable income and low educational level in the parents results in inadequate nutrition which in turn leads to low intellectual functioning in their children. Furthermore, it was argued that low income results in living in crowded dwellings with consequent low parental attention, restriction of the child and again low intellectual functioning. However, in their study in Bogota, Colombia, outlined in the same chapter, they found that a strong relationship exists between malnutrition, (measured by physical growth measures), and intellectual functioning even when the effects of social and health factors are controlled. It is necessary however to recognize that malnutrition occurs with other aspects of poverty and disadvantage which may themselves lead to poor cognitive status. Duncan et al. (1994) reported that family income and poverty status are correlates of cognitive development, even after accounting for family structure and maternal schooling. On the other hand, Guo and Harris (2000) broke down aspects of poverty which they identified in a structural equation model and showed that the specific factors of cognitive style, physical environment, parenting style, and child's health, all mediate children's intellectual development. They also showed that cognitive stimulation in the home is a mediating factor which is affected by lack of income and influences intellectual development. It is thus apparent that it is necessary to take into account a wide range of factors of disadvantage when studying the deleterious effects of malnutrition.

Malnutrition and Schizophrenia

Susser and Lin, (1992) and Susser, et al., (1996) reported an increased risk for schizophrenia in those whose mothers were exposed in the early stages of pregnancy to the height of the Dutch Famine winter at the end of World War II. Hoek, Brown, and Susser, (1998) and Hoek, et al., (1996) also reported that there was a greater risk of schizophrenia spectrum disorders and schizoid personality disorder in those conceived at the height of the Famine winter. However, the caveat expressed above that these were the effects of a discrete period of malnutrition needs to be borne in mind. Importantly, there do not appear to be any findings on ongoing postnatal malnutrition as a risk factor for schizophrenia.

In this connection it is necessary to take into account social factors which may be associated with schizophrenia and which may be associated with malnutrition. Classic papers in the literature have reported excesses of schizophrenics in lower socio-economic populations ((Goldberg and Morrison, 1963; Hollingshead and Redlich, 1954; Redlich, et al., 1953). However, Goldberg and Morrison, (1963) showed that the social class distribution of the fathers of schizophrenics was the same as that of the general population and in consequence formulated the "drift" hypothesis, namely that the lower social class of schizophrenics was due to their inability to occupy higher social class occupations by which their socio-economic status would be defined. Kohn, (1968) in questioning the "drift" hypothesis suggested that "in all probability, lower class families produce a disproportionate number of schizophrenics". In support of this, Kety, (1980) suggested that insofar as malnutrition might play a role, its impact would be exaggerated in the lower classes. Castle, Scott, Wessley, and Murray, (1993) also " challenge the conventional wisdom that the excess of schizophrenics in deprived areas and the mal-distribution of these individuals with regard to social class is due entirely or predominantly to "drift". Consequently, individuals who later manifest schizophrenia are disproportionately likely to have suffered the disadvantages of social deprivation *in utero* and in early life".

Cognitive Status and Schizophrenia

The evidence that there is an association between intellectual status and schizophrenia has been reviewed in detail by Aylward, Walker, and Bettes, (1984) who carried out a meta-analysis of studies on the relation between IQ and schizophrenia. In summarizing their findings they comment: "…taken together the findings suggest that early onset and adult onset schizophrenia are associated with intellectual deficits across the life span" (p.430). There is also evidence that cognitive dysfunction is related to schizotypy. Barrantes-Vidal, et al., (2003); Chapman, Chapman, and Raulin, (1976); Chapman, Chapman, and Raulin, (1978); and Voglmaier, Seidman, Salisbury, and McCarley, (1997) all found that cognitive functioning was impaired in subjects meeting the criteria for DSM-III Schizotypal Personality Disorder (SPD). However, Trestman, et al., (1995), while showing that SPD patients exhibited deficits on the Wisconsin Card Sorting test and Trial Making Part B, did not show impairment on the WISC-R.

Sex Differences in Neurodevelopment

Castle and Murray (1991) reviewed differences in the way that schizophrenia manifests itself in the two sexes. They suggested that because males are more susceptible to neurodevelopmental disorders, they are more prone to show those structural brain aspects of the disease such as increased ventricular size (related to negative symptomatology), cognitive impairment, early onset, poor clinical outcome and poor employment record. These are also characteristic of male schizophrenics, and furthermore Bogerts, (1991) reported that hippocampal volume is reduced in male but not female schizophrenics. Mednick, et al., (1978) in the Copenhagen high risk study showed that in men there was a link between obstetric complications, autonomic system anomalies and schizophrenia which did not exist in females in whom it was suggested that genetic influences might be more important. This view was supported by Goldstein, Santangelo, Simpson, and Tsuang, (1990) and Goldstein, Seidman, Santangelo, Knapp, and Tsuang, (1994) who concluded that " schizophrenic men may be at higher risk for developmental deficits than women".

It is clear from the above that risk factors for schizophrenia that impact neurodevelopment may differ across the sexes. Consequently, in our examination of the relation between malnutrition, IQ and schizotypy we examined these relations separately in the two sexes.

THE STUDY: MALNUTRITION, COGNITIVE ABILITY, AND SCHIZOTYPY

We report here initial findings from our analysis of malnutrition at age 3, its relation to cognitive ability at age 3 and 11 years, and later adolescent and adult schizotypy This study is concerned, in the first instance, with an attempt to define three factors of disadvantage that may be related to impaired development and then to show how one or more of these factors is related to lower intelligence. Lastly we aim to assess whether adolescent and adult schizotypal status is directly related to early disadvantage or is instead indirectly related via impaired intellectual level. The questions are examined by the use of structural equation modelling and the data used in the study are taken from the Mauritius Child Health study (see Bell et al. (1975), Venables (1978) and the Appendix to this book).

The focus is on schizotypy rather than schizophrenia because among the 1,795 children entering the study started in 1972 only 7 have a definite diagnosis of schizophrenia 30 years later, making impossible the use of structural equation modelling with schizophrenic diagnosis as one of the variables. Arguments concerning the extent to which schizotypy may be considered as a proxy for schizophrenia have been presented by Raine and Lencz, (1995) and Venables (1995). That there may be neuro-mechanistic differences between schizophrenics and schizotypals is suggested by Trestman, et al., (1995) who argued that "SPD patients, like schizophrenic patients, may have an underlying neurodevelopmental impairment that affects their frontal cortical function" (p. 133). However, they also argue that "that schizotypal individuals may be spared from chronic psychosis by their lower propensity for psychosis associated subcortical upward regulation of the dopamine system secondary to the cortical impairment" (p. 134).

The study is also limited in its measurement of disadvantage to those variables collected at the start of the study. Those used here may be briefly described as parental economic and educational status, conditions of crowding, housing and malnutrition. To address the role of socio-economic status the variables available were the educational level of the mother and father and the income level of the father, thus using variables that have been traditionally used in this field. Galle, Gove, and McPherson, (1972) reported that even after holding social class constant, population density, measured by variables such as rooms per housing unit, and numbers of persons per room was related to admissions to mental hospitals. Similar variables were available in the present study.

The measurement of malnutrition, however, requires more discussion. Liu, Raine, Venables, Dalais, and Mednick, (2003), Liu, Raine, Venables, and Mednick, (2004), and Liu et al. (this volume) have used measures reflecting indicators of vitamin, zinc and iron deficiency as measures of malnutrition where levels of these indicators are used as factors in analyses of variance. In the present study using statistics with a correlational basis, the more general and continuous measures of stunting (height for age) as a measure of protein-energy malnutrition (PEM) and anaemia as a measure of iron deficiency are used . Gibson, (1990) states that " Height for age (stunting) can be used as an index of the nutritional status of population groups as it estimates past or chronic nutritional status... The condition results from extended periods of inadequate food intake ... and is highest in the second or third year of life." (p. 175). The measure of stunting thus seems to be particularly appropriate in the present instance. Further, stunting and anaemia have been used more extensively in measures of malnutrition in developing countries. For instance Chang, Walker, Grantham-McGregor, and Powell, (2002), Chang, et al., (1994),; Dangour, Hill, and Ismail, (2002),; and Rivera and Sepulveda Amor, (2003) all report that stunting and anaemia are indicators of malnutrition in under-nourished populations and that these two variables are substantially related. However, Pollitt, (1995) notes that the effects which are attributed to PEM may be instead determined by iron deficiency.

In the present study the choice of indicators was also partly determined by an initial analysis which was undertaken to examine how the measures used were related to those used by Liu, Raine, Venables, Dalais, and Mednick (2003) and Liu, Raine, Venables, and Mednick (2004). An Exploratory Factor Analysis (EFA) of the variables anaemia, stunting, angular stomatitis, hair colour, and hair sparseness produced two orthogonal factors with loadings of 0.49 (anaemia), 0.45 (stunting) and 0.42 (mucous membrane) on the first factor and 0.77 (hair colour), 0.41 (hair sparseness) and 0.37 (angular stomatitis) on the second. The studies by Liu et al. had used angular stomatitis, hair colour (dyspigmentation), sparseness of hair and anaemia (on a 2 point scale) to produce a measure of malnutrition, whereas the present study used stunting, anaemia (as a continuous measure) and mucous membrane colour on a 3 point scale. The overlap between the measures used in the present study and those by Liu et al. is in the use of the variable anaemia which as Pollitt, (1995) indicates may be the most important variable in the measurement of malnutrition.

METHOD

Participants

Participants were drawn from a birth cohort of 1,795 children from the island of Mauritius. Based on vaccination records, all children born in 1969-1970 in two main towns on the island were recruited into the study when aged 3 years between September 1972 and August 1973. The two towns (Vacoas and Quatre Bornes) were chosen in order to be representative of the ethnic distribution of the whole island. The sample consisted of both males (51.4%) and females (48.6%). Mauritius has a multi-racial society and its ethnic distribution was in 1970: 68.7% of Indian origin, 25.7% "General Population", 1.8% Chinese, 0.1% English, 0.1% French, and 3.6% "other". The Indian group is comprised largely of descendants of indented labour brought to the island by the British after the abolition of slavery in 1835 (Bowman, 1991). The term "General Population" is a term used officially to represent those known locally as "creoles" who are largely descendants of slaves brought to the island by the French between 1670 and 1810 from Madagascar, the East African Coast, West Africa and India (Barker, 1996; Filliot, 1974). Patois créole is the language commonly used amongst all ethnic groups, although the official languages are English and French.

Informed consent was obtained from the mothers of the participants in the early phases, and from participants themselves after the age of 17. Early research activities were conducted according to the principles outlined in the Declaration of Helsinki (World Medical Association 1964) that prevailed in 1972 when the research was initiated, while research activities in later years were conducted using principles outlined in Belmont (1969) IRB approval for later research phases and retrospective data analyses was obtained from the University of Southern California (see Appendix)

Sample Used in the Study

The variables used in the structural equation modelling are described below. The analysis requires that it is carried out on a sample with no missing variables. A sample to meet this criterion contained 339 subjects. An analysis was carried out to assess whether this sample was significantly different on key variables from those subjects from the total population who were omitted from the analysis. It was found that the sample of 339 subjects contained an excess of males (M/F ratio 57.9/42.1 as against 50.4/49.6 in the omitted group ($p = .012$). There were no significant differences in any of the other variables used in the study between the included and non-included groups. As it was intended to analyse the data from males and females separately, all the subjects were retained. Because some of the subjects in the sample were included in those who received additional nutrition in the nursery schools which were started as part of the total project (see Raine, Mellingen, Liu, Venables, and Mednick, 2003, and Raine, et al., 2001) it was thought that inclusion of these subjects would bias the analyses. They were therefore omitted, resulting in sample sizes of 171 males and 130 females.

Variables Used in the Analysis

Measures of Disadvantage

Variable names used on the path diagrams are given in brackets

(a) Status

(1)Years of Father's schooling (Fa Educ), (2) Years of Mother's schooling (Mo Educ), (3) Father's occupational status (Fa Occup). Occupational status was measured on an eight point scale (e.g. 1= unemployed, 2 = part-time labourer, 8= head of a moderate or large business or academic). These variables were measured when the subject was aged 3 in 1972.

(b) Crowding

(1) Number of persons per room (No in Rooms3), (2) number of persons per house (No in House), (3) number of persons per room (No in Rooms11), Ss aged 11. These measures were provided from the standard reports of social workers who visited subjects homes. The first two variables were measured at age three and the latter at age 11.

(c) Malnutrition

(1) Anaemia, assessed by laboratory testing of blood drawn from the child in terms of haemoglobin level in g/dl , labelled (Anaemia, positive values = high anaemia), (2) To provide an additional measure of anaemia the variable colour of the mucous membrane which had been rated by visiting doctors was also used (Muc Memb, positive values = paleness of mucous membranes), (3) Stunting (Stunting, positive values = high stunting) expressed as observed height as a percentage of expected height for the same age. It seemed inappropriate to use Western norms to give estimates of expected height. For this reason the heights of children from social classes > 1sd from the mean SES were used as norms. Furthermore differences in heights were shown between the various racial groups making up the sample measures of stunting were therefore calculated separately within each racial group and subsequently combined and standardized. Analyses showed no racial differences in the measure eventually used.

Measures of Intelligence

Age 3

Verbal, (VIQ3) and spatial (PIQ3) measures of cognitive ability (denoted as verbal and performance IQ for the purposes of labelling in analyses below) were derived from 6 subtests of a modified version of the Boehm Test of Basic Concepts- Preschool version (Boehm, 1986) which assesses verbal and visuo-spatial concepts involved in early school achievement. Full details of measurement, factor structure, reliability and validity, together with modifications of the original version of the test to make it suitable for use with Mauritian children are given in Raine, Yaralian, Reynolds, Venables, and Mednick, (2002).

Age 11

Seven sub-tests of the Wechsler Preschool and Primary Scale of Intelligence (Wechsler, 1967) was used to provide measures of Verbal IQ, (similarities and digit span), (VIQ11) and Performance IQ, (block design, object assembly, coding, mazes, and picture completion) (PIQ11).

Measures of Schizotypy

Age 17

Positive schizotypy (including unusual perceptual experiences, magical thinking and cognitive disorganization) was measured by the schizophrenism (SZism) scale of a self report instrument developed for the measurement of schizotypy in Mauritius. Details of the scoring of the scale, its item content, reliability and validity are given in Venables, (1990) and Venables, Wilkins, Mitchell, Raine, and Bailes, (1990).

Age 23

Schizotypal personality was assessed using the self-report Schizotypal Personality Questionnaire (SPQ, Raine, 1991) where the reliability and validity of this scale are also given. Confirmation of its three factor structure when used in Mauritius are provided by Reynolds, Raine, Mellingen, Venables, and Mednick, (2000). The three factors are

"Cognitive-Perceptual deficits"(COGPERC) , "Interpersonal deficits"(INTERPER), and "Disorganization" (DISORG).

Both scales used were translated into patois créole and then back translated into English to assure accuracy of translation.

Analysis

Structural Equation Modelling was carried out using the EQS program (Bentler, 1995). Modelling was carried out in steps, examining first the relationship between measures of disadvantage, then their relationship to measures of cognitive ability and finally the relation of both of these to measures of schizotypy.

Goodness of fit of these models to the data was examined by the Normed Fit Index (NFI), the Non-normed Fit Index (NNFI) (Bentler and Bonett, 1980), and the Comparative Fit Index (CFI) developed by Bentler, (1990) to take account of sample size. A value of these indices which is greater than 0.9 is taken to indicate a good fit. To enable the use of these indices to be compared to those using LISREL (Joreskog and Sorbom, 1989), the Goodness of Fit Index (GFI) and the Adjusted Goodness of Fit Index (AGFI) are also presented. Values of 0.9 are taken to indicate a good fit for GFI and 0.8 for AGFI. Lastly, the standardized root mean residual (SRMR) is provided. Bentler, (1995) suggests that this index is better than any other at discriminating between fitting and mis-specified models. Values <0.05 indicate a good fit.

Significance values of measurement equations (paths linking factors or variables) are provided in EQS output as the parameter estimate divided by its standard error. Based on an α level of 0.05, the test statistic needs to be greater than 1.96 for the hypothesis to be rejected.

The Langrage Multiplier (LM) test (Lee and Bentler, 1980) was used to examine the effect of adding free parameters to a model. In making use of this test to add parameters, we implemented the warning of Byrne, (1994), that the researcher needs to take account of psychological theory before adopting the suggestions of adding parameters on a purely statistical basis.

When examining the relation of disadvantage to IQ or schizotypy, all hypothesised paths were included in the first models tested. Subsequently, those paths which proved to be non-significant were removed and the model retested. These retested models are those whose fit is reported below. Indices for the fit of models are shown in Table 1. Models are labelled "m" and "f" to indicate the fit for analyses carried out on male and females samples.

Table 1. Goodness of fit indices for male (m) and female (f) samples for the 6 models. NFI = Normed Fit Index, NNFI = Non-normed Fit Index (NNFI) CFI = Comparative Fit Index (CFI)GFI = Goodness of Fit Index (GFI), AGFI = Adjusted Goodness of Fit Index, SRMR = standardized root mean residual (SRMR)

Model	NFI	NNFI	CFI	GFI	AGFI	SRMR
1m	.633	.599	.699	.889	.815	.095
1f	.619	.607	.705	.886	.811	.097
2m	.629	.416	.650	.879	.717	.124
2f	.713	.582	.749	.895	.754	.115
3m	.902	.888	.940	.966	.912	.072
3f	.925	.959	.978	.974	.932	.057
4m	.891	.955	.974	.967	.930	.049
4f	.825	.863	.920	.948	.890	.064
5m	.875	1.02	1.00	.957	.928	.048
5f	.749	.818	.874	.914	.854	.065
6m	.839	.978	.983	.929	.898	.057
6f	.759	.875	.901	.886	.837	.066

RESULTS

Models of Disadvantage

The first analysis examined whether all the variables under "status", "crowding" and "malnutrition" outlined above are accounted for by a single "disadvantage" or "poverty" factor. A confirmatory factor analysis (CFA) using the nine variables shows that a single factor solution is not a good fit to the data for either sex (Model 1).

A CFA carried out on the six "social" measures of disadvantage, using "status" and "crowding" variables shows that these are not best accounted for by a single factor, the fit to the data is poor (Model 2).

A two factor solution using the variables defining "status" and "crowding" separately is a reasonable fit for the data for male subjects and a good fit for the data for female subjects (Model 3). For each data set all six variables make a significant contribution to the solution. The factors are significantly correlated.

A three factor solution including the biological "malnutrition" variables with the social variables defining "status" and "crowding" was shown in preliminary analyses combining male and female samples to be a good fit to the data. However, for the males but not the females the Langrange Multiplier test indicated that a better fit to the data was made if the variable "mothers education" was loaded on the malnutrition factor. As this was an extension of the model which made psychological sense, indicating that the effect of malnutrition might be minimized in households with a better educated mother, its contribution was examined. This model was examined separately for the male and female samples. Model 4m is a good fit to the data and "mother's education" is loaded significantly (-.33) on the malnutrition factor. Model 4f is not such a good fit and mother's education is not significantly (-.18) loaded on the malnutrition factor suggesting a different treatment, in this culture, of male and female children. All variables are loaded significantly on the relevant factors for each gender sample and the covariance of each factor with the others is significant. These models are seen graphically on the left hand side of Figures 1 and 2 which show the significant interrelationships for each sample.

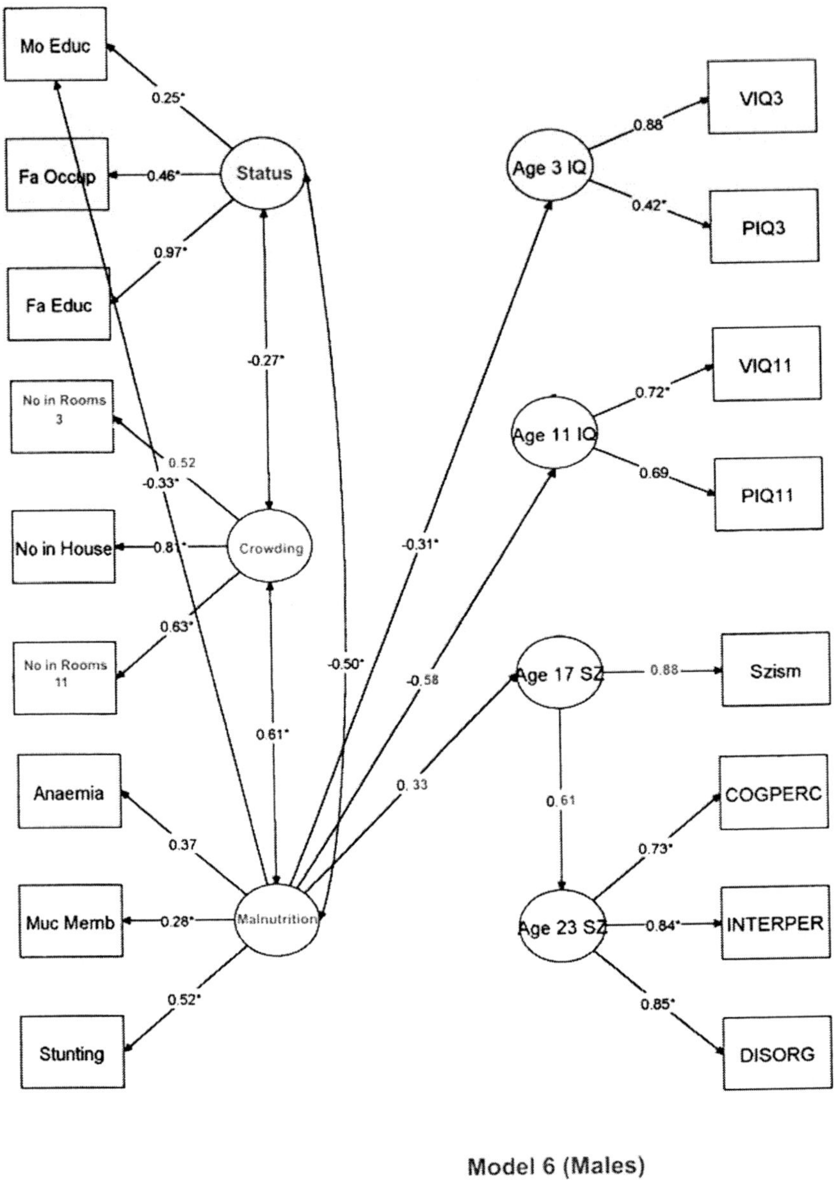

Figure 1. Model 6 showing significant relations between measures of disadvantage, IQ and schizotypy for males

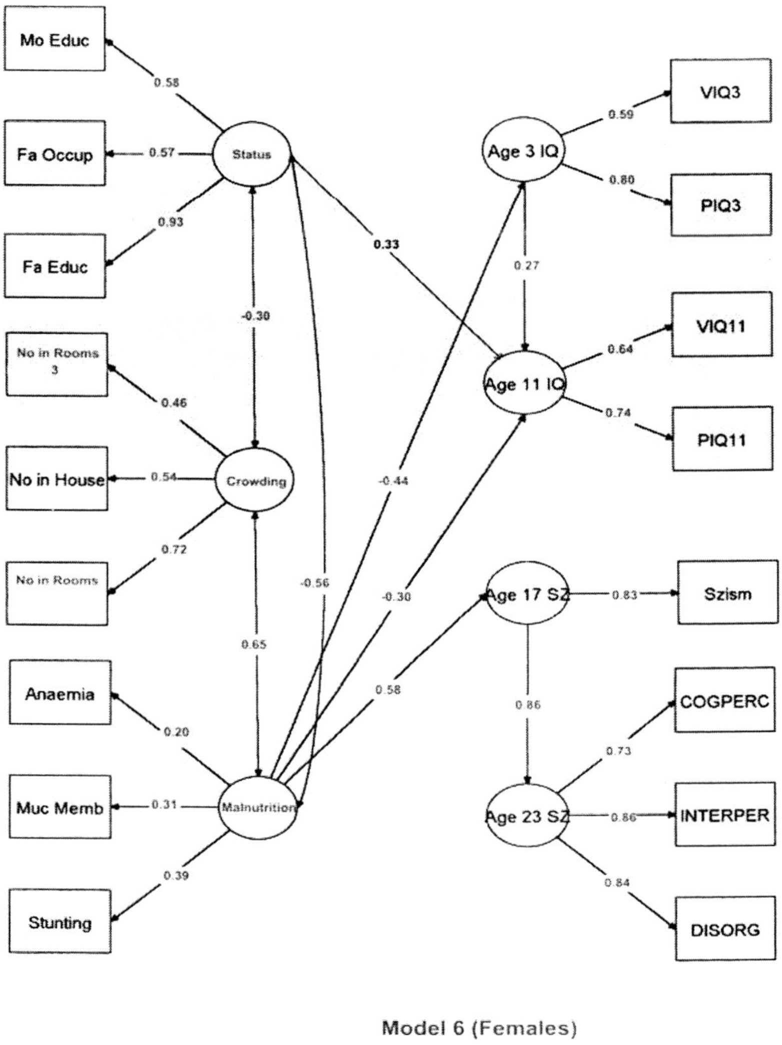

Figure 2. Model 6 showing significant relations between measures of disadvantage, IQ and schizotypy for females

In summary, the outcome of these analyses indicates that, although correlated, the three "disadvantage" or "adversity" factors are best thought of as three separate factors.

The Relation of Disadvantage to Cognitive Ability

In Model 5 the three "disadvantage" variables were related to a factor of cognitive ability defined by verbal and performance IQ at age 3 and at age 11 separately for males and females (see Figures 1 and 2). Non-significant paths were removed.

The fit to the data was very good for males, but not such a good fit for females although the fit would have been accepted as adequate using the LISREL indices GFI and AGFI.

For the males, of the three "disadvantage" variables only malnutrition is related to cognitive ability, the loading for IQ at age 3 being -0.31 and for IQ at age 11 being -0.58. The lack of relation between status or crowding and IQ is noteworthy but it is the consequences of poverty indexed by these two "social" variables in producing malnutrition that is apparently responsible for impaired cognitive ability in this sample. The relation between IQ measures at age 3 and 11 is not significant apparently because both are independently affected by malnutrition.

For the females a somewhat different pattern emerges. Although, as with the males IQ is significantly affected by malnutrition at age 3 (-0.44) and at age 11 (-.30), there is an effect of family status on IQ at age 11, with those of higher status having more intelligent females offspring (0.33). Also, in contrast to males, IQ at age 3 is significantly related to IQ at age 11 (0.27).

The Relation of Disadvantage to Cognitive Ability and Schizotypy

In Model 6 the factors of schizotypy at age 17 and at age 23 are added. The interrelationships between variables are shown in Figures 1 and 2 for males and females respectively. As before non-significant paths were removed before final model fit testing. The models for males and females are essentially the same although the fit is much better for males than it is for females (see Table 1). In both sexes schizotypy at age 17 is significantly related to malnutrition, those who were shown to be malnourished at age 3 having higher schizotypy scores than those not malnourished. There is however no direct relation between malnourishment at age 23 and malnutrition for either males or females. In both sexes there is a relation between schizotypy at age 17 and schizotypy at age 23. What is particularly noteworthy is the absence of any relationship between IQ at age 3 or at age 11 and schizotypy at age 17 or 23. There are no relationships between either of the "social" disadvantage variables and schizotypy.

Discussion

Disadvantage

The results indicate that although highly correlated, the measures of "Disadvantage" namely, "Status", "Crowding" and "Malnutrition" which are used in this study are best modelled as three separate factors. This means that when one of these factors is related to IQ or schizotypy the effect of the other factors is taken into account. As might be expected the parameter estimates for the 3 factor solution are very similar for the samples of children of both sexes. The only difference in the structure of the models is that for the males the Lagrange multiplier test suggested a better model fit if Mother's education were loaded on malnutrition. A significant parameter of –0.33 suggests that there is less malnutrition in households where the mother is better educated. This does not hold for female children.

It is suggested that this is a finding which may be dependent on the culture in this society and may not be capable of wider generalization A study by Ghosh, Kilaru, and Ganapathy,

(2002) carried out in rural India, which may have some of the same cultural characteristics as the present sample showed that when intervention in the form of counselling of mothers on better nutritional practices took place, there was a greater effect on female infants, suggesting that these children had previously been neglected. Wachs (1995) in discussing the effects of mild to moderate malnutrition (which characterises the conditions in the present study) finds that postnatal malnutrition is associated with a variety of cognitive and behavioural defects across the lifespan. He suggests that research should include an emphasis on the interaction between specific psychosocial and nutritional risk factors and the ways in which individual (e.g. gender) or cultural characteristics can moderate nutrition-development relations. What should nevertheless be recognised in the present study is that although a three factor solution provides the best fit to the data, the factors are substantially correlated, indicating that malnutrition is part of a general climate of disadvantage which is undoubtedly found worldwide.

In both male and female samples stunting and anaemia both contributed to the factor of malnutrition, confirming the findings in the literature that these two variables are consistently associated (e.g. (Chang, et al., 1994 and Dangour, Hill, and Ismail, 2002). It should be noted that in both male and female samples the contribution of stunting to the malnutrition factor is greater than that of the "anaemia" variables, thus throwing into question the view of Pollitt, (1995) that iron deficiency is the most important variable to be considered.

Apart from the fact that the factor of crowding was highly correlated to the other two measures of disadvantage, crowding did not itself have significant associations with either IQ or schizotypy. The data thus did not directly support the studies (e.g. (Galle, Gove, and McPherson, 1972) which have produced relations between crowding and pathology or the once influential idea of the "behavioural sink" where increased population density of rats produced a variety of pathologies (Calhoun, 1962; Calhoun, 1967). Again, the important effect of population density may, as was shown by Calhoun (1962, 1967), be through the effect on crowding on the availability of food.

IQ-Disadvantage Relationships

A striking finding is that for males, it is only malnutrition that is related to IQ at both ages. The influence of parental education and status is not shown, neither is there an effect of crowding. This complements the report of Liu, Raine, Venables, Dalais, and Mednick, (2003) who find the effect of malnutrition (although measured differently) is present when the effect of other adversity variables are taken into account. What may also be noted is the lack of a relationship between IQ at age 3 and IQ at age 11. Examination of the simple correlations between these variables showed that while the correlation for verbal IQ at both ages was significant ($r(185) = 0.26$ $p<.000$), that for performance IQ was not ($r(185) = 0.14$, ns). It will be noted from Figure 1 that verbal IQ has a greater loading on the age 3 IQ factor than performance IQ.

For females the pattern is somewhat different. Although, as with the males, there is a strong effect of malnutrition on IQ at both ages, there is an effect of status on the Age 11 IQ factor. It is suggested (Scarr, 1997) that although social class (which is contained in the present "status" variable) may be said to combine both environmental and genetic factors, behaviour-genetic research offers evidence that "differences in intelligence by social class arise in large part from genetic variability and not from differences in opportunities to learn" (p.29).

As far as the possibility of genetic influence is concerned, two questions arise. One, why is the effect only on IQ age 11 and two, why is the effect only found in females? There is now an increasing body of work which shows that the variance in intelligence due to genetic factors differs over the age of the subject. For their findings, Cherney, Fulker, and Hewitt, (1997) reported that for genetic influences, " the amount of variation appears to be decreasing through age 4 but rises substantially at age 7" (p. 477). The same type of finding but over a longer age period was reported by Loehlin, Horn, and Willereman, (1997) who found an increase in genetic variance up to the age of 17. The present finding of an effect on intelligence of "status" a factor with a strong genetic component at age 11 but not at age 3 is consistent with these findings. The suggestions reviewed earlier (see Castle, Abel, Takei, and Murray, 1995) that genetic effects may be greater in females but that neurodevelopmental factors may be more prominent in males may explain why the "status"-IQ effect is shown only in the female sample.

IQ-Schizotypy Relationships

The finding that there is no relation between IQ at age 3 or 11 and schizotypy at age 17 or 23 is very surprising in view of the strong findings reviewed earlier and summarized by (Aylward, Walker, and Bettes, 1984) that "...taken together the findings (of their meta-analysis) suggest that early onset and adult onset schizophrenia are associated with intellectual deficits across the life span". Furthermore, (Barrantes-Vidal, et al., 2003; Chapman, Chapman, and Raulin, 1976; Chapman, Chapman, and Raulin, 1978; Voglmaier, Seidman, Salisbury, and McCarley, 1997) reported that schizotypy was negatively related to cognitive performance. These studies do not take into account the presence of a third variable, such as in the present case, malnutrition, which may effect both IQ and the tendency to schizotypy/schizophrenia separately. In the present sample where evidently malnutrition is a strong source of variance, independence is shown between IQ and schizotypy.

Malnutrition–Schizotypy Relationships

In the context of direct malnutrition – schizotypy relationships, the main point to be noted is that there is no direct effect of malnutrition on schizotypy at age 23 even though there are strong correlations between measures of schizotypy at age 17 and 23. It is conceivable therefore that the influence of malnutrition on mechanisms that are involved in the development of schizotypy have been implemented by age 17 and that the results of this disordered mechanism are continued in some fashion at age 23.

Malnutrition-IQ-Schizotypy Relationships

As outlined above, the finding that cognitive status and schizotypy are independently affected by malnutrition suggests that the mechanisms by which malnutrition is having its effect are different in each case. Liu, Raine, Venables, Dalais, and Mednick, (2003) reviewed the evidence to suggest that iron deficiency leads to a general defect in DNA synthesis, neurotransmitter function and white matter formation and provided evidence that it was anaemia which was the variable measured in their study which overall affected measures of IQ. It thus appears that it is a general effect of malnutrition on nervous structure and function that may be responsible for impaired cognitive function. On the other hand Brown, et al. (1996) suggested that malnutrition has effects on mechanisms that are specifically found to be disordered in schizophrenia, specifically the hippocampus. It should be noted however that Brown et al. (1996) are referring to the effects on pregnant women of the Dutch Famine winter (Susser, et al., 1996) and these considerations are not necessarily applicable to the present study where malnutrition was measured postnatally when the subjects were aged 3 years. It is nevertheless likely in this study that subjects who are malnourished at age 3 are likely to be those who come from families in which the mother was malnourished while pregnant.

The independence of effects of teratogenic factors on IQ and schizotypy may be illustrated by studies on the effect of mothers' exposure to the influenza virus in the second trimester of pregnancy. Seeking to replicate the findings of Mednick, Huttunen, and Machon, (1994) on the effects of influenza exposure on schizophrenia, Venables, (1996) carried out a study in Mauritius on the effect of influenza exposure on schizotypy (measured in the same way at age 17 as in the present study). It was found that there was an increased incidence of schizotypy in the offspring of those mothers who were exposed to influenza in the second trimester of pregnancy. It has been suggested (see reviews by Mednick, Huttunen, and Machon, (1994) and Venables, (1996) that the areas of the brain which are affected by influenza exposure are those which are found to be disorganized in schizophrenia and those suggested by Brown, et al., (1996) to be disturbed by malnutrition. To examine whether exposure to influenza had an effect on cognitive performance, a subsidiary analysis was carried out on the dataset used in the Venables (1966) study. It was found that there was no significant effect of influenza exposure on IQ ($F(4,485) = 1.41$, $p=.23$. This suggests that the teratogenic effect of influenza exposure was specific to schizotypy / schizophrenia and did not have an effect on the more generally determined level of cognitive function. This would appear to offer support to the findings of the present study where the effects of malnutrition on IQ and schizotypy were apparently differentiated.

Conclusions and Implications

The key point to emphasize from this chapter is that malnutrition in the early postnatal years is associated with increased schizotypy at age 17 years, but not age 23 years. These findings extend the work of Hoek, Brown, and Susser, (1998) and Hoek, et al., (1996) on the effects of prenatal malnutrition on adult schizotypy by showing similar effects for postnatally-assessed malnutrition. An important caveat on this conclusion is that while the fit to the models tested is good in the case of male subjects, it is less good in the case of females. This may be because in the female sample there are other untested factors which might have produce better fits, because the error variance of the variables was larger in the female sample or because the female sample was smaller. Given the stronger findings for males, future studies should probably take into account not only simple sex differences but also the interaction of cultural differences in the developmental life history of boys and girls and the ways in which genetics and environmental factors affect the sexes differently.

If poor nutrition is of etiological significance in relation to schizotypal personality and schizophrenia, then one potentially important intervention / prevention implication is that better nutritional care early in life could potentially reduce the rate of adult schizophrenia. Intervention resources might be most effectively targeted at the at-risk offspring of parents with schizophrenia. Findings of the current study also suggest that such interventions might be particularly effective in males for whom stronger effects were obtained. The fact that one early prevention study of schizotypy included a strong nutritional component (Raine et al. 2003) provides further support for taking nutrition into account in future prevention / intervention studies.

The fact that cognitive ability did not mediate the malnutrition – schizotypy relationship has implications for future studies, We speculate here that while the effects of malnutrition on impacting the brain structures underlying cognitive ability may be generalized, the pathway in which malnutrition increases the risk of schizotypy may be more regionally-specific. While the hippocampus may be one candidate, future brain imaging studies which assess the effects of malnutrition on brain structure / function, schizotypy, and neurocognition could importantly clarify the brain circuits the malnutrition – schizotypy relationship.

Finally, the evidence for a link between poor postnatal nutrition and schizotypal personality should be viewed within the wider context of risk factors for crime and schizophrenia. Previous work has shown a link between poor prenatal nutrition and both crime and schizophrenia / schizotypy (Susser et al. 1996; Hoek et al. 1996; Neugebauer et al. 1990). New research presented here and elsewhere is now beginning to show a link between postnatal malnutrition and both antisocial / aggressive behaviour and schizotypal personality (Liu et al. 2004). Poor pre- and post-natal malnutrition may therefore be a common etiological process that simultaneously gives rise to both crime and schizophrenia, and may account for some of the comorbidity between these constructs.

REFERENCES

Aylward, E., Walker, E., and Bettes, B. (1984). Intelligence in schizophrenia: Meta-analysis of the research. *Schizophrenia Bulletin*, *10*, 430-459.

Barker, A.J. (1996). *Slavery and anti-slavery in Mauritius*. Basingstoke: Macmillan Press Ltd.

Barrantes-Vidal, N., Fananas, L., Rosa, A., Caparros, B., Dolors Riba, M., and Obiols, J.E. (2003). Neurocognitive, behavioural and neurodevelopmental correlates of schizotypy clusters in adolescents from the general population. *Schizophrenia Research*, *61*(2-3), 293-302.

Belmont, Report. (1979). *The Belmont Report: Ethical Principles and Guidelines for the Protection of Human Subjects of Biomedical and Behavioral Research*. US Dept of Health and Human Services.

Bentler, P.M. (1990). Comparative fit indices in structural models. *Psychological Bulletin*, *107*, 238-246.

Bentler, P.M. (1995). *EQS Structural Equations Program Manual.* (3.0 ed.). Encino, CA: Multivariate Software Inc.

Bentler, P.M., and Bonett, D.G. (1980). Significance tests and goodness of fit in the analysis of covariance structures. *Psychological Bulletin, 88*, 588-606.

Boehm, A. (1986). Boehm Test of Basic Concepts-Preschool version. San Antonio: Psychological Corporation.

Bogerts, B. (1991). The neuropathology of schizophrenia: pathophysiological and neurodevelopmental implications. In S.A. Mednick, T.D. Cannon, C.E. Barr, and M. Lyon (Eds.), *Fetal neural development and adult schizophrenia* (pp. 153-173). Cambridge: Cambridge University Press.

Bowman, L.W. (1991). *Mauritius: Democracy and development in the Indian Ocean.* London: Westview Press.

Brown, A.S., Susser, E.S., Butler, P.D., Richardson Andrews, R., Kaufmann, C.A., and Gorman, J.M. (1996). Neurobiological plausibility of prenatal nutritional deprivation as a risk factor for schizophrenia. *Journal of Nervous and Mental Disease, 184*(2), 71-85.

Byrne, B.M. (1994). *Structural Equation Modelling with EQS and EQS/Windows.* Thousand Oaks CA: Sage Publications Inc.

Calhoun, J.B. (1962). Population density and social pathology. *Scientific American, 206*, 139-148.

Calhoun, J.B. (1967). Ecological factors in the development of behavioral anomalies. *Proceedings of the Annual Meeting American Psychopathological Association, 55*, 1-51.

Castle, D.J., Abel, K., Takei, N., and Murray, R.M. (1995). Gender differences in schizophrenia: Hormonal effect or subtypes? *Schizophrenia Bulletin, 21*, 1-12.

Castle, D.J., and Murray, R.M. (1991). The neurodevelopmental basis of sex differences in schizophrenia. *Psychological Medicine, 21*, 565-575.

Castle, D.J., Scott, K., Wessley, S., and Murray, R.M. (1993). Does social deprivation during gestation and ealy life predispose to later schizophrenia? *Social Psychiatry and Psychiatric Epidemiology, 28*, 1-4.

Chang, S.M., Walker, S.P., Grantham-McGregor, S., and Powell, C.A. (2002). Early childhood stunting and later behaviour and school achievement. *Journal of Child Psychology and Psychiatry, 43*, 775-83.

Chang, Y., Zhai, F., Li, W., Ge, K., Jin, D., and de Onis, M. (1994). Nutritional status of preschool children in poor rural areas of China. *Bulletin of the World Health Organization, 72*, 105-12.

Chapman, L.J., Chapman, J.P., and Raulin, M.L. (1976). Scales for physical and social anhedonia. *Journal of Abnormal Psychology, 85*, 374-382.

Chapman, L.J., Chapman, J.P., and Raulin, M.L. (1978). Body-image aberration in schizophrenia. *Journal of Abnormal Psychology, 87*, 399-407.

Cherney, S.S., Fulker, D.W., and Hewitt, J.K. (1997). Cognitive development from infancy to middle childhood. In R.J. Sternberg and E.L. Grigorenko (Eds.), *Intelligence, heredity and environment* (pp. 463-482). Cambridge: Cambridge University Press.

Dangour, A.D., Hill, H.L., and Ismail, S.J. (2002). Height, weight and haemoglobin status of 6 to 59-month-old Kazakh children living in Kzyl-Orda region, Kazakhstan. *European Journal of Clinical Nutrition, 56*, 1030-8.

Filliot, J.M. (1974). *La traite des esclaves vers mascareignes au XVIII siecle.* Paris: ORSTOM.

Galle, O.R., Gove, W.R., and McPherson, J.M. (1972). Population density and pathology: what are the relations for man? *Science*, *176*, 23-30.

Ghosh, S., Kilaru, A., and Ganapathy, S. (2002). Nutrition education and infant growth in rural Indian infants: narrowing the gender gap? *Journal of the Indian Medical Association*, *100*, 483-4,

Gibson, R.S. (1990). *Principles of Nutritional Assessment*. New York: Oxford University Press.

Goldberg, E.M., and Morrison, S.L. (1963). Schizophrenia and social class. *British Journal of Psychiatry*, *109*, 785-802.

Goldstein, J.M., Santangelo, S.L., Simpson, J.C., and Tsuang, M.T. (1990). The role of gender in identifying subtypes of schizophrenia: A latent class analytic approach. *Schizophrenia Bulletin*, *16*, 263-275.

Goldstein, J.M., Seidman, L.J., Santangelo, S., Knapp, P.H., and Tsuang, M.T. (1994). Are schizophrenic men at higher risk for developmental deficits than schizophrenic women? Implications for adult neuropsychological functions. *Journal of Psychiatric Research*, *28*, 483-498.

Hoek, H.W., Brown, A.S., and Susser, E. (1998). The Dutch famine and schizophrenia spectrum disorders. *Social Psychiatry and Psychiatric Epidemiology*, *33*, 373-9.

Hoek, H.W., Susser, E., Buck, K.A., Lumey, L.H., Lin, S.P., and Gorman, J.M. (1996). Schizoid personality disorder after prenatal exposure to famine. *American Journal of Psychiatry*, *153*, 1637-9.

Hollingshead, A.B., and Redlich, F.C. (1954). Schizophrenia and social structure. *American Journal of Psychiatry*, *110*, 695-701.

Joreskog, K.G., and Sorbom, D. (1989). *LISREL 7*. (2nd ed.). Chicago: SPSS Inc.

Kety, S.S. (1980). The syndrome of schizophrenia. *British Journal of Psychiatry*, *136*, 421-436.

Kohn, M.L. (1968). Social class and schizophrenia: a critical review. In D. Rosenthal and S.S. Kety (Eds.), *The Transmission of Schizophrenia* (pp. 155-173). Oxford: Pergamon Press.

Lee, S.-Y., and Bentler, P.M. (1980). Some asymtotic properties of contrained generalized least squares estimamtion in covariance structure models. *South African Statistical Journal*, *14*, 121-136.

Liu, J., Raine, A., Venables, P.H., Dalais, C., and Mednick, S.A. (2003). Malnutrition at age 3 years and lower cognitive ability at age 11 years: independence from psychosocial adversity. *Archives of Pediatric Adolescent Medicine*, *157*, 593-600.

Liu, J., Raine, A., Venables, P.H., and Mednick, S.A. (2004). Malnutrition at age 3 and externalizing behavior problems at ages 8, 11 and 17 years. *American Journal of Psychiatry*, *161*, 2005-2013.

Loehlin, J.C., Horn, J.M., and Willereman, L. (1997). Herdedity, environement and IQ in the Texas Adoption Project. In R.J. Sternberg and E.L. Grigorenko (Eds.), *Intelligence, heredity and environment* (pp. 105-125). Cambridge: Cambridge University Press.

Mednick, S.A., Huttunen, M.O., and Machon, R.A. (1994). Prenatal influenza infections and adult schizophrenia. *Schizophrenia Bulletin*, *20*, 263-7.

Mednick, S.A., Machon, R.A., Huttenen, M.O., and Bonett, D. (1988). Adult schizophrenia following prenatal exosure to an influenza epidemic. *Archives of General Psychiatry*, *45*, 189-192.

Mednick, S.A., Schulsinger, F., Teasdale, T.W., Schulsinger, H., Venables, P.H., and Rock, D.R. (1978). Schizophrenia in High-Risk children: Sex differences in predisposing factors. In G. Serban (Ed.), *Cognitive defects in the development of mental illness* (pp. 169-204). New York: Brunner/Mazel.

Neugebauer, R., Hoek, H W, and Susser, E. (1999). Prenatal exposure to wartime famine and development of antisocial personality disorder in early adulthood. *JAMA: Journal of the American Medical Association, 282*, 455-462.

Pollitt, E. (1995). Functional significance of the covariance between protein energy malnutrition and iron deficiency anemia. *Journal of Nutrition, 125*(8 Suppl), 2272S-2277S.

Raine, A. (1991). The SPQ: A scale for the assessment of Schizotypal Personality Disorder based on DSM-III-R criteria. *Schizophrenia Bulletin, 17*, 555-564.

Raine, A., and Lencz, T. (1995). Conceptual and theoretical issues in schizotypal personality research. In A. Raine, T. Lencz, and S.A. Mednick (Eds.), *Schizotypal Personality* (pp. 3-15). Cambridge: Cambridge University Press.

Raine, A., Mellingen, K., Liu, J., Venables, P., and Mednick, S.A. (2003). Effects of environmental enrichment at ages 3-5 years on schizotypal personality and antisocial behavior at ages 17 and 23 years. *American Journal of Psychiatry, 160*, 1627-35.

Raine, A., Venables, P.H., Dalais, C., Mellingen, K., Reynolds, C., and Mednick, S.A. (2001). Early educational and health enrichment at age 3-5 years is associated with increased autonomic and central nervous system arousal and orienting at age 11 years: Evidence from the Mauritius Child Health Project. *Psychophysiology, 38*, 254-266.

Raine, A., Yaralian, P.S., Reynolds, C., Venables, P.H., and Mednick, S.A. (2002). Spatial but not verbal cognitive defects at age 3 in persistently antisocial individuals. *Developmental Psychopathology, 14*, 25-44.

Redlich, F.C., Hollingshead, A.B., Roberts, B.H., Robinson, H.A., Freedman, L.Z., and Myers, J.K. (1953). Social structure and psychiatric disorders. *American Journal of Psychiatry, 109*, 729-734.

Reynolds, C.A., Raine, A., Mellingen, K., Venables, P.H., and Mednick, S.A. (2000). Three factor model of schizoptypal personality: Invariance across culture, gender, religious affiliation, family adversity and psychpathology. *Schizophrenia Bulletin, 26*, 603-618.

Rivera, J.A., and Sepulveda Amor, J. (2003). Conclusions from the Mexican National Nutrition Survey 1999: translating results into nutrition policy. *Salud Publica Mexicana, 45 Suppl 4*, S565-75.

Scarr, S. (1997). Behavior-genetic and socialization theories of intelligence; Truce and reconciliation. In R.J. Sternberg and E.L. Grigorenko (Eds.), *Intelligence, heredity and environment* (pp. 3-41). Cambridge: Cambridge University Press.

Susser, E., Neugebauer, R., Hoek, H.W., Brown, A.S., Lin, S., Labovitz, D., and Gorman, J.M. (1996). Schizophrenia after prenatal famine. Further evidence. *Archives of General Psychiatry, 53*(1), 25-31.

Susser, E.S., and Lin, S.P. (1992). Schizophrenia after prenatal exposure to the Dutch Hunger Winter of 1944-1945. *Archives of General Psychiatry, 49*, 983-8.

Trestman, R.L., Keefe, R.S.E., Mitropoulou, V., Harvey, P.D., deVegvar, M.L., LeesRoitman, S., Davidson, M., Aronson, A., Silverman, J., and Siever, L.J. (1995). Cognitive function and biological correlates of cognitive performance in schizotypal personality disorder. *Psychiatry Research, 59*, 127-136.

Venables, P.H. (1990). The measurement of schizotypy in Mauritius. *Personality and Individual Differences*, *11*, 965-971.

Venables, P.H. (1995). Schizotypal status as a developmental stage in studies of risk for schizophrenia. In A. Raine, T. Lencz, and S.A. Mednick (Eds.), *Schizotypal Personality* (pp. 107-131). Cambridge: Cambridge University Press.

Venables, P.H. (1996). Schizotypy and maternal exposure to influenza and to cold temperature: The Mauritius study. *Journal of Abnormal Psychology*, *105*, 53-60.

Venables, P.H., Wilkins, S., Mitchell, D.A., Raine, A., and Bailes, K. (1990). A scale for the measurement of schizotypy. *Personality and Individual Differences*, *11*, 481-495.

Voglmaier, M.M., Seidman, L.J., Salisbury, D., and McCarley, R.W. (1997). Neuropsychological dysfunction in schizotypal personality disorder: A profile analysis. *Biological Psychiatry*, *41*(5), 530-540.

Wachs, T.D. (1995). Relation of mild-to-moderate malnutrition to human development: correlational studies. *Journal of Nutrition*, *125*(8 Suppl), 2245S-2254S.

Wechsler, D. (1967). *Wechsler Pre-school and Primary Scale of Intelligence*. San Antonio Texas: Psychological Corporation.

World Medical Association. (1964). *Declaration of Helsinki, Recommendations guiding doctors in clinical research Adopted by the 18th World Medical Assembly. Helsinki, Finland.*

In: Crime and Schizophrenia: Causes and Cures
Editor: Adrian Raine, pp. 151-163
ISBN 1-59454-609-6

Chapter 8

NEURODEVELOPMENT AND POSTNATAL MATURATION: A DIACHRONIC FRAMEWORK TO EXAMINE GENE /ENVIRONMENT INTERACTIONS IN PSYCHIATRIC DISORDERS

Marie-Odile Krebs*
E0117 Inserm - Paris 5, Hôpital Sainte- Anne, Paris

INTRODUCTION

Several psychiatric disorders are now viewed as "neurodevelopmental" disorders. More generally, events related to neurodevelopment are thought to have long-lasting influence on behavior and personality characteristics. Schizophrenia is the disease in which the evidence for a neurodevelopmental origin are the most convincing. Indeed, despite a delayed onset during teenage years, the neurodevelopmental origin for schizophrenia is supported by the high prevalence of structural cerebral and of functional neurocognitive abnormalities noticed since early childhood in patients. Those abnormalities, also found in healthy relatives, are thought to underlay the vulnerability to schizophrenia. However, the processes responsible for the delayed transformation of a "vulnerability" into a schizophrenic disorder remain poorly understood. Schizophrenia's pathophysiology is complex and involves a genetic predisposition and environmental factors (Mueser and McGurck, 2004). The way the environment interacts with the genetic vulnerability is critical to understand in order to decipher the mechanisms that explain why and how a predisposition becomes an actual illness (Sawa and Snyder, 2002).

The diachronic perspective is one of the most promising ways of viewing major psychiatric diseases such as schizophrenia or bipolar disorders, as well as conduct disorders including and violent behavior. This view integrates the notion of vulnerability together with the transition that results in the pathological condition. Besides clinical and epidemiological

* krebs@broca.inserm.fr

studies, animal models are of particular interest since they allow testing of the influence of post-natal interventions on the outcome of prenatal disruption during neurodevelopment. In this paper, the main issues in the diachronic approach in schizophrenia will be presented with a brief review of the evidence supporting the neurodevelopmental hypothesis of schizophrenia. We will also present clinical and preclinical evidence supporting the rationale for the continuum of neurodevelopment and post-natal maturation.

SCHIZOPHRENIA : THE END OF A TRAJECTORY

When looking backward in the past history of an individual with recent-onset psychosis, premorbid behavioral changes or functional impairment frequently preceeds the onset. These changes usually begin one or two year before the onset and are thought to reflect a "prodromal phase" (Yung et al, 2003). Before that, some patients display slight neurocognitive dysfunctions and sometimes behavioral characteristics (Cannon et al, 2002, Walker et al, 1994). Those earlier mild abnormalities are more likely to reflect vulnerability to schizophrenia. Indeed, the same neurocognitive impairments or behavorial characteristics are seen in non-psychotic first-degree relatives of patients with schizophrenia (Ismail et al, 1998; Egan et al, 2001). Altogether, schizophrenia appears as the end of a trajectory from vulnerability, to "prodromes", "first episode psychosis" and *in fine* schizophrenia.

A delay of 2 years usually occurs between the first psychotic symptoms and an appropriate treatment (Mueser et McGurck , 2004). Recent clinical data have emphasized the benefits of earlier recognition and treatment of psychosis before schizophrenia is diagnosed (Cornblatt et al, 2002 ; Yung et al, 2003 ; McGorry and Yung, 2003). This early detection is believed to benefit the patients in terms of decreased comorbidity (in particular decreased incidence of substance abuse, or suicidal attempts) but also in reducing the transition to chronic psychosis (McGorry et al, 2004 ; Mc Gorry et al, 2002). These strategies raise multiple ethical, sociological, clinical (which subjects should be treated and when) and therapeutic (antipsychotics, antidepressant, CBT, education) issues (McGorry et al, 2003) . It also raises new theoretical issues.

Indeed, a patient with schizophrenia is not born with the disease; but with a particular vulnerability, which in turn has evolved into schizophrenia. Studying the pathophysiology of schizophrenia thus requires addressing different phases of the disease. These include processes underlying the vulnerability, the "prodromal phase", the onset of "first episode psychosis", and lastly the processes underlying schizophrenia itself. The specificity and potential reversibility of these different phases are unclear. It is obvious that not all vulnerable subjects will develop schizophrenia (approximately 10% only will succumb to schizophrenia). From the pioneering studies of "prodromal" patients, it is now accepted that not all patients characterized as prodromal will present a first episode psychosis (at least in the period of observation). In line with this, it has thus been suggested to name this phase of disease "at risk mental state" instead of "prodrome" (Yung et al, 2003). Lastly, "first episode" studies have shown that some patients displaying typical psychotic episodes will not develop schizophrenia, but instead develop bipolar disorders or other psychotic disorders. In other words, when looking prospectively, we are dealing with "risk of disease" rather than the disease itself. Among subjects displaying markers of vulnerability, it is hard to detect those in whom the disease will progress until we know more about the processes underlying the transition toward psychosis, until we better identify when the subject is still only "vulnerable" to schizophrenia, and until the progression of the disease has already started.

Thus, identifying clinical or cognitive dysfunctions occurring during the different phases is of crucial interest, as well as detecting abnormalities associated with the transition leading to the first psychotic episode (Yung et al, 2004; Cornblatt et al, 2002). It is also of importance to be able to understand what are the phenomena that precipitate vulnerable subjects into the disease and, if the environment plays a role, to identify by which processes the response to the environment can be modulated (Strohman , 2002). For instance, some alleles of the gene encoding the enzyme monoamine oxidase A (MAO-A) moderate the response of children to maltreatment (Caspi et al, 2002). It has also been suggested that the occurrence of psychosis or mood disorder could be a maladaptative response to stress (Walker et al, 1997 ; Harrison and Weinberger, 2004) and/or a "bad encounter" with toxic substances / street drugs (Arsenault et al, 2004). These observations suggest in turn that post-natal neuroplasticity is a key figure in psychiatric disorders.

The crucial clinical issues of "early detection/intervention" programs are : (i) can we detect "at risk states " (and distinguish them from vulnerability), and (ii) can we prevent schizophrenia ? The answers to these questions lay in the understanding of the pathophysiology. The diachronic approach is the clinical translation of the vulnerability model : congenital vulnerability resulting from the interaction of environmental factors with a genetic background will evolve, or not, into the disease.

It remains for us to identify not only the genes that are responsible for the vulnerability, but also those responsible for the response to the environment (together with the identification of the precipitating factors) and whether some interventions could reverse or prevent the evolution. Some genetic factors could account for both. Indeed numerous so-called "developmental " factors that play a crucial role during development are now recognized as having specific post-natal patterns of expression, which could reflect their role in neuronal plasticity. These factors, if deregulated and/or dysfunctional, could lead to both neurodevelopmental anomalies and dysfunctional plasticity. In this context, the neurodevelopmental hypothesis is of particular interest.

Anomalies in Neurodevelopment

Experimental research in human and animal models, as well as clinical studies, has brought forward compelling evidence that the vulnerability to psychosis is related to a disturbance of neurodevelopment. The neurodevelopmental hypothesis of schizophrenia is supported by the presence of brain structural anomalies in post-mortem or in MRI studies (Weinberger, 1995, see Harrison and Weinberger, 2004; Mueser, 2004 for reviews).

Among these anomalies, the most convergent findings are ventricular enlargement and atrophy of fronto-temporal structures, in particular the hippocampus (Shenton et al, 2001; Wright et al, 2000). Sub-cortical structures (basal ganglia, cerebellum) are also affected (Ishimiya et al, 2001). Interestingly, the brain volumes appear related to outcome in recent-onset schizophrenia (vanHaren et al, 2003). In addition, evidence has been reported of abnormal gyration in the cortex, and which is necessarily of neurodevelopmental origin

(Vogeley et al, 2000) and is present before the onset of the disease (Yucel et al, 2003). Lastly, abnormalities are found in the relatives of patients though to a lesser degree (Staal et al, 2000), suggesting that at least part of the structural brain characteristics are related to vulnerability to schizophrenia. The precise neuropathology of schizophrenia is still a matter of debate, although there is evidence for abnormalities in the cortex (reduction in thickness) and in the hippocampus. Reduction of neuronal size or number of neurons have been suggested, in particular of the GABAergic neurons (see Harrison and Weinberger, 2004; Knable et al 2002).

Clinically, physical minor anomalies (MPA) (Guy et al, 1983; Green et al, 1994; Ismail et al, 1998), including abnormal dermatoglyphic (Fananas et al, 1990), are frequent in schizophrenia and are a risk factor for future schizophrenia, as reported in birth cohort (Cannon et al, 2003; Schiffman et al, 2004).

Early motor abnormalities and/or delayed acquisition of psychomotor milestones have been reported as risk factors in birth cohort studies (Jones, 1994; Rosso et al, 2000; Leask et al, 2002) as well as in studies conducted in the offspring of patients with schizophrenia (Walker et al, 1994; Schiffman et al, 2004). Neurological soft signs (NSS) are more frequently seen in patients with schizophrenia, even during their 'first episode' and in neuroleptic naive patients (see Dazzan et al, 2002 ; Keshavan et al, 2003 ; Krebs et al, 2000). NSS are also more frequent in the first degree relatives of schizophrenic patients (Ismail et al, 1998, Yazici 2002) than in the general population. The NSS are also significantly correlated to MPAs (Gourion et al, 2004) and are transmitted within families (Gourion et al, 2003 ; Gourion et al, 2004). Lastly, epidemological studies have provided further evidence by demonstrating that pre- or peri-natal complications are associated with increased risk for schizophrenia (Mednick et al, 1988; Cannon et al, 2002).

Anomalies in Neurodevelopment and Maturation?

Although there is clear evidence that abnormal neurodevelopment (from genetic or environmental origin) is involved, the evolution of the disease is still a matter of debate and the precise mechanisms associated with the onset of disease (psychotic transition) remain largely unknown. The historical debate of "neurodenegerative" vs "neurodevelopmental" disease has gone back and forth evolution since the first historical descriptions of the disorder (Weinberger, 1995; McClure et Lieberman, 2003). While a neurodegenerative processes is eliminated by the neuropathology (and in particular the absence of gliosis), there is also evidence for some evolution, at least contemporary of the onset.

This question has been recently re-activated by observations suggesting that grey matter atrophy is increased during the transition (Pantelis et al, 2003). This suggests that the onset of the disease is an active or at least evolving process (Walker et Bollini, 2002, Walker et al, 2004; Weinberger, 1987; McClure et Lieberman, 2003) in line with the vulnerability model. Whether this reflects the physiological maturation of a previously disordered brain or a dysfunctional maturation due to an abnormal response to the environment is unclear, these two hypothesis being not necessarly antinomic. Puberty is a period of major changes in structural and functional connectivity in the brain (see Sowell et al, 2004) and the elimination of synapses, reduction of dendritic spines as well as the improved connectivity in the limbic system due to myelination of the connecting fibers are an important feature of the brain maturation and probably not unrelated to the fact that behaviors are notably changed during adolescence as well as when comparing before and after puberty (Walker et al, 2002; 2004).

Actually, neurodevelopment does not end at birth and the brain is now viewed as a "neotenic" structure, expressing many "developmental" factors expressed in the embryo and in which the post-natal maturation changes occur thoughout the whole lifetime. The adult brain has different forms of plasticity: modulation in the efficacy of synapses in response to a stimulus or synaptic plasticity, neurogenesis, growth and branching of dendrites, remodeling of synaptic contacts. Much of this plasticity is observed in limbic regions that are important for cognition and control of mood and emotion (like the prefrontal cortex, amygdala and hippocampus) although neurogenesis appears limited to two areas of the brain: the dentate gyrus (Gould et al, 1998) and the olfactory bulb. During the past decade, results from in vivo neuroimaging studies and post mortem cytoarchitecture analysis have identified significant abnormalities in frontolimbic brain regions in psychiatric pathologies and in particular in depression. These different alterations could reflect a decrease in functional and structural plasticity, that could be superimposed with neurodevelopmental abnormalities. In addition, impairments in signaling pathways that regulate neural plasticity, synaptic plasticity and cell survival have been recently identified in depressive and psychotic disorders (Duman, 2002; Manji et al., 2001; 2003; Konradi and Heckers, 2001).

Postmortem studies suggest that schizophrenia is associated with anomalous synaptogenesis that particularly affects glutamatergic transmission (Harrison and Weinberger, 2004; Konradi and Heckers, 2003 ; Knable et al, 2002). The reduction of the number of dendrites and synapses seen in the brain of patients with schizophrenia could be due to abnormal formation or stabilization of synapses. In the cortex, there is a reduction of (a) GABAergic and glutamatergic markers, (b) presynaptic markers and (c) of reelin. The expression of reelin, a protein involved in neuronal migration in laminar structures such as cortex, hippocampus and cerebellum, was concordantly found decreased in post-mortem frontal cortex and hippocampus of patients with schizophrenia or bipolar disorders (Guidotti et al, 2000; Knable et al, 2002). These changes of expression are related to "post natal" synthesis of reelin by GABAergic interneurons. The signalling pathways involve the phosphorylation of the protein Dab1. The BDNF (Brain Derived Neurotrophic Factor) is modified in the cortex and hippocampus of post-mortem brains of patients with schizophrenia (Takahashi et al, 1998). During development, BDNF plays an important role in the differentiation and survival of dopaminergic neurons (Hyman et al. 1991). More recently, it has been demonstrated that BDNF participates in the effect of antidepressant drugs, in particular in reversing the influence of stress on hippocampal plasticity (Duman, 2002).

The proteins with homeodomain are crucial in the development of the embryo and more specifically in the development of the nervous brain system (Rubinstein et al, 1994). More recently, it has been shown that several of these are still expressed in the adult brain with a specific pattern and could be involved in synaptic plasticity. For instance, HoxB8, only found in the caudal part of CNS during development is expressed in the adult in the specific region of the orbitofrontal cortex and in the caudate nucleus. Mice with defective hox B8 display repetitive grooming reminiscent of obsessive compulsive disorders (Greer and Capechi, 2002).

Altogether, these factors could plays a role not only during development but also in post-natal life, assuming that post-natal neuronal plasticity share some mechanisms with neurodevelopmental plasticity. Neuronal and synaptic plasticity could be the core of the pathophysiology of psychiatric disorders. This allows for the consideration that some interventions, chemical or not, could accelerate the remission or even stop the progression of the disease by facilitating neuroplasticity (Konradi and Heckers, 2001).

Animal Model for Schizophrenia

In line with the neurodevelopmental hypothesis of schizophrenia, new animal models have been proposed that use pre- or early post-natal insults to induce schizophrenia-like behavioral or cognitive changes, e.g. neonatal ventral hippocampal lesions, maternal deprivation (Ellenbroek et al, 2004), and social isolation (Lipska and Weinberger, 2000). The most consistent results have been obtained using neonatal excitotoxic lesion of the ventral hippocampus using ibotenic acid (Lipska et al, 1993). Taken together, findings show that the rats with lesions to the ventral hippocampus (VHL) display behavioral changes that are reminiscent of positive, negative, and cognitive symptoms of schizophrenia. For instance, they have spontaneous locomotor hyperactivity, a deficit in sensory gating (PPI), and hyper-reactivity to dopaminergic (amphetamine) or antiglutamatergic (MK-801) drugs (Lipska, 2004). They also have deficits in social interaction, working memory impairments, and anhedonia. As would be predicted, most of these features appear to be reversed by antipsychotic drugs. Interestingly, most of those behavioral changes appear after puberty, thus providing a valid model for studying the influence of different factors on phenotypes.

Because this model is based on direct lesions of the hippocampus, lesions which are not similar to what is seen in schizophrenia, other models have been developed. Prenatal mitotoxin exposure on specific days of gestation can induce structural brain abnormalities which are relatively specific in relation to the timetable of neuronal development. When methylazoxymethanol acetate (MAM), an antimitotic agent, is administered intraperitoneally to pregnant rat dams at embryonic day 17 (E17), the cells further implicated in hippocampo-prefrontal cortex network undergo major divisions (Cattabeni and Di Luca, 1997).

Rats prenatally exposed to MAM exhibited working memory deficits in a radial arm-maze task in adulthood (Gourevitch et coll., 2004), suggesting a disrupted hippocampo-cortical network in these animals. The behavioral profile of the MAM-exposed rats shows that they exhibited spontaneous hyperactivity in adulthood, as well as hypersensitivity to the motor activating effects of a glutamatergic antagonist, MK-801 (Le Pen et al., submitted). At adulthood, spatial recognition memory disturbances have been observed in MAM rats in a two-trial memory task. Interestingly, the hyperactivity only emerged after puberty. The prepulse inhibition paradigm showed that MAM rats also exhibited sensorimotor gating deficits at adulthood. In addition, we showed that MAM rats exhibited social interaction deficits at both pre- and post-puberty (as was found in VHL rats). Those results are in line with those in the literature using the same paradigm, showing hyper-reactivity to amphetamine with increased subcortical dopamine release (Flagstadt et al, 2004).

Because the course of development and post- natal maturation is much more rapid in the mice or rat, developmental models in those species are adapted to test the influence of concurrent enviromental factors or of physiological dysregulation. For instance, sensitivity to stress in animals with development abnormalities can be assessed (Lipska et al, 1993). It has also been recently reported that treatment with a cannabinoid during puberty in the rat induces cognitive and PPI impairments in the adult (Schneider and Koch, 2004), suggesting a specific influence of cannabis during the puberty period.

Another interesting question to address is the influence of sex hormones. Clinical data have revealed that schizophrenia in women is generally less severe (Castle et al, 1998) and that estrogen acts as a protective factor against stress-induced cellular modification in the hippocampus (Behl, 2002). It is also well known that estrogens and antiandrogens attenuate violent behaviors in violent patients, including violent schizophrenic patients. Developmental models are well adapted to test the influence of hormonal exposure at different phases of development and/or post natal neuromaturation. Animal models should thus provide promising paradigms for understanding schizophrenia. Lastly, it would also be interesting to investigate up to what point the structural and biological changes observed in these developmental models are reminiscent of the changes observed in post-mortem brains of patients with schizophrenia. Such studies could finally provide evidence for the underlying pathophysiology of schizophrenia.

CONCLUSIONS

The diachronic approach of psychiatric disorders relies on the assumption that brain maturation or plasticity is a lifetime ongoing process. As a consequence, the behavior observed at a particular time depends on the interaction of the environment with the pre-existent vulnerability. An implicit consequence is that "nurture " modulates "nature " up to a point that nurture can both precipitate and hamper the emergence of the behavioral consequences of early insult and/or genetic background. This approach takes its full value when considering the early detection / intervention in patients with ultra-high risk of schizophrenia. In those subjects with "at risk mental state ", prospective studies have shown that some patients will not develop the disease. Nevertheless, we still need to identify which factors will precipitate the disease and especially which are the factors (or treatments) that will allow the subject to escape their fate. This heuristic model can also be applied to other mental disorders or to components of those complex phenotypes.

The results obtained in animals are supporting the value of developmental models mimicing some of the features seen in schizophrenia. It is noteworthy though that no difference in agressivity has been observed in any of these developmental models. This is not in line with the observation that violence is more frequent in patients than in other populations (Taylor and Gunn, 1984 ; Arsenault et al, 2000). This is also not in line with observations that some neurocognitive abnormalites, potentially related to development and/or maturational abnormalities, are associated with later antisocial individuals (Raine et al 2002), given that those individuals are more likely to have impulsive and sometimes violent behaviors than other individuals. Lastly, in longitudinal studies, MPA has been identified as a risk factor for later violent behavior in adolescence (Arsenault et al, 2000).

The absence of "violence " of aggression in developmental animal studies of schizophrenia does not exclude the possibility that violence can stem from neurodevelopment abnormalitites. Nevertheless, it suggests that violence in schizophrenia is related to an additional aetiological component either related to an "independant " process (for instance, abnormal seroroninergic dysregulation due to genetic background or to independant environmental factors) or it is related to the same etiological factor acting at a different time during development and/or in a different brain site (leading for instance to abnormal development of the serotonin nucleus). As a matter of fact, violent behavior could indeed be associated with an abnormal regulation of serotonin, as reported in several diagnostic categories. Accordingly, we found that the functional 5HTTLPR polymorphism in the serotonin transporter was associated with more violent suicidal attempts in schizophrenic patients (Bayle et al, 2003), as has been previously reported in other clinical populations (Bondy et al., 2000; Courtet et al., 2001). In addition, an association with this genotype was found with violent behavior in early onset type 2 alcoholism (Hallikainen et al., 1999) and violence in adolescents (Zalsman et al, 2001). On the other hand, we could also speculate that the same developmental factors could be responsible for both developmental disuption and serotoninergic dysregulation, since some develepental genes are still expressed in serotoninergic neurons. Nevertheless, violent behavior in schizophrenia, as with other clinical feature of schizophrenia, is most likely related to have multifactorial origins, with a pre-determined predisposition interacting with physiological and environmental factors (Arsenault et al, 2000), as well as with clinical characteristics of schizophrenia itself (i.e. lack of insight, Buckley et al, 2004).

In summary, the diachronic approach accurately offers a frame for understanding the interaction between nature and nurture which stimulate the development of valuable models for understanding the relation between schizophrenia and violence.This chapter has presented the main issues of the diachronic approach in schizophrenia as well as the evidence supporting the rationale for a continuum between neurodevelopment and post-natal maturation. Although schizophrenia is viewed as a neurodevelopmental disorder, the processes that are responsible for the delayed transformation of a "vulnerability" into a schizophrenic disorder remain poorly understood. The diachronic perspective is one of the most promising ways of thought in major psychiatric diseases since it integrates the notion of vulnerability together with the evolution or transition that results in the pathological condition.

REFERENCES

Arango C, Calcedo Barba A, Gonzalez-Salvador, Calcedo Ordonez A (2000). Violence in inpatients with schizophrenia: a prospective study. *Schizophr Bull, 25*, 493-503.

Arseneault L, Cannon M, Witton J, Murray RM. (2004) Causal association between cannabis and psychosis: examination of the evidence. *British Journal of Psychiatry,* 184, 110-117.

Arseneault L, Tremblay RE, Boulerice B, Seguin JR, Saucier JF (2000). Minor physical anomalies and family adversity as risk factors for violent delinquency in adolescence. *Am J Psychiatry*, *57*, 917-23.

Arseneault, L., Moffitt, T.E., Caspi, A., Taylor, P.J. and Silva, P.A. (2000). Mental disorders and violence in a total birth cohort: results from the Dunedin study. Arch. *Gen. Psychiatry, 57*, 968–979.

Bayle FJ, Leroy S, Gourion D, Millet B, Olie JP, Poirier MF, Krebs MO (2003). 5HTTLPR polymorphism in schizophrenic patients: further support for association with violent suicide attempts. *Am J Med Genet, 119*B, 13-7.

Behl C. (2002) Oestrogen as a neuroprotective hormone, Nature rev. *Neuroscience, 2,* 433-442.

Bondy B, Erfurth A, de Jonge S, Kruger M, Meyer H (2000). Possible association of the short allele of the serotonin transporter promoter gene polymorphism (5-HTTLPR) with violent suicide. *Mol Psychiatry, 5*, 193-195.

Buckley PF, Hrouda DR, Friedman L, Noffsinger SG, Resnick PJ, Camlin-Shingler K (2004). Insight and its relationship to violent behavior in patients with schizophrenia. *Am J Psychiatry, 161*, 1712-1714.

Cannon M, Caspi A, Moffitt TE, Harrington H, Taylor A, Murray RM, Poulton R (2002). Evidence for early-childhood, pan-developmental impairment specific to schizophreniform disorder: results from a longitudinal birth cohort. *Arch Gen Psychiatry, 59*, 449-56.

Cannon M, Jones PB, Murray RM (2002). Obstetric complications and schizophrenia: historical and meta-analytic. *Am J Psychiatry. 159,* 1080-92.

Cannon TD, van Erp TG, Bearden CE, Loewy R, Thompson P, Toga AW, Huttunen MO, Keshavan MS, Seidman LJ, Tsuang MT (2003). Early and late neurodevelopmental influences in the prodrome to schizophrenia: contributions of genes, environment, and their interactions. *Schizophr Bull,* 29, 653-69.

Caspi A, McClay J, Moffitt TE, Mill J, Martin J, Craig IW, Taylor A, Poulton R (2002). Role of genotype in the cycle of violence in maltreated children. *Science, 297,* 851-4.

Castle D, Sham P, Murray R (1998) Differences in distribution of ages of onset in males and females with schizophrenia. *Schizophr Res, 33*, 179-83.

Cattabeni F, Di Luca M (1997): Developmental models of brain dysfunctions induced by targeted cellular ablations with methylazoxymethanol. *Physiol Rev, 77,* 199-215.

Cornblatt BA.The New York high risk project to the Hillside recognition and prevention (RAP) program (2002). *Am J Med Genet,* 8, 114, 956-66.

Courtet P, Baud P, Abbar M, Boulenger JP, Castelnau D, Mouthon D, Malafosse A, Buresi C (2001). Association between violent suicidal behavior and the low activity allele of the serotonin transporter gene. *Mol Psychiatry, 6*, 338-341.

Dazzan P, Murray RM (2002). Neurological soft signs in first-episode psychosis: a systematic review. *Br J Psychiatry Suppl, 43*, s50-s57.

Duman RS (2002) Pathophysiology of depression: the concept of synaptic plasticity. *Eur Psychiatry, 17,* Suppl 3, 306-10.

Egan MF , Goldberg TE, Gscheidle T, Weirich M, Rawlings R, Hyde TM, Bigelow L, and Weinberger DR (2001). Relative Risk for Cognitive Impairments in Siblings of Patients with Schizophrenia. *Biol Psychiatry, 50,* 98–107

Fananas L, Moral P, Bertranpetit J (1990). Quantitative dermatoglyphics in schizophrenia: study of family history subgroups. *Hum Biol,* 62, 421-7.

Flagstad P, Mork A, Glenthoj BY, van Beek J, Michael-Titus AT, Didriksen M (2004). Disruption of Neurogenesis on Gestational Day 17 in the Rat Causes Behavioral Changes Relevant to Positive and Negative Schizophrenia Symptoms and Alters Amphetamine-Induced Dopamine Release in Nucleus Accumbens. *Neuropsychopharmacology, 29,* 2052-64.

Geyer, M. A., Wilkinson, L. S., Humby, T. and Robbins, T. W (1993). Isolation rearing of rats produces a deficit in prepulse inhibition of acoustic startle similar to that in schizophrenia. *Biol Psychiatry, 34,* 361-72.

Gould E, Tanapat P, McEwen BS, Flugge G, Fuchs E. (1998) Proliferation of granule cell precursors in the dentate gyrus of adult monkeys is diminished by stress. *Proc Natl Acad Sci U S A, 95*, 3168-71.

Gourevitch, R., Rocher, C., Le Pen, G., Krebs, M. O. and Jay, T. M (2004). Working memory deficits in adult rats after prenatal disruption of neurogenesis. *Behav Pharmacol 15*, 287-92.

Gourion D, Goldberger C, Bourdel MC, Bayle FJ, Loo H, Krebs MO (2004). Minor physical anomalies in patients with schizophrenia and their parents: prevalence and pattern of craniofacial abnormalities. *Psychiatry Res*, *125,* 21-8.

Gourion D, Goldberger C, Bourdel MC, Bayle FJ, Millet B, Olie JP, Krebs MO (2003). Neurological soft-signs and minor physical anomalies in schizophrenia: differential transmission within families. *Schizophr Res, 63*, 181-7.

Gourion D, Goldberger C, Olie JP, Loo H, Krebs MO. (2004). Neurological and morphological anomalies and the genetic liability to schizophrenia: a composite phenotype. *Schizophr Res, 67,* 23-31.

Green, M.F., Satz, P. and Christenson, C. (1994a). Minor physical anomalies in schizophrenia patients, bipolar patients, and their siblings. *Schizophr Bul., 20*, 433-40.

Greer JM, Capecchi MR (2002). Hoxb8 is required for normal grooming behavior in mice. *Neuron, 33*, 23-34.

Guidotti A, Auta J, Davis JM, Di-Giorgi-Gerevini V, Dwivedi Y, Grayson DR, Impagnatiello F, Pandey G, Pesold C, Sharma R, Uzunov D, Costa E (2000). Decrease in reelin and glutamic acid decarboxylase67 (GAD67) expression in schizophrenia and bipolar disorder: A postmortem brain study. *Arch Gen Psychiatry,* 57, 1061-9.

Guy, J.D., Majorski, L.V., Wallace, C.J. and Guy, M.P (1983). The incidence of minor physical anomalies in adult male schizophrenics. *Schizophr Bul., 9,* 571-82.

Hallikainen T, Saito T, Lachman HM, Volavka J, Pohjalainen T, Ryynanen OP, Kauhanen J, Syvalahti E, Hietala J, Tiihonen J (1999). Association between low activity serotonin transporter promoter genotype and early onset alcoholism with habitual impulsive violent behavior. *Mol Psychiatry, 4,* 385-388.

Harrison PJ and Weinberger DR (2004). Schizophrenia genes, gene expression, and neuropathology: on the matter of their convergence. *Mol Psychiatry,* 10, 40-68.

Hyman C, Hofer M, Barde YA, Juhasz M, Yancopoulos GD, Squinto SP, Lindsay RM (1991). BDNF is a neurotrophic factor for dopaminergic neurons of the substantia nigra. *Nature,* 350, 230-2.

Ismail B, Cantor-Graae E, McNeil TF (1998). Minor physical anomalies in schizophrenic patients and their siblings. *Am J Psychiatry,* 155, 1695-702.

Jones, P., Rodgers, B., Murray, R. and Marmot, M (1994). Child development risk factors for adult schizophrenia in the British 1946 birth cohort. *Lancet, 344,* 1398-402.

Keshavan MS, Sanders RD, Sweeney JA, Diwadkar VA, Goldstein G, Pettegrew JW, Schooler NR (2003). Diagnostic specificity and neuroanatomical validity of neurological abnormalities in first-episode psychoses. *Am J Psychiatry,* 160, 1298-304.

Knable MB, Barci BM, Bartko JJ, Webster MJ, Torrey EF (2002). Molecular abnormalities in the major psychiatric illnesses: Classification and Regression Tree (CRT) analysis of post-mortem prefrontal markers. *Mol Psychiatry;* 7, 392-404.

Konradi C, Heckers S (2003). Molecular aspects of glutamate dysregulation: implications for schizophrenia and its treatment. *Pharmacol Ther, 97,* 153-79.

Konradi C and Heckers S (2001): Antipsychotic Drugs and Neuroplasticity: Insights into the Treatment and Neurobiology of Schizophrenia. *Biol Psychiatry, 50,* 729–742

Krebs MO, Gut-Fayand A, Bourdel MC, Dischamp J, Olie JP (2000). Validation and factorial structure of a standardized neurological examination assessing neurological soft signs in schizophrenia. *Schizophr Res, 45,* 245-60.

Leask SJ, Done DJ, Crow TJ (2002). Adult psychosis, common childhood infections and neurological soft signs in a national birth cohort. *Br J Psychiatry,* 181, 387-92.

Lipska, B. K. and Weinberger, D. R (2000). To model a psychiatric disorder in animals: schizophrenia as a reality test. *Neuropsychopharmacology, 23,* 223-39.

Lipska, B. K (2004). Using animal models to test a neurodevelopmental hypothesis of schizophrenia. *J Psychiatry Neurosci, 29,* 282-6.

Lipska, B. K., Jaskiw, G. E. and Weinberger, D. R (1993). Postpubertal emergence of hyperresponsiveness to stress and to amphetamine after neonatal excitotoxic hippocampal damage: a potential animal model of schizophrenia. *Neuropsychopharmacology, 9,* 67-75.

McClure RK and Lieberman JA (2003). Neurodevelopmental and neurodegenerative hypotheses of schizophrenia: *a review and critique Current Opinion in Psychiatry, 16,* (Suppl 2), S15–S28.

McGorry PD, Yung AR, Phillips LJ, Yuen HP, Francey S, Cosgrave EM, Germano D, Bravin J, McDonald T, Blair A, Adlard S, Jackson H (2002). Randomized controlled trial of interventions designed to reduce the risk of progression to first-episode psychosis in a clinical sample with subthreshold symptoms. *Arch Gen Psychiatry,* 59, 921-8.

McGorry PD, Yung AR, Phillips LJ (2003). The "close-in" or ultra high-risk model: a safe and effective strategy for research and clinical intervention in prepsychotic mental disorder. *Schizophr Bull, 29,* 771-90.

McGorry PD, Yung AR (2003). Early intervention in psychosis: an overdue reform. *Aust N Z J Psychiatry, 37,* 393-8.

Mednick, S. A., Machon, R. A., Huttunen, M. O. and Bonett, D (1988). Adult schizophrenia following prenatal exposure to an influenza epidemic. *Arch Gen Psychiatry, 45,* 189-92.

Mueser KT, McGurk SR (2004). Schizophrenia. *Lancet,* 363, 2063-72.

Pantelis C, Velakoulis D, McGorry PD, Wood SJ, Suckling J, Phillips LJ, Yung AR, Bullmore ET, Brewer W, Soulsby B, Desmond P, McGuire PK (2003). Neuroanatomical abnormalities before and after onset of psychosis: a cross-sectional and longitudinal MRI comparison. *Lancet,* 361, 281-8.

Pantelis C, Velakoulis D, McGorry PD, Wood SJ, Suckling J, Phillips LJ, Yung AR, Bullmore ET, Brewer W, Soulsby B, Desmond P, McGuire PK (2003). Neuroanatomical abnormalities before and after onset of psychosis: a cross-sectional and longitudinal MRI comparison. *Lancet,* 361, 281-8.

Rubinstein JLR, Martinez S, Shimamura K Puelles L (1994). The embryonic Vertebrate forebrain : The prosomeric model. Science, 266, 578-80.

Sawa A and Snyder SH (2002). Schizophrenia : diverse approaches to a complex disease. *Science,* 296, 692-695.

Schiffman J, Ekstrom M, LaBrie J, Schulsinger F, Sorensen H, Mednick S (2002). Minor physical anomalies and schizophrenia spectrum disorders: a prospective investigation. *Am J Psychiatry, 159*, 238-43.

Schiffman J, Walker E, Ekstrom M, Schulsinger F, Sorensen H, Mednick S (2004). Childhood videotaped social and neuromotor precursors of schizophrenia: a prospective investigation. *Am J Psychiatry, 161*, 2021-7.

Shenton ME, Dickey CC, Frumin M, McCarley RW (2001) A review of MRI findings in schizophrenia. *Schizophr Res, 49*, 1-52.

Schneider M , and Koch M (2003). Chronic Pubertal, but not Adult Chronic Cannabinoid Treatment Impairs Sensorimotor Gating, Recognition Memory, and the Performance in a Progressive Ratio Task in Adult Rats *Neuropsychopharmacology, 28*, 1760–1769.

Sowell ER, Thompson PM, Toga AW (2004). Mapping the changes in the human cortex throughout the span of life. *Neuroscientist, 10*, 372-92.

Staal WG, Hulshoff Pol HE, Schnack HG, Hoogendoorn ML, Jellema K, Kahn RS (2000). Structural brain abnormalities in patients with schizophrenia and their healthy siblings. *Am J Psychiatry,* 157, 416-21.

Strohman R (2002). Maneuvering in the Complex Path from Genotype to Phenotype : *Science, 296,* 701-703

Takahashi M, Shirakawa O, Toyooka K, Kitamura N, Hashimoto T, Maeda K, Koizumi S, Wakabayashi K, Takahashi H, Someya T, Nawa H (2000). Abnormal expression of brain-derived neurotrophic factor and its receptor in the corticolimbic system of schizophrenic patients. *Mol Psychiatry*, 5, 293-300.

Van Haren NE, Cahn W, Hulshoff Pol HE, Schnack HG, Caspers E, Lemstra A, Sitskoorn MM, Wiersma D, Van Den Bosch RJ, Dingemans PM, Schene AH, Kahn RS (2003). Brain volumes as predictor of outcome in recent-onset schizophrenia: a multi-center MRI study. *Schizophr Res,* ;64, 41-52.

Vogeley K, Tepest R, Pfeiffer U, Schneider-Axmann T, Maier W, Honer WG, Falkai P (2001). Right frontal hypergyria differentiation in affected and unaffected siblings from families multiply affected with schizophrenia: a morphometric mri study. *Am J Psychiatry, 158*, 494-6.

Walker E, Kestler L, Bollini A, Hochman KM (2004). Schizophrenia: etiology and course. *Annu Rev Psychol, 55*, 401-30.

Walker EF, Diforio D (1997). Schizophrenia: a neural diathesis-stress model. *Psychol Rev. 104*, 667-85.

Walker EF, Savoie T, Davis D (1994). Neuromotor precursors of schizophrenia. *Schizophr Bull, 20,* 441-51.

Walker, E. and Bollini, A. M (2002). Pubertal neurodevelopment and the emergence of psychotic symptoms. *Schizophr Res, 54,* 17-23.

Weinberger D.R (1995). From neuropathology to neurodevelopment. *Lancet, 346,* 552-557.

Weinberger D.R (1987). Implications of the normal brain development for the pathogenesis of schizophrenia. *Arch. Gen. Psychiatry, 44*, 660-669.

Wright I.C, RabeHesketh S, Woodruff .W, David AS, Murray RM, Bullmore ET (2000). Meta-analysis of regional brain volumes in schizophrenia. *Am. J. Psychiatry; 157*, 16-25.

Yazici AH, Demir B, Yazici KM, Gogus A (2002). Neurological soft signs in schizophrenic patients and their nonpsychotic siblings. *Schizophr Res, 58,* 241-6.

Yucel M, Wood SJ, Phillips LJ, Stuart GW, Smith DJ, Yung A, Velakoulis D, McGorry PD, Pantelis C. (2003). Morphology of the anterior cingulate cortex in young men at ultra-high risk of developing a psychotic illness. *Br J Psychiatry,* 182 , 518 - 524

Yung AR, Phillips LJ, Yuen HP, Francey SM, McFarlane CA, Hallgren M, McGorry PD (2003). Psychosis prediction: 12-month follow up of a high-risk ("prodromal") group. *Schizophr Res, 60*, 21-32.

Yung AR, Phillips LJ, Yuen HP, McGorry PD (2004). Risk factors for psychosis in an ultra high-risk group: psychopathology and clinical features. *Schizophr Res,* 67, 131-42.

Zalsman G, Frisch A, Bromberg M, Gelernter J, Michaelovsky E, Campino A, Erlich Z, Tyano S, Apter A, Weizman A (2001). Family-based association study of serotonin transporter promoter in suicidal adolescents: No association with suicidality but possible role in violence traits. *Am J Med Genet, 105*, 239-245.

PART 5. RISK FACTORS COMMON TO CRIME AND SCHIZOPHRENIA

In: Crime and Schizophrenia: Causes and Cures
Editor: Adrian Raine, pp. 167-177
ISBN 1-59454-609-6

Chapter 9

FETAL NEURAL DEVELOPMENT AND DEVIANCE

Ricardo A. Machón*[1]*, Sarnoff A. Mednick*[2]*,
***Matti O. Huttunen*[3] *and Antti Tanskanen*[4]**
[1]Loyola Marymount University Los Angeles
[2]University of Southern California
[3]University of Helsinki and National Public Health Institute of Finland
[4]National Public Health Institute of Finland

This chapter examines the weight of the evidence for a prenatal neurodevelopmental disturbance as one basis for a variety of deviant outcomes, including schizophrenia spectrum and major affective disorders, and violent crime. The following questions will be discerned: Is second trimester exposure to maternal influenza associated with increased risk for schizophrenia spectrum disorders, major affective disorders, and violence? Is second trimester exposure to other, non-viral stressors (such as analgesics and earthquakes) also associated with deviant psychological outcomes? Is it possible to narrow the window of vulnerability to deviant outcomes? What are the likely mechanisms of action in the pathogenesis of these deviant outcomes? Lastly, this chapter will also examine the critical question: what is the more important factor in explaining the above findings, the *type* of stressor vs. the *timing* of the stressor?

In the nineteenth century, it became clear that exogenous chemical and physical conditions could adversely affect the embryonic development of many species. This conclusion was based on studies of species whose fertilization and development took place outside the mother (cnidarians, echinoderms, amphibians, and fish). Since their fertilization and development were better protected and took place at an almost constant temperature, mammalian embryos were held to be relatively impervious to potentially teratogenic agents. Malformations of newborn mammals were, nevertheless, observed (McClure, 1995). With the mammalian fetus so well protected, it was reasoned that these malformations must be genetic anomalies. This prevailing view held until the 1930s when Hale (1933) reported a litter of eleven piglets born without eyeballs. The parents had normal eyes and were previously (and subsequently) able to produce offspring with normal eyes. Hale traced the deficit of this litter to a diet lacking in Vitamin A during the ill-fated pregnancy.

In more recent decades it has been demonstrated that the mammalian fetus may be highly sensitive to specific untoward influences. The level of this sensitivity has been shown to vary markedly as a function of the type of the teratogen, the dose and (perhaps most important) its timing relative to stage of gestation. Examples of such teratogens include alcohol, smoking, drugs (e.g., thalidomide), and infections such as rubella. These agents often produce anomalies observable at the time of birth (McClure, 1995).

There is another class of teratogen which may be associated with more subtle effects on the human fetus; this class of teratogen may be more difficult, or impossible, to detect at birth, because its influence may not become manifest before adolescence or adulthood. For example, exposure of the developing fetal brain to moderate levels of ionizing radiation during a sensitive period of gestation may produce no anomalies which are immediately observable in the infant at the time of the birth; such radiation exposure, nevertheless, is associated with deviant psychological functioning in adulthood (Otake and Schull, 1984). Third trimester exposure to Phenobarbital (via maternal medical treatment) is associated with significant deficits in later adult intelligence. These deficits are not detectable at birth (McClure, 1995).

INFLUENZA AND SCHIZOPHRENIA

Infection with H_2N_2 subtype influenza A virus during the first trimester was identified by Hakosalo and Saxén (1971) as a likely teratogen associated with elevated rates of central nervous system anomalies in the newborn. The Hakosalo and Saxén research examined individuals whose mothers were exposed to this influenza virus during the 1957 pandemic in Helsinki, Finland. We have studied psychiatric outcomes for adults whose mothers very likely suffered an influenza infection during this same Helsinki 1957 pandemic (Mednick, Machón, Huttunen and Bonett, 1988; Mednick, Huttunen and Machón, 1994). We found that maternal influenza during the second trimester was associated with significantly elevated rates of adult schizophrenia in the offspring. No such increase was observed in those fetuses exposed in their first or third trimester. This basic finding for the same 1957 and other pandemics has been replicated in a wide range of national settings (O'Callaghan, Sham, Takei, Glover and Murray, 1991; Kendall, and Kemp, 1989; Kunugi, Nankos and Takei, 1992; McGrath, Pemberton, Welham, and Murray, 1994; Fahy, Jones, Sham, Takei and Murray, 1993; Barr, Mednick and Munk-Jørgenson, 1990); some recent failures to replicate also have been noted (Crow and Done, 1992; Bowler and Torrey, 1990; Selten and Slaets, 1994; Susser, Lin, Brown, Lumey and Erlenmeyer-Kimling, 1994). In a major review of the extant literature, Bagalkote, Pang and Jones (2001) conclude that despite recent failures to replicate the basic prenatal influenza and schizophrenia findings, the data are nevertheless compelling and the "gun continues to smoke" (p. 16).

We have interpreted this association between fetal influenza and adult schizophrenia outcome to be a product of an influenza-based disturbance in fetal neural development during a period of rapid growth in schizophrenia-relevant brain regions, particularly involving the mesolimbic system, the thalamus and entorhinal regions. The maternal influenza infection may disturb the generation of young neurons, interfere with the migration, positioning or connections of the young neurons, or disturb programmed cell death, thus potentially causing errors in brain development, and therefore increasing the risk for later, adult deviance.

Analgesics and Schizophrenia

The above findings provide evidence that maternal influenza in the second trimester of gestation may disturb fetal neural development. Is the *timing* of the teratogen more important than the *type* of teratogen? We tested this hypothesis in a Copenhagen cohort born 1959-1961, comprising 9,125 consecutive births. This cohort was identified and intensively examined as part of an obstetrical study. The pregnancy, delivery and post natal period was carefully described by Danish pediatricians and obstetricians. This description included notation of the timing and administration of analgesics.

Animal studies suggest a neurobehavioral teratogenic effect elicited by strong analgesics (opioids). Prenatal exposure of mice to heroin during mid to late gestation produced marked deficits in hippocampus-related behaviors (Yanai, Vatury and Slotkin, 2002). An observational study in humans found that prenatal exposure to aspirin, but not acetaminophen was associated with negative long-term impact on the CNS, affecting behavior and intellectual performance in children (Streissguth, Treder and Barr, 1987).

On the basis of these studies, we speculated that prenatal exposure to certain types of analgesic drugs might interfere with early neurodevelopment and also render the exposed individuals more vulnerable to the development of schizophrenia later in life.

The analgesics noted in our study, included: (1) aspirin; (2) phenacetin (or aspirin) and codeine; (3) morphine (very rare); (4) mixtures of aspirin and opioids; and (5) non-steroid anti-inflammatory antipyrine. Across the first, second and third trimesters, the rate of prescription of analgesics ranged from 0.9 to 1%.

Cases of schizophrenia diagnoses in the cohort were identified by cross-checking the birth cohort in the Danish Psychiatric Central Register. Individuals exposed to analgesics in the second trimester of fetal life had significantly higher levels of schizophrenia than non-exposed controls or those exposed in trimesters one or three ($P < .001$, Odds Ratio = 5.61). We removed all cases with parental schizophrenia and the results remained the same. When we examined cases separately by sex, the overall pattern of results was the same. Similarly when cases with severe birth complications (maternal diabetes, severe eclampsia, staining) in the 4th, 5th or 6th months of pregnancy were removed, the overall pattern of results was the same. Regrettably, the relatively low number of cases did not permit additional analyses by type of analgesic or month of exposure.

Influenza and Major Affective Disorder

Is schizophrenia the only psychiatric disorder that may have a neurodevelopmental origin? Magnetic resonance imaging findings, particularly the presence of medial temporal lobe (i.e., hippocampus or amygdala complex) hypoplasia and reduction of total cerebral volume, have been interpreted as providing support for a neurodevelopmental etiology for bipolar affective disorder (Nasrallah, 1991; Olsen et al., 1990). These neurostructural findings appear to parallel those of schizophrenia.

Thus, we examined the hypothesis that exposure to the 1957 influenza pandemic in greater Helsinki, Finland during the second trimester of gestation would increase the risk for adult major affective disorders (ICD-8 code: 296) compared with controls born in the same months of the year but in the 6 years before the 1957 pandemic (Machón, Mednick, and Huttunen, 1997). For these analyses, we removed anyone with a lifetime history of schizophrenia diagnosis (ICD-8 code: 295). For those exposed to influenza during trimesters 1 or 3, major affective disorder was diagnosed in a similar proportion of subjects in the Index and Control groups. Among those exposed to influenza during their second trimester of fetal life, subjects in the Index group had a significantly elevated proportion of major affective disorder diagnoses (13%) relative to total psychiatric admissions compared with Control subjects (2%) (2-tailed Fisher exact test, $P < .001$). The above pattern remained statistically significant for males exposed in the second trimester (16% vs. 2%; 2-tailed Fisher exact test, $P < .001$); it did not reach statistical significance for females exposed in the second trimester (8% vs. 3%; 2-tailed Fisher exact test, $P > .05$) but it was in the same direction as the males.

Since the ICD-8 diagnosis code of 296 includes unipolar and bipolar forms of affective disorder, we also examined whether the above findings extended in a similar fashion to both unipolar and bipolar forms. Subjects in the Index group who were exposed to influenza during the second trimester had a significantly higher proportion of *unipolar* (depressive) forms of major affective disorder (7.1%) compared with their controls (0.5%) (Fisher exact test, $P < .002$). Those Index subjects exposed to influenza during the second trimester did not have a significantly different proportion of *bipolar* forms of major affective disorder (5.4%) compared with their controls (1.6%) (Fisher exact test, $P > .05$) although it was in a similar direction as the unipolar group.

Influenza and Schizotypal Personality

Our initial research report showed a significant increase in *schizophrenia* diagnoses among those exposed to influenza in their second trimester of fetal life (Mednick et al., 1988). We have carried out additional studies in an attempt to address two related research questions: Is second trimester exposure to influenza associated with adult schizophrenia *spectrum* disorder, in particular schizotypal personality? With a large enough sample size, is it possible to narrow the window of vulnerability to psychiatric disorder?

Peter Venables (1996) previously examined the relationship between influenza exposure during gestation and scores on a schizotypy scale administered to 17-year-olds as part of the Mauritius Study. The findings indicated that those exposed to maternal influenza as fetuses evidenced significantly elevated Schizophrenism (positive symptoms of schizotypy) scale scores as compared to controls. When Venables examined the relationship by month of exposure, he noted a significant increase in Schizophrenism scores among those exposed to the influenza epidemic in the 5th month of gestation. No significant elevation was noted for the Anhedonia (negative symptoms of schizotypy) factor.

Thus, we undertook a study to attempt to replicate the intriguing findings of Venables (1996). Each year, 30,000 Finnish men are eligible to start their compulsory military service. They are routinely administered a whole battery of tests, including several complete scales from the original Minnesota Multiphasic Personality Inventory (MMPI). We constructed a Schizotypal Personality disorder scale by summing the 7 (Psychasthenia) and 8 (Schizophrenia) scales. The totaled score of these scales has been reported by Meyer (1993) to be a clinical indicator of schizotypal personality disorder (SPD or schizotypy). In 1969 there was a worldwide pandemic caused by the H_3N_2 subtype influenza virus which struck Helsinki, Finland beginning the week of January 12, reaching a peak during the week of January 26, diminishing rapidly at the end of February, and ending the week of February 23.

The findings from our study were recently published in a report that examined a database containing MMPI scores for all male conscripts in Finland (Machón et al., 2002). We identified individuals who, as fetuses, were exposed to the severe influenza epidemic (the "Hong Kong flu") of 1969. We also identified a group of Controls born during a relatively low year (1971) for infectious epidemics; for these two groups, we compared the pattern of their MMPI scale scores, indicative of SPD characteristics. As hypothesized, a significantly higher proportion of *6th month* exposed Index subjects (39%) had "elevated" (in the highest quartile) Schizotypal Personality Characteristics Scale scores as compared to their Controls (26%) ($P< .003$). Further analyses revealed that these differences were accounted for by those exposed to the influenza epidemic in Week 23 (51% vs. 24%) of the sixth month ($P< .005$). Exploratory analyses for the other months did not reveal any significant differences. These findings replicated those of Venables (1996). (Note: Although the Venables study used a different standard for defining the pregnancy period [9 months vs. 40 weeks or 10 months], both studies report that exposure to maternal influenza *5 months prio*r to the birth of the fetus is associated with increased risk for schizotypy.)

The above findings (Machón et al., 2002) and those of Venables (1996) point to the relationship between positive features of schizotypy and prenatal influenza. We have previously reported that among patients with schizophrenia, those exposed to influenza in the second trimester had significantly higher levels of positive symptoms (delusions of jealousy, delusions of reference and suspiciousness) as compared to schizophrenics exposed in the first or third trimester or Controls (Machón et al., 1995). There is compelling evidence suggesting, "that schizotypal personality is related to schizophrenia in terms of common phenomenological, outcome and treatment response characteristics" (Siever, Bernstein, and Silverman, 1995, p. 71). This may suggest that maternal exposure to second trimester influenza increases the risk for some specific personality organization (positive features of schizotypy), which then places the individual at increased risk for later decompensation for schizophrenia depending on additional psychosocial and neuromaturational factors.

EARTHQUAKE (A NON-VIRAL "STRESSOR") AND SCHIZOTYPAL PERSONALITY

On 28 July 1976, a 7.9 (Richter scale) earthquake struck Tangshan, People's Republic of China. The epicenter of the quake was 5 miles east-by-northeast of Tangshan. The devastating effects of the quake included widespread destruction of houses and disruption of basic services. Countless numbers of Tangshan residents were injured; an estimated 240,000 people were killed. This catastrophic event (unpredictable and uncontrollable) represents a natural, quasi-experiment since all Tangshan women who were pregnant were stressed by the quake at the same instant. In a series of analyses recently completed, we assessed symptoms of schizotypal personality disorder in a group of 18-year-old high school students whose mothers experienced the Tangshan earthquake at various stages of pregnancy (the "Index" group). Their controls, born a year later, were not subjected to the earthquake (the "Control" group).

One aim of this study was to try to replicate, in an independent sample, our earlier findings from Finland implicating the sixth month, and in particular the 23rd week of gestation, and later schizotypal personality characteristics (Machón et al., 2002). For this study, we employed Raine's Schizotypy Personality Questionnaire-B (SPQ-B) to assess "schizotypy" (Raine et al., 1994; Raine and Benishay, 1995). The SPQ-B, which yields a total score and three subscale scores (Cognitive Perceptual disturbance; Interpersonal Deficit; and Disorganization), has been translated and validated in a Chinese population (Chen, Hsiao, and Lin, 1997).

It was hypothesized that among fetuses exposed to the 1976 Tangshan earthquake in their sixth month (weeks 21-24) of gestation (the Index group), we would observe higher mean scores on the SPQ-B as compared to their Controls born in the same month of the year but who were not exposed to the earthquake. We further predicted that among those Index subjects exposed in the sixth month, those in their 23rd week of gestation would show the highest SPQ-B scores as compared to their Controls.

The results indicated that Index subjects exposed in their sixth month of gestation (weeks 21-24 combined) showed a statistically significant higher mean SPQ-B Total Scale score as compared to their sixth month Controls (t [97.7] =2.04, $P < 0.04$). Index subjects exposed in their sixth month also showed a statistically significant higher mean SPQ-B subscale Cognitive Perceptual score as compared to their sixth month Controls (t [95.8] =2.0, $P < 0.049$). Index subjects exposed in the sixth month did not differ in their mean SPQ-B subscale Interpersonal Deficits score as compared to their sixth month Controls (t (122) =1.1, $P > 0.05$). There was a trend for Index subjects exposed in their sixth month to show higher mean SPQ-B subscale Disorganization scores as compared to their Controls but these differences did not reach statistical significance (t [122] =1.8, $P < 0.07$).

Based on our recent Finnish findings implicating the 23rd week in the sixth month of gestation as being relevant to schizotypal personality characteristics (Machón et al., 2002), we then tested whether the observed differences in the sixth month were attributable to differences in the 23rd week of gestation in this Chinese sample. As predicted, those Index subjects exposed in their 23rd week of gestation showed significantly higher mean SPQ-B Total Scale scores as compared to their 23rd week Controls (t [39] =2.1, $P < 0.039$). There was a trend for Index subjects exposed in their 23rd week of gestation to show higher SPQ-B subscale Cognitive Perceptual scores as compared to their Controls but these differences did not reach statistical significance (t (39) =1.6, $P < 0.10$). Index subjects exposed in the 23rd week did not differ in SPQ-B subscale Interpersonal Deficits score (3.2) as compared to their sixth month Controls (2.5) (t (39) =1.2, $P > 0.05$). Index subjects exposed in their 23rd week of gestation exhibited significantly higher SPQ-B subscale Disorganization scores (3.1) as compared to their Controls (1.9) (t (39) =2.3, $P < 0.028$).

Index subjects exposed in the 21st, 22nd or 24th weeks of gestation did not differ from Controls on either the SPQ-B Total Scale or the 3 SPQ-B subscales. We also compared Exposed Index group scores with their corresponding Controls on SPQ-B Total Scale and the 3 SPQ-B subscales for the other nine months of gestation (1-5 and 7-10) for which we had no hypothesis, adjusting the alpha level for these analyses with a Bonferroni correction set at 0.0055. No significant differences were noted.

Influenza and Violent Offenses

We then posed the following question: is second trimester exposure to maternal influenza associated with increased risk for violent criminal behaviors? To test this hypothesis we examined the same Helsinki cohort which had been exposed to the 1957 influenza pandemic (Mednick et al., 1988; Machón et al., 1997). We scanned the Criminal Registers in Finland for any evidence of criminal convictions. Routinely, less severe offenses are removed from the register after 2 years. Violent offenses are never removed (Tehrani, Brennan, Hodgins, and Mednick, 1998).

No statistically significant relationship was observed between exposure to maternal influenza in trimesters one, two or three and *property* crime. Convictions for violent crimes, however, were significantly related to exposure to second trimester maternal influenza. Those exposed to maternal influenza in trimester two evidenced significantly elevated convictions for severe violent offenses (41%) as compared to those exposed in trimester one (23%) or trimester three (26%) (Chi squared= 6.2, $P < .01$).

Critical Risk Period and Type of Deviance

Does the critical risk period differ for *type* of deviance? In order to address this question, we have examined the specific distribution of deviant outcomes (schizophrenia, major affective disorder and violent offenses) by month of birth of exposure. The results revealed a significantly larger cluster of the major affective disorder diagnoses in the *fifth* month of gestation. A significantly greater cluster of those with schizophrenia diagnoses tended to have been exposed to influenza in their *sixth* month of fetal life while those convicted for violent offenses tended to have been exposed to influenza in their *sixth and seventh* months of gestation. In toto, these findings seem to suggest that neurodevelopmental disturbances at different critical periods are associated with distinct deviant outcomes.

Mechanism of Action in the Pathogenesis of the Schizophrenia Spectrum

What mechanism or mechanisms might explain the pathogenesis of the schizophrenia spectrum findings? Huttunen (1971) previously reported that rats subjected to prenatal stress evidenced disturbances in brain neurochemistry and behavior after their births. More recent findings point to the key role that heat stress proteins play in regulating both the genetically and environmentally induced apoptosis of neuronal cells (Srivastava, 2002). These proteins represent a central reaction of the body cells against all kinds of stress and their levels are increased during fever, stress, etc. Their increase is known to distract the metabolism of fetal neurons from synaptic formation. This process may result in a failure of connection of the crucial neurons at a critical period (in the 23rd week) of the formation of connections.

McGlashan and Hoffman (2000) have proposed a model of schizophrenia as a disorder of developmentally reduced synaptic connectivity. Early neurobiological lesions (neurodevelopmental deficits) are major determinants of childhood synaptic density and vulnerability to psychosis. Deterioration to full-blown schizophrenia results from the vulnerable-to-psychosis brain system being subjected to a normal or abnormal, developmentally driven synaptic pruning process, which is accelerated during adolescence and young adulthood. Friston (2002) has posited an alternative mechanism. He proposes that the pathophysiology of schizophrenia is a disorder marked by synaptic abnormalities and dysfunctional connectivity. Thus, is schizophrenia a disorder of abnormal structural or functional/synaptic plasticity? Though these systems are commonly regarded as separate, they may represent two manifestations of a common, underlying process. A paradigm that integrates these two "non-independent" processes will undoubtedly advance our understanding of the etiology of schizophrenia spectrum disorders.

The Importance of Type of "Stressor" vs. Timing of the Stressor

The bulk of the epidemiological studies supporting the neurodevelopmental hypothesis has shown the importance of exposure to prenatal influenza and later adult psychiatric outcomes (Mednick et al., 1988; Bagalkote et al., 2001; Machón et al., 1997). Huttunen and Niskanen (1978) reported elevated rates of psychosis in the offspring of mothers who were informed during their second trimester of pregnancy that their husbands had been killed during war. Otake and Schull (1984) have noted that Hiroshima survivors who were second-trimester fetuses when the atomic bomb exploded later evidenced increased levels of adult, cognitive disturbances (mainly mental retardation). More recently, Selten et al. (1997) have reported that prenatal maternal exposure to severe stress (1953 Dutch flood) was associated with an increased risk for psychosis in the offspring. The recent Tanhshan China earthquake findings reported above are the first to link exposure to an earthquake with adverse psychological outcomes in young adulthood. These findings, as a whole, tend to support the interpretation that the timing of the "stressor" during relevant and critical brain neurodevelopment is the more salient factor than is the type of "stressor."

Conclusions and Future Directions

This paper examined the supporting evidence for a prenatal neurodevelopmental disturbance as one basis for a variety of deviant outcomes, including schizophrenia spectrum and major affective disorders, and violent crimes. A solid body of evidence has emerged suggesting that schizophrenia and other deviant outcomes may have, as one of their bases, an underlying neurodevelopmental etiology. This neurodevelopmental hypothesis posits that risk for deviant outcomes is produced by a disruption of normal brain development (particularly involving the mesolimbic system, the thalamus and the entorhinal regions) during a critical prenatal risk period in the second trimester. Disruptions in these neural processes, in turn, increase the probability of adult schizophrenia and other major mental disorders and crime. The studies reviewed above demonstrated links between a variety of teratogens (including influenza exposure, maternal stress, flood, earthquakes and radiation) and later, adult deviant outcomes. The evidence suggested that the timing of the teratogen is more critical than the type of teratogen in disrupting brain processes to increase the risk for these deviant outcomes.

This paper also examined whether the risk period differed as a function of type of deviance. Perhaps the most intriguing findings were that influenza exposure in the *sixth month only* was associated with increased schizophrenia diagnoses while exposure in the *sixth and seventh months* of fetal life was associated with an increase in convictions for violent crime. Is it possible that this overlap in risk period for both schizophrenia and violent crime explains the increased tendency for violence in a subpopulation of patients with schizophrenia? Further research is necessary to both replicate this basic finding and to more closely examine the pathogenesis of the violent crime-schizophrenia condition.

Acknowledgements

Ricardo A. Machón, Department of Psychology, Loyola Marymount University Los Angeles, One LMU Drive, Suite 4700, Los Angeles, California, 90045-2659, USA; E-mail RMACHON@LMU.EDU; Sarnoff A. Mednick, Social Science Research Institute, University of Southern California; Matti O. Huttunen, Department of Psychiatry, University of Helsinki, and Department of Mental Health and Alcohol Research, National Public Health Institute of Finland; and Antti Tanskanen, Department of Mental Health and Alcohol Research, National Public Health Institute of Finland.

This study was realized through funding from Dr. Joseph Jabbra, Academic Vice President, Loyola Marymount University Los Angeles (awarded to Dr. Machón). Dr. Machón wishes to recognize his Loyola Marymount University students who provided valuable assistance in the preparation of this manuscript---Ann Marie Dolan, Summer Tawalbeh, Maneka Deanna Brooks and Emma Zeledón.

References

Barr, C. E., Mednick, S. A., and Munk-Jørgenson, P. (1990). Exposure to influenza epidemics during gestation and adult schizophrenia: A 40-year study. *Archives of General Psychiatry, 47*, 869-874.

Bowler, A. E., and Torrey, E.F. (1990). Influenza and schizophrenia: Helsinki vs. Edinburgh. *Archives of General Psychiatry, 47*, 876-877.

Chen, W.J., Hsiao, C.K., and Lin, C.C.H., (1997). Schizotypy in community samples: The three-factor structure and correlation with sustained attention. *Journal of Abnormal Psychology, 106*, 649-654.

Crow, T. J., and Done, D. J. (1992). Prenatal exposure to influenza does not cause schizophrenia. *British Journal of Psychiatry, 161*, 390-392.

Fahy, T. A., Jones, P. B., Sham, P. C., Takei, N., and Murray, R. M. (1993). Schizophrenia in Afro-Caribbeans in the UK following prenatal exposure to the 1957 A_2 influenza pandemic. *Schizophrenia Research, 9*, 132.

Friston, K.J., 2002. Dysfunctional connectivity in schizophrenia. *World Psychiatry, 1*, 66-71.

Hakosalo, J. K., and Saxén, L. (1971). Influenza epidemic and congenital defects. *Lancet, 2*, 1346-1347.

Hale, F. (1933). Pigs born without eye balls. *Journal of Heredity, 24*, 104-106.

Huttunen, M.O., 1971. Persistent alteration of turnover of brain noradrenalin in the offspring of rats subjected to stress during pregnancy. *Nature, 35*, 53-55.

Huttunen, M.O., and Niskanen, P., (1978). Prenatal loss of father and psychiatric disorders. *Archives of General Psychiatry, 35*, 429-431.

Kendell, R., and Kemp, I. W. (1989). Maternal influenza in the etiology of schizophrenia. *Archives of General Psychiatry, 46*, 878-882.

Kunugi, H., Nankos, S., and Takei, N. (1992). Influenza and schizophrenia in Japan. *British Journal of Psychiatry, 160*, 274-275.

Machón, R. A., Huttunen, M. O., Mednick, S. A., Sinivuo, J., Tanskanen, A., Watson, J. et al. (2002). Adult schizotypal personality characteristics and prenatal influenza in a Finnish birth cohort. *Schizophrenia Research, 54*, 7-16.

Machón, R. A., Mednick, S. A., and Huttunen, M. O. (1995). Fetal viral infection and adult schizophrenia: Empirical findings and interpretation. In S. A. Mednick and J. M. Hollister (Eds.), *Neural development and schizophrenia: Theory and research. NATO ASI series. Series A: Life sciences Vol. 275* (pp 191-202). New York: Plenum Press.

Machón, R. A., Mednick, S. A., and Huttunen, M. O. (1997). Adult major affective disorder after prenatal exposure to an influenza epidemic. *Archives of General Psychiatry, 54*, 322-328.

McClure, W.O. (1995). Fetal development and schizophrenia: Historical observations from teratology. In S. A. Mednick and J. M. Hollister (Eds.), *Neural development and schizophrenia: Theory and research. NATO ASI series. Series A: Life sciences Vol. 275* (pp 13-25). New York: Plenum Press.

McGlashan, T.H., and Hoffman, R.E., (2000). Schizophrenia as a disorder of developmentally reduced synaptic connectivity. *Archives of General Psychiatry, 57*, 637-648.

McGrath, J. J., Pemberton, M. R., and Welham, J. L., (1993). Schizophrenia and the influenza epidemics of 1954, 1957 and 1959: A southern hemisphere study. *Schizophrenia Research, 14*, 1-8.

Mednick, S. A., Huttunen, M. O. and Machón, R. A. (1994). Prenatal influenza infections and adult schizophrenia. *Schizophrenia Bulletin, 20*(2), 263-267.

Mednick, S. A., Machón, R. A., Huttunen, M. O., and Bonett, D. (1988). Adult schizophrenia following prenatal exposure to an influenza epidemic. *Archives of General Psychiatry, 45*, 189-192.

Meyer, R. G. (1993). *The clinician's handbook: Integrated diagnostics, assessment and intervention in adult and adolescent psychopathology* (3rd ed.). Needham Heights, MA: Allyn and Bacon.

Nasrallah, H. A. (1991). Neurodevelopmental aspects of bipolar affective disorder. *Biological Psychiatry, 29*, 1-2.

O'Callaghan, E., Sham, P., Takei, N., Glover, G., and Murray, R. M. (1991). Schizophrenia after prenatal exposure to 1957 A_2 influenza epidemic. *Lancet, 337*, 1248-1250.

Olsen, S. C., Bogerts, B., Coffman, J. A., Schwarzkopf, S. B., and Nasrallah, H. A. (1990). Medial-temporal and ventricular abnormalities by MRI: Comparing major psychoses. *Biological Psychiatry, 27*, 59A-60A.

Otake, M., and Schull, M. J. (1984). In utero expsosure to A-bomb radiation and mental retardation: A reassessment. *British Journal of Radiology, 57*, 409-414.

Raine, A., and Benishay, D. (1995). The SPQ-B: A brief screening instrument for schizotypal personality disorder. *Journal of Personality Disorders, 9*, 346-355.

Raine, A., Reynolds, C., Lencz, T., Scerbo, A., Triphon, N., and Kim, D. (1994). Cognitive-perceptual, interpersonal and disorganized features of individual differences in schizotypal personality in the general population. *Schizophrenia Bulletin, 21*, 191-201.

Selten, J-P., and Slaets, J. P. J. (1994). Evidence against maternal influenza as a risk factor for schizophrenia. *British Journal of Psychiatry, 164*, 674-676.

Selten, J.P., van Duursen, R., van der Graaf, C., Gispen, W., and Kahn, R.S., (1997). Second-trimester exposure to maternal stress is a possible risk factor for psychotic illness in the child. *Schizophrenia Research 24*, 258.

Siever, L. J. Bernstein, D. P., and Silverman, J. M. (1995). Schizotypal personality disorder. In W. J. Livesley (Ed.), *The DSM-IV personality disorders* (pp. 71-90). New York: Guilford Press.

Srivastava, P., 2002. Roles of heat-shock proteins in innate and adaptive immunity. *Nature Reviews Immunology, 2,* 185-194.

Streissguth, A. P., Treder, R. P., and Barr, H. M. (1987). Aspirin and acetaminophen use by pregnant women and subsequent child IQ and attention decrements. *Teratology, 35*, 211-219.

Susser, E., Lin, S. P., Brown, A. S., Lumey, L. H., and Erlenmeyer-Kimling, L. No relation between risk of schizophrenia and prenatal exposure to influenza in Holland. *American Journal of Psychiatry, 151*, 922-924.

Tehrani, J. A., Brennan, P. A., Hodgins, S., and Mednick, S. A. (1998). Mental illness and criminal violence. *Social Psychiatry and Psychiatric Epidemiology, 33*, 81-85.

Venables, P. H. (1996). Schizotypy and maternal exposure to influenza and to cold temperature: The Mauritius study. *Journal of Abnormal Psychology, 105*(1), 53-60.

Yanai, J., Vatury, O., and Slotkin, T. A. (2002). Cell signaling as a target and underlying mechanism for neurobehavioral teratogenesis. *Annals of the New York Academies of Sciences, 965*, 473-478.

In: Crime and Schizophrenia: Causes and Cures
Editor: Adrian Raine, pp. 179-201

ISBN 1-59454-609-6

Chapter 10

FETAL ORIGINS OF ANTISOCIAL PERSONALITY DISORDER AND SCHIZOPHRENIA: EVIDENCE FROM THE DUTCH HUNGER WINTER 1944-45

Richard Neugebauer[1, 2, 3, 4] and Ezra Susser[1,5]
[1] Epidemiology of Developmental Brain Disorders Department, New York State Psychiatric Institute, New York, NY
[2] G.H. Sergievsky Center, Columbia University, New York, NY
[3] International Program on Refugee Trauma, New York, N.Y.
[4] The Department of International Health and Development, School of Public Health and Tropical Medicine, Tulane University
[5] Department of Epidemiology, Mailman School of Public Health, Columbia University, New York, N.Y.

INTRODUCTION

Risk factors for mortality and morbidity are divisible into three categories: those present before conception, others occurring postpartum and finally, those that operate in the interval between conception and birth. Until comparatively recently, this last period received limited attention in epidemiological research on psychiatric and (to a lesser degree) other disorders first emerging beyond the childhood years. One notable exception is the early and sustained interest in possible prenatal viral etiology of schizophrenia. Nonetheless, the operation of genetic factors, present at conception, and of macro and micro-level environmental factors, in the postnatal period were the primary focus of attention.

The past two decades have witnessed a growing interest in the prenatal and perinatal origins of adolescent and adult onset somatic and psychiatric diseases. Early, ground breaking work by Ravelli in the 1970s on prenatal nutrition and adult onset obesity (Ravelli et al., 1976) was followed two decades later by studies on low birth weight and raised risk for cardiovascular disease (Barker, 2003a; Barker, 2003b; Roseboom et al., 2001; Leon, 2001; Harding, 2001) A separate vein of research, emerging in the 1980s, examined prenatal and perinatal factors in risk for psychiatric disorders, initially motivated by an interest in a 'neurodevelopmental hypothesis' of schizophrenaia (Cannon, Kendell, Susser and Jones, 2003), now broadened to include a life course approach to neuropsychiatric disorders (Terry and Susser, 2001). These two research initiatives link the knowledge of established perinatal risk factors for diseases of early life, acquired through several decades of pediatric and perinatal epidemiologic research, with an equally extensive literature on the distribution and determinants of adult onset disorders, thereby creating conditions for a greatly enhanced understanding of both the proximal and distal etiologies of disease and dysfunction across the life span. Some initial scientific insights yielded by this approach in the area of psychiatric disorders, specifically, of ASPD (ASPD) and schizophrenia, are the subject of the present chapter.

HISTORICAL DISASTER, EPIDEMIOLOGICAL OPPORTUNITY: DUTCH HUNGER WINTER 1944-1945

In October 1944, the German army blockaded food supplies to the Western Netherlands as punishment for Dutch involvement in the planned Allied invasion of Europe. Before the October blockade, the food supply had been adequate; in May 1945, following the German retreat, it became plentiful again. In the intervening months, however, the Dutch population, particularly in the larger cities, received increasingly meager food rations, a circumstance that was rendered even more difficult by an especially harsh winter (Burger, Drummond, and Sandstead, 1947). Hence, Dutch women who were pregnant in October 1944, and others who conceived in the following months, experienced declining food supplies at varying points in gestation.

This wartime catastrophe, occurring in a previously well nourished industrialized nation, created a strategic epidemiological opportunity to examine the association of prenatal nutritional deficiency of varying intensity imposed at different points in intrauterine development with postnatal health and cognitive outcomes. Zena Stein and Mervyn Susser were the first researchers to appreciate the potential of this historical disaster to yield a rich harvest of epidemiological good. The fundamental design of the present analyses is based upon the initial work of these investigators, Famine and Human Development (Stein et al., 1975). While the work of Stein and Susser focused on the impact of prenatal malnutrition on measured intelligence of male offspring at age 18, the historical conditions created by the Dutch Famine continue to offer a unique research opportunity for evaluating the increasingly longer term effects of this complex prenatal exposure on health and disease at each stage of the advancing life cycle of the exposed individuals.

The findings reported in this chapter link in utero famine exposure to ASPD and schizophrenia, thereby providing important evidence of a possible association between prenatal nutrition, brain development and subsequent postnatal psychopathology. The sections on each disorder begin with a brief account of findings from other investigations adopting a neurodevelopmental perspective, followed by a detailed account of our study methods, analysis, findings and conclusions. With each set of findings, we include an essential examination of alternative explanations and study limitations.

ANTISOCIAL PERSONALITY DISORDER

Background

The causes of antisocial behavior, of ASPD and of its developmental precursor, conduct disorder, have received macro-level research attention for many decades. Striking regional differences and rapid secular variations in rates of violent crime argue persuasively for the profound influence of social, economic and community forces on antisocial behavior (Olds et al., 1998; Sampson, Raudenbush and Earls,1997). Nonetheless, biological, especially micro-level environmental, risk factors for antisocial behavior, including prenatal and perinatal factors, have garnered increasing scientific, public health, and policy interest, (Reiss, and Roth., 1993) especially when such factors may be amenable to intervention.

Most research in this field on humans (as contrasted with animal models) has necessarily been confined to observational studies. Numerous case control investigations have examined whether perinatal or obstetric complications occur more frequently among persons with a criminal record as compared with non-criminals (Raine, 1993). Prospective studies have tested whether the offspring of women with prenatal or obstetric complications have an increased risk for violent criminal offending as compared with offspring of women with comparatively unremarkable pregnancies. The authors of one study (Raine et al., 1994) found that such complications conferred risk only when conditioned on maternal rejection in the first postnatal year.

Despite the design strengths of these studies, especially of the cohort studies, research to date has several limitations both general and specific to the disorder under investigation. As with all non-experimental work, it is not possible to rule out confounding or alternative explanations of associations observed between hypothesized risk factors and health outcomes of interest. With regard to alternative explanations, for example, it is noteworthy that several risk factors (e.g., socioeconomic status, neighborhood crime rates) for adverse reproductive outcomes (e.g., obstetric complications) are also independent risk factors for antisocial behavior. As a consequence, findings of an association between perinatal complications and violent criminal offending may be entirely artifactual.

Many studies measure perinatal risk with a single numerical index that combines maternal, pregnancy, obstetric, and neonatal complications. Some of these conditions pertain to the mother's health and are often present before and throughout the pregnancy (e.g., maternal chronic illness). Other adversities arise only late in gestation, at the time of labor or delivery (e.g., breach presentation). Yet others pertain to the neonate (e.g., prolonged respiratory distress). Collapsing these diverse complications into a single index creates difficulties for identifying critical periods and distinct factors in embryonic life crucial to the development of behavioral disturbance. It also obscures clues to neuropathological mechanisms and to the appropriate timing of possible intervention strategies.

We hypothesized a priori that exposure to maternal nutritional deficiency during gestation increases offspring's risk for ASPD. Early gestation as contrasted with later gestation was seen as a potentially critical period of risk since prenatal insults and toxic exposures in the 1st and 2nd trimesters had been implicated in raised rates of central nervous system anomalies and neurodevelopmental disorders (Stein et al., 1975; Kline, Stein, and

Susser, 1989). In addition, minor physical anomalies originating early in gestation are reported in excess in persons with conduct disorder and aggression in childhood and violent offending in adulthood (Mednick and Kandel, 1988; Brennan, Mednick, and Kandel, 1993; Baker and Mednick, 1984; Paulus and Martin, 1986; Halverson and Victor , 1976; Waldrop et al., 1978).Nonetheless, since temporally precise understanding of embryonic development and antisocial behavior was sparse, we elected not to advance any more specific hypotheses regarding risk periods a priori (Neugebauer et al., 1999).

Methods for Studying Antisocial Personality Disorder

Exposure

Geographic Regions and Cities

Food was rationed weekly in Holland during World War II. For rationing purposes, the government divided the country into 3 regions. The first, Western Holland, was the region where the blockade exerted its greatest force. Consequently, it is hereafter referred to as the "Famine Region". The remaining area was split into North and South, which for parsimony, we combine analytically into a single "Non-famine Region". We studied men born only in the cities throughout the Netherlands with populations exceeding 40 000 (in the Famine Region, Amsterdam, Haarlem, Leiden, Rotterdam, Utrecht and Hague) since the blockade was felt most strongly in larger urban areas (Stein et al., 1975).

Nutritional Intake .Estimates of maternal nutritional intake are based on the caloric content of the food rations and calculated for each trimester of pregnancy. Moderate nutritional deficiency is defined as mean daily rations of 1000-1500 k calories (kcal/d); severe nutritional deficiency, mean daily rations of less than 1000 kcal for the duration of a given trimester. The biological validity of the 1000 kcal/d cut point is supported by a previous finding that risk for perinatal mortality increased only at or below this level. In the Famine Region, the rations declined to less than 1000 k cal/d from February 1945 through early May 1945. Special supplements to pregnant women, available previously, were discontinued; those for infants through the first postnatal year were maintained. In the Non-Famine Region, daily rations declined to less than 1500 kcal/d but not less than 1000 kcal/d. Natural ingenuity and social privileged moderated the impact of war to some degree. Rations were enhanced by nutritional intake from other sources such as foraging for food in rural areas. The upper classes generally had more access to non-ration food than did the low classes. Nevertheless, data on fertility and other outcomes indicate a high correlation between actual food intake and official rations.

Specification of Exposures by Trimester

Men born between January 1, 1944 and December 31, 1946 inclusive are divided into 36 monthly birth cohorts. For each cohort in each region (Famine, Non-Famine) mean daily caloric content of the official ration during the 1st, 2nd and 3rd trimesters of their intrauterine life, were calculated. Moderate food deprivation occurred in both regions during 1944-1945; severe nutritional deficiency, only in the Famine Region.

Famine Region

Using the above approach, males born from February 1945 through December 1945 in the famine region (corresponding to conceptions from May 1944 through March 1945) were classified as prenatally exposed to severe nutritional deficiency. Among these individuals, men born in February, March, and April were exposed to severe nutritional deficiency in the 3rd trimester only; in May, June, and July, in the 2nd trimester only; born in August and September, in the 1st and 2nd trimesters only; born in October through December, in the 1st trimester only. Men born from September 1944 through January 1945 and in January 1946 (corresponding to conceptions from December 1943 through April 1944 and conceptions in April 1945) were classified as moderately exposed during one or more trimesters and otherwise adequately nourished. The remaining men--those born before the calendar period of moderate or severe nutritional deficiency and those conceived after these periods--were combined to form a single unexposed comparison group. The mean daily maternal food ration per trimester for these months always exceeded 1500 kcal.

Non-Famine Region

In the Non-Famine Region, men born in the north from September 1944 to November 1945 and in the south from 1944 to August 1945 were classified as prenatally exposed to moderate nutritional deficiency. The remaining monthly birth cohorts, during which maternal mean daily intake per trimester always exceeded 1500 kcal, constitute the unexposed comparison group.

Measure of Outcome

In the 1960s, when the surviving male children born during the period 1944-1946 reached their 18th birthday, they were called up for military service and received physical, psychiatric and IQ examinations at induction centers. The examinee's date and place of birth indexed whether, to what degree and in which trimesters he was exposed to prenatal malnutrition. Linkage of any psychiatric diagnostic information with these data on date and place of birth permits a test of the association of prenatal exposure to maternal nutritional deficiency with development of ASPD by age 18 years. The diagnoses of institutionalized individuals (e.g., persons with severe mental retardation) were made based on requested medical records. Each individual could receive up to 2 diagnoses. Clergy, police, long-term prisoners, emigrants, and men with 3 older brothers who had been in the service, comprising altogether roughly 3% of potentially eligible individuals, were exempt from examination (Stein et al., 1975).

Diagnostic Criteria

Examining physicians performed psychiatric evaluations using the Dutch version of the International Classification of Diseases, Sixth Edition (ICD6) (World Health Organization, 1948; Manual of International Classification of Diseases, Injuries, and Causes of Death, Adapted 1948). While formal diagnostic criteria are not delineated in the early ICDs, descriptions of "ASPD" in Dutch psychiatric texts (Carp, 1947; Zeldenrust, 1966) from the late 1940s to the 1960s make clear that it approximates current criteria enumerated in the

Diagnostic and Statistical Manual of Mental Disorders, Fourth Edition (American Psychiatric Association, 1994) ASPD was characterized by aggression, failure to conform to social norms with respect to lawful behavior (e.g., thievery and other frank criminal acts), and disregard for the truth (e.g., swindling, conning, etc.). In addition, behavioral instability and unreliability, outbursts of anger, and other interpersonal problems marked the person's childhood. In the current study persons with a primary or secondary diagnosis of ASPD constitute cases.

Other Variables in the Military Induction Examination Data Base

In addition to birth date and place, the records also contain information on social class (indexed by father's occupation), IQ (i.e., Ravens Progressive Matrices), sibship size, birth order, height, and weight.

Data Analysis

The association of nutritional deficiency with ASPD was estimated using odds ratios (ORs), 95% confidence intervals (CIs), and, in multivariate analyses, maximum likelihood logistic regression (Hosmer and Lemeshow, 1989). The first analyses are conducted in the Famine Region. The odds of having ASPD among men exposed prenatally to severe nutritional deficiency and moderate nutritional deficiency are compared with the reference odds of having ASPD among men unexposed either to severe or moderate malnutrition. The second analysis is conducted in the Non-Famine Region. The odds of having ASPD among men exposed to moderate nutritional deficiency is compared with the odds among unexposed men. In the third analysis, the odds of having ASPD following severe prenatal nutritional deficiency in the Famine Region is refined further by specifying trimester(s) of exposure. Under the conditions prevailing in the current study, rarity of disease outcome, the odds ratios generated by these analyses approximates a risk ratio.

Based on a review of the published literature we identified the following potential confounding variables and other correlates of conduct disorder and ASPD: birth order, height, weight, and body mass index (BMI, calculated as weight in kilograms divided by the square of height in meters), IQ, sibship size and social class (Pine et al., 1986; Raine, 1994). Using a change of greater than 10% in the odds ratio of interest as the criterion for retaining a variable in the logistic model, only social class was a requisite covariate in the multivariable model. Both observed odds ratios and odds ratios adjusted for social class are presented in the tables while only adjusted odds ratios are discussed in the text.

In the Famine Region, an increased odds of having ASPD in severely exposed cohorts compared with unexposed cohorts might reflect a coincidental countrywide excess for the calendar period corresponding to famine exposure. We tested this question with a fourth analysis based on the entire sample of Dutch men entering terms for the main effect of region, social class, and famine exposure months, and an interaction term for region by exposure months. Specific probability values at $p<.10$ or less are reported in the text. However, in all analyses, statistical significance was set at $p<.05$.

Sample

Military examinations were conducted for 100,543 Dutch men born in Holland's larger cities (defined previously) from January 1944 to December 1946 who were residing in Holland at age 18 years. Analyses presented below pertain to this group only. (Table 1) Among the 68,932 men born in the Famine Region, 14,310 were exposed prenatally to severe nutritional deficiency during 1 or more trimesters of intrauterine life; 9615 to moderate nutritional deficiency only; 31, 45,007 were unexposed. Among the 31611 individuals born in the Non-Famine region, 10 517 were exposed prenatally to moderate nutritional deficiency; 21,094 were unexposed.

Table 1. Distribution of Men Born in Major Dutch Cities* 1944 -1946 Residing in the Netherlands at Age 18 Years by Geographic Region, Calendar Year and Prenatal Exposure to Maternal Nutritional Deficiency

		Exposed (Born 1944-1946)					
			Severe Exposure (<1000 kcal/d)± Trimester of Exposure:				
Geo-graphic Region	Unexposed (>1500 kcal/d, Born 1944) ++	Moderate Exposure (1000-1500kcal/d) §	1st Only	1st/ 2nd Only	2nd Only	3rd Only	Unexposed (>1500 kcal/d Born 1945-1946)^
Western Holland	13929	9615	2443	2223	4586	5058	31078
Northern/ Southern Holland¶	6335	10517	...	...	...	...	14759

*Major Dutch cities comprise cities with populations exceeding 40,000 people

± Groups comprise in western Holland, men born from October through December 1945 with first-trimester exposure only, men born in August through September 1945 with first and second-trimester exposure, men born from May through July 1945 with second-trimester exposure only, and men born February through April 1945 with third-trimester exposure only

++ Groups comprise men born between January and August 1944 in western, southern and northern Holland

§ Groups comprise, in western Holland, men born from September 1944 through January 1945 and in January 1946, in northern Holland, men born from September 1944 through November 1945, and in southern Holland, men born from September 1944 through August 1945. Men born in January 1946 were exposed to moderate prenatal nutritional deficiency in the first trimester of pregnancy but were well nourished thereafter.

^Groups comprise, in western Holland, men born from February through December 1946, in northern Holland, men born from December 1945 through December 1946, in southern Holland, men born from September 1945 through December 1946.

In northern Holland, 2761, 4889, and 6154 were unexposed in 1944, moderately exposed in 1944-1945, and unexposed in 1945-1946, respectively. The corresponding figures in southern Holland were 3574, 5628, and 8605. Ellipses indicate persons that residing in northern and southern Holland were not exposed to severe nutritional deficiency.

Results

In the Famine Region, the odds of ASPD were elevated among men with severe but not with moderate prenatal nutritional deficiency. The adjusted odds ratios were 2.0 (95% CI 1.2-3.3) and 0.7 (0.3-1.6), respectively (Table 2) These individuals in the Famine Region were sub-grouped further by trimester of exposure to severe nutritional deficiency (Table 3) to examine whether the increased odds of ASPD applied equally throughout gestation, varied by trimester or was possibly confined to only one or two trimesters. Odds ratios for 1st and/or 2nd-trimester exposures ranged from 2.1 to 3.0 and did not differ significantly from each other. The odds of ASPD were not increased as a consequence of exposure to third-trimester nutritional deficiency. (The difference in odds between 1st and/or 2nd-trimester exposure and third-trimester exposure was statistically significant at P<.10.)

Table 2. Association Between Antisocial Personality Disorder (ASPD) in Dutch Men at Age 18 Years and Moderate or Severe Prenatal Nutritional Deficiency: Western Holland (Famine Region), 1944-1946

Level of Nutritional Deficiency*	Population N	Cases of ASPD N	Prevalence of ASPD per 10,000	OR (95% CL), Observed/Adjusted±
Severe (<1000 kcal/d)	14310	26	18.2	1.6 (1.02-2.6)/2.0 (1.2-3.3)
Moderate (1000-1500 kcal/d)	9615	10	10.4	0.9 (0.6-1.9)/0.7 (0.3-1.6)
Unexposed (>1500 kJcal/d)	45007	50	11.1	Reference

*Value pertains to average daily rations during 1 or more trimesters of pregnancy. For calendar birth dates corresponding to exposure categories, see "Methods" section of text.

± OR indicates odds ratio; CI, confidence interval, ORs to the right of the virgules are adjusted for social class (manual laborers including farmers and nonmanual laborers). The comparison between the odds of antisocial personality disorder associated with moderate vs severe exposure is statistically significant; the comparison between the moderately exposed and unexposed is not

Table 3. Association Between Antisocial Personality Disorder and Severe Prenatal Nutritional Deficiency in Dutch Men at Age 18 Years Over and by Trimester of Exposure: Western Holland (Famine Region), 1944-1946

Trimester of Exposure*	Population N	Cases of ASPD N	Prevalence of ASPD per 10,000	OR (95% CI), Observed/Adjusted ±
1, 2, or 3	14310	26	18.2	1.6 (1.02-2.6)/2.0 (1.2-3.3)
1 and/or 2	9252	20	21.6	2.0 (1.2-3.5)/2.5 (1.5-4.2)
1 only	2443	6	24.6	2.2 (0.95-5.0)/2.9 (1.2-6.7)
1 and 2 only	2223	6	27.0	2.4 (1.04-5.7)/3.0 (1.3-7.0)
2 only	4586	9	19.6	1.8 (0.9-3.6)/2.1(1.03-4.4)
3 only	5058	5	9.9	0.9 (0.4-2.2)/1.1 (0.4-2.7)
Unexposed	45007	50	11.1	Reference

*Values pertain to average daily rations during 1 or more trimesters of pregnancy. For calendar birth dates corresponding to exposure categories, see "Methods" section of text.

±OR indicates odds ration; CI, confidence interval. ORs to the right of the virgules are adjusted for social class (manual laborers (including farmers) and nonmanual laborers).

In the Non-Famine Region, the odds of ASPD was not associated with moderate nutritional deficiency (adjusted OR, 1.0; 95% CI, 0.6-1.7). In a nation wide analysis the elevated odds of having ASPD was restricted to men born in the Famine Region exposed to severe nutritional deficiency. Individuals conceived in the Non-Famine Region during the same calendar period of the blockade at its severest point, but unexposed to severe maternal nutritional deficiency, did not exhibit increased rates of ASPD. Thus, the excess ASPD rate was confined to the Famine Region and the calendar period of severe nutritional deficiency.

SCHIZOPHRENIA

Background

Our schizophrenia investigation (Susser, Neugebauer and Hoek, 1996) predated and served as the template for the work on ASPD. The neurodevelopmental hypothesis of the etiology of schizophrenia, like that for ASPD, posits that a disruption of early brain development produced in the prenatal or perinatal period exercises a causal role in a substantial proportion of schizophrenia cases. This hypothesis is supported by converging evidence from a variety of fields, including longitudinal studies of high risk offspring and research on neuro-imagining and neuropathology (Marenco and Weinberger, 2000; Murray, Jones, Susser, Van Os and Cannon, 2003).

If the interval from conception to birth comprises a period of biological vulnerability to factors that influence risk for schizophrenia, what particular factors warrant attention? A host of plausible risk factors have been advanced, in addition to the nutritional hypothesis considered here, including season of birth, i.e., an excess of winter/spring births; Rhesis incompatibility; obstetric complications as well as certain neonatal infections (Cannon, Kendell, Susser, Jones, 2003).

Two other factors warrant brief separate mention: prenatal infection and maternal stress. Suspected prenatal infectious, notably viral, etiologies have a long pedigree. Most studies have demonstrated that individuals in utero during influenza epidemics evidence increased rates of schizophrenia, with 2nd trimester exposure contributing most to these results. Rubella, a known cause of neurodevelopmental anomalies and a risk factor for autism, has been implicated in our own recent work in risk for non-affective psychosis, including schizophrenia (Susser, Brown and Matte, 1999; Brown et al., 2004).

Three studies of the potential role of prenatal maternal stress in the etiology of schizophrenia in offspring are especially noteworthy in the current context. One investigation reported increased risk for schizophrenia among the posthumous children of men who died in the Russo-Finnish war in 1939 (Huttenen and Niskanen, 1978); a second, increased risk for schizophrenia among individuals in utero at the time of the May 1940 German invasion of the Netherlands (Van Os and Selden, 1998); a third, increased risk for schizophrenia associated with prenatal exposure to a severe tornado (Kinney, Hyman, Geetham and Tramer, 1999) Extensive animal literature affords evidence that prenatal maternal stress alters fetal brain development and subsequent offspring behavior (Suomi, 1997), an effect thought to be mediated by the impact of glucocorticoid on the fetal hypothalamo-pituitary-adrenal axis (Cannon, Kendell, Susser, Jones, 2003) However, stress-related depressed appetite and consequent reduction in food intake associated with bereavement (in the case of the Finnish study) or with distress generally might also contribute to these findings.

Methods for Studying Schizophrenia and Famine

The methods of determining kcal/d, applying these values to trimesters, and the division into Famine and Non-Famine Regions are the same as in the study of ASPD, both patterned on Stein et al. (1975).

Exposure

Geographic Regions and Cities

Preliminary work on famine and schizophrenia (Susser and Lin, 1992) investigated the possible impact of prenatal exposure to varying degrees of maternal nutritional deficiency in the Famine and Non-Famine Regions. Given space limitations here we focus exclusively on the subsequent, definitive elaboration of findings for the Famine Region only.

Refinement of Exposure Criteria: Restriction by Severity and Trimester

The identification of the 1st and 2nd trimesters of gestation as critical periods for the later development of ASPD, while striking, was nonetheless largely post hoc. By contrast, previous work examining neurodevelopmental hypotheses for schizophrenia enabled us to proceed with a more precise a prior hypothesis regarding both the timing and the degree of the prenatal nutritional insult. Consequently, we were able to formulate a strict exposure algorithm.

Three criteria were used to define exposed birth cohorts: (1) low maternal food rations during the 1st trimester of intrauterine life, (2) conception at the height of the famine, and (3) increased frequency of congenital neural defects among individuals comprising the cohort. Regarding the first criterion, average food rations during the 1st trimester were below 1000 kcal/d for individuals born between August and December 1945. These cohorts were defined as exposed to low rations. All other birth cohorts were defined as unexposed. For the second criterion, we relied on the documented health outcomes of the famine period, indicating that the height of the famine was toward the end of the Hunger Winter (February through April 1945). The population was nutritionally depleted, and the effects on morbidity and mortality most severe (Stein et al., 1975; Burger, Drummond, and Sandstead, 1947). Among the cohorts of August through December 1945, only the later born (October 15 through December 31, 1945) were conceived during the height of the famine and, therefore, also met our second criterion for exposure. We shall refer to these later born as the EX2 cohort. The earlier born (August 1 through October 14, 1945) were conceived in the early months of the Hunger Winter and did not meet our second criterion for exposure. Owing to the timing of their conception, the EX2 cohort was marked by fertility below 50% of previous levels; the EX1 cohort suffered a smaller decline in fertility.

With regard to the third exposure criterion, we computed the risk in the EX2, EX1 and unexposed cohorts for congenital neural defects with established or strongly suspected links with early prenatal nutritional deficiency. (For details on databases and computational methods employed in these analyses see Susser et al., 1975.) The EX2 cohort had a detectable excess of congenital neural defects, while the EX1 cohort did not exhibit any such excess. Examination of secular trends for the entire period 1944-46 also provided compelling evidence of a pronounced peak in risk for congenital neural defects in the EX2 cohort. Thus, the exposed birth cohorts comprised two distinct groups: the EX2 cohort which met all three exposure criteria's the EX1 cohort met only one of the three criteria.

Outcome

Since the median age of onset for schizophrenia is in the 20's, the military induction examination data were not useful for investigation of this outcome. Consequently, we utilized the Dutch National psychiatric registry to ascertain cases of schizophrenia for the proposed analyses. At the time of our study, registry data were available for 1970 through 1992, comprising persons 24 to 48 years of age for the birth cohorts of 1944 through 1946. Data on cases were derived from psychiatric and university hospitals, which account for more than 90% of psychiatric admissions in the Netherlands. Data on each case included ICD-8-ICD-9 (World Health Organization, 1938) diagnosis, place of birth, and week of birth.

Two definitions of schizophrenia were employed: narrow and broad. "Narrowly defined" included only those cases in which the ICD-8ICD-9 diagnosis was that of paranoid, hebephrenic, residual, or catatonic schizophrenia,' in accordance with the modern criteria for the disorder (American Psychiatric Association, 1994). While severely limiting the number of cases available for analysis, this definition reduced the risk of misclassifying affective psychoses as schizophrenia. "Broadly defined" comprised all cases with an ICD-9 diagnosis of schizophrenia, irrespective of the subtype. Individuals were classified based on their most recent discharge diagnosis.

Other Variables in the Dutch Psychiatric Registry Data Base

For each case reported by the registry, the only data provided were the birth date, birth place, gender, number and date of each psychiatric admission and diagnosis at each admission.

Data Analysis

The risks for schizophrenia in the EX2 cohort, the EX I cohort, and the unexposed cohort were computed by dividing the number of schizophrenia cases by the number of births minus deaths up to age 18 years in each cohort. Each quotient was expressed as a cumulative incidence per 1000 persons. Relative risks (RR) were calculated together with 95% CLs (Fleiss, 1981). The chi-square statistic was used to test the null hypothesis of no association between exposure and disease. Seasonal and other fluctuations in the rate of schizophrenia were examined by dividing the birth cohorts of 1944-46 into smaller cohorts, each of 2 months duration. However, to maintain the integrity of the EX 1 and EX2 cohorts, the period of May through December 1945 was divided into just three periods: May through July, August 1 through October 14 (EX1), and October 15 through December 31 (EX2). (For further details regarding both the rationale and mechanics of these computations see Susser, Neugebauer and Hoek, 1996)

Sample

The entire study cohort comprised 146,347 individuals with 93.4% classified as unexposed to severe prenatal malnutrition in their 1st trimester. Among the remaining individuals, 2.9% were in the EX1 cohort (n=5466) and 3.7% in the EX2 (n=4190) cohort.

Results

With regard to narrowly defined schizophrenia, risk was significantly higher in the EX2 cohort than in the unexposed cohort (Table 4) (RR=2.0; 95% CI = 1.2 to 3.4; P<.01). The RR did not vary by gender; among men, the RR=1.9 (95% Cl = 1.0 to 3.7; P=.05), and among women, the RR = 2.2 (95% Cl = 1.0 to 4.7; P=.04). The risk for schizophrenia was not increased in the EX1 cohort. The Figure shows the risk for schizophrenia in 17 successive two month birth cohorts of 1944 through 1946. The risk for schizophrenia peaked in the EX2 cohort and was otherwise stable.

We reanalyzed the finding for the EX2 cohort under a broad definition of schizophrenia and using other procedures for selecting the diagnosis. The association between early prenatal exposure to famine and schizophrenia was consistent under six approaches.

Table 4. Schizophrenia* in Birth Cohorts Exposed± and Unexposed± to Early Prenatal Nutritional Deficiency During the Dutch Hunger Winter of 1944 Through 1945: Cumulative Incidence Data

Level of Nutritional Deficiency	Population N	Cumulative Incidence per 1000 persons++(N cases)	Relative risk at age 24-48 y (95% CI) P
Total			
EX 2	4190	3.8 (16)	2.0 (1.2 – 3.4) <.01
EX 1	5466	2.0 (11)	1.1 (0.6 – 2.0) .82
Unexposed	136,691	1.9 (257)	-----
Men			
EX 2	2184	4.1 (9)	1.9 (1.0-3.7) .05
EX 1	2800	2.5 (7)	1.2 (0.5-2.5) .70
Unexposed	69,943	2.2 (151)	-----
Women			
EX 2	2006	3.5 (7)	2.2 (1.0-4.7) .04
EX 1	2666	1.5 (4)	0.9 (0.4-2.6) .91
Unexposed	68,748	1.6 (106)	-----

*Schizophrenia narrowly defined, ie, ICD-9 (International Classification of Diseases, Ninth Revision) 295.1,2,3,6.

± EX2 indicates exposed birth cohort of October 15 through December 31, 1945; EX1, exposed birth cohort of August 1 through October 14, 1945; and unexposed, all other births of 1944 through 1946 in famine cities.

++ Denominators are live births minus deaths up to age 18 years

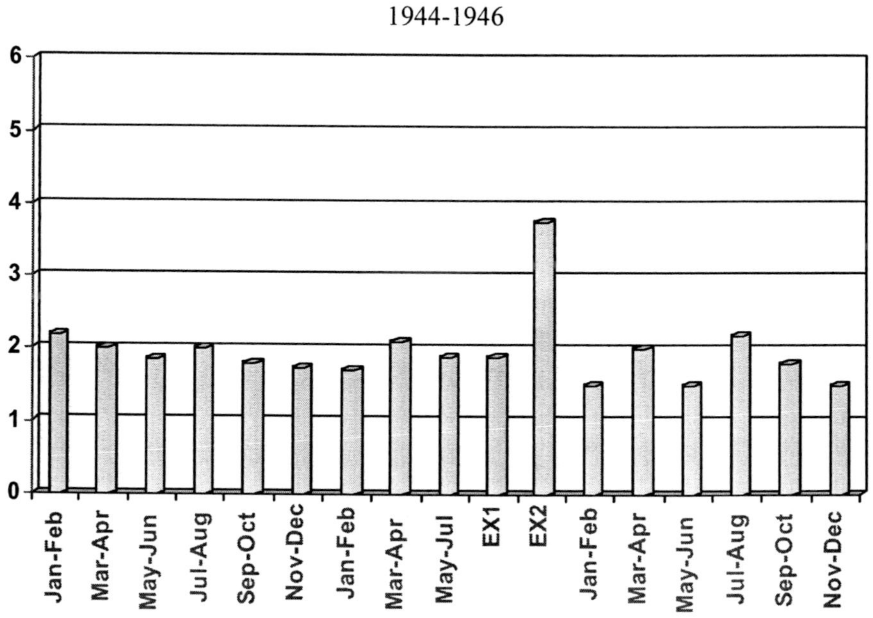

Figure 1. Schizophrenia in adulthood (hospitalized cases of 24 to 48 years of age) in Dutch birth cohorts of 1944 through 1946. EX1 and EX2 represent cohorts born August 1 - October 14, 1945, and October 15 - December 31, 1945, respectively; bar, 95% confidence limits

Summary of Findings for Antisocial Personality Disorder and Schizophrenia

These studies offer evidence of a relationship between early prenatal nutritional deficiency and the risk for ASPD and for schizophrenia in offspring. The ASPD findings suggest that exposure to severe nutritional deficiency in the 1st and/or 2nd trimesters of intrauterine life is associated with a 2-3 fold increased risk for development of ASPD among males. Exposure at other times and to only moderate nutritional deficiency does not confer risk. No information was available on this question for females. The schizophrenia findings suggest that exposure early in gestation at the height of the Dutch Hunger Winter (EX2) doubled risk for schizophrenia both in males and females. This increased risk was evident under all definitions of schizophrenia, but most marked under a narrow definition consistent with modern criteria. Taken together, the notable specificity in these outcomes and in the exposure enhances the credibility of these findings for both disorders.

Strength of the Study Design

The origin of the nutritional exposure under study in a large-scale, geographically and temporally delimited historical conflict, driven by forces extrinsic to those that pattern disease in Dutch society, confers several methodological and inferential strengths on these findings.

First, the Dutch Hunger Winter permits an examination of the effect of a relatively specific antenatal insult--nutritional deprivation. Second, the timing of the exposure in prenatal development can be identified with unique precision. Third, the community-wide nature of the exposure and its imposition by military force created a quasi-experimental condition likely to reduce the effect of potentially confounding factors.

Pursuing the example of potential confounding offered at the outset of this chapter, in peacetime low socioeconomic status is a risk factor for adverse reproductive outcomes such as birth complications which have been implicated in violent criminal offending in adulthood. Low socioeconomic status is also a risk factor for antisocial behavior. An observed association between birth complications and antisocial behavioral therefore may be an artifact of confounding. By contrast, the specific risk factor under study here—severe nutritional deficiency—was introduced by foreign blockade whose distribution, timing and to a large degree intensity was governed by forces acting entirely independent of the class structure of Dutch society. Fourth, the absence of severe nutritional deficiency in the Non-Famine Region allows a test of whether the increased odds of developing ASPD or schizophrenia reflected some countrywide rise in 1944-45 unrelated to the nutritional crisis. Finally, the restriction of the sample to 18-year old men in the ASPD analysis eliminated an extraneous source of variance, i.e., age, in the dependent measure, thereby affording a more precise estimate of effect.

Replication of the Dutch Famine Schizophrenia Findings: Study of the Chinese Famine 1959-61

A recent study of schizophrenia among persons exposed in utero to the Chinese Famine that occurred in 1959-61 offers a substantial and important replication of the Dutch results (St. Clair, Zu, Wang , Yu, Fang, Zhang, Zheng, Gu, Feng, Sham , He , 2005). Among persons born in a famine-affected region in China 1960, the adjusted relative risk for schizophrenia (based on psychiatric hospital inpatient and outpatient data) was 2.30 (95% CI 1.99-2.65). These results, based on altogether different historical and cultural circumstances, afford strong independent confirmation of the neurodevelopmental and specifically prenatal nutritional hypothesis for schizophrenia. Further details of the Chinese work, as it helps to address certain limitations in the original Dutch findings, are discussed below.

Limitations

Ecological Nature of the Measurement of Exposure

Despite the strengths of the Dutch study several limitations--both intrinsic to our study design and to observational studies generally—prompt some caution in accepting these results. A primary limitation is the ecological measurement of nutritional status. The nutritional status of individual pregnant women was not directly measured but was based on official government food rations. Redistribution of food rations within households, supplementation from the black market, or foraging in the countryside could introduce misclassification into our estimates. Considerable evidence from different sources indicates that whatever the degree of misclassification, it enjoyed sufficient true variance to achieve discernable effects. Other studies of these birth cohorts document associations between famine exposure, measured ecologically, and immediate reproductive and intergenerational health outcomes (Ravelli et al., 1976; Ravelli et al., 1998; Lumey, Stein and Ravelli, 1995; Susser and Lin, 1992; Hoek et al., 1996; Brown et al, 1995; Brown and Susser, 1997). Macro level historical data confirm the near ubiquity of the famine for urban populations. Furthermore, while the famine's force varied somewhat by social class, (Susser, Neugebauer and Hoek, 1998) reflecting the fact that even calamities can become socialized, this differential is adjusted for in our analyses of ASPD and did not require adjustment in the case of schizophrenia.

Doubts attending the ecological measurement of exposure are further defused by the Chinese findings, despite the fact that it also utilized an ecological measure of nutritional intake. By replicating the Dutch findings under vastly different historical conditions, the Chinese results reduce the likelihood that some third factor, coinciding with but distinct from the famine, accounts for the association of nutritional deprivation with schizophrenia risk. Furthermore, the far greater severity, extent and duration of the Chinese famine, involving an 80% decline in birth rate, makes it extremely unlikely that more privileged social groups in the population escaped the famine's force and operated as a confounder in the analysis. Hence, the consistency of the Chinese and Dutch results reinforce our premise that ecologically measured and individual level nutritional intake are highly correlated under famine conditions, a conclusion that also serves to strengthen the ASPD findings.

Dates of conception were also not directly measured, producing error in the assignment of individuals to exposure category. However, neither random misspecification of exposure status nor of timing of exposure would threaten the validity of our positive findings. Rather, such measurement errors would produce underestimates, not overestimates, of risk (Rothman and Greenland, 1998).

Other limitations of the schizophrenia study included the use of registry diagnoses, the absence of patients younger than 24 years of age, and, for both investigations, the loss to emigration of a small number of cohort members. Because each of these factors would likely affect the exposed and unexposed cohorts in the same way, they would not account for the reported associations. Rather, they would tend to diminish the observed association owing to nondifferential misclassification.

Other Neurodevelopmental Toxins and Viral Etiologies

Famine could lead to eating of food substitutes, e.g., tulip bulbs, constitute a severe stressor affecting prenatal maternal hormones, (Huttenen and Niskanen, 1978) and was followed by rapid nutritional repletion with the Allied victory. In theory these exposures could exert toxic effects on the developing brain.

Finally, a thorough search was undertaken to locate evidence of non-nutritional exposures that coincided with the height of the famine in the Netherlands and that could account for our findings. None were identified. It is true that a nationwide rise in infant infections, including tuberculosis, typhoid and dysentery, occurred in the months afterward (Stein et al., 1975). Arguably, one or more of these conditions could have played an etiologic role in one or both of the conditions studies. However, none of these factors followed a temporal or geographic pattern that could account for effects that were restricted to the Famine region and to the first two trimesters of pregnancy. Hence, they are unsatisfactory as competing explanatory factors. The Chinese results, arising of course in the absence of tulip bulb consumption and characterized by a very gradual recovery from starvation, further diminishes the reasonableness of any of these competing explanations.

Diagnostic Validity and Case Ascertainment

Antisocial Personality Disorder

Clinical descriptions of ASPD in the 1960s readily concur with current criteria and the descriptive epidemiology of this entity in the military data, e.g., inverse relationship with social class, affords evidence of constructive validity. However, given the relatively low frequency of this diagnosis among recruits, it is reasonable to conclude both that ASPD was under diagnosed and the individuals so diagnosed comprised the more severe cases.

Case Ascertainment Unbiased by the Criminal Justice System

In many studies of ASPD and of criminal offending more generally, cases comprise individuals arrested or arrested and successfully prosecuted for criminal behavior. Such individuals, while typical of one segment of the prison population, are unlikely to be representative of antisocial individuals in general. Additionally, some cases will in fact be innocent of the commission of a crime. Therefore, risk factors identified in such studies may represent risk for detection, arrest and conviction rather than for the commission of antisocial acts per se. Hence, strength of the current study is that it achieves case ascertainment largely independently of the individual's relationship to the legal system.

The one exception to this statement pertains to long-term prisoners -- many probably meeting criteria for ASPD (Kaplan and Sadock,1991) – who were exempt from military induction. However, few 18-year-old Dutch men are likely to fall into this category. Moreover, any unascertained cases of ASPD would only threaten the validity of our positive findings if length of incarceration were directly associated with 1st- and/or 2nd-trimester exposure. Unbiased case under ascertainment per se will not inflate the OR (Rothman and Greenland, 1998)

Schizophrenia

The schizophrenia findings rely on the use of hospitalized cases of the disorder. Consequently, the question arises as to whether the apparent increased risk for schizophrenia reflects simply an increased likelihood of ascertainment and hospitalization of cases exposed to famine early in gestation. Apart from the inherent implausibility of such a specific bias in hospitalization patterns, two independent findings further reduce the reasonableness of this alternative explanation. First, Chinese famine results derived from a study of outpatient and inpatient cases, thereby requiring that the bias in hospitalization patterns also extended to outpatient care. Second, conception at the height of the Dutch famine has also been implicated in increased risk for schizophrenia spectrum personality disorder, a finding based on the same military data as were employed in the ASPD analyses(Hoek, Susser, Buck, Lumey, Lin, and Gorman,1996). Diagnoses in the military records are entirely independent of treatment status and hence, free of any possible bias pertaining to entry into treatment. These results for schizoid personality disorder help to counter the concerns raised here regarding reliance on treated cases of schizophrenia.

Selection Bias

Selective Conception

Did couples at elevated risk of having antisocial offspring enjoy superior fertility under famine conditions? If so, the apparent association between ASPD and famine could be artifactual. For example, sociopathic parents might circumvent equitable official food rationing, thereby securing a reproductive advantage over more rule bound couples. However, fertility was most affected by nutritional deficiency at time of conception and mortality in the first year of life was most affected by nutritional deficiency in the third trimester. Thus, such differential fertility, even if present, cannot explain the increased risk of ASPD associated with 2nd trimester famine exposure. More simply, the excess rate of offspring with ASPD and reproductive advantage among such couples would have to be extraordinarily high to have an appreciable impact on the adjusted ORs.

Selective conception is also unlikely to account for the schizophrenia findings. Hypothetically, individuals carrying susceptibility alleles for schizophrenia might be more inclined to maintain efforts at conception during the famine. Poor nutrition was probably the most critical factor influencing conception. Therefore, we would expect such women to have reduced conception rates because they were less effective in competing for black market and other *extra food rations.*

Selective Survival

Live births in the exposed cohorts comprise conceptions that survived arduous intrauterine circumstances. It has been argued that schizophrenia's persistence in the population, despite reduced fertility and survival of affected individuals, may be explained by the relevant genes conferring a selective survival advantage in some contexts, for example, in the context of fetal wastage owing to severe malnutrition. An analogous causal model could be advanced for ASPD, which is also characterized by increased adult mortality rates for affected individuals. However, at present, no evidence is available to directly support this causal model.

The Chinese famine study investigated this question of selective reproduction directly by examining the frequency of mental disorder among the family members of cases. The proportion of cases having relatives with psychiatric illness did not differ among those born before, during or after the famine years, a result that diminishes the plausibility of the selective procreation hypothesis (St. Clair, Zu, Wang , Yu, Fang, Zhang, Zheng, Gu, Feng, Sham , He , 2005). However, the absence of comparisons specific to schizophrenia and the unreliability of family history data generally mean that appreciable differences in genetic susceptibility to schizophrenia might still be present but obscured by measurement error (Neugebauer, 2005).

Mediating Mechanisms

As previously noted, obstetric complications have been associated both with an increased risk for ASPD and for schizophrenia. Therefore, prenatal nutritional deficiency may have exerted its pathogenic effects indirectly though such perinatal complications. Individual level data to test this proposed mediating mechanism are unfortunately not available. However, perinatal complications are reflected in perinatal mortality rates and these rates were elevated among famine births. However, some of the unexposed birth cohorts of 1944-1946 were also afflicted by high perinatal mortality, for other reasons, yet these cohorts did not experience elevated rates of ASPD or schizophrenia.

Pregnancy complications may compromise maternal-child interactions, for example, by raising maternal or offspring risk for physical illness, thereby increasing offspring's risk for behavioral problems (Cohler et al., 1975; Robinson and Robinson, 1965; Field et al., 1986; Grigoroiu-Servanescu, 1984; McGee et al., 1984). However, the similarity in rates of physical morbidity between exposed cases and exposed noncases, together with the absence of a 3rd trimester effect of severe nutritional deficiency on the outcomes studied, renders these proposed intervening mechanisms implausible. Finally, the excess of ASPD among exposed cohorts is not explained by an independent effect of nutritional deficiency on measured physical illness, depressed IQ, sibship size, or BMI.

Limitations on Generalizability of Findings

Assuming adequate internal validity for these findings, to what extent can these results be generalized beyond our samples? Regarding our ASPD findings for 18 year olds males, we do not know whether they apply to antisocial behavior of prepubital origin, (Lyons et al., 1995) or to women. Furthermore, estimations of the magnitude of the contribution of prenatal factors to antisocial behavior is necessarily relativistic. In certain social environments (e.g., communities characterized by high concentrations of economic disadvantage, political disenfranchisement, and limited "collective efficacy" (Sampson, Raudenbush and Earls, 1997)) postnatal risk factors may dwarf the independent role of prenatal ones.

Early prenatal nutritional deficiency could produce the observed effects either because of general malnutrition or of a specific micronutrient deficiency. Severe prenatal protein-calorie malnutrition is a rare exposure that occurs mainly in developing countries. In developed countries, it could account only for a small number of cases in special circumstances. A specific prenatal micronutrient deficiency, on the other hand, might play an important role in developed as well as in developing countries (Stein et al., 1975; Baker and Mednick, 1984; Paulus and Martin, 1986).

The findings for neural tube defects such as spina bifida and anencephaly exemplify this point. Early prenatal folate deficiency has remained an important causative factor for neural tube defects in wealthy societies. The incidence appears to depend on the specific micronutrient composition of the diet, and on the genetic background of the population, rather than on overall food intake, and it follows no simple gradient across rich and poor societies.

These findings may also have implications for societies that are victimized by ongoing civil wars. The Dutch Hunger Winter imposed conditions of severe nutritional deficiency on a population that was reasonably well nourished prior to the blockade and in its immediate aftermath. The implications of these findings for developing countries, where episodes of maternal starvation, often associated with civil war, natural disaster, forced migration, and refugee status (Neugebauer, 1997) are superimposed on conditions of endemic under nutrition, await clarification. Future efforts at replication and extension of these results to more heterogeneous samples, including samples in developing countries, are needed

While we conclude that prenatal nutritional deficiency offers the most compelling and parsimonious explanation for these findings, a prenatal nutritional contribution to risk for ASPD and schizophrenia does not preclude or outrank other explanatory factors; indeed, it may depend upon other factors to exert appreciable effects.. With regard to the ASPD findings, we note that the results for 1st and/or 2nd-trimester nutritional deficiency are compatible with separate genetic and pregnancy or postnatal environmental contributions to risk. The folate model proposed above for schizophrenia is suitable here as well. Periconceptional nutritional deficiency increases risk for neural tube defects but possibly only or primarily among genetically at-risk individuals (Elwood, Little and Elwood, 1992). On the other hand, nutritional deficiency early in pregnancy may enhance fetal susceptibility to obstetric insults. Furthermore, these findings do not preclude a substantial contribution of poverty, social disadvantage, and early family environment to the development of antisocial behaviors, especially because maternal nutritional deficiency reflects in part the prenatal operation of social and economic forces. Finally, intrauterine factors can mimic genetic patterns of disease transmission. Therefore, identification of intrauterine factors in offspring's risk for antisocial behavior may improve estimation and specification of possible genetic contributions, an issue whose place in history and current politics is naturally highly charged (Gershon, 1995).

With regard to the schizophrenia findings we note that prenatal nutritional deficiency could act in conjunction with either genetic factors or other prenatal exposures (Susser, Neugebauer and Hoek, 1996). In this regard too, neural tube defects may serve as a useful paradigm. These defects are influenced by genetic *factors, as well as by prenatal* nutrition, and comprise several types that may be genetically distinct. Recent findings, that in the presence of an impairment in homocysteine metabolism, which may be genetically determined, a higher than average periconceptional intake of vitamin B_{12} or of folate may compensate by overcoming the metabolic defect and, thereby, reduce the risk for neural tube defects in offspring.

Advances in our knowledge of DNA methylation now make folic acid a candidate micronutrient, not just an exemplar, in efforts to understand nutrition and schizophrenia. Levels in the diet of methyl-donor components, for example, of folic acid, affect DNA methylation. In turn DNA methylation at cystosines in cytosine guanine dinucleotides can alter gene expression and functioning without perturbing the primary DNA sequence (Neugebauer, 2005). Recent research documents a role for such DNA-methylation alternations in DNA expression early in development and also in several adult-onset disorders. In a 2005 meta-analysis, Lewis and colleagues (Lewis, Zammit, Gunnell and Smith, 2005) found a link between the MTHFR C677T genotype, known to exercise a role in folate metabolism, with risk for schizophrenia, thereby identifying a direct connection between folate metabolism and the intracellular availability of folate metabolites for methylation with the development of schizophrenia. These results, while still preliminary, support our conceptualization of schizophrenia as a genetic neurodevelopmental disorder that may entail prenatal nutritional alternation of gene expression. The distant possibility is raised, therefore, of primary prevention strategies for this most destructive of psychiatric disorders.

Conclusion

The strength of the reported associations, the security of the temporal order, specificity of 1st- and/or 2nd trimester effect, and the coherence with findings in collateral research support the view that early prenatal nutritionally related insults to the developing brain are implicated as risk factors for antisocial behavior and schizophrenia. Much future work is required to identify the specific mechanisms of action by which particular nutritional deficiencies operate at precise stages of embryonic development to achieve such devastating and crippling impediments to normal human development.

References

American Psychiatric Association. (1994). *Diagnostic and Statistical Manual of Mental Disorders*. (4th ed.). Washington, DC: American Psychiatric Association.

Baker, R.L., Mednick, B.R. (1984). *Influences on Human Development: A Longitudinal Perspective*. Boston: Kluwer-Nijhoff.

Barker, D.J. (2003a). Commentary: Developmental origins of raised serum cholesterol. *International Journal of Epidemiology,* 32, 876-877.

Barker, D.J. (2003b). The developmental origins of adult disease. *European Journal of Epidemiology*, 18, 733-736.

Brennan, P., Mednick, S.A., Kandel, E. (1993). Congenital determinants of violent and property offending. In D.J. Pepler and K.H. Rubin (Eds). *The Development and Treatment of Childhood Aggression (pp.* 81-92). Hillsdale, NJ: Lawrence Erlbaum Associates.

Brown, A., Susser, E., Lin, S.P., Neugebauer, R. and Gorman, J.M. (1995). Increased risk for affective disorders in males after second trimester prenatal exposure to the Dutch Hunger Winter of 1944-45. *British Journal of Psychiatry*, 166, 601-606.

Brown, A.S., Begg, M.D., Gravenstein, S., Schaefer, C.A., Wyatt, R.J., Bresnahan, M., Babulas, V.P., Susser, E.S. (2004). Serologic evidence of prenatal influenza in the etiology of schizophrenia. *Archives of General Psychiatry*, 61, 774-780.

Brown, A.S. and Susser, E.S. (1997). Sex differences in prevalence of congenital neural defects after periconception famine exposure. *Epidemiology,* 8, 555-558.

Burger, G.C.E., Drummond, J.C.,and Sandstead, H.R.,(Eds). (1947) Malnutrition and Starvation in the Western Netherlands: September 1944-July 1945. The Hague: General Printing Office.

Cannon M, Kendell R, Susser E and Jones P. (2003). Chapter 5. Prenatal and perinatal risk factors for schizophrenia. IN The Epidemiology of Schizophrenia. Eds Murray RM, Jones PBN, Susser E and Van Os J, Cannon M. (2003) Cambridge University Press, London. Chapter 5, pp. 74-99.

Carp, E.A.D.E. (1947). Medische Psychologie en Pathopsychologie. Part 3. Amsterdam: Scheltema and Holkema.

Cohler, B.J., Gallant, D.H., Gruenbaum, H.U., Weiss, J.L. and Gamer, E. (1975). Pregnancy and birth complications among mentally ill and well mothers and their children. *Social Biology*, 22, 269-277.

Diagnostic and Statistical Manual of Mental Disorders, Fourth Edition.(1994). Washington, DC: American Psychiatric Press;

Elwood, J.M., Little, J. and Elwood, J.H. (1992). *Epidemiology and Control of Neural Tube Defects*. New York: Oxford University Press.

Field, T.M., Sandberg, D., Garcia, R., Vega-Lahr, N., Goldstein, S., and Guy, L. (1985). Pregnancy problems, postpartum depression, and early mother-infant interactions. *Developmental Psychology*, 21, 1152-1156.

Gershon, E.S. (1995). Antisocial behavior. *Archives of General Psychiatry,* 52, 900-901.

Grigoroiu-Servanescu, M. (1984). Intellectual and emotional development and school adjustment in preterm children at 6 and 7 years of age. *International Journal of Behavioral Development*, 7, 307-320.

Halverson, C.F. and Victor, J.B. (1976). Minor physical anomalies and problem behavior in elementary school children. *Child Development*, 47, 281-285.

Harding, J.E. (2001). The nutritional basis of the fetal origins of adult disease. *International Journal of Epidemiology*, 30, 15-23.

Hoek, H.W., Susser, E., Buck, K.A., Lumey, L.H., Lin, S.P., Gorman, J.M. (1996). Schizoid personality disorder after prenatal exposure to famine. *American Journal of Psychiatry*, 153, 1637-1639.

Hosmer, D.W. and Lemeshow, S. (1989). *Applied Logistic Regression.* New York: John Wiley and Sons Inc.

Huttenen, M. and Niskanen, P. (1978). Prenatal loss of father and psychiatric disorders. *Archives of General Psychiatry*, 35, 429-431. *International Journal of Epidemiology* (2001) 30.

Kaplan, H.I., and Sadock, B.J. (Eds.). (1991). Personality disorders. In: *Synopsis of Psychiatry*. (6th ed.).

Kinney DK, Hyman W, Greetham C and Tramer S. (1999). Increased relative risk for schizophrenia and prenatal exposure to a severe tornado. *Schizophrenia Research* 36: 45-46.

Kline, J, Stein, Z. and Susser, M. (1989). *Conception to Birth: Epidemiology of Prenatal Development*. New York: Oxford University Press.

Leon, D.A. (2001). Commentary: Getting to grips with fetal programming-aspects of a rapidly evolving agenda. *International Journal of Epidemiology*, 30, 96-98.

Lewis SJ, Zammit S, Gunnell D and Smith GD. (2005). A meta-analysis of the MTHFR C677T polymorphism and schizophrenia risk. *Am J Med Genet B Neuropsychiatr Genet.* 135, 2-4.

Lumey, L.H., Stein, A.D., Ravelli, A.C. (1995). Timing of prenatal starvation in women and birth weight in their first and second born offspring. *European Journal of Obstetrics, Gynecology and Reproductive Biology,* 61, 23-30.

Lyons, M.J., True, W.R., Eisen, S.A., et al. (1995). Differential heritability of adult and juvenile antisocial traits. *Archives of General Psychiatry*. 52: 906-915.

Manual of the International Classification of Diseases, Injuries and Causes of Death, Sixth Revision [translated and edited for the Netherlands in 6 decimals by Dr. I.J. van der Mandele]. Adapted 1948.

Marenco S, Weinberger DR. (2000). The neurodevelopmental hypothesis of schizophrenia: following a trail of evidence from cradle to grave. *Developmental Psychopathology*. 12:501-527.

McGee, R., Silva, P.A., and Williams, S. P. (1984). Perinatal, neurological, environmental and developmental characteristics of seven-year-old children with stable behaviour problems. *Journal of Child Psychology and Psychiatry,* 25, 573-586.

Mednick, S.A., Kandel, E. (1988). Genetic and perinatal factors in violence. In: S.A. Mednick, T. Moffitt, (Ed). *Biological Contributions to Crime Causation (pp.* 331). Dordrecht: Martinus Nijhoff.

Murray RM, Jones PB, Susser E, Van Os J and Cannon M. (2003). The Epidemiology of Schizophrenia. Cambridge University Press, New York, N.Y.

Neugebauer R. (2005). Accumulating evidence for prenatal nutritional origins of mental disorders. *JAMA*.294, 621-623.

Neugebauer, R.N., Hoek, H.W., Susser, E. (1999). Prenatal exposure to wartime famine and development of antisocial personality disorder in early adulthood. *Journal of the American Medical Association,* 282, 455-462.

Neugebauer R. (1997). The uses of psychosocial epidemiology in promoting refugee health. *American Journal of Public Health*, 87, 726-728.

Olds, D., Henderson, C.R. Jr, Cole, R., et al. (1998). Long-term effects of nurse home visitation on children's criminal and antisocial behavior: 15-year follow-up of a randomized controlled trial. *Journal of the American Medical Association*, 280, 1238-1244.

Paulhus, D.L., Martin, C.L. (1986). Predicting adult temperament from minor physical anomalies. *Journal of Personality and Social Psychology*, 50, 1235-1239.

Pine, D.S., Cohen, P., Brook, J., and Coplan, J.D. (1997). Psychiatric symptoms in adolescence as predictors of obesity in early childhood. *American Journal of Public Health*, 87, 1303-1310.

Raine, A., Brennan, P., Mednick, S.A. (1994). Birth complications combined with early maternal rejection at age 1 year predispose to violent crime at age 18 years. *Archives of General Psychiatry*, 51, 984-988.

Raine, A. (1993). *The Psychopathology of Crime: Criminal Behavior as a Clinical Disorder*. San Diego: Academic Press.

Ravelli, G.P., Stein, Z.A., Susser, M.W. (1976). Obesity in young men after famine exposure in utero and early infancy. *New England Journal of Medicine*. 295, 349-353.

Ravelli, A.C., van der Meulen, J.H., Michels, R.P., et al. (1998). Glucose tolerance in adults after prenatal exposure to famine. *Lancet.,* 351,173-177.

Reiss, A.J. and Roth, J.A. (Eds.). (1993). *Understanding and Preventing Violence, Vol. 1.* Washington, DC: National Academy Press.

Robinson, N.M. and Robinson, H.B.(1965) A follow-up study of children of low birth weight and control children at school. *Pediatrics.* ,35:425-433.

Roseboom, T.J., van der Meulen, J.H., Ravelli, A.C., Osmond, C., Barker, D.J., Bleker, O.P. (2001). Effects of prenatal exposure to the Dutch famine on adult disease in later life: an overview. *Twin Research.* Rothman, K.J. and Greenland, S. (1998). *Modern Epidemiology.* (2nd ed.), Philadelphia: Lippincott-Raven Publishers.

St. Clair D, Zu M, Wang P, Yu Y, Fang Y, Zhang F, Zheng X, Gu N, Feng G, Sham P and He L. (2005). Rates of adult schizophrenia following prenatal exposure to the Chinese Famine of 1959-1961. *JAMA* 294, 557-62.

Sampson, R.J., Raudenbush, S.W., Earls, F. (1997). Neighborhoods and violent crime: a multilevel study of collective efficacy. *Science.* 277, 918-924.

Stein, Z., Susser, M., Saenger, G., Marolla, F. (1975). Famine and Human Development The Dutch Hunger Winter of 1944-45. New York: Oxford University Press.

Stein, Z., Susser, M., Saenger, G., Marolla, F. (1973). Nutrition and mental performance. *Science.* 178(62), 708-713.

Suomi S.J. (1997). Long-term effects of different early rearing experiences on social, emotional and pyshiological development in nonhuman primates. In: Neurodevelopement and Adult Psychopathology. Ch. 8, Keshavan MS, Murray RM, eds, Cambridge, UK: Cambridge University Press, pp. 104-116.

Susser, E., Hoek, H.W., Brown, A. (1998). Neurodevelopmental disorders after prenatal famine: The story of the Dutch Famine Study. *American Journal of Epidemiology.* 147, 213-216.

Susser, E. and Lin, S.P. (1992). Schizophrenia after prenatal exposure to the Dutch Hunger Winter of 1944-45. *Archives of General Psychiatry.* 49, 983-988.

Susser, E., Neugebauer, R., Hoek, H.W., et al. (1996). Schizophrenia after prenatal famine: Further evidence. *Archives of General Psychiatry.* 53, 25-31.

Terry, M.B. and Susser, E. (2001). Commentary: The impact of fetal and infant exposures along the life course. *International Journal of Epidemiology.* 30, 95-96.

Van Os J, Selten J-P (1998). Prenatal exposure to maternal stress and later schizophrenia: the May 1940 invasion of the Nehterlands. *British Journal of Psychiatry* 172, 324-326.

Waldrop, M.F., Bell, R.Q., McLaughlin, B. and Halverson, C.F. (1978). Newborn minor physical anomalies predict short attention span, peer aggression, and impulsivity at age 3. *Science*, 199, 536-565.

World Health Organization. (1948). *Manual of the International Classification of Diseases, Injuries and Causes of Death,* (6th ed). Geneva: World Health Organization.

World Health Organization. (1938). *Manual of the International Statistical Classification of Diseases, Injuries, and Causes of Death.* Geneva: World Health Organization.

Zeldenrust ELK. (1966) Psychopathie. Ned Tijdschr Geneeskd. 110:1737-1745.

In: Crime and Schizophrenia: Causes and Cures
Editor: Adrian Raine, pp. 203-217
ISBN 1-59454-609-6

Chapter 11

SCHIZOPHRENIA AND VIOLENCE: A COMMON DEVELOPMENTAL PATHWAY?

David Gourion
Universitary Dept of Sainte-Anne Hospital (SHU). Paris, France and INSERM unit 0117, 7 rue Cabanis, 75014 Paris. France

INTRODUCTION

In general, about 10% of serious violence, including homicide, has been attributed to various psychoses combined, and ~5% of homicide to schizophrenia (Walsh et al., 2001). An epidemiological study conducted in the United States found a prevalence for violence in 8% of schizophrenic persons as against 2% in persons without mental illness (Swanson et al., 1990). This well established comorbidity between schizophrenia and violence could be determined by common developmental pathways:

- For schizophrenia, the hypothesis of a neurodevelopmental basis leading to the disorder has been proposed by many investigators for more than two decades and this hypothesis is supported by strong and converging lines of evidences (Pilowsky et al., 1993).
- For violence, longitudinal studies of young patients with conduct disorders and antisocial personality have shown that early developmental factors represent predictors of later aggressive or violent behaviors (Tremblay et al., 2004).

A better knowledge of common developmental pathways between schizophrenia and antisocial behaviors could help to open new insights into the pathophysiology of the biological, cognitive and clinical determinants that underlie both the two disorders.

In the first part of this chapter, we are going to define some of the developmental abnormalities leading to schizophrenia and violence and intend to suggest an integrative model. In the second part, we will introduce a phenotype-genotype strategy in the context of the neurodevelopmental model of schizophrenia.

I. Schizophrenia and Violence: Developmental Pathways

1. Schizophrenia: A Pan-Developmental Disorder?

Major evidence in a neurodevelopmental model theory is the delayed onset of the disease preceded by a premorbid vulnerability. In schizophrenia, a range of early clinical signs and prodromal symptoms can be found in children go on to develop schizophrenia, which could lead us to consider this disease as a "pan-developmental" disorder (Cannon et al., 2002).

Abnormalities in brain development and maturation seem to begin prenataly but may continue throughout childhood, and the observed changes during these periods must have consequences for the neuronal circuitry and connectivity. Advances in brain imaging have now led to the identification of a great number of brain abnormalities in schizophrenia. The most consistently replicated structural anomaly present in the brains of patients with chronic schizophrenia is ventricular enlargement (Elkis et al., 1995). Abnormalities have also been found in medial temporal lobe structures (which include the amygdala, hippocampus, and parahippocampal gyrus), and neocortical temporal lobe regions (superior temporal gyrus). Futhermore, there is some evidence for frontal lobe abnormalities, particularly prefrontal gray matter and orbitofrontal regions. Similarly, parietal lobe and subcortical abnormalities have been reported. However, it is possible that the brain structural abnormalities observed in schizophrenia are not only due to neurodevelopmental anomalies, but also to an alteration in cortical plasticity and maturation processes that occurs over the long course of the disease.

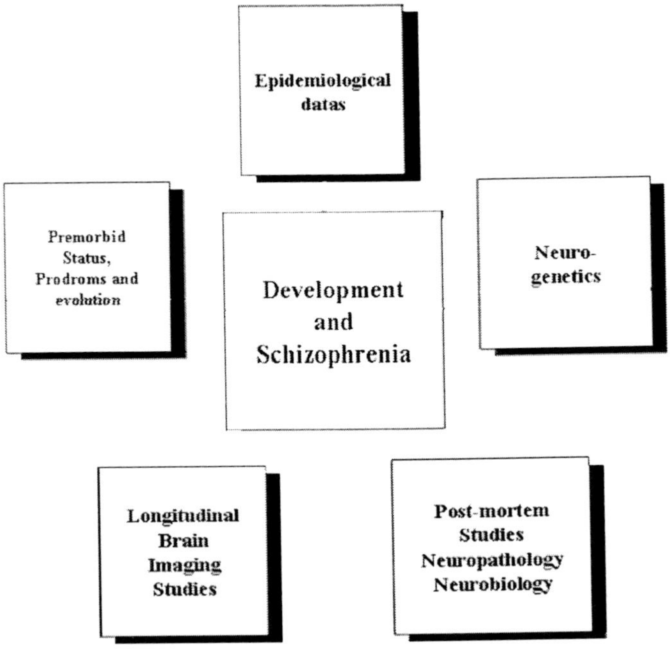

Figure 1. Schizophrenia and neurodevelopment

Moreover, schizophrenia is not only a brain disorder; patients may also display body dysmorphic abnormalities. Minor physical anomalies, manifesting as slight anatomical defects of the head, hair, eyes, mouth, hands, and feet, as dematoglyphic fluctuating asymmetries, are due to some injury ocuring during the first or second trimester of fetal life, and are more common among patients with schizophrenia and their unaffected siblings than in the general population.

2. Clinical Predictors of Violence in Patients with Schizophrenia

The usefulness of clinical variables in predicting aggression and violence in individuals with mental illness remains unclear. The discrepancies between studies to date are probably discrepant probably due to the use of varying definitions of aggression and violence and to the paucity of standardized, validated instruments to assess aggressive or violent acts. To date, at least four clinical factors have been suggested to identify those patients with psychosis at increased risk of committing violent acts:

1) Comorbid Substance Misuse

Comorbid substance abuse is probably the best established risk factor for aggressive behaviours in patients with schizophrenia (Walsh et al., 2001; Swanson et al., 1990; Tiihonen et al., 1996; Brennan et al., 2000; 9).

Asking patients about substance misuse and routinely testing urine in all patients with first episode psychosis may help identify those at risk of aggressive behaviour owing to substance misuse.

2) Medication Noncompliance

Individuals with poor insight are at increased risk of medication noncompliance and aggression following admission, suggesting that strategies to improve insight merit further evaluation (Swartz et al., 1998).

3) Active Psychotic Symptoms

Active psychotic symptoms, especially in paranoid subtypes of schizophrenia represent well established risk factors for violence (Swanson et al., 1990;Taylor, 1985;Swanson et al., 1996). At a phenomenological level, it is interesting to note that the catatonic subtype of schizophrenia presents mostly psychomotor disturbances alternating between lack of activity and violent excitement, typically characterized by unpredictable motor hyperactivity.

4) Involuntary Hospitalisation

The relationship between aggression and admission status may be bi-directional: aggressive behaviour may increase the need for involuntary admission, and involuntary admission may, in turn, exacerbate the patient's aggression. In a recent study (Walsh et al., 2004), 271 patients with schizophrenia were interviewed using a standardized battery of instruments. Assault was measured from multiple data sources over the next 2 years and criminal records were obtained. The sociodemographic and clinical significant predictors among variables measured at baseline were: history of recent assault (OR 2.33; 95% CI [1.17–4.61]), a previous violent conviction (OR 2.02; 95% CI [1.04–3.87]), having received special education (OR 2.76; 95% CI [1.22–6.26]) and alcohol abuse (OR 3.55; 95% CI [1.24–10.2]). In this study, although low premorbid IQ did not predict violence, a need for special education did.

3. Neuropsychology of Aggressive Behaviors and Schizophrenia

Intended volitional action constitutes the very foundation of human relations and action behavior at its highest level of neural integration and is mediated by functions of the prefrontal cortex. The anatomical maturation of the prefrontal cortex occurs late during development, normally extending beyond puberty to adulthood.

Neuropsychological studies examining cognitive functioning in violent groups have frequently cited the relationship between neural dysfunction and violence (Barkataki et al., In Press). These studies have generally aimed to identify the cognitive deficits that may underlie certain patterns of psychopathology. Jones (1992) proposed a model with multiple neuropsychopathological factors contributing to violent behaviour including reduced inhibition, as well as impairment in memory, attention and concentration.

Executive Functions and Behavioral Dyscontrol

Neuropsychological assessments of patients with schizophrenia have shown deficits in a wide range of cognitive domains including impairments in attention, cognitive processing, memory and IQ (Sharma et al., 2003). Basically, schizophrenia has been linked to poor performance on several dimensions of executive functioning using tests of working memory (Pantelis et al., 1997), planning (Morris, 1997) and inhibition (Perlstein et al., 1998). One study comparing non-aggressive and aggressive schizophrenia patients (Rasmussen et al., 1995), reported that the aggressive group performed poorly compared to the non-aggressive group on tasks of frontal functioning.

There are some common cognitive impairments between patients with schizophrenia and patients with antisocial personality disorders, that still exhibit deficits in executive function and inhibitory control. Published neuropsychological investigations of antisocial personality disorder and schizophrenia with violence have mainly focused exclusively on each group versus control, and there are very few direct comparisons.

The neuropsychological analysis of action behavior has already specifically pointed to the prefrontal cortex, also supporting abnormal behaviors in other developmental neuropsychiatric disorders like Attention Deficit disorder with Hyperactivity (ADHD).

Theory of Mind and Violent Behaviors in Patients with Schizophrenia

The ability to infer mental states is known in the literature as 'theory of mind' (Abu-Akel et al., 2004). Theory of mind is essential for our understanding of social and behavioral functioning (Mitchell, 1997), including the ability to empathize (Batson et al., 1987) and (Marshall et al., 1995) and feel guilt (Baron-Cohen, 1995). Three levels of theory of mind occur during development from childhood to adulthood: First-order theory of mind, which is acquired around 5 years of age, refers to the ability to understand that other people can have a belief that is different from our own. Second-order theory of mind is acquired around 7 years of age and refers to the ability to understand that one can have a false belief about the belief of another. Lastly, the Third-order theory of mind is acquired around 10 years of age, and refers to the ability to understand situations when someone says something inappropriate ("faux-pas") and involves inferring thoughts and empathic inferences.

Studies in schizophrenia have confirmed that patients with schizophrenia have deficits in theory of mind, especially at the second-order level (Mazza et al., 2001; Pickup et al., 2001).

In violent patients with schizophrenia, Murphy (1998) found that, though they showed no specific deficits in First-order theory of mind compared to patients with personality disorder, they were significantly more impaired in Second-order theory of mind. In a recent study (Abu-Akel et al., 2004), patients with paranoid schizophrenia were divided into violent and nonviolent groups. Results showed that violent patients have more difficulties than nonviolent patients in tasks involving empathic inferencing, and but shared a better ability to infer cognitive-mental states in others.

Patients with early-onset damage to the prefrontal cortex, despite normal performance on intellectual tasks, seem to have little or no empathy, significant impairments on moral reasoning, and are verbally and physically abusive to others (Anderson, 1999).

4. Neurobiology of Violence and Schizophrenia

At a neurobiological level, increases in violent behaviour have been associated with various biological modifications, with:

- Reductions in dopamine (Berman et al., 1998)
- Reductions in serotonin (Soderstrom et al., 2001)
- Increases in testosterone (Book et al., 2001)

Neuroimaging studies have suggested that certain structural brain abnormalities could be linked with violent behaviour (Chesterman et al., 1994), especially in two neural regions that have been consistently cited in relation to violent behaviour in both antisocial personality disorder and schizophrenia (Das et al., 2002):

- *The prefrontal cortex (PFC)* mediates executive functions and social conduct, in addition to exerting an inhibitory influence on certain behaviours, such as aggression (Damasio, 1995). Furthermore, neuroimaging studies examining this region have reported structural abnormalities in both schizophrenia (Buchanan et al., 1998) and antisocial personality disorder (Raine et al., 2000).
- *The limbic system* is involved in processing emotional stimuli and relaying it into emotional response (Aggleton, 1992), and studies have demonstrated abnormal limbic structure and function in both schizophrenia (Chesterman et al., 1994) and antisocial personality disorder (Laakso et al., 2001).

5. Toward an Integrative Model of Violence in Schizophrenia

An integrative model of violence in schizophrenia could be based on the common cognitive, neurobiological and neuroanatomical defects found in schizophrenia and antisocial personality disorders.

The finding that prefrontal and mesolimbic dysfunctions are associated with impulsive and violent behavior leaves open the possibility that these behaviors may be due to impaired connectivity between these cerebral structures.

Table A. A global comparison between deficits in schizophrenia and antisocial personality disorders

Cognitive deficits	**Schizophrenia**	**Antisocial Personality disorders**
IQ	+++	+
Attention	+++	+
Executive functions	+++	+
Inhibitory control	+	+++
Theory of Mind	+++	+
Neurobiological abnormalities		
Dopamine	+++	+
Serotonin	+	+++
Testosteron	+	+++
Abnormal brain structures		
Prefrontal cortex	+++	+
Mesolimbic system	+++	+++

+ Soft dysfunctions; +++ significant dysfunctions

Davidson (1992) proposed that violent behavior was related to dysfunction in a circuit involving the orbitofrontal cortex, the anterior cingulate, and the amygdala. Impaired connectivity between these regions might be observed as an alteration in white matter microstructure. Diffusion tensor imaging is a new magnetic resonance imaging technology that provides information on the directionality and coherence of the self-diffusion of water along the direction of the myelinated axons and this technique may, have some relevance for understanding connectivity between brain regions (Weinberger et al., 1995). Reductions in white matter fractional anisotropy (which represents an increase in axonal disorganization)- have been found in schizophrenia (Buchsbaum et al., 1998, Lim et al., 1999, Foong et al., 2002).

Using Diffusion tensor imaging, Hoptman et al., (2002) examined the relationship between frontal white matter microstructure and both impulsivity and aggression in men with schizophrenia and showed that lower fractional anisotropy in right inferior frontal white matter was significantly associated with higher motor impulsiveness and with aggressiveness.

Finally, the occurrence of violent behaviours in patients with schizophrenia could be modelized as the result of a neurodevelopmental disconnectivity between the prefrontal cortex and mesolimbic structures. The mesolimbic dopaminergic hyperactivity leading to paranoid delusion and hallucinations can be dramatically increased by substance misuse. The co-occurrence of paranoid delusions and of thought disorganization due to the prefrontal dysfunction could result in the emergence of violent behaviors.

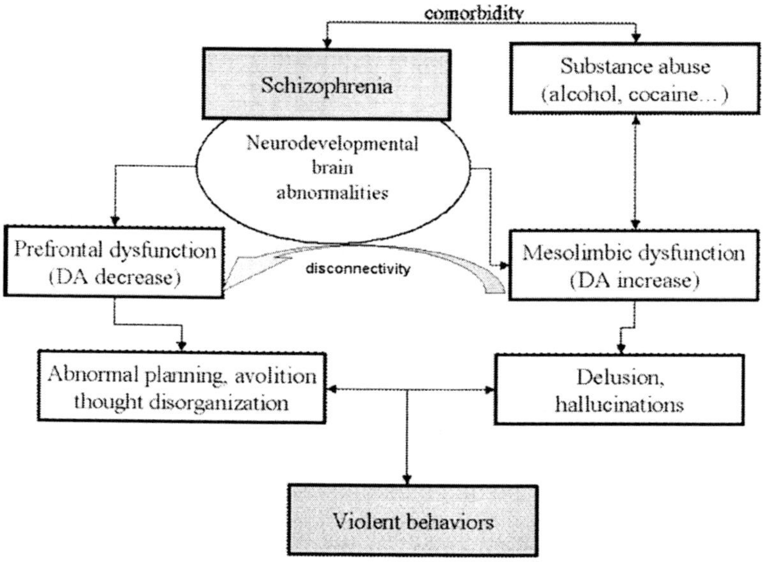

Figure II. Schizophrenia and violence: An integrative model

II. Phenotype-Genotype Strategies in the Context of the Neurodevelopmental Hypothesis

1. Dissecting the Developmental Phenotype of Patients with Schizophrenia

Dissecting the phenotype in schizophrenia, as in other complex mental disorders, appears as one of the major challenges of the decade. Despite intensive efforts, relationships between phenotypes and genotypes in patients with schizophrenia remain unclear.

One part of the issue could be due to the fact that schizophrenia is probably not represented by one homogeneous phenotype, but by the interaction of several simple, intermediate phenotypes: the heterogeneity of the disease is probably due to. the complex aggregation of these phenotypes.

Beyond the dissection of these phenotypes, future investigations need to be directed to investigate whether these phenotypes are transmitted within families (Gourion et al., 2003), how they aggregate within the different subgroups of the disease, and why they could be found in certain healthy relatives. This approach could provide a better support for the optimization of phenotype-genotype molecular studies in schizophrenia.

2. Minor Physical Anomalies and Neurological Soft Signs: Two Quantitative Phenotypes that Could Be Relevant in the Context of the Developmental Hypothesis

Some clinical phenotypes are particularly relevant in terms of developmental origin, as minor physical anomalies that are considered to have a prenatal origin and seem to be increased in patients with neurodevelopmental disorders like schizophrenia, autism, mental retardation, but also antisocial personality disorders. Minor physical anomalies, such dermatoglyphic abnormalities and neurological soft signs are thus frequently found in patients with schizophrenia, probably reflecting a common developmental background noise. These phenotypes can be easily and quickly clinically assessed, and their relevance as developmental phenotypes in patients with schizophrenia is widely consistent be widely consistent in the literature.

Minor physical anomalies (MPAs) are mild errors of the morphogenesis leading to subtle alterations in the development of various bodily structures in the face, eye, ear, mouth, hand and feet areas. MPAs are considered to have a prenatal origin, possibly during the first and second trimester, when most ectodermic derivatives are under development (Smith, 1976, Green et al., 1994). Because of their common embryonic origin with that of the brain, minor physical anomalies probably represent indices of disturbance in early neurodevelopment (O'Callaghan et al., 1995). MPAs have been increasingly found in a range of developmental disorders including conduct disorders, mental retardation, autism, hyperactivity, epilepsy, fetal alcohol syndrome and schizophrenia. The excess of MPAs in subjects with schizophrenia compared with other psychiatric populations and control subjects is now well established (Gualtieri et al., 1982, Guy et al., 1983, Green et al., 1994b, Lane et al., 1997, Ismail et al., 1998), supporting the neurodevelopmental hypothesis of schizophrenia.

Nevertheless, the precise pattern of physical anomalies and their specificity remains unclear, stressing the need for an improvement of the clinical tools used for the phenotypic characterization of these patients.

Very few studies have explored the relationship between MPAs and violence since Waldrop suggested a possible association between MPAs and impulsivity (Waldrop et al., 1968). In one report (Arseneault et al., 2000), MPAs were assessed in a sample of 170 adolescents boys with a low socioeconomic status that had been enrolled in a longitudinal study since their kindergarten year and delinquency was measured by auto-questionnaires and by a search of official criminal records. Results showed that the total count of MPAs, and especially anomalies of the mouth, was significantly associated with an increased risk of violent delinquency in adolescence. This result was consistent with the findings of another longitudinal study (Kandel et al., 1989).

In this context, it would be of great interest to explore, in patients with schizophrenia, if MPAs represent a predictor of aggressive and violent behaviours.

Neurological soft-signs (NSS): Several studies have reported a high prevalence of neurological 'subtle' or 'soft' signs (NSS) in patients suffering from schizophrenia (Buchanan et al., 1989), even in first episode and in drug-naïve patients (Krebs et al., 2000).

In addition, the high prevalence of these signs in schizophrenic patients' relatives suggests that they could be associated with the genetic liability (Ismail et al., 1998b).

To date, only one investigation (Braun et al., 1995) aimed to explore the correlations between neurological soft signs and violence in patients with schizophrenia; levels of lifetime violence did not correlate significantly with neurological soft signs but there was a strong association between soft-signs and impulsivity. However, this study was carried out on a small sample of 31 men with schizophrenia.

Implementation of a strategy allowing a better phenotypic characterization of the healthy biological relatives

Among biological parents of patients with schizophrenia, "presumed carriers" of the genetic loading can be identified on the basis of their own family history if another ascendant and/or collateral is also affected by the illness. This approach enables us to determine the phenotypic markers that cosegregate with the genetic loading. For instance, (Ross et al., 1998) suggested that abnormal smooth pursuit eye movements were related to the presumed genetic risk in schizophrenia and several authors have used similar strategies for brain-imaging studies in schizophrenia (Steel et al., 2002).

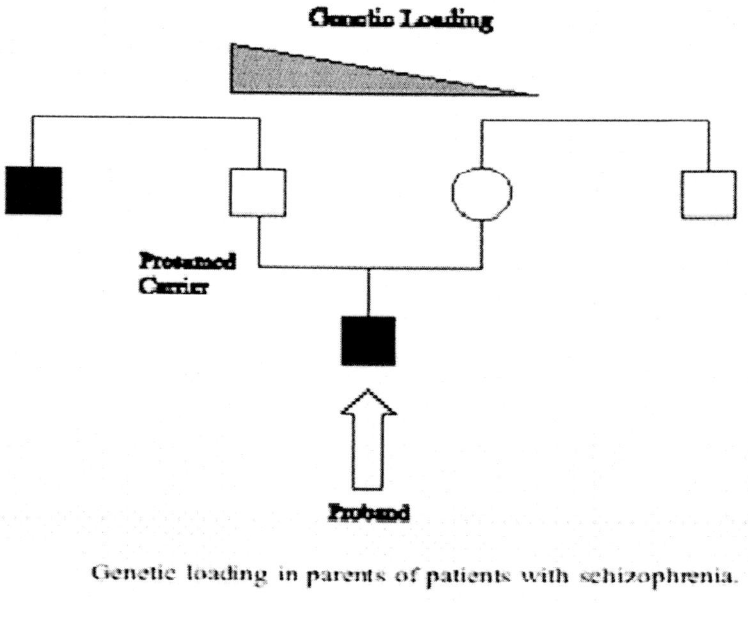

Figure III. Dichotomization of the healthy biological relatives on the basis of their genetic loading: Presumed and non presumed carriers for the genes of the disease

As NSS and MPA may both represent intermediate phenotypes of particular interest, we aimed to investigate whether NSS and/or MPA cosegregate with the genetic liability.

Patients with schizophrenia, nonpsychotic parents of these patients and healthy comparison subjects took part in the study. Parents were further classified as "presumed carriers" of the genetic loading if they had a second relative with schizophrenia in their ascendants and/or collaterals (first or second degree) or as "presumed noncarriers". In this sample of patients with schizophrenia and their non psychotic relatives, we found that both NSS and MPA were higher in patients with schizophrenia than in controls, and that NSS cosegregate with the genetic loading in the nonpsychotic first-degree relatives (Gourion et al., 2004). Indeed, NSS were higher in presumed-carrier parents than in presumed noncarriers in terms of total scores and, more specifically, in two particular functional domains: motor coordination and motor integration. MPA were higher in patients with schizophrenia and in parents than in controls, albeit not significantly different between presumed-carrier parents and presumed noncarriers.

In an exploratory study, we explored whether the combination of two phenotypes was better than each phenotype separately to classify as presumed or non presumed carriers a population of healthy relatives of patients with schizophrenia, blindly from their family history (Gourion et al., 2004b).

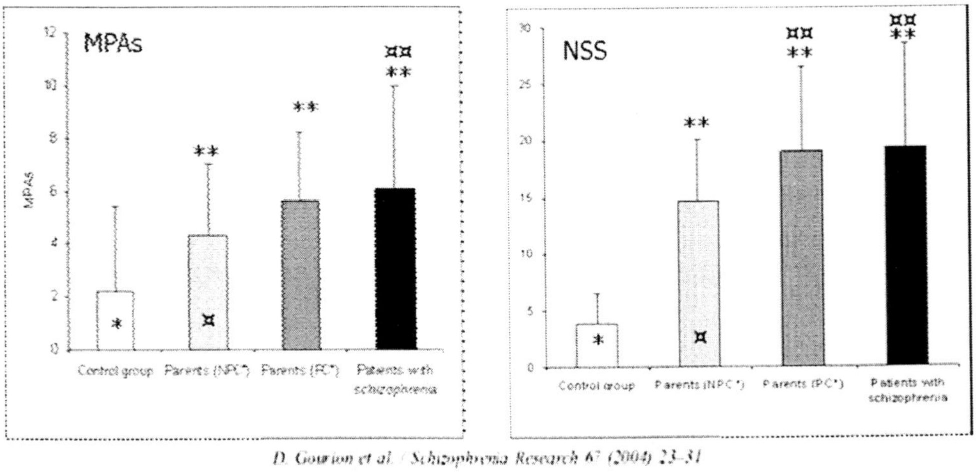

Figure IV. Comparisons of Minor Physical Anomalies (left) and Neurological Soft Signs (right) between patients with schizophrenia, their parents classified as Presumed Carriers (PC) or Non Presumed Carriers(NPC) and controls (Gourion et al., 2004)

Using a linear discriminant function, about 70% of the healthy relatives were correctly classified as presumed carriers or non presumed carriers, with two linear equations using NSS and MPAs as variables (Gourion et al., 2004b), whereas using each phenotype separately allowed a lower quality of classification (less than 50%).

This example indicates that the construction of a composite phenotype could strongly optimize the classification of relatives on the basis of their own genetic loading.

Conclusion

When violence occurs in schizophrenia, the prefrontal dysfunctions that underlie volitional intent and planning probably play a role altogether with abnormal content of thought under the impact of delusions and/or hallucinations (Pontius, 2004). Converging neuroimaging results suggest prefrontal and mesolimbic brain abnormalities in schizophrenia. The finding that prefrontal and mesolimbic dysfunctions are associated with impulsive and violent behavior leaves open the possibility that these behaviors may be due to impaired connectivity between these cerebral structures, potentially occurring during neurodevelopment. This disconnectivity could result in a mesolimbic dopaminergic hyperactivity worsened by substance abuse. The combination of delusion (mesolimbic dopaminergic hyperactivity) and of abnormal planning (prefrontal dopaminergic hypoactivity) could lead to the occurrence of aggressive behaviors.

Despite intensive efforts over the last decade, molecular genetic studies have failed to find the genetic risk factors for genes linked to schizophrenia. In this context, it has become essential now to try to implement new phenotype-genotype strategies. Violence in patients with schizophrenia could also represent an overt behavioral phenotype underlied by prefrontal abnormalities related to executive dysfunctions, which could be succesfully exploited by the genetic studies of the disease. To illustrate this approach, some data support the hypothesis that the 5HTTLPR polymorphism could represent a risk factor for violent suicidal behavior in patients with schizophrenia (Bayle et al., 2003).

Dissecting and refining the phenotype of such a heterogeneous disease is probably only part of the solution, and we need to improve our clinical assessments beyond a purely phenomenological level and we have given an exemple of a such characterization at a developmental level with the assessment of minor physical anomalies and neurological soft-signs.

References

Abu-Akel, A., and Abushua'leh, K. (2004). 'Theory of mind' in violent and nonviolent patients with paranoid schizophrenia. *Schizophrenia Research*, 69 (1):45-53.

Aggleton, J. (1992). *The* Amygdala. Neurobiological Aspects of Emotion, Memory and Mental Dysfunction. New York: Wiley-Liss.

Anderson, R.L., and Lewis, D.A. (1999). Clinical characteristics and service use of persons with mental illness living in an intermediate care facility. *Psychiatry Service*, 50(10):1341-5.

Arseneault, L., Tremblay, R.E., Boulerice, B., Seguin, J.R., Saucier, J.F. (2000). Minor physical anomalies and family adversity as risk factors for violent delinquency in adolescence. *American Journal of Psychiatry*, 157(6):917-23.

Arseneault, L., Moffitt, T.E., Caspi, A., Taylor, P.J. and Silva, P.A. (2000). Mental disorders and violence in a total birth cohort: results from the Dunedin study. *Arch. Gen. Psychiatry* 2000, 57: 968–979.

Barkataki, I., Kumari, V., Das, M., and al. In Press. A neuropsychological investigation into violence and mental illness, *Schizophrenia Research*.

Baron-Cohen, S. (1995). *Mindblindness: An Essay on Autism and Theory of Mind.* Cambridge: MIT Press.

Batson, C.D., Fultz, J. and Schoenrade P.A. (1987). *Adults' emotional reactions to the distress of others.* Cambridge: Cambridge Univ. Press (Empathy and its Development):163–185.

Bayle, F.J., Leroy, S., Gourion, D., Millet, B., Olie, J.P., Poirier, M.F., Krebs, M.O. (2003). 5HTTLPR polymorphism in schizophrenic patients: further support for association with violent suicide attempts. *American Journal of Medical Genetics.* 2003; 119B (1):13-7.

Berman, M.E., and Cocarro, E.F. (1998). Neurobiologic correlates of violence: revelance to criminal responsibility. *Behavioral Science,* 16: 303-318.

Book, A.S., Starzyk, K.B. and Quinsey, V.L. (2001). The relationship between testosterone and aggression: a meta-analysis. *Aggressive and Violent Behaviors,* 6:579–599.

Braun, C.M. J., Lapierre, D., Hodgins, S., Toupin, J., Leveille, S. and Constantineau, C. (1995). Neurological soft signs in schizophrenia: Are they related to negative or positive symptoms, neuropsychological performance, and violence? *Archives of Clinical Neuropsychology,* 10 (6): 489-509.

Brennan, P.A., Mednick, S.A. and Hodgins, S. (2000). Major mental disorders and criminal violence in a Danish birth cohort. *Archives of General Psychiatry,* 57: 494–500.

Buchanan, R.W. and Heinrichs, D.W. (1989). The Neurological Evaluation Scale (NES): a structured instrument for the assessment of neurological signs in schizophrenia. *Psychiatry Research.* 27, pp. 335–350.

Buchanan, R.W., Buchanan, K., Vladar, P.E. and al. (1998). Structural evaluation of the prefrontal cortex in schizophrenia. *American Journal of Psychiatry,* 155: 1049–1055.

Buchsbaum, M.S., Buchsbaum, C.Y., Tang, S., Peled, H., Gudbjartsson, D., Lu, E.A. Hazlett, et al., (1998). MRI white matter diffusion anisotropy and PET metabolic rate in schizophrenia. *Neuroreport,* 9:425–430.

Cannon, M., Caspi, A., Moffitt, T.E., Harrington, H., Taylor, A., Murray, R.M., Poulton, R. (2002). Evidence for early-childhood, pan-developmental impairment specific to schizophreniform disorder: results from a longitudinal birth cohort. *Archives of General Psychiatry,* 59 (5):449-56.

Chesterman. L., Taylor, P., Cox, T., Hill, M., and Lumsden J. (1994). Multiple measures of cerebral state in dangerous mentally disordered inpatients. *Crim. Behav. Ment., Health 4* : 228–239.

Damasio, A.R. (1995). On some functions of the human prefrontal cortex, Ann. N.Y. Acad. Sci., 769 : 241–251.

Das, M., Barkataki, I., Kumari V., and Sharma, T. (2002). Neuroimaging violence in the mentally ill: what can it tell us? *Hosp. Med,* 63 : 604–609.

Davidson, R.J. (1992). Anterior cerebral asymmetry and the nature of emotion. *Brain Cogn,* 20 :125–151.

Elkis, H., Friedman, L., Wise, A., Meltzer, H.Y. (1995). Meta-analyses of studies of ventricular enlargement and cortical sulcal prominence in mood disorders. Comparisons with controls or patients with schizophrenia. *Archives of General Psychiatry,* 52(9):735-46.

Foong, J., Symms, M.R., Barker, G.J., Maier, M., Miller, D.H., Ron, M.A. (2002). Investigating regional white matter in schizophrenia using diffusion tensor imaging. *Neuroreport,* 4;13(3):333-6.

Gourion, D., Goldberger, C., Bourdel, M.C., Bayle, F.J., Lôo, H. and Krebs, M.O. (2004). Minor physical anomalies in patients with schizophrenia and their parents: prevalence and pattern of craniofacial abnormalities. *Psychiatry Research,* 125, (1): 21-28.

Gourion, D., Goldberger, C., Bourdel, M.C., Bayle, F.J., Millet, B., Olie, J.P. and Krebs, M.O. (2003). Neurological soft-signs and minor physical anomalies in schizophrenia: differential transmission within families. *Schizophrenia Research*, 63, (1-2):181-187.

Gourion, D., Goldberger, C., Olie, J.P., Lôo, H. and Krebs, M.O. (2004b). Neurological and morphological anomalies and the genetic liability to schizophrenia: a composite phenotype. *Schizophrenia Research*, 67 (1) :23-31

Green, M.F., Bracha, H.S., Satz, P., and Christenson, C.D. (1994). Preliminary evidence for an association between minor physical anomalies and second trimester neurodevelopment in schizophrenia. *Psychiatry Research*, 53: 119–127.

Green, M.F., Satz, P., and Christenson, C.D. (1994b). Minor physical anomalies in schizophrenia patients, bipolar patients, and their siblings. *Schizophrenia Bulletin*, 20(3):433-40.

Gualtieri, C.T., Gualtieri, I., and Mele, C. (1982). Minor physical anomalies in alcoholic and schizophrenic adults and hyperactive and autistic children. *American Journal of Psychiatry,* 5: 640–643.

Guy, J.D., Majorski, L.V., Wallace C.J., and Guy, M.P. (1983). The incidence of minor physical anomalies in adult male schizophrenics. *Schizophrenia Bulletin*, 9: 571–582.

Hoptman, M.J., Volavka, J., Johnson, G., Weiss, E., Bilder, R.M., and Kelvin, O.L. (2002). Frontal white matter microstructure, aggression, and impulsivity in men with schizophrenia: a preliminary study. *Biological Psychiatry*, 52(1) : 9-14.

Ismail, B. Cantor-Graae E. and McNeil, T.F. (1998). Minor physical anomalies in schizophrenic patients and their siblings. *American Journal of Psychiatry*, 155: 1695–1702.

Ismail, B. Cantor-Graae E. and McNeil, T.F. (1998b). Neurological abnormalities in schizophrenic patients and their siblings. *American Journal of Psychiatry*, 155: 84–89.

Jones, H. (1992). Neuropsychology of violence. *Forensic Rep*, 5 : 221–233.

Kandel, E., Brennan, P.A., Mednick, S.A., Michelson, N.M. (1989). Minor physical anomalies and recidivistic adult violent criminal behavior. *Acta Psychiatrica Scandinavia*, 79(1):103-7.

Krebs, M.A., Gut-Fayand, A., Bourdel, M.C., Dischamp, J. and Olié, J.P. (2000). Validation and factorial structure of a standardized neurological examination assessing neurological soft signs in schizophrenia. *Schizophrenia Research*, 45 (3): 245-260.

Laakso, M., Vaurio, O., Koivisto, E., Savolainen, L., Eronen, M., Aronen, H., Soininen, H., and Tiihonen, J. (2001). Psychopathy and the posterior hippocampus, *Behav. Brain Res.*2001, 118:187-93.

Lane, A., Kinsella, A., Murphy, P., Byrne, M., Keenan, J., Colgan, K., Cassidy, B., Sheppard, N., Horgan, R., Waddington, J.L., Larkin C., and O'Callaghan, E. (1997). The anthropometric assessment of dysmorphic features in schizophrenia as an index of its developmental origins. *Psychological Medi*cine, 27: 1155–1164.

Lim, K.O., Hedehus, M., Moseley, M., de Crespigny, A., Sullivan E.V., and Pfefferbaum, A. (1999). Compromised white matter tract integrity in schizophrenia inferred from diffusion tensor imaging. *Arch Gen Psychiatry* , 1999, 56: 367–374.

Marshall, W.L., Hudson, S.M., Jones, R., and Fernandez, Y.M. (1995). Empathy in sex offenders. *Clin. Psychol. Rev.*, 15: 99–113.

Mazza, M., De Risio, A., Surian, L., Roncone, R. and Casacchia, M. (2001). Selective impairments of theory of mind in people with schizophrenia. *Schizophrenia Res*earch, 47: 299–308.

Mitchell, P. (1997). *Introduction to Theory of Mind: Children, Autism and Apes*. London: Arnold.

Morris, R.G., Rushe, T., Woodruffe, P.W., and Murray, R.M. (1995). Problem solving in schizophrenia: a specific deficit in planning ability. *Schizophrenia Res*earch, 14: 235–246.

Murphy, D. (1998). Theory of mind in a sample of men with schizophrenia detained in a special hospital: it's relationship to symptom profiles and neuropsychological tests. *Crim. Behav. Ment. Health,* 1998, 8:13–26.

O'Callaghan, E., Buckley, P. , Madigan, C., Redmond, O., Stack, J.P., Kinsella, A., Larkin, C., Ennis, J.T., and Waddington, J.L. (1995). The relationship of minor physical anomalies and other putative indices of developmental disturbance in schizophrenia to abnormalities of cerebral structure on magnetic resonance imaging. *Biological Psychiatry*, 38:516–524.

Pantelis, C. Barnes, T.R. Nelson, H.E. Tanner, S. Weatherley, L. Owen A.M. and Robbins, T.W. (1997). Frontal-striatal cognitive deficits in patients with chronic schizophrenia. *Brain*, 120:1823–1843.

Perlstein, W.M. Carter, C.S. Barch D.M. and Baird, J.W. (1998).The Stroop task and attention deficits in schizophrenia: a critical evaluation of card and single-trial Stroop methodologies. *Neuropsychology*, 12:414–425.

Pickup, G. and Frith, C. (2001). Theory of mind impairments in schizophrenia: symptomatology, severity and specificity. *Psychological Medecine*, 31:207–220.

Pilowsky, L.S., Kerwin, R.W., Murray, R.M. (1993). Schizophrenia: a neurodevelopmental perspective. *Neuropsychopharmacology*, 9 (1):83-91.

Pontius A. (2004). Violence in schizophrenia versus limbic psychotic trigger reaction: Prefrontal aspects of volitional action. *Aggression and Violent Behavior,* 9, (5): 503-521.

Raine, A., Lencz, T., Bihrle, S., LaCasse L., and Colletti, P. (2000). Reduced prefrontal gray matter volume and reduced autonomic activity in antisocial personality disorder. *Archives of. General Psychiatry*, 57:119–127.

Rasmussen, K., Levander S., and Sletvold H. (1995). Aggressive and non-aggressive schizophrenics: symptom profile and neuropsychological differences. *Psychol. Crime, Law 2*:119–129.

Ross, R.G., Olincy, A., Harris, J.G., Radant, A., Adler, L.E., Freedman, R. (1998). Anticipatory saccades during smooth pursuit eye movements and familial transmission of schizophrenia. *Biological Psychiatry*, 44(8):690-7.

Sharma, T. and Antonova, L. (2003). Cognitive function in schizophrenia. Deficits, functional consequences, and future treatment. *Psychiatr. Clin. North Am*, 26:25–40.

Smith, D.W. (1976). *Recognizable Patterns of Human Malformations: Genetic, Embryologic and Clinical Aspects*. Philadelphia: WB Saunders.

Soderstrom, H., Blennow, K., Manheim A., and Forsman, A. (2001). CSF studies in violent offenders. 5-HIAA as a negative and HVA as a positive predictor of psychopathy. *J. Neural Transm,* 108:869–878.

Steel, R.M., Whalley, H.C., Miller, P., Best, J.J., Johnstone, E.C., Lawrie, S.M. (2002). Structural MRI of the brain in presumed carriers of genes for schizophrenia, their affected and unaffected siblings. *J Neurol Neurosurg Psychiatry*, 72(4):455-8.

Swanson, J.W., Holzer, C.E., Ganju, V.K. and Jono, R.T. (1990). Psychotic symptoms and disorders and the risk of violent behaviour in the community. Crim. Behav. *Ment. Health*, 6:309–329.

Swartz, M.S., Swanson, J.W., Hiday, V., Borum, R., Wagner, H.R. and Burns, B.J. (1998). Violence and severe mental illness: the effects of substance abuse and nonadherence to medication. *American Journal of Psychiatry*,155:226–231.

Taylor, P.J. (1985). Motives for offending among violent and psychotic men. *British Journal of Psychiatry,* 147:491–498.

Tiihonen, J., Isohanni, M., Räsänen, P., Koiranen, P. and Moring, J. (1997). Specific major mental disorders and criminality: a 26-year prospective study of the 1966 northern Finland birth cohort. *American Journal of Psychiatry*, 154:840–845.

Tremblay, R.E., Nagin, D.S., Seguin, J.R., Zoccolillo, M., Zelazo, P.D., Boivin, M., Perussed Japel, C. (2004). Physical aggression during early childhood: trajectories and predictors. *Pediatrics*, 114 (1):e43-50.

Waldrop, M.F., Pedersen, F.A., and Bell, R.Q. (1968). Minor physical anomalies and behavior in pre-school children. *Child Development,* 1968, 39:391–400

Walsh, E., Gilvarry, C., Samele, C., Harvey, K., Manley, C., Tattan, T., Tyrer, P., Creed, F., Murray, R., Fahy, T. and the UK700 Group. (2004). Predicting violence in schizophrenia: a prospective study. *Schizophrenia Research*, 67, (2-3):247-252.

Walsh, E., Buchanan, A. and Fahy, T. (2001). Violence and schizophrenia: Examining the evidence. *British Journal of Psychiatry*, 180:490–495.

Weinberger, D.R., Lipska, B.K. (1995). Cortical maldevelopment, anti-psychotic drugs, and schizophrenia: a search for common ground. *Schizophrenia Research*, 1; 16(2):87-110.

In: Crime and Schizophrenia: Causes and Cures
Editor: Adrian Raine, pp. 219-245
ISBN 1-59454-609-6

Chapter 12

NEUROANATOMICAL AND GENETIC INFLUENCES ON SCHIZOPHRENIA AND CRIME: THE SCHIZOPHRENIA-CRIME ASSOCIATION

***Tyrone D. Cannon*[1] *and Adrian Raine*[2]**

[1] Department of Psychology,
University of California, Los Angeles
[2] Department of Psychology and Neuroscience Program,
University of Southern California

INTRODUCTION

Several lines of evidence converge in implicating disturbances of early brain development in the etiology of schizophrenia. By "early", we mean occurring during the formation of the brain during the intrauterine period and the first few years after birth. This evidence includes recent work indicating that reductions in gray matter volume in certain cortical and subcortical regions, including the hippocampus, derive at least in part from the interacting influences of an inherited genotype for schizophrenia and hypoxic complications in utero (Cannon et al. 2002a; Cannon et al. 2002c; Van Erp et al. 2002). Such evidence is consistent with the view that the neuropathology leading to the development of schizophrenia is partly present from birth and may therefore explain motor, language and social-affective delays and other deficits in neurocognitive functioning in children who later develop schizophrenia (Cannon et al. 2000a).

Nevertheless, formal diagnostic symptoms and signs of schizophrenia do not manifest typically until late adolescence and early adulthood. This pattern, combined with evidence from some longitudinal imaging studies of anatomical deterioration in the early phase of schizophrenia (Thompson et al. 2001), suggests that additional factors active during the late adolescent through early adult period (i.e., the "late" period) participate in the deterioration in functioning associated with the onset of schizophrenia. In fact, the primary brain maturational changes occurring in the normal adolescent through early adult period are regressive in nature

(Andersen 2003), leading to a reduction in dendritic arborization and synaptic contacts on cortical neurons (Keshavan and Hogarty 1999). A reduction in cortical neuropil volume, without a loss of cell bodies, is precisely the pattern observed in a number of recent postmortem studies of schizophrenic patients (Glantz and Lewis 2000). Together, these observations suggest that later neurodevelopmental influences may also play a role in the etiology and pathophysiology of schizophrenia.

Compared to research on schizophrenia, there has been much less empirical work on antisocial and criminal behavior. Indeed, a decade ago, brain imaging research on antisocial behavior was in its infancy. Nevertheless, a recent, burgeoning body of brain imaging evidence now attests to the fact that links exist between brain deficits and antisocial, violent behavior. Most of this research has assessed the functioning of the brain using PET (positron emission tomography, measuring glucose metabolism), SPECT (single photon emission computerized tomography assessing blood flow), MRS (magnetic resonance spectroscopy assessing neural density) or fMRI (functional magnetic resonance imaging, measuring blood flow). Some recent studies have employed MRI to assess brain structure (aMRI). These supercede the older imaging studies using computerized tomography (CT) which suffer from relatively poor spatial resolution. To date, the key brain areas that have been shown to be abnormal in antisocial individuals include the prefrontal cortex, temporal cortex, the amygdala-hippocampal complex, and the corpus callosum.

This chapter focuses on the structural brain impairments that have been found to be common to both schizophrenia and crime. Going beyond anatomical MRI, we also discuss initial work on molecular genetic processes underlying the structural brain abnormalities found in schizophrenia, and speculate on the genes that give rise to both antisocial behavior and frontal structural impairments in antisocial personality disorder. Finally, we provide an initial hypothesis on anatomical and genetic abnormalities that may give rise to both crime and schizophrenia which can be pursued in future studies.

Neural System Abnormalities in Schizophrenia

While the specific neurobiological processes that underlie schizophrenic symptoms have not yet been definitively isolated, disturbances in prefrontal and temporal-limbic systems and their interconnections are likely to play critical roles (Cohen and Servan-Schreiber 1992; Grace et al. 1998; Gray et al. 1991). The prefrontal cortex is more highly evolved in humans than in non-human primates and supports higher-order cognitive processes such as working memory, the strategic allocation of attention, reasoning, planning, and other forms of abstract thought (Goldman-Rakic 1995).

In concert with the prefrontal cortex, the medial temporal lobe structures (i.e., hippocampus, amygdala) and adjacent temporal cortex are involved in learning and recall of episodic information, emotion (especially the amygdala) and certain aspects of language processing (Squire and Zola 1996). For example, functional neuroimaging studies have revealed that both prefrontal cortical regions (Braver et al. 2001) and temporal lobe regions (Eldridge et al. 2000) are activated during encoding and retrieval in long-term memory (Braver et al. 2001), as well as during maintenance and manipulation of information in working memory (D'Esposito et al. 1999), and disruptions to working memory during encoding have been shown to dramatically decrease episodic memory (Gardiner and Parkin 1990). Further, performance on both working memory and long-term memory tasks is associated with disturbed dorsolateral prefrontal cortex activation in schizophrenia (Barch et al. 2002).

Neuropsychological studies have shown that, against a background of generalized cognitive deficit, schizophrenic patients show profound deficits in the areas of long-term and working memory (Cannon et al. 2000b). These deficits appear not to be merely secondary effects of impaired attention, disease chronicity, or neuroleptic treatment (Cirillo in press.). Such findings have been corroborated by evidence of abnormal physiologic activity (i.e., altered blood flow) in prefrontal and temporal lobe regions in patients with schizophrenia during performance of tests assessing these same domains of functioning (Callicott et al. 1998; Yurgelun-Todd et al. 1996).

At the structural-anatomical level, schizophrenic patients show a variety of volumetric changes throughout the brain, including reduced cortical, hippocampal, and thalamic volumes and increased sulcal and ventricular volumes (Pfefferbaum and Marsh 1995). Recent neuroimaging work indicates a relatively greater degree of reduction in frontal and temporal cortical volumes compared with posterior cortical volumes (Cannon et al. 1998).

Prefrontal Cortex and Working Memory Deficits

Given that the genetic basis of schizophrenia has thus far proved elusive, and is likely to involve multiple genes of small effect which contribute to increasing risk for the disorder (Moldin and Gottesman 1997), the search for schizophrenia genes may be aided by the study of central nervous system indicators of the inherited vulnerability state, or "endophenotypes" (Cannon et al. 2002b). Several lines of evidence suggest that working memory deficits and associated abnormalities in prefrontal cortical structure and function are reflective of an inherited diathesis to schizophrenia, and thus represent promising candidate endophenotypic markers for the disorder. In a Finnish twin sample, we found that impaired performance on tests of spatial working memory and structural abnormalities in polar and dorsolateral prefrontal regions on MRI varied in a dose-dependent fashion with degree of genetic loading for schizophrenia (Cannon et al. 2000b; Cannon et al. 2002a; Glahn et al. 2002). Figure 1 illustrates the cortical maps showing the magnitude of liability-related gray-matter deficits in polar and dorsolateral prefrontal regions. Interestingly, global and dorsolateral prefrontal volumetric deficits have been found to correlate with performance deficits on tests sensitive to working memory processes (Maher et al. 1995). It has been suggested that a reduction of interneuronal neuropil in the prefrontal region in patients with schizophrenia results in impaired working memory functioning due to hypoactive dopaminergic (i.e., D1-receptor-mediated) modulation of pyramidal cell activity (Goldman-Rakic and Selemon 1997).

This prediction has been supported by a PET investigation which found significantly decreased D1-receptor binding in the prefrontal cortex of neuroleptic-naïve and medication-free schizophrenic patients compared with controls (Okubo et al. 1997). Notably, D1-receptor reduction predicted negative symptomatology and working memory impairment. However, a more recent D1-receptor imaging study found increased D1-receptor binding in the dorsolateral prefrontal cortex of schizophrenic patients compared to controls, which also correlated with reduced working memory performance in schizophrenia (Abi-Dargham et al.

2002), suggesting that more work with a variety of tracers is needed in this area. It is also of interest in this context that treatment with an atypical antipsychotic drug (Risperidone) is associated with normalization of blood flow in the prefrontal cortex and increased behavioral accuracy during performance of a working memory test (Honey et al. 1999).

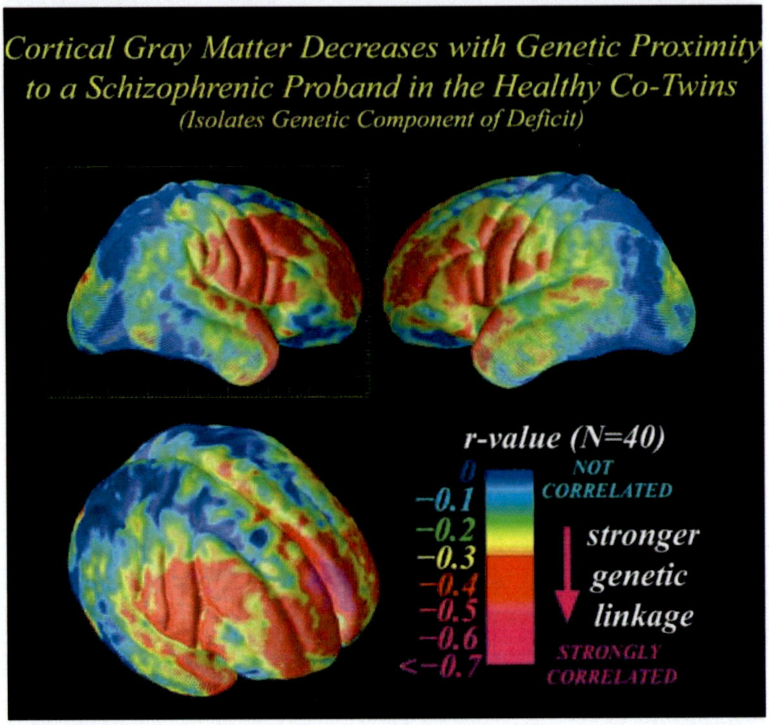

Figure 1. Cortical maps showing the magnitude of liability-related gray-matter deficits viewed from the right, left, and right-oblique perspectives. "R-value" refers to the correlation between gray-matter density and genetic liability to schizophrenia, modeled as highest among unaffected MZ co-twins of probands (n=10), intermediate among unaffected DZ co-twins of probands (n=10), and lowest among normal control twins (n=20, where one co-twin was chosen at random from each pair). The map reveals liability-related deficits primarily in polar and dorsolateral prefrontal regions, the significance of which survived correction for multiple comparisons. Most of the remaining cortex is significantly less affected than the average deficit in the frontal cortex. Reprinted from (Cannon et al. 2002a) with permission from the National Academy of Sciences of the United States of America

Given that abnormalities of working memory and prefrontal structure and function are associated with genetic liability to schizophrenia, it should be possible to identify specific genes that underlie these disturbances. Weinberger and colleagues have reported evidence of one such genetic influence – the MET/VAL polymorphism of the COMT gene (located on chromosome 22), with VAL alleles promoting more rapid breakdown of synaptic dopamine leading to prefrontal hypofunction in patients with schizophrenia (Egan et al. 2001). We have been interested in another potential susceptibility locus that may affect prefrontal function in schizophrenia, this one on chromosome 1. St. Clair and colleagues (St Clair et al. 1990) identified a large Scottish kindred showing linkage between schizophrenia and a balanced translocation involving chromosomes 1 and 11 t(1;11)(q42.1;q14.3) with a maximum LOD score of 6.0. Sequence analysis of the chromosome 1 site revealed the disruption of two overlapping and antiparallel genes in the 1q41 region (DISC1 and DISC2) (Millar et al. 2000), located approximately 0 – 1.5 cMs from marker D1S2833. Notably, in a national sample of affected sib-pairs drawn from the general Finnish population, Ekelund et al. (Ekelund et al. 2000) observed significant linkage of the 1q41 region with schizophrenia, with maximal evidence of linkage at marker D1S2833.

To further elucidate the nature and location of this potential susceptibility locus, we performed linkage and association analyses across the chromosome 1 region of interest using quantitative neuropsychological measures of liability in our sample of dizygotic twins discordant for schizophrenia (Gasperoni et al. 2003). Analyses with a composite measure of liability yielded suggestive evidence for linkage at marker D1S2833 ($P = 0.04$). Follow-up analyses of the individual trait measures revealed that the Spatial Span subtest of the Wechsler Memory Scale (WMS), an indicator of spatial working memory function, was uniquely sensitive to marker D1S2833 ($P = 0.007$). Association analysis confirmed that allelic variation in D1S2833 is associated with variation in spatial working memory performance as measured by the Spatial Span subtest ($P = 0.003$), the significance of which was confirmed in an analysis of 10,000 Monte Carlo permutations. These findings implicate a gene near the D1S2833 marker (most probably the DISC1 locus) in the etiology of spatial working memory deficits in schizophrenic patients and their relatives.

The DNA sequence of the DISC1 gene is most homologous to proteins involved in axon guidance, synaptogenesis, and intracellular axonal and dendritic transport. Recently, the protein was shown to promote neurite outgrowth (Ozeki et al. 2003). This function may help to explain the reductions in neuropil volume observed in postmortem studies of schizophrenia.

Together, these findings strongly implicate genetic factors as playing a role in the abnormalities of prefrontal cortex and working memory in schizophrenia. Because deficits on tests sensitive to working memory have also been observed in children at elevated genetic risk (Cosway et al. 2000), it is tempting to conclude that disturbances in the prefrontal cortex in schizophrenia are reflective of an inherited vulnerability to the disorder that is present from early in life. Nevertheless, patients with schizophrenia have been found to show even greater disturbances in DLPFC function and structure than their non-ill MZ co-twins (Cannon et al. 2002a). Thus, while genetic factors may cause patients and some of their first-degree relatives to share a certain degree of compromise in prefrontal cortical systems, non-genetic disease-related influences cause the DLPFC to be further deviant in the patients.

The timing of the appearance of this disease-related increase in DLPFC abnormality is not known, but could conceivably reflect both early and late neurodevelopmental influences. The DLPFC is one of the regions to mature the latest in the mammalian brain, with apoptotic and synaptic pruning processes occurring maximally in the adolescent to early adult period (Huttenlocher 1979). Given that both members of a discordant MZ twin pair pass through this period of development with the same genetic make-up, a non-genetic influence, if experienced by one co-twin preferentially, could potentially interact with pruning processes to result in lower DLPFC volume in some individuals as they become affected with schizophrenia. Consistent with this point of view is evidence from recent longitudinal neuroimaging studies of patients with schizophrenia showing structural changes within the same patients over time, especially in the early stages of illness (Thompson et al. 2001; Wood et al. 2001). In early-onset schizophrenia in particular, striking anatomical profiles of accelerated gray matter loss have been detected; using brain mapping algorithms, such deficits were observed to move in a dynamic pattern, beginning in parietal association cortices and proceeding frontally to envelop dorsolateral prefrontal cortex and temporal cortices (Thompson et al. 2001 - see Figure 2).

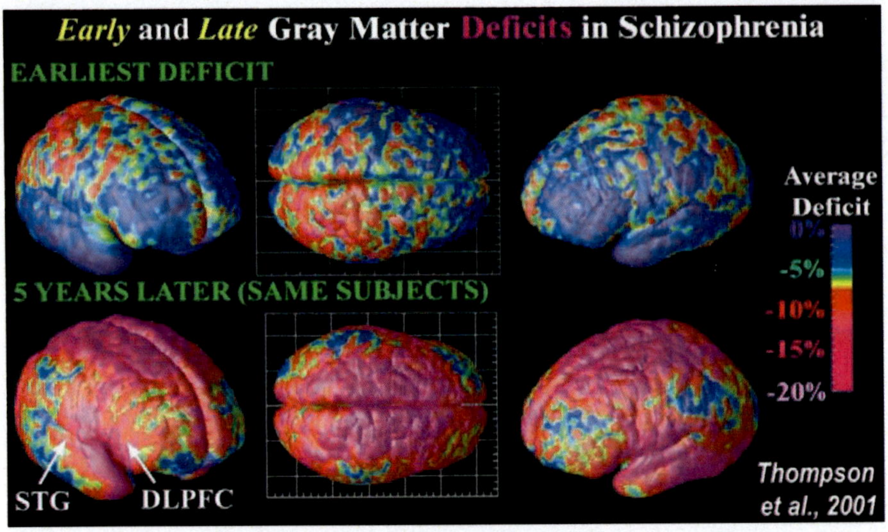

Figure 2. Mapping Early and Late Deficits in Schizophrenia. Deficits occurring during the development of schizophrenia are detected by comparing average profiles of gray matter between patients and controls at their first scan (age 13; top row) and their last scan 5 years later (age 18; bottom row). Although severe parietal, motor and diffuse frontal loss has already occurred (top row), and subsequently continues (Figs. 1,2), the temporal and dorsolateral pre-frontal loss characteristic of adult schizophrenia is not found until later in adolescence (bottom row), where a process of fast attrition occurs over the next 5 years. The color code shows the significance of these effects. Reprinted from (Thompson et al. 2001) with permission from the National Academy of Sciences of the United States of America

However, involvement of early neurodevelopmental influences in prefrontal cortical deficits in schizophrenia cannot be excluded. In an MRI study of a Helsinki birth cohort, we found that a history of fetal hypoxia was associated with significant decreases in gray matter density in both prefrontal and temporal lobe regions among patients with schizophrenia and their healthy siblings, but not in controls at low genetic risk for the disorder, and more so in the patients than in their siblings (Cannon et al. 2002c). We interpreted this pattern as consistent with a genotype-environment interaction. At the cellular level, the neural sequelae of hypoxia vary in severity from alterations in neurite outgrowth to neuronal cell death (Nyakas et al. 1996). In the former case, immature neurons may survive the hypoxic insult but still have a compromised elaboration of synaptic interconnections (Nyakas et al. 1996). Studies in fetal sheep have shown that hypoxia secondary to chronic placental insufficiency is associated with reduced cortical thickness and increased cortical neuronal density, without any observable neuronal loss (Rees et al. 1998).

The pattern of morphologic changes associated with hypoxia in our human study is thus compatible with an animal model of chronic fetal hypoxia and with the observed cellular pathology in schizophrenic patients. Note that this account would not exclude involvement of cortical synaptic pruning during late adolescence and early adulthood (Feinberg 1982; Keshavan et al. 1994), as these later maturational events could interact with the earlier hypoxia-related effects in lowering interneuronal connectivity to below a threshold critical for integrated cognitive activity, leading to further behavioral deterioration at that time.

Temporal Lobe and Episodic Memory Deficits

Several microscopic abnormalities of the hippocampus have been documented in schizophrenia including alterations in neuronal density (Zaidel et al. 1997), size (Arnold 2000), and orientation (Conrad et al. 1991). Hippocampal volume decreases appear to be present at disease onset (Bilder et al. 1995), and several postmortem and MRI studies have reported positive correlations between hippocampal volume and age at onset (Stefanis et al. 1999; Van Erp et al. 2002). Hippocampal volume reductions also appear to be present in healthy biological relatives of schizophrenia probands (Seidman et al. 2002).

Only one study to date has compared structural hippocampal measures between high-risk subjects who later developed a psychotic illness and those who did not (Phillips et al. 2002); contrary to expectation, findings indicated that *larger* left hippocampal volume in prodromal subjects at intake was associated with the subsequent development of acute psychosis, rather than smaller volumes. These results appear to be inconsistent with the genetic high-risk studies described above, and point to the need for more longitudinal research on prodromal subjects who are both genetically at-risk for psychosis and exhibiting early symptoms.

From a neurocognitive perspective, impaired declarative memory processes that depend on the integrity of the hippocampus (Faraone et al. 2000) have been reported in both high-risk adolescents (Byrne et al. 1999) and non-psychotic relatives of schizophrenics (Cannon et al. 1994), suggesting that they derive in part from an inherited genotype. However, because long-term memory deficits are specifically more pronounced in patients compared with their own healthy MZ co-twins, non-genetic, disease-related factors must also be involved (Cannon et al. 2000b). Importantly, two studies have shown a significant relationship between deficits in verbal declarative memory and smaller hippocampal volumes in relatives of schizophrenia patients (Seidman et al. 2002). Initial evidence indicates that impairment in long-term verbal memory and, to a lesser extent, executive function is associated with the occurrence of psychotic symptoms in prodromal high-risk subjects, suggesting that such deficits may mark the pathophysiological processes underlying functional deterioration during the prodromal phase of schizophrenia (Cosway et al. 2000).

The hippocampus in particular is acutely vulnerable to hypoxic-ischemic damage (Zola and Squire 2001). Obstetric complications (i.e., oxygen deprivation) have been linked with hippocampal abnormalities in schizophrenia (McNeil et al. 2000). Specifically, in MZ twins discordant for schizophrenia, relatively small hippocampi in the ill twin were significantly related to labor-delivery complications and to prolonged labor, both risk factors associated with fetal oxygen deprivation (McNeil et al. 2000). We have previously found, in a Helsinki birth cohort, that schizophrenia probands who experienced fetal hypoxia have smaller hippocampal volumes than in those who did not, a difference not noted within unaffected siblings and healthy comparison subjects (Van Erp et al. 2002). At the same time, hippocampal volume differences occurred in a stepwise fashion with each increase in genetic load for schizophrenia (Seidman et al. 2002), suggesting that, in patients with schizophrenia spectrum disorders, hippocampal volume is influenced in part by schizophrenia susceptibility genes and an interaction of these genes with fetal hypoxia.

Additionally, there is growing evidence that fetal hypoxia predicts early-onset schizophrenia (Cannon et al. 2000c) and that adolescent-onset schizophrenic patients perform worse than adult-onset patients on cognitive functions involving the hippocampus, such as remote memory (Johnstone et al. 1989), recent memory and executive functions (Basso et al. 1997). In our twin sample, we found shared and unique environmental effects on hippocampal gray matter volumes in schizophrenia. Specifically, probands' hippocampal volumes were smaller than those of their non-schizophrenic MZ and DZ co-twins and healthy subjects, and probands' non-ill co-twins' hippocampal volumes were smaller than those of healthy subjects, but non-ill MZ and DZ co-twins of schizophrenic patients did not differ from each other. The intraclass correlations (ICCs) for hippocampal volumes among healthy MZ pairs were larger than those among healthy DZ pairs, but the ICCs for hippocampal volumes among discordant MZ and DZ pairs were equivalent. Together, these findings indicate that while hippocampal volume in healthy subjects is under substantial genetic control, hippocampal volume in schizophrenic patients and their relatives appears to be influenced to a greater extent by unique and shared environmental factors (van Erp submitted).

Course of Change in Prodromal Patients

The only study to date to examine whether progressive structural changes occur in prodromal subjects is that of Pantelis and colleagues (Pantelis 2002); findings indicate striking baseline differences in regional grey-matter volume between those who subsequently developed a psychotic illness and those who did not; specifically, those who developed psychosis had less gray matter in the right medial temporal, lateral temporal, and inferior frontal cortex, and in the cingulate cortex bilaterally. In the longitudinal comparison, when re-scanned, individuals who had developed psychosis showed a reduction in gray matter in the left parahippocampal, fusiform, orbitofrontal and cerebellar cortices, and the cingulate gyri, whereas longitudinal changes were restricted to the cerebellum in those who did not become psychotic.

While this is a fascinating and important first study, this study did not distinguish between outcomes of schizophrenia and other psychotic illness, and obtained MRI outcome data on only 21 of the original 75 patients. Moreover, normal comparison subjects were not scanned twice. Thus, replication is warranted in a larger sample, with comparisons with comparable test-retest scan designs, and the question of whether there is a core neuropathology of schizophrenia that can be detected prior to illness onset remains to be answered.

Such a progressive developmental pathophysiology of the illness during adolescence (Woods 1998) may result from several factors working singly, or in combination. First, genetic factors may predispose to an excess synaptic elimination, increased neuronal apoptosis, decreased cell somal size or a combination of these processes during adolescence. Such changes might result from altered expression of genes that are critical for neurodevelopmental processes such as glutamatergic NMDA/AMPA receptor expression (Olney and Farber 1995), brain derived neurotrophic factor levels (Nawa et al. 2000), or altered dynamics of dopaminergic and GABAergic neurotransmitter systems (Costa et al.

2001). Second, hormonal changes, especially of the reproductive steroids, could modulate brain maturational processes such as synaptic pruning and/or myelination (Amateau and McCarthy 2002). This possibility is supported by observations that age related gray matter volume reductions during adolescence in healthy males might be steeper than those of healthy females (De Bellis et al. 2001). Third, psychosocial environmental factors might play a significant role as well. It is known that environmental enrichment leads to increased spine density and dendritic arborization (Globus et al. 1973). Likewise, environmental impoverishment or stress could conceivably lead to the opposite, i.e. an increased fall-out of synapses and/or neurons (Teicher et al. 2002), and decreased neuronal viability (De Bellis et al. 2001).

PREFRONTAL IMPAIRMENTS IN ANTISOCIAL PERSONALITY

Turning from schizophrenia to brain mechanisms involved in criminal and antisocial personality, neurological research studies have shown that those suffering significant prefrontal damage develop an antisocial, psychopathic-like personality (Damasio et al. 1994). These patients also show electrodermal arousal and orienting deficits to socially meaningful events, a finding consistent both with the role played by the prefrontal cortex in modulating emotion, arousal, and attention (Davidson et al., 2000) and also the psychophysiological impairments found in psychopathic offenders (Patrick et al., 1997).

Alternatively, these neurological patients have major structural prefrontal deficits, and the relevance and generalizability of such findings to individuals with APD and psychopathy in both society and prison could be questioned. To address this issue, we reversed the standard neurological paradigm (starting with individuals with major prefrontal trauma and assessing outcome behavior) by instead taking as the starting point community individuals with APD, and using structural MRIs to assess prefrontal gray volume. We found that APDs showed an 11% reduction in prefrontal gray compared with normal controls, substance dependence controls, and psychiatric controls (Raine et al., 2000), deficits that could not be explained by psychosocial factors. This deficit was relative in that no difference in whole brain volume was observed, and was specific to prefrontal gray matter as opposed to white. APDs also showed reduced skin conductance and cardiovascular reactivity to a social stressor eliciting secondary emotions of shame, embarrassment, and fear. Furthermore, within the APDs, those with prefrontal gray volume reductions had lower skin conductance activity during the stressor than those without reduced prefrontal gray, indicating a structure-function relationship. Taken together, findings from this first anatomical MRI study of APD are consistent with a somatic marker hypothesis of APD (Bechara et al., 1997; Damasio, 1994) and extend and amplify findings from neurological research. They also show that different clinical neuroscience paradigms are beginning to converge on the conclusion that there is a significant brain basis to APD, and that these neurobehavioral processes are relevant to understanding violence in everyday society.

Nevertheless, there are some important limitations to this research. The sample size for APDs is modest (N = 21) and replicability can be questioned. There appear to be only three other MRI studies which bear on this issue. Woermann et al. (2000) found significantly reduced left prefrontal gray volumes in aggressive epileptic patients. Laakso et al. (2002) found reduced left prefrontal gray volumes (dorsolateral, orbito-frontal, and medial), in alcoholics with antisocial personalities compared to controls, but argued for an abolition of these findings when duration of alcoholism was employed as a covariate. This conclusion may not be warranted because this covariate is very heavily correlated with group membership (i.e. all controls have a zero age of alcoholism onset, while all alcoholic antisocial subjects have some age of onset); as such, the covariate analysis is almost synonymous with controlling for group membership. Finally, Dolan, et al., (2002) did not find significantly reduced frontal volumes in patients with impulsive aggressive personality disorder. Overall, initial studies neither refute the original findings nor convincingly support them.

Assuming that a prefrontal structural impairment is observed in APDs, an important question concerns its precise localization within the prefrontal cortex. Different theoretical perspectives make differential predictions on which prefrontal sector is most impaired.

Orbitofrontal / Ventral Cortex

To date, the strongest prediction is that any prefrontal impairment in APD is localized to the orbitofrontal/ventral region. Several lines of evidence support this prediction. First, orbitofrontal damage has been traditionally viewed as resulting in personality disorders and impaired emotion and behavioral inhibition, features common to APD (Stuss and Levine, 2002). Second, data based on acquired damage to the prefrontal cortex in civilians (e.g. Damasio, 1994) and soldiers (e.g. Grafman et al., 1996) implicate the ventromedial and orbitofrontal sub-regions in antisocial behavior. Third, some neuropsychological studies of APDs and other antisocial groups have claimed that orbitofrontal functions are most impaired (Dinn and Harris, 2000). Fourth, moral judgments in normals activate the ventromedial cortex bilaterally (Heekeren et al. 2003), suggesting that immoral behavior may result from impairment to this region. Fifth, psychopaths with APD fail to show the differential CS+/CS- activation that normals show in the right orbitofrontal cortex during the acquisition phase of aversive classical conditioning (Veit et al., 2002). Sixth, the orbitofrontal cortex has important connections with other cortical and subcortical brain regions implicated in emotion regulation (Davidson et al., 2000).

In theoretical terms, the hypothesis that APDs will particularly show orbitofrontal / ventral impairments is consistent with Damasio's somatic marker hypothesis. Patients with orbito-frontal / ventral damage fail to give anticipatory skin conductance responses to choice options that are risky, and make bad choices even when aware of the more advantageous option (Bechara et al., 1997). This inability to reason and to take appropriate decisions in risky situations may contribute to the impulsivity, rule-breaking, and reckless, irresponsible behavior that make up four of the seven traits of DSM-IV APD. The linkage of ventral/orbitofrontal damage with the failure to develop somatic markers is consistent with reduced autonomic anticipatory fear found in both child and adolescent antisocial / psychopathic individuals (Raine, 1993; Patrick et al. 1994; Fung et al., 2005). For both theoretical and empirical reasons therefore, it is reasonable to speculate that prefrontal structural impairments in APDs are localized to the orbitofrontal / ventral region.

Dorsolateral Prefrontal Cortex (DLPFC)

An alternative hypothesis is that prefrontal structural impairments may be localized to the DLPFC. The DLPFC is critically involved in cognitive flexibility and response perseveration. Because recidivistic, antisocial behavior can be conceptualized as perseverative, unmodifyable behavior in the face of repeatedly punished responses, APD could be the product of the cognitive inflexibility and response perseveration that follows from damage to the DLPFC. Furthermore, individual studies and a meta-analysis indicate that deficits in executive function tasks do indeed exist in antisocial individuals (Morgan and Lilienfeld, 2000; Ishikawa and Raine, 2003). Additionally, PET and MRI studies have found that violent offenders have widespread reductions in prefrontal functions that include the DLPFC (Raine et al. 1997), while one fMRI study has found reduced prefrontal activation to response inhibition (Go/Nogo tack) localized to the left DLPFC in psychopaths (Smith, 2000). At a structural level, reduced volume of the DLPFC has been found in antisocial alcoholics (Laakso et al., 2002).

A further reason to implicate the DLPFC in APD lies at the endophenotypic level of analysis. Functional imaging and neurological research shows that individual APD traits are linked to DLPFC. For example, empathic and forgivable judgments have been found to activate the left superior frontal gyrus in addition to the orbitofrontal gyrus (Farrow et al., 2001), while moral judgments in contrast to non-moral control judgments activate the middle frontal gyrus (Eslinger et al. 2002) and the left DLPFC (Heekeren et al., 2003). Furthermore, patients with either left or right DLPFC lesions have impaired empathy and reduced cognitive flexibility (Grattan et al., 1994). Because APDs lack empathy (American Psychiatric Association, 1994), they could be expected to show DLPFC impairments. APDs also lack planning ability (American Psychiatric Association, 1994), and fMRI studies implicate the DLPFC in planning and task manipulation (Cazalis et al., 2003). Taking together these lines of thinking, there are several reason to expect DLPFC impairments in APDs.

Widespread Prefrontal Impairment

A third, alternative model is that prefrontal structural impairments in APDs are not localized but are instead spread throughout all prefrontal sectors. As outlined above, there are reasonable empirical reasons to believe that *both* orbitofrontal / ventral and dorsolateral regions may be impaired in APDs. Taking this argument to a broader level, APD is clearly a complex personality disorder that is made up of a relatively broad array of behavioral, cognitive, and emotional traits that are pervasive from childhood to adulthood. These multiple characteristics are more likely to be predicated on impairment to *multiple* regions of the prefrontal cortex rather than originating from the same source. In support of this, one of the very few studies to date on prefrontal structural impairments in APDs which has also segmented the prefrontal cortex finds impairments in all dorsolateral, orbitofrontal, and medial prefrontal regions (Laakso et al., 2002).

Furthermore, there are clearly prefrontal regions other than the DLPFC and orbital / ventral regions that may be implicated in the multiple traits that define APD. For example, fMRI studies indicate that the mesial prefrontal cortex is one of a number of areas activated by multiple inhibitory response tasks (Rubia et al. 2001). Furthermore, a meta-analysis of 330 functional brain imaging studies indicate that emotional activation tasks produce a greater likelihood of activation in the medial prefrontal compared to cognitive tasks, with the medial prefrontal boundary between emotion and cognitive activation being supra-genual (Steele and Lawrie, 2004). Given that a lack of behavioral inhibition and emotion regulation are thought to be central to a number of APD features, structural impairments to the medial prefrontal cortex is conceivable.

Amygdala and Hippocampal Impairments in Antisocial Groups

It is clear that the prefrontal cortex plays a critical regulatory role in a larger brain circuit involved in emotion regulation, decision-making, and the inhibition of aggressive and antisocial behavior (Damasio, 1994). Neural processes underlying antisocial behavior are complex and cannot be simplistically reduced to single brain mechanisms causing APD in a direct, causal fashion (Raine et al., 2000). Other structures may well be implicated, particularly those connected to the prefrontal cortex, including the amygdala, hippocampus, anterior cingulate, and the corpus callosum.

Amygdala

Blair (2003) has speculated that abnormalities in the amygdala in part underlie psychopathic behavior. The amygdala is critically involved in fear conditioning (LeDoux, 1996) and in the processing of fearful and sad facial expressions (Adolphs et al. 1996). Relatedly, psychopathic and criminal offenders show impairments in both fear conditioning and processing fear and sadness in others (Blair, 2001), and also emotion-modulation of the startle-blink reflex (Patrick, 1994). Because the amygdala plays a crucial role in emotional processes in animals and humans (Davidson et al., 2000), amygdala impairments could partly explain the emotional and learning deficits observed in psychopathic, antisocial individuals.

Brian imaging research on the amygdala in antisocial populations is sparse. Findings to date include an abnormal functional asymmetry in murderers using PET (Raine et al. 1997), reduced activation to negative affect stimuli in psychopaths (Kiehl et al., 2001), and reduced N-acetyl aspartate (NAA) in the amygdala-hippocampal complex (Critchley et al., 2000). Anatomically, one study observed reduced amygdala volumes in psychopaths (Tiihonen et al., 2000) but another study failed to show amygdala pathology in aggressive patients (Elst et al. 2000).

To date, there appear to be no studies on structural integrity of the amygdala in APDs. Because the amygdala is reciprocally connected to the ventromedial cortex (Davidson et al., 2000), linked volumetric reduction in both regions could exist in antisocial groups. Alternatively, two conditioning studies have shown either *increased* activation in the amygdala in APDs / psychopaths (Schneider et al., 2000) or conversely an appropriate amygdala response (Veit et al., 2002). Consequently, normal or even exaggerated amygdala volume cannot be ruled out. For example, the descending pathway between the medial prefrontal cortex and amygdala is inhibitory. Conceivable, ventro-medial damage combined with an *unimpaired* amygdala could result in reduced inhibitory control over the amygdala's response to threat stimuli and inappropriate evaluation of the social context by the orbitofrontal cortex, resulting in impulsive, aggressive behavior. As such, both structures which play a critical role in emotion regulation, aversive classical conditioning, and emotional expression may be together implicated in antisocial behavior.

Hippocampus

The hippocampus is a key structure in the limbic circuit that is thought to regulate emotional behavior (Swanson, 1999), and has been implicated in aggressive, antisocial behavior in animals and humans. In animals, the hippocampus regulates aggression via projections to midbrain peri-aqueductal gray and the perifornical lateral hypothalamus, structures important in mediating both defensive rage and predatory attack (Gregg and Siegel, 2001). Structurally, aggressive male mice show size reductions in intra- and infra-pyramidal mossy fiber terminal fields in the hippocampus (Hensbroek et al., 1995) while rats with hippocampal lesions at birth show increased aggressive behavior in adulthood (Becker et al. 1999).

Abnormal structure and function have been reported in human antisocial populations. Our earlier functional imaging work on violent offenders had observed an unusual asymmetry in hippocampal functioning, with lower left but increased right functioning in violent offenders (Raine et al., 1997). We recently took this finding into the structural domain, and found that unsuccessful psychopaths showed an exaggerated right greater than left structural hippocampal asymmetry relative to both successful psychopaths and controls (Raine et al., 2004), findings which were localized to the anterior region. Atypical anterior hippocampal asymmetries in unsuccessful psychopaths may reflect an underlying neurodevelopmental abnormality that disrupts hippocampal-prefrontal circuitry, resulting in affect dysregulation, poor contextual fear conditioning, and insensitivity to cues predicting capture.

Using the same population, Yang et al. (2005) revealed a significant 18-23% reduction in prefrontal gray matter only in unsuccessful psychopaths compared to both successful psychopaths and controls. We believe these findings are broadly consistent with a somatic marker hypothesis of antisocial, sociopathic behavior (Damasio, 1994). Because unsuccessful psychopaths also show reduced autonomic stress reactivity and executive function deficits (Ishikawa et al. 2001), poor decision-making, reduced autonomic reactivity to cues predicting punishment, and reduced prefrontal gray may render them less sensitive to environmental cues signaling danger and capture, hence making them more prone to conviction.

We do not believe that prefrontal structural impairments, in and of themselves, cause antisocial, psychopathic behavior. Instead, it is more likely that there is more complex disruption to neural circuitry, albeit involving the prefrontal cortex, which predisposes to psychopathic traits. One such candidate circuit is the septo-hippocampal-frontal system. Given our conjoint findings of both prefrontal and hippocampal structural impairments in unsuccessful psychopaths (Raine et al., 2004; Yang et al., 2005), anterior hippocampal abnormality may be associated with unsuccessful psychopathy by signaling disruption to frontal-subcortical neural circuitry. Earlier animal research has also found that lesions to the septo-hippocampal-frontal system result in behavioral disinhibition and a hypersensitivity to immediate reward (Gorenstein and Newman, 1980), while in humans disruption to circuits involving the prefrontal cortex and hippocampus have been implicated in both disrupted emotion regulation and antisocial / aggressive behavior (Davidson, 2000). Given that the orbito-frontal cortex likely exerts control over the anterior hippocampus through entorhinal-hippocampal projections (Pansky et al., 1988) and given also our prior findings, impairments in criminals may be specific to the orbito-frontal region of the prefrontal cortex and the anterior hippocampus.

Further research supports the hypothesis of hippocampal impairments in antisocial groups. Similarly, reduced left parahippocampal gyral activation has been found in psychopaths (Muller et al., 2003) together with reduced activation in the amygdala-hippocampal complex (Kiehl et al., 2001). Structural impairments are indicated by reduced N-acetyl aspartate (NAA) in the amygdala-hippocampal complex in violent offenders (Critchley et al., 2000), and left hippocampal atrophy has been reported in 6 of 10 violent APD patients (Chesterman et al. 1994). One structural MRI study has found reduced *right* hippocampal volume reductions in violent offenders with APD (Laakso et al., 2001).

At a theoretical level the hippocampus is involved in the retrieval of emotional memories and contextual fear conditioning (LeDoux, 1996), and hippocampal pathology could also help explain classical conditioning theories of psychopathic / criminal behavior (Patrick et al., 1994). At the level of the amygdala, the uncoupling of the hippocampus from the amygdala could result in inappropriate emotional expression to the social context, and also in poor insight into emotional states (LeDoux, 1996). At the prefrontal level, a compromised hippocampus could signal disruption to frontal-subcortical neural circuitry that contributes to affect dysregulation and the impulsive, disinhibited behavior observed in psychopaths.

As outlined above for the amygdala, conjoint impairment of the hippocampus and prefrontal cortex may provide a more complete explanation of APD. Indeed, hippocampal abnormalities per se may not raise the incidence of APD. Instead, hippocampal abnormalities may most likely predispose to aggressive, inappropriate, and psychopathic behavior when combined with prefrontal impairments that decrease behavioral inhibition and regulation over the amygdala. Structural impairments of these conjoint structures may therefore be central to a neurobiological explanation of antisocial and criminal behavior.

Molecular Genetics, Structural Brain Abnormalities, and Antisocial Behavior

An uncharted research area concerns the molecular genetic basis to brain impairments in APD. A key question concerns whether brain impairments have a molecular genetic underpinning. Relatedly, does this same gene(s) differentiate APDs from controls? We focus here on just three possible candidates – BDNF, NOTCH4, and COMT.

BDNF (brain derived neurotrophic factor) is a neurotrophin that plays a key role in the regulation of the survival and structure of CNS neurons, and also influences cortical dendrite growth (Huang and Reichardt, 2001). Mutant mice with BDNF selectively restricted in the forebrain have a thinner cortex at five weeks due to neuronal shrinkage, indicating a role of BDNF in the maintenance of neural size and dendritic structure (Gorski et al., 2003). Furthermore, a human fMRI study found the BDNF val66met polymorphism linked to reduced hippocampal functioning (Hariri et al. 2003), and also reduced hippocampal N-acetyl aspartate, a marker of neuronal integrity (Egan et al., 2003) - again linking BDNF with neural structure. Regarding aggression, mutant mice deficient in BDNF become highly aggressive and risk-taking (Einat et al., 2003; Lyons et al., 1999). Because the BDNF gene is linked to both reduced cortical thickness *and* increased aggression a nonconservative val to met substitution at codon 66 in the BDNF gene may represent a frequent polymorphism that underlies both structural cortical impairments (particularly cortical thinning) and also APD.

A second gene linked to both impaired brain structure and also increased antisocial behavior is the developmentally-expressed NOTCH4 gene which is involved in neuronal stem cell differentiation, cell determination, and outgrowth of axons and dendrites. In normals, a $(CTG)_n$ in exon one of NOTCH4 (6 CTG repeats) is associated with both reduced prefrontal gray volume and reduced frontal lobe (WCST) functioning (Wassink et al., 2003). In human normal controls, the NOTCH4 SNP2 variant has been associated with both increased irritability and also increased activity and extraversion, personality traits that have been correlated with APD (Carmine et al., 2003). Consequently, NOTCH allele variability could partly mediate both APD and also the structural prefrontal gray abnormalities we have previously found in APDs.

In humans, a polymorphism on the COMT gene has been cross-culturally linked to aggressive personality in U.S., German, and Italian clinical and non-clinical populations (Rujescu et al., 2003; Mazzanti et al., 1999; Volavka et al., 2004). In animals, catechol-o-methyl transferase gene (COMT) knockout mice show high levels of aggression (Gogos et al., 1998). Neurocognitive, psychophysiological, and imaging studies also implicate a common polymorphism in the COMT gene in prefrontal functioning in both adults and children (Egan et al., 2001; Diamond et al., 2004). Particularly given links between prefrontal structure / function and APD (see above) as well as this cross – animal/human linkage, this would be a reasonable candidate gene for further exploration.

Schizophrenia and Crime: Common Brain and Genetic Risk Factors?

Genes, Brain Impairments, and Schizophrenia-Crime Comorbidity

We have argued above that prefrontal and temporal-limbic structural brain abnormalities have been observed in schizophrenia patients, and that they may account for the working memory impairments found in these patients. It was also argued that while genetic processes (particularly DISC1 and COMT genes) may partly account for the prefrontal functional impairments in schizophrenia, environmental influences included anoxia at birth contribute to the hippocampal structural brain impairments that have also been observed in schizophrenia.

In a similar fashion, we have also argued that prefrontal structural impairments are also observed in antisocial populations, and indeed, that prefrontal structural impairment can in a causal fashion predispose to antisocial, psychopathic-like behavior. We have also argued that structural hippocampal impairments have also been observed in antisocial groups, and that a polymorphism on the COMT gene has been related to aggressive personality in several studies.

Juxtaposing these two perspectives, it is speculated that the significant comorbidity that has been documented between crime and schizophrenia (Brennan and Alden, in press) could be partly accounted for by common brain impairments. We suggest that structural impairment to the prefrontal cortex and the hippocampus may be part of the neurobiological commonality between schizophrenia and crime. We further speculate that a common set of genes may be implicated in both schizophrenia and crime and that they partly account for the comorbidity by acting on common brain structures. These genes include COMT, NOTCH4, and BDNF.

As outlined above, the COMT gene has been linked to both schizophrenia and also aggression in both humans and animals. Based on a review of the literature linking schizophrenia with crime together with data from three additional Danish cohort studies, Silverton (1988a; 1988b) argued that the link between schizophrenia and crime is genetically-mediated, with specific environmental stressors interacting with this genotype to produce either schizophrenia or antisocial behavior. Because the COMT gene has also been linked to prefrontal functional impairments, and because such impairments are well-replicated correlates of both schizophrenia and crime, it may reflect part of a genetic linkage between schizophrenia and crime.

Similarly, as outlined above the BDNF (brain derived neurotrophic factor) gene has been linked to aggression in mice. In addition, it has recently been reported that the val66met single-nucleotide polymorphism of this gene has been associated with schizophrenia (Neves-Pereira et al., 2005). Because imaging research has demonstrated that this polymorphism is related to reduced hippocampal functioning (Hariri et al. 2003) and also reduced hippocampal N-acetyl aspartate (Egan et al., 2003), it could conceivably account for the hippocampal impairments found in both schizophrenia and antisocial populations. The empirical data are clearly very sparse, but this is one example of how an individual gene can give rise to a brain impairment that in turn predisposes to both schizophrenia and crime, and in doing so is a part-explanation for the comorbidity between schizophrenia and crime.

With respect to NOTCH4, we outlined above how allele variability is both associated with prefrontal structural and functional impairments, and also with increased irritability. In addition however, a recent meta-analysis has resulted in the conclusion that several NOTCH4 polymorphisms (including (TAA)(n), (CTG)(n), SNP1, and SNP2) are associated with schizophrenia (Glatt et al., 2005). It is conceivable therefore that NOTCH4 in part results in prefrontal impairment which in turn predisposes to both schizophrenia and crime.

Memory, Birth Complications, and Crime

If part of the genetic predisposition to schizophrenia is reflected in both prefrontal structure and also prefrontal function as indicated by spatial memory deficits (Cannon et al. 2002a), and if there is indeed a genetic link between crime and schizophrenia, then it would be predicted that in addition to structural prefrontal impairments, antisocial individuals should also show working memory impairments, including spatial memory deficits. We recently tested this proposition using a community sample of 325 schoolboys in whom a variety of neurocognitive measures were assessed at age 16-17 years (Raine et al. 2005). Antisocial behavior measures collected from age 7 to 17 years were used to identify those boys who were persistently antisocial across all ages. Those on the Life-Course Persistent path were found to be particularly impaired on both visual and verbal memory, involving both immediate and delayed memory functions. These findings are consistent with other studies which have found memory impairments in antisocial and violent groups (e.g. Dolan and Park,

2002b; Moffitt and Caspi, 2001; Seguin et al. 2002). Consequently, if a genetic linkage between crime and schizophrenia does indeed exist, it may manifest itself through the hippocampal and prefrontal impairments that in turn predispose to memory impairments.

The notion that hypoxia at birth could contribute to the memory impairments in schizophrenia patients raises the possibility that birth complications could also contribute to the memory impairments observed in antisocial populations. Consistent with this possibility, a number of studies have shown that birth complications are associated with later antisocial and violent behavior (Raine et al., 1994; Piquero and Tibbetts, 1999; Hodgins et al. 2001; Kemppainen et al. 2001; Werner, 1997; Brennan et al. 1993). On the other hand, these studies have indicated that birth complications increase the risk for antisocial and violent behavior only in the presence of other psychosocial risk factors such as maternal rejection of the child and a disruptive family environment. Consequently, although schizophrenia and crime may share the common risk factor of birth complications and hippocampal impairments, the absence of an adverse family environment may predispose to schizophrenia and not crime, while the presence of psychosocial risk factors may result in both crime and schizophrenia.

Conclusions

The latter point emphasizes an important issue. Theoretical explanations for the comorbidity between schizophrenia and crime have to take into account not only common mechanisms that help explain the comorbidity, but also processes which explain differential outcome. There is an enormous empirical literature documenting social and environmental risk factors for crime (Wilson and Petersilia, 2002) which stands in contrast to a very limited literature on social causation of schizophrenia. As such, the presence or absence of psychosocial adversity in those sharing the same diathesis for schizophrenia clearly represents a possible explanation for why some but not others go on to develop criminal behavior.

In addition, differential *neurobiological* processes may also help account for differential outcome. For example, genetic and environmental processes that impair both ventromedial and dorsolateral prefrontal structure / function may result in an individual manifesting both crime and schizophrenia. However, impairment only to the ventromedial PFC (resulting in disinhibited behavior) may result in crime but not schizophrenia, while impairment only to the DLPFC (resulting in cognitive-perceptual impairments) may result in schizophrenia but not crime. Alternatively, impairments to the amygdala may result in reduced fear conditioning and antisocial behavior in those with the diathesis for schizophrenia, while sparing of the amygdala may result only in outcome for schizophrenia.

Currently, we can only speculate as to the possible brain and genetic mechanisms that may help explain the comorbidity between schizophrenia and crime. To date, researchers have not utilized brain imaging and molecular genetic techniques to probe neurobiological commonalities of schizophrenia and crime outcome in the same population. We emphasize that our hypotheses regarding links between individual genes (specifically NOTCH4, COMT, and BDNF), structural brain impairments, and psychiatric outcome (schizophrenia and antisocial personality) are very speculative and currently based on very provisional and limited evidence. Nevertheless, greater attention to the comorbidity issue in future brain imaging and molecular genetic studies would not only help provide a stronger empirical basis for theories on the comorbidity issue, but would also increase our understanding of both schizophrenia and crime in their own right.

ACKNOWLEDGEMENTS

This paper was written with the support of an Independent Scientist Award from NIMH (K02 MH01114-01) to the second author.

REFERENCES

Abi-Dargham, A.; Mawlawi, O.; Lombardo, I.; Gil, R.; Martinez, D.; Huang, Y.; Hwang, D.R.; Keilp, J.; Kochan, L.; Van Heertum, R.; Gorman, J.M.; and Laruelle, M. Prefrontal dopamine D1 receptors and working memory in schizophrenia. *J Neurosci*, 22(9):3708-19, 2002

Adolphs, R., Damasio, H, Tranel, D, and Damasio, A R. (1996). Cortical systems for the recognition of emotion in facial expressions. *Journal of Neuroscience, 16*, 7678-7687.

Amateau, S.K., and McCarthy, M.M. (2002). A novel mechanism of dendritic spine plasticity involving estradiol induction of prostaglandin-E2. *J Neurosci, 22* 8586-96.

American Psychiatric Association. (1994). *Diagnostic and statistical manual of mental disorders*. (4th ed.). Washington, D.C.: American Psychiatric Association.

Andersen, S.L. (2003). Trajectories of brain development: point of vulnerability or window of opportunity. *Neuroscience and Behavioral Reviews, 27*, 3-18.

Barch, D.M.; Csernansky, J.G.; Conturo, T.; and Snyder, A.Z. (2002). Working and long-term memory deficits in schizophrenia: is there a common prefrontal mechanism? *J Abnorm Psychol, 111*, 478-94.

Arnold, S.E. (2000). Cellular and molecular neuropathology of the parahippocampal region in schizophrenia. *Annals of the New York Academy of Sciences, 911*, 275-92.

Basso, M.R.; Nasrallah, H.A.; Olson, S.C.; and Bornstein, R.A. (1997). Cognitive deficits distinguish patients with adolescent- and adult- onset schizophrenia. *Neuropsychiatry Neuropsychol Behav Neurol, 10*, 107-12.

Bechara, A., Damasio, H, Tranel, D, and Damasio, A R. (1997). Deciding advantageously before knowing the advantageous strategy. *Science, 275*, 1293-1294.

Becker, A., Grecksch, G, Bernstein, H G, Hollt, V, and Bogerts, B. (1999). Social behaviour in rats lesioned with ibotenic acid in the hippocampus: quantitative and qualitative analysis. *Psychopharmacology, 144*, 333-338.

Bilder, R.M.; Bogerts, B.; Ashtari, M.; Wu, H.; Alvir, J.M.; Jody, D.; Reiter, G.; Bell, L.; and Lieberman, J.A. (1995). Anterior hippocampal volume reductions predict frontal lobe dysfunction in first episode schizophrenia. *Schizophr Res, 17*, 47-58.

Blair, R. J. R., Colledge, E, Murray, L, and Mitchell, D G V. (2001). A selective impairment in the processing of sad and fearful expressions in children with psychopathic tendencies. *Journal of Abnormal Child Psychology, 29*, 491-498.

Blair, R. J. R. (2003). Neurobiological basis of psychopathy. *British Journal of Psychiatry, 182*, 5-7.

Braver, T.S.; Barch, D.M.; Kelley, W.M.; Buckner, R.L.; Cohen, N.J.; Miezin, F.M.; Snyder, A.Z.; Ollinger, J.M.; Akbudak, E.; Conturo, T.E.; and Petersen, S.E. (2001). Direct comparison of prefrontal cortex regions engaged by working and long-term memory tasks. *Neuroimage, 14*, 48-59.

Brennan, P. A., Mednick, B. R., and Mednick, S. A. (1993). Parental psychopathology, congenital factors, and violence. In S. Hodgins (ed.) *Mental disorder and crime* (pp. 244-261). Thousand Oaks: Sage.

Brennan, P.A. and Alden, A. (in press). Schizophrenia and Violence: The Overlap. In A. Raine (ed.) in A. Raine (ed). *Crime and schizophrenia: Causes and cures*. New York: Nova Science Publishers.

Byrne, M.; Hodges, A.; Grant, E.; Owens, D.C.; and Johnstone, E.C. (1999). Neuropsychological assessment of young people at high genetic risk for developing schizophrenia compared with controls: Preliminary findings of the Edinburgh High Risk Study (EHRS). *Psychological Medicine, 29*, 1161-1173.

Callicott, J.H.; Ramsey, N.F.; Tallent, K.; Bertolino, A.; Knable, M.B.; Coppola, R.; Goldberg, T.; van Gelderen, P.; Mattay, V.S.; Frank, J.A.; Moonen, C.T.; and Weinberger, D.R. (1998). Functional magnetic resonance imaging brain mapping in psychiatry: methodological issues illustrated in a study of working memory in schizophrenia. *Neuropsychopharmacology, 18*, 186-96.

Cannon, T.D.; Bearden, C.E.; Hollister, J.M.; Rosso, I.M.; Sanchez, L.E.; and Hadley, T. (2000a). Childhood cognitive functioning in schizophrenia patients and their unaffected siblings: a prospective cohort study. *Schizophr Bull, 26*, 379-93.

Cannon, T.D.; Huttunen, M.O.; Lonnqvist, J.; Tuulio-Henriksson, A.; Pirkola, T.; Glahn, D.; Finkelstein, J.; Hietanen, M.; Kaprio, J.; and Koskenvuo, M. (2000b). The inheritance of neuropsychological dysfunction in twins discordant for schizophrenia. *Am J Hum Genet, 67*, 369-82.

Cannon, T.D.; Thompson, P.M.; van Erp, T.G.; Toga, A.W.; Poutanen, V.P.; Huttunen, M.; Lonnqvist, J.; Standerskjold-Nordenstam, C.G.; Narr, K.L.; Khaledy, M.; Zoumalan, C.I.; Dail, R.; and Kaprio, J. (2002a). Cortex mapping reveals regionally specific patterns of genetic and disease-specific gray-matter deficits in twins discordant for schizophrenia. *Proc Natl Acad Sci U S A, 99*, 3228-33.

Cannon, T.D.; van Erp, T.G.; Huttunen, M.; Lönnqvist, J.; Salonen, O.; Valanne, L.; Poutanen, V.P.; Standertskjöld-Nordenstam, C.G.; Gur, R.E.; and Yan, M. (1998). Regional gray matter, white matter, and cerebrospinal fluid distributions in schizophrenic patients, their siblings, and controls. *Archives of General Psychiatry, 55*, 1084-91.

Cannon, T.D.; van Erp, T.G.; and Glahn, D.C. (2002b). Elucidating continuities and discontinuities between schizotypy and schizophrenia in the nervous system. *Schizophr Res, 54*, 151-6.

Cannon, T.D.; van Erp, T.G.; Rosso, I.M.; Huttunen, M.; Lonnqvist, J.; Pirkola, T.; Salonen, O.; Valanne, L.; Poutanen, V.P.; and Standertskjold-Nordenstam, C.G. (2002c). Fetal hypoxia and structural brain abnormalities in schizophrenic patients, their siblings, and controls. *Archives of General Psychiatry, 59*, 35-41.

Cannon, T.D.; Zorrilla, L.E.; Shtasel, D.; Gur, R.E.; Gur, R.C.; Marco, E.J.; Moberg, P.; and Price, R.A. (1994). Neuropsychological functioning in siblings discordant for schizophrenia and healthy volunteers. *Archives of General Psychiatry, 51*, 651-61.

Carmine, A., Chheda, M G, Jonsson, E G, Sedvall, G C, Farde, L, Gustavsson, J P, Bergman, H, Anvret, M, Buervenich, S, and Olson, L. (2003). Two NOTCH4 polymorphisms and their relation to schizophrenia susceptibility and different personality traits. *Psychiatric Genetics, 13*, 23-28.

Cazalis, F., Valabregue, R, Pelegrini-Issac, M, Asloun, S, Robbins, T W, and Granon, S. (2003). Individual differences in prefrontal cortical activation on the Tower of London planning task: implication for effortful processing. *European Journal of Neuroscience, 17*, 2219-2225.

Chesterman, L. P., Taylor, P J, Cox, T, Hill, M, and Lumsden, J. (1994). Multiple measures of cerebral state in dangerous mentally disordered inpatients. *Criminal Behaviour and Mental Health, 4*, 228-239.

Cirillo, M.S., LJ. (in press). Verbal declarative memory dysfunctions in schizophrenia: From clinical assessment to genetics and brain mechanisms. *Neuropsychology Review.*

Cohen, J.D., and Servan-Schreiber, D. (1992). A neural network model of disturbances in the processing of context in schizophrenia. *Psychiatric Annals*, *22*, 131-136.

Conrad, A.J.; Abebe, T.; Austin, R.; Forsythe, S.; and Scheibel, A.B. (1991). Hippocampal pyramidal cell disarray in schizophrenia as a bilateral phenomenon. *Arch Gen Psychiatry*, *48*, 413-7.

Costa, E.; Davis, J.; Grayson, D.R.; Guidotti, A.; Pappas, G.D.; and Pesold, C. (2001). Dendritic spine hypoplasticity and downregulation of reelin and GABAergic tone in schizophrenia vulnerability. *Neurobiol Dis*, *8*, 723-42.

Cosway, R.; Byrne, M.; Clafferty, R.; Hodges, A.; Grant, E.; Abukmeil, S.S.; Lawrie, S.M.; Miller, P.; and Johnstone, E.C. (2000). Neuropsychological change in young people at high risk for schizophrenia: Results from the first two neuropsychological assessments of the Edinburgh High Risk Study. *Psychological Medicine*, *30*, 1111-1121.

Critchley, H. D., Simmons, A, Daly, E M, Russell, A, van Amelsvoort, T, Robertson, D M, Glover, A, and Murphy, D G M. (2000). Prefrontal and medial temporal correlates of repetitive violence to self and others. *Biological Psychiatry, 47*, 928-934.

Damasio, A. (1994). *Descartes' error: Emotion, reason, and the human brain.* New York: GP Putnam's Sons.

Davidson, R. J., Putnam, K M, and Larson, C L. (2000). Dysfunction in the neural circuitry of emotion regulation--a possible prelude to violence. *Science, 289*, 591-594.

De Bellis, M.D.; Keshavan, M.S.; Beers, S.R.; Hall, J.; Frustaci, K.; Masalehdan, A.; Noll, J.; and Boring, A.M. (2001). Sex differences in brain maturation during childhood and adolescence. *Cereb Cortex*, *11*, 552-7.

D'Esposito, M.; Postle, B.R.; Ballard, D.; and Lease, J. (1999). Maintenance versus manipulation of information held in working memory: An event-related fMRI study. *Brain and Cognition*, *41*, 66-86.

Diamond, A., Briand, L, Fossella, J, and Gehlbach, L. (2004). Genetic and neurochemical modulation of prefrontal cognitive functions in children. *American Journal of Psychiatry, 161*, 125-132.

Dinn, W. M., and Harris, C L. (2000). Neurocognitive function in antisocial personality disorder. *Psychiatry Research, 97*, 173-190.

Dolan, M. C., Deakin, J F W, Roberts, N, and Anderson, I M. (2002). Quantitative frontal and temporal structural MRI studies in personality-disordered offenders and control subjects. *Psychiatry Research-Neuroimaging, 116*, 133-149.

Dolan, M., and Park, I. (2002b). The neuropsychology of antisocial personality disorder. *Psychological Medicine, 32*, 417-427.

Egan, M. F., Goldberg, T E, Kolachana, B S, Callicott, J H, Mazzanti, C M, Straub, R E, Goldman, D, and Weinberger, D R. (2001). Effect of COMT Val(108/158) Met genotype on frontal lobe function and risk for schizophrenia. *Proceedings of the National Academy of Sciences of the United States of America, 98*, 6917-6922.

Egan, M. F., Kojima, M, Callicott, J H, Goldberg, T E, Kolachana, B S, Bertolino, A, Zaitsev, E, Gold, B, Goldman, D, Dean, M, Lu, B, and Weinberger, D R. (2003). The BDNF val66met polymorphism affects activity-dependent secretion of BDNF and human memory and hippocampal function. *Cell, 112*, 257-269.

Einat, H., Manji, H K, Gould, T D, Du, J, and Chen, G. (2003). Possible involvement of the ERK signaling cascade in bipolar disorder: Behavioral leads from the study of mutant mice. *Drug News and Perspectives, 16*, 453-463.

Ekelund, J.; Lichtermann, D.; Hovatta, I.; Ellonen, P.; Suvisaari, J.; Terwilliger, J.D.; Juvonen, H.; Varilo, T.; Arajarvi, R.; Kokko-Sahin, M.L.; Lonnqvist, J.; and Peltonen, L. (2000). Genome-wide scan for schizophrenia in the Finnish population: evidence for a locus on chromosome 7q22. *Hum Mol Genet, 9*, 1049-57.

Eldridge, L.L.; Knowlton, B.J.; Furmanski, C.S.; Bookheimer, S.Y.; and Engel, S.A. (2000). Remembering episodes: A selective role for the hippocampus during retrieval. *Nature Neuroscience, 3*, 1149-1152.

Elst, L. T. v., Woermann, F G, Lemieux, L, Thompson, P J, and Trimble, M R. (2000). Affective Aggression in Patients with Temporal Lobe Epilepsy: A Quantitative MRI Study of the Amygdala. *Brain, 123* , 234-243.

Eslinger, P. J., Moll, J, and Oliveira-Souza, R. (2002). Emotional and cognitive processing in empathy and moral behavior. *Behavioral and Brain Sciences, 25*, 34-+

Faraone, S.V.; Seidman, L.J.; Kremen, W.S.; Toomey, R.; Pepple, J.R.; and Tsuang, M.T. (2000). Neuropsychologic functioning among the nonpsychotic relatives of schizophrenic patients: the effect of genetic loading. *Biol Psychiatry, 48*, 120-6.

Farrow, T. F. D., Zheng, Y, Wilkinson, I D, Spence, S A, Deakin, J F W, Tarrier, N, Griffiths, P D, and Woodruff, P W R. (2001). Investigating the functional anatomy of empathy and forgiveness. *Neuroreport: For Rapid Communication of Neuroscience Research, 12*, 2433-2438.

Feinberg, I. (1982). Schizophrenia: Caused by a fault in programmed synaptic elimination during adolescence? *Journal of Psychiatric Research, 17*, 319-334.

Fung, M.T., Raine, A., Loeber, R., Lynam, D.R., Steinhauer, S.R., Venables, P.H., and Stouthamer-Loeber, M. (2005). Reduced electrodermal activity in psychopathy-prone adolescents *Journal of Abnormal Psychology, 114*, 187-196

Gardiner, J.M., and Parkin, A.J. (1990). Attention and recollective experience in recognition memory. *Mem Cognit, 18*, 579-83.

Gasperoni, T.L.; Ekelund, J.; Huttunen, M.; Palmer, C.G.; Tuulio-Henriksson, A.; Lonnqvist, J.; Kaprio, J.; Peltonen, L.; and Cannon, T.D. (2003). Genetic linkage and association between chromosome 1q and working memory function in schizophrenia. *Am J Med Genet, 116*, 8-16.

Glahn, D.C.; Kim, J.; Cohen, M.S.; Poutanen, V.P.; Therman, S.; Bava, S.; Van Erp, T.G.; Manninen, M.; Huttunen, M.; Lonnqvist, J.; Standertskjold-Nordenstam, C.G.; and

Cannon, T.D. (2002). Maintenance and manipulation in spatial working memory: dissociations in the prefrontal cortex. *Neuroimage, 17*, 201-13.

Glantz, L.A., and Lewis, D.A. (2000). Decreased dendritic spine density on prefrontal cortical pyramidal neurons in schizophrenia. *Arch Gen Psychiatry, 57*, 65-73.

Glatt, S. J., Wang, R S, Yeh, Y C, Tsuang, M T, and Faraone, S V. (2005). Five NOTCH4 polymorphisms show weak evidence for association with schizophrenia: evidence from meta-analyses. *Schizophrenia Research, 73*, 281-290.

Globus, A.; Rosenzweig, M.R.; Bennett, E.L.; and Diamond, M.C. (1973). Effects of differential experience on dendritic spine counts in rat cerebral cortex. *J Comp Physiol Psychol, 82*, 175-81.

Gogos, J. A., Morgan, M, Luine, V, Santah, M, Ogawa, S, and Pfaff, D. (1998). Catechol-O-methyltransferase-deficient mice exhibit sexually dimorphic changes in catecholamine levels and behavior. *Proceedings of the National Academy of Sciences, 95*, 9991-9996.

Goldman-Rakic, P.S. (1995). Architecture of the prefrontal cortex and the central executive. *Annals of the New York Academy of Sciences, 769*, 71-83.

Goldman-Rakic, P.S., and Selemon, L.D. (1997). Functional and anatomical aspects of prefrontal pathology in schizophrenia. *Schizophrenia Bulletin, 23*, 437-458.

Gorenstein, E. E., and Newman, J P. (1980). Disinhibitory psychopathology: A new perspective and a model for research. *Psychological Review, 87*, 301-315.

Gorski, J. A., Zeiler, S R, Tamowski, S, and Jones, K R. (2003). Brain-derived neurotrophic factor is required for the maintenance of cortical dendrites. *Journal of Neuroscience, 23*, 6856-6865.

Grace, A.A.; Moore, H.; and O'Donnell, P. (1998). The modulation of corticoaccumbens transmission by limbic afferents and dopamine: a model for the pathophysiology of schizophrenia. *Adv Pharmacol, 42*, 721-4.

Grafman, J., Schwab, K, Warden, D, Pridgen, A, Brown, H R, and Salazar, A M. (1996). Frontal lobe injuries, violence, and aggression: A report of the Vietnam Head Injury Study. *Neurology, 46*, 1231-1238.

Grattan, L. M., Bloomer, R H, Archambault, F X, and Eslinger, P J. (1994). Cognitive flexibility and empathy after frontal lobe lesions. *Neuropsychiatry, Neuropsychology, and Behavioral Neurology, 7*, 251-259.

Gray, J.A.; Feldon, J.; Rawlins, J.N.; and Hemsley, D.R. (1991). The neuropsychology of schizophrenia. *Behavioral and Brain Sciences, 14*, 1-84.

Gregg, T. R., and Siegel, A. (2001). Brain structures and neurotransmitters regulating aggression in cats: Implications for human aggression. *Progress in Neuro-Psychopharmacology and Biological Psychiatry, 25*, 91-140.

Hariri, A.R., Goldberg, T.E., Mattay,V.S., Kolachana,B.S., Callicott, J.H., Egan, M.F., and Weinberger, D.R. (2003). Brain-derived neurotrophic factor val(66)met polymorphism affects human memory-related hippocampal activity and predicts memory performance. *Journal of Neuroscience, 23,* 6690-6694.

Heekeren, H. R., Wartenburger, I, Schmidt, H, Schwintowski, H P, and Villringer, A. (2003). An fMRI study of simple ethical decision-making. *Neuroreport, 14*, 1215-1219.

Hensbroek, R. A., Sluyter, F, Guillot, P V, van Oortmerssen, G A, and Crusio, W E. (1995). Y-chromosomal effects on hippocampal mossy fiber distributions in mice selected for aggression. *Brain Research, 682*, 203-206.

Hodgins S, Kratzer L, and McNeil TF (2001). Obstetric complications, parenting, and risk of criminal behavior. *Archives of General Psychiatry, 58,* 746-752.

Honey, G.D.; Bullmore, E.T.; Soni, W.; Varatheesan, M.; Williams, S.C.; and Sharma, T. (1999). Differences in frontal cortical activation by a working memory task after substitution of risperidone for typical antipsychotic drugs in patients with schizophrenia. *Proc Natl Acad Sci U S A, 96,* 13432-7.

Huang, E. J., and Reichardt, L F. (2001). Neurotrophins: Roles in neural development and function. *Annual Review of Neuroscience, 24,* 677-736.

Huttenlocher, P.R. (1979). Synaptic density in human frontal cortex - developmental changes and effects of aging. *Brain Res, 163,* 195-205.

Ishikawa, S. S., and Raine, A. (2003). The neuropsychiatry of aggression. In B. S. Fogel, R. B. Schiffer, and S. M. Rao (Eds.), *Neuropsychiatry.* (pp. 660-679). Philadelphia: Lippincott Williams and Wilkins.

Ishikawa, S. S., Raine, A, Lencz, T, Bihrle, S, and LaCasse, L. (2001). Autonomic stress reactivity and executive functions in successful and unsuccessful criminal psychopaths from the community. *Journal of Abnormal Psychology, 110,* 423-432.

Johnstone, E.C.; Owens, D.G.; Bydder, G.M.; Colter, N.; Crow, T.J.; and Frith, C.D. (1989). The spectrum of structural brain changes in schizophrenia: age of onset as a predictor of cognitive and clinical impairments and their cerebral correlates. *Psychol Med, 19,* 91-103.

Kemppainen, L., Jokelainen, J., Jaervelin, M. R., Isohanni, M., and Raesaenen, P. (2001). The one-child family and violent criminality: A 31-year follow-up study of the Northern Finland 1966 birth cohort. *American Journal of Psychiatry, 158,* 960-962.

Keshavan, M.S.; Anderson, S.; and Pettegrew, J.W. (1994). Is schizophrenia due to excessive synaptic pruning in the prefrontal cortex? The Feinberg hypothesis revisited. *J Psychiatr Res, 28,* 239-65.

Keshavan, M.S., and Hogarty, G.E. Brain maturational processes and delayed onset in schizophrenia. *Dev Psychopathol, 11,* 525-43, 1999.

Kiehl, K. A., Smith, A M, Hare, R D, Mendrek, A, Forster, B B, Brink, J, and Liddle, P F. (2001). Limbic abnormalities in affective processing by criminal psychopaths as revealed by functional magnetic resonance imaging. *Biological Psychiatry, 50,* 677-684.

Laakso, M. P., Gunning-Dixon, F, Vaurio, O, Repo-Tiihonen, E, Soininen, H, and Tiihonen, J. (2002). Prefrontal volumes in habitually violent subjects with antisocial personality disorder and type 2 alcoholism. *Psychiatry Research-Neuroimaging, 114,* 95-102.

Laakso, M. P., Vaurio, O, Koivisto, E, Savolainen, L, Eronen, M, Aronen, H J, Hakola, P, Repo, E, Soininen, H, and Tiihonen, J. (2001). Psychopathy and the posterior hippocampus. *Behavioural Brain Research, 118,* 187-193.

LeDoux, J. (1996). *The emotional brain* . New York: Simon and Schuster.

Lyons, W. E., Mamounas, L A, Ricaurte, G A C V, Reid, S W, Bora, S H W C, and Koliatsos, V E T L. (1999). Brain derived neurotrophic factor-deficient mice develop aggressiveness and hyperphagia in conjunction with brain serotonergic abnormalities. *Proceedings of the National Academy of Sciences, 96,* 15239-15244.

Maher, B.A.; Manschreck, T.C.; Woods, B.T.; and Yurgelun-Todd, D.A. (1995). Frontal brain volume and context effects in short-term recall in schizophrenia. *Biological Psychiatry, 37,* 144-150.

Mazzanti, R. A., Lunardi, C M, Gonnelli, A, Pardini, C, Tiano, L, Bouanani, L, Bandettini, S, Bozak, A, Vyas, D, Dell'Orso, G, and Cassano, L. (1999). Evidence for association of the catechol-O-methyltransferase gene with bipolar disorder and aggressive behavior. *Molecular Psychiatry, 4*, S100.

McNeil, T.F.; Cantor-Graae, E.; and Weinberger, D.R. (2000). Relationship of obstetric complications and differences in size of brain structures in monozygotic twin pairs discordant for schizophrenia. *Am J Psychiatry*, *157*, 203-12.

Millar, J.K.; Wilson-Annan, J.C.; Anderson, S.; Christie, S.; Taylor, M.S.; Semple, C.A.; Devon, R.S.; Clair, D.M.; Muir, W.J.; Blackwood, D.H.; and Porteous, D.J. (2000). Disruption of two novel genes by a translocation co-segregating with schizophrenia. *Hum Mol Genet*, *9*, 1415-23.

Moffitt, T. E. and Caspi, A. (2001). Childhood predictors differentiate life-course persistent and adolescence-limited antisocial pathways among males and females. *Development and Psychopathology, 13,* 355-375.

Moldin, S.O., and Gottesman, II. (1997). At issue: genes, experience, and chance in schizophrenia--positioning for the 21st century. *Schizophr Bull*, *23*, 547-61.

Morgan, A. B., and Lilienfeld, S O. (2000). A meta-analytic review of the relation between antisocial behavior and neuropsychological measures of executive function. *Clinical Psychology Review, 20*, 113-156.

Muller, J. L., Sommer, M, Wagner, V, Lange, K, Taschler, H, Roder, C H, Schuierer, G, Klein, H E, and Hajak, G. (2003). Abnormalities in emotion processing within cortical and subcortical regions in criminal psychopaths: Evidence from a functional magnetic resonance imaging study using pictures with emotional content. *Biological Psychiatry, 54*, 152-162.

Nawa, H.; Takahashi, M.; and Patterson, P.H. (2000). Cytokine and growth factor involvement in schizophrenia--support for the developmental model. *Mol Psychiatry*, *5*, 594-603.

Neves-Pereira, M., Cheung, J, Pasdar, A, Zhang, F, Breen, G, Yates, P, Sinclair, M, Crombie, C, Walker, N, and St Clair, D M. (2005). BDNF gene is a risk factor for schizophrenia in a Scottish population. *Molecular Psychiatry, 10*, 208-212.

Nyakas, C.; Buwalda, B.; and Luiten, P.G. (1996). Hypoxia and brain development. *Prog Neurobiol*, *49*, 1-51.

Okubo, Y.; Suhara, T.; Suzuki, K.; and Kobayashi, K. (1997). Decreased prefrontal dopamine D1 receptors in schizophrenia revealed by PET. *Nature*, *385*, :634-636.

Olney, J.W., and Farber, N.B. (1995). Glutamate receptor dysfunction and schizophrenia [see comments]. *Archives of General Psychiatry*, *52*, 998-1007.

Ozeki, Y.; Tomoda, T.; Kleiderlein, J.; Kamiya, A.; Bord, L.; Fujii, K.; Okawa, M.; Yamada, N.; Hatten, M.E.; Snyder, S.H.; Ross, C.A.; and Sawa, A. (2003). Disrupted-in-Schizophrenia-1 (DISC-1): mutant truncation prevents binding to NudE-like (NUDEL) and inhibits neurite outgrowth. *Proc Natl Acad Sci U S A*, *100*, 289-94.

Pansky, B, Allen, D J, and Budd, G C. (1988). *Review of neuroscience*. (2nd ed.). New York: Macmillan Publishing Company.

Pantelis, C., Velakoulis, D, McGorry, PD, Wood, SJ, Suckling, J, Phillips, LJ, Yung, AR, Bullmore, ET, Brewer, W, Soulsby, B, Desmond, P, McGuire, PK. (2002). Neuroanatomical abnormalities before and after onset of psychosis: a cross-sectional and longitudinal MRI comparison. *Lancet*.

Patrick, C. J. (1994). Emotion and psychopathy: Startling new insights. *Psychophysiology, 31*, 319-330.

Patrick, C. J., Cuthbert, B N, and Lang, P J. (1994). Emotion in the criminal psychopath: Fear image processing. *Journal of Abnormal Psychology, 103*, 523-534.

Patrick, C. J., Zempolich, K A, and Levenston, G K. (1997). Emotionality and violent behavior in psychopaths: A biosocial analysis. In Anonymous, *Biosocial bases of violence*. (pp. 145-161). New York: Plenum.

Pfefferbaum, A., and Marsh, L. (1995). Structural brain imaging in schizophrenia. *Clinical Neuroscience, 3*, 105-11.

Phillips, L.J.; Velakoulis, D.; Pantelis, C.; Wood, S.; Yuen, H.P.; Yung, A.R.; Desmond, P.; Brewer, W.; and McGorry, P.D. (2002). Non-reduction in hippocampal volume is associated with higher risk of psychosis. *Schizophr Res, 58*, 145-58.

Piquero, A, and Tibbetts S. (1999). The impact of pre/perinatal disturbances and disadvantaged familial environment in predicting criminal offending. *Studies on Crime and Crime Prevention, 8*, 52-70.

Raine, A., Ishikawa, S S, Arce, E, Lencz, T, Knuth, K H, Bihrle, S, LaCasse, L, and Colletti, P. (2004). Hippocampal structural asymmetry in unsuccessful psychopaths. *Biological Psychiatry, 55*, 185-191.

Raine, A. (1993). *The psychopathology of crime: Criminal behavior as a clinical disorder*. San Diego: Academic Press.

Raine, A., Brennan, P., and Mednick S.A. (1994). Birth complications combined with early maternal rejection at age 1 year predispose to violent crime at age 18 years. *Archives of General Psychiatry, 51*, 984-988.

Raine, A., Buchsbaum, M, and LaCasse, L. (1997). Brain abnormalities in murderers indicated by positron emission tomography. *Biological Psychiatry, 42*, 495-508.

Raine, A., Lencz, T, Bihrle, S, LaCasse, L, and Colletti, P. (2000). Reduced prefrontal gray matter volume and reduced autonomic activity in antisocial personality disorder. *Archives of General Psychiatry, 57*, 119-127.

Raine, A., Moffitt, T.E., Caspi, A., Loeber, R., Stouthamer-Loeber, M., and Lynam, D. (2005). Neurocognitive impairments in boys on the life-course persistent antisocial path. *Journal of Abnormal Psychology 114* 38-49.

Rees, S.; Mallard, C.; Breen, S.; Stringer, M.; Cock, M.; and Harding, R. (1998). Fetal brain injury following prolonged hypoxemia and placental insufficiency: a review. *Comp Biochem Physiol A Mol Integr Physiol, 119*, 653-60.

Rubia, K., Russell, T., Overmeyer,S., Brammer, M.J., Bullmore, E.T., Sharma, T., Simmons,A., Williams, S.C.R., Giampietro, V., Andrew, C.M., and Taylor,E. (2001). Mapping motor inhibition: Conjunctive brain activations across different versions of go/no-go and stop tasks. *Neuroimage, 13*, 250-261.

Rujescu, D., Giegling, I, Gietl, A, Hartmann, A M, and Moller, H J. (2003). A functional single nucleotide polymorphism (V158M) in the COMT gene is associated with aggressive personality traits. *Biological Psychiatry, 54*, 34-39.

Schneider, F., Habel, U, Kessler, C, Posse, S, Grodd, W, and Muller-Gartner, H W. (2000). Functional imaging of conditioned aversive emotional responses in antisocial personality disorder. *Neuropsychobiology, 42*, 192-201.

Seguin, J.R., Arseneault, L., Boulerice, B., Harden, P.W., Tremblay, R.E. (2002). Response perseveration in adolescent boys with stable and unstable histories of physical aggression: the role of underlying processes. *Journal of Child Psychology and Psychiatry 43* 481-484.

Seidman, L.J.; Faraone, S.V.; Goldstein, J.M.; Kremen, W.S.; Horton, N.J.; Makris, N.; Toomey, R.; Kennedy, D.; Caviness, V.S.; and Tsuang, M.T. (2002). Left hippocampal volume as a vulnerability indicator for schizophrenia: a magnetic resonance imaging morphometric study of nonpsychotic first- degree relatives. *Arch Gen Psychiatry, 59,* 839-49..

Silverton, L. (1988a). The genetic relationship between antisocial bchavior and schizophrenia: a review of the literature. In W. Buikbausen (Ed.), *Explaining Crime.* Brill, Holland.

Silverton, L. (1988b). Crime and the schizophrenia spectrum: a study of three Danish cohorts. In T.E. Moffitt and S.A. Mednick (Eds.), *Biological contributions to crime causation.* Dordrecht, Martinus Nijhoff.

Smith, A. M. (2000). An fMRI investigation of frontal lobe functioning in psychopathy and schizophrenia during a go/no go task. *Dissertation Abstracts International: Section B: The Sciences and Engineering, 61*, 128

Squire, L.R., and Zola, S.M. (1996). Structure and function of declarative and nondeclarative memory systems. *Proc Natl Acad Sci U S A, 93*, 13515-22.

St Clair, D.; Blackwood, D.; Muir, W.; Carothers, A.; Walker, M.; Spowart, G.; Gosden, C.; and Evans, H.J. (1990). within a family of a balanced autosomal translocation with major mental illness. *Lancet, 336*, 13-6.

Stefanis, N.; Frangou, S.; Yakeley, J.; Sharma, T.; O'Connell, P.; Morgan, K.; Sigmudsson, T.; Taylor, M.; and Murray, R. (1999). Hippocampal volume reduction in schizophrenia: effects of genetic risk and pregnancy and birth complications. *Biol Psychiatry, 46*, 697-702.

Steele,J.D., and Lawrie,S.M. (2004). Segregation of cognitive and emotional function in the prefrontal cortex: a stereotactic meta-analysis. *Neuroimage, 21*, 868-875.

Stuss,D.T., and Levine,B. (2002). Adult clinical neuropsychology: Lessons from studies of the frontal lobes. *Annual Review of Psychology, 53*, 401-433.

Swanson, L. W. (1999). Limbic system. In G. Adelman and B. H. Smith (Eds.), *Encyclopedia of neuroscience.* (pp. 1053-1055). Amsterdam: Elsevier.

Thompson, P.M.; Vidal, C.; Giedd, J.N.; Gochman, P.; Blumenthal, J.; Nicolson, R.; Toga, A.W.; and Rapoport, J.L. (2001). Mapping adolescent brain change reveals dynamic wave of accelerated gray matter loss in very early-onset schizophrenia. *Proc Natl Acad Sci U S A, 98*, 11650-5.

Teicher, M.H.; Andersen, S.L.; Polcari, A.; Anderson, C.M.; and Navalta, C.P. Developmental neurobiology of childhood stress and trauma. (2002). *Psychiatr Clin North Am, 25*, 397-426.

Tiihonen, J., Hodgins, S., and Vaurio, O. Amygdaloid volume loss in psychopathy. *Society for Neuroscience Abstracts* 20017.

Van Erp, T.G.; Saleh, P.A.; Rosso, I.M.; Huttunen, M.; Lonnqvist, J.; Pirkola, T.; Salonen, O.; Valanne, L.; Poutanen, V.P.; Standertskjold-Nordenstam, C.G.; and Cannon, T.D. (2002). Contributions of genetic risk and fetal hypoxia to hippocampal volume in patients with schizophrenia or schizoaffective disorder, their unaffected siblings, and healthy unrelated volunteers. *Am J Psychiatry, 159*, 1514-20.

Veit, R., Flor, H, Erb, M, Hermann, C, Lotze, M, Grodd, W, and Birbaumer, N. (2002). Brain circuits involved in emotional learning in antisocial behavior and social phobia in humans. *Neuroscience Letters, 328*, 233-236.

Volavka, J., Kennedy, J L, Ni, X, Czobor, P, Nolan, K, and Sheitman, B. (2004). COMT158 polymorphism and hostility. *American Journal of Medical Genetics Part B-Neuropsychiatric Genetics, 127*, 28-29.

Wassink, T. H., Nopoulos, P, Pietila, J, Crowe, R R, and Andreasen, N C. (2003). NOTCH4 and the frontal lobe in schizophrenia. *American Journal of Medical Genetics Part B-Neuropsychiatric Genetics, 118B*, 1-7.

Weinberger, D. R., Egan, M F, Bertolino, A, Callicott, J H, Mattay, V S, Lipska, B K, Berman, K F, and Goldberg, T E. (2001). Prefrontal neurons and the genetics of schizophrenia. *Biological Psychiatry, 50*, 825-844.

Werner, E. E. (1987). Vulnerability and resiliency in children at risk for delinquency: A longitudinal study from birth to young adulthood. In J.D. Burchard and S. N. Burchard (Eds.), *Primary prevention of psychopathology* (pp. 16-43). Newbury Park, CA: Sage.

Wilson, J.Q. and Petersilia, J. (2002). *Crime: Public Policies For Crime Control.* San Francisco: ICS Press.

Woods, B.T. (1998). Is schizophrenia a progressive neurodevelopmental disorder? Toward a unitary pathogenetic mechanism. *Am J Psychiatry, 155*, 1661-70, 1998.

Wood, S.J.; Velakoulis, D.; Smith, D.J.; Bond, D.; Stuart, G.W.; McGorry, P.D.; Brewer, W.J.; Bridle, N.; Eritaia, J.; Desmond, P.; Singh, B.; Copolov, D.; and Pantelis, C. A. (2001). longitudinal study of hippocampal volume in first episode psychosis and chronic schizophrenia. *Schizophr Res, 52*, 37-46.

Woermann, F. G., Van Elst, L T, Koepp, M J, Free, S L, Thompson, P J, Trimble, M R, and Duncan, R D. (2000). Reduction of frontal neocortical grey matter associated with affective aggression in patients with temporal lobe epilepsy: an objective voxel by voxel analysis of automatically segmented MRI. *Journal of Neurology, Neurosurgery, and Psychiatry, 68*, 162-169.

Yang, Y., Raine, A., Lencz, T., Bihrle, S., Lacasse, L. and Colletti, P. (2005). Volume reduction in prefrontal gray matter in unsuccessful criminal psychopaths. *Biological Psychiatry 57* 1103-1108.

Yurgelun-Todd, D.A.; Waternaux, C.M.; Cohen, B.M.; Gruber, S.A.; English, C.D.; and Renshaw, P.F. (1996). Functional magnetic resonance imaging of schizophrenic patients and comparison subjects during word production. *American Journal of Psychiatry, 153*, 200-5.

Zaidel, D.W.; Esiri, M.M.; and Harrison, P.J. (1997). Size, shape, and orientation of neurons in the left and right hippocampus: investigation of normal asymmetries and alterations in schizophrenia. *Am J Psychiatry, 154*, 812-8.

Zola, S.M., and Squire, L.R. (2001). Relationship between magnitude of damage to the hippocampus and impaired recognition memory in monkeys. *Hippocampus, 11*, 92-8.

PART 6. PREVENTION / TREATMENT OF CRIME AND SCHIZOPHRENIA

In: Crime and Schizophrenia: Causes and Cures
Editor: Adrian Raine, pp. 249-265
ISBN 1-59454-609-6

Chapter 13

PREVENTING CRIME AND SCHIZOPHRENIA USING EARLY ENVIRONMENTAL ENRICHMENT

***Adrian Raine*[1], *Jianghong Liu*[2], *Peter Venables*[1,3] *and Sarnoff A. Mednick*[2]**

[1] Department of Psychology, University of Southern California, Los Angeles, CA 90089-1061

[2] Social Science Research Institute, University of Southern California, Los Angeles, CA 90089-1061

[3] Department of Psychology, University of York, Heslington, York, England

INTRODUCTION

While schizophrenia is a major mental illness that can be treated, primary prevention of this disorder is elusive. Nevertheless, one population-based strategy for preventing this debilitating mental disorder may be to tackle not so much the end-state of the disease process itself, but instead to develop primary prevention programs that tackle the milder, prodromal features of the disorder, i.e. schizotypal personality (American Psychiatric Association, 1994; Cornblatt, Lencz, and Obuchowski, 2002). If primary prevention programs could be developed to attenuate individual difference in schizotypal features in the general population (e.g. unusual perceptual experiences, no close friends, disorganization), such efforts could provide the basis for developing new programs aimed at preventing schizophrenia (Tsuang, Stone, and Faraone, 2000). To date however, no such primary prevention programs have been developed for either schizophrenia or schizotypal personality (McGorry, 2000).

International epidemiological studies have increasingly shown increased rates of criminal offending in schizophrenia patients (Volavka, Laska, Baker, and Meisner, 1997; Volavka, 1999; Raine, 1993; Raesaenen et al., 1998; Fishbein, 1999). A number of the neurobiological and psychological risk factors for schizophrenia are also risk factors for crime (Volavka, 1999; Raine, 1993). Consequently, primary prevention efforts for schizotypy and schizophrenia may also reduce rates of conduct disorder and criminal behavior. Violence and crime is being increasingly viewed as a major public health problem with its origins in the early years of life (Fishbein, 2001; Mercy and Hammond, 1999; Guerra, Tolan, and Hammond, 1994), and prevention of this behavior is one of the most important and pressing issues in society today. Yet very few primary prevention studies have intervened in the early years of life to tackle the root causes of conduct disorder. Because animal research has clearly shown that environmental enrichment benefits both brain structure and function (Kempermann, Kuhn, and Gage, 1997; van Praag, Kempermann, and Gage, 1999; Pham, Soderstrom, Winblad, and Mohammed, 1999), and because there is increasing evidence from brain imaging and neuropsychological studies of brain dysfunction in both schizophrenia and antisocial behavior (Andreasen, 1999; Buchsbaum and Hazlett, 1998; Raine, Buchsbaum, and LaCasse, 1997a; Raine, Lencz, Bihrle, LaCasse, and Colletti, 2000; Volavka, 1999a; Gur et al., 2000; Siever et al., 2002; Raine, Buchsbaum, and LaCasse, 1997; Raine, Lencz, Bihrle, LaCasse, and Colletti, 2000; Cannon, van Erp, and Glahn, 2002), it is conceivable that an early environmental enrichment could reduce both schizotypal personality and antisocial behavior.

Nutrition may be an important component of early environmental enrichment. Nutritional deficits have been implicated in both antisocial personality and schizophrenia / schizoid personality (Fishbein and Pease, 1994; Hoek et al., 1996; Raine, 1993b; Tsuang, 2000), and animal experimental studies have demonstrated the importance of nutrition on cognitive and brain functioning (Lim and Suzuki, 2001; Salvati, Attorri, Avellino, Di Biase, and Sanchez, 2000). One of most successful early interventions for antisocial behavior to date involved nurse home visitations to mothers in which nutritional advice was an important component (Olds et al., 1998). Consequently, an enrichment that provides better early nutrition could reduce schizotypal personality and antisocial behavior, especially in those with poor nutritional status at the start of the prevention program.

We describe below the effects of an early environmental enrichment from ages 3-5 years that included a nutritional component on later antisocial behavior and schizotypal personality (Raine, Mellingen, Liu, Venables, and Mednick, 2003). We also assess whether any beneficial effects are maximized in children with poor nutrition, and whether early psychosocial adversity alters the effect of the enrichment.

The Early Environmental Enrichment Program

Subjects were drawn from a larger population of 1,795 children from Mauritius and are described in full in Venables (1978). All children born in 1969-1970 in two towns were recruited into the study when aged 3 years. This total sample consisted of both males (51.4%) and females (48.6%). Ethnic distribution was as follows: Indian (68.7%), Creoles (25.7%), and others (5.6%). After complete description of the study to the subjects, verbal informed consent was obtained from the mothers of the participants for the age 3-5 test phase, while written informed consent was obtained for later collection phases.

Stratified random sampling was conducted to select which 100 of the 1,795 would enter the enrichment, with sampling conducted using random number tables. The remaining 1,695 experienced the community control condition. The 100 were stratified on autonomic functioning in order to assess the moderating effects of autonomic activity on the enrichment (see Venables, (1978) for further details). Controls were then selected from the remaining

1,695 community sample to match the enriched group on autonomic functioning as well as other key age three variables that could influence outcome. Of the original 100 in the Enriched group, 83 could be followed up on outcome data. This enriched group were matched on ten age 3 variables (ethnicity, gender, age, nutritional status, cognitive ability, temperament, autonomic reactivity, parental social class, social adversity, and mother's age at birth) with 355 of the Controls on whom outcome data were available. At age 17, 438 participants (83 in the enriched group) had complete data on behavior problems. At age 23-26, 359 (75 enriched) had complete data on schizotypy. Those in the analysis (N = 438) did not differ to the remainder of the population (N = 1,357) on age, ethnicity, and gender.

Enrichment and Community Control Conditions

The enriched and control conditions have been described in full in(Raine et al. (2001). Briefly, the enrichment started at age 3 years, had a duration of two years, and consisted of three key elements: nutrition, education, and physical exercise. The enrichment was conducted in two specially constructed nursery schools with a teacher / pupil ratio of 1 to 5.5. Staff training included physical health (nutrition, hygiene, anatomy and physiology, childhood disorders), physical activities (gymnastics and rhythm activities, outdoor activities, physiotherapy), and education (multi-modal stimulation, use of toys, art, handicrafts, drama, music). A special feature of the nurseries was the emphasis on nutrition, health care, basic hygiene, and exercise (Venables, 1978). A structured nutrition program provided milk, fruit juice, a hot meal of fish or chicken or mutton, and a salad each day to the children. A program of physical exercise was incorporated into the afternoon session of each day consisting of gym lessons, structured outdoor games, and free play. Another special feature of the enrichment was the incorporation of walking field trips, basic hygiene skills, and medical inspections (every two months) into the curriculum (Raine et al., 2001). There was an average of 2.5 hours of physical activities each day. Educational activities focused on verbal skills, visuo-spatial coordination, conceptual skills, memory, and sensation and perception.

The children in the Control condition underwent the traditional Mauritius experience which consisted of attendance at "petite ecoles" (Raine et al., 2001). These schools focused on a tradition ABC curriculum with a teacher / pupil ration of 30/1. No lunch, milk, or structured exercise was provided. For lunch children typically ate bread only, rice and bread, or rice only.

Effects of the Enrichment on Later Schizotypy, Conduct Disorder, and Crime

Ratings of behavior problems were also obtained on the subjects using the Revised Behavior Problem Checklist (Quay and Peterson, 1987) at age 17 years. This instrument assesses six dimensions of behavior problems: Conduct Disorder, Motor Excess, Attention Problems, Psychotic Behavior, Anxiety-Withdrawal, and Socialized Aggression. Details of reliability and validity are provided in(Quay et al. (1987).

As indicated in Figure 1, by age 17, children who had experienced the enrichment were found to have significantly lower scores on ratings of Conduct Disorder and Motor Excess compared to controls. On the other hand, as will be seen from Figure 1, the effects of the enrichment were selective in that it did not affect scores on Attention Problems, Socialized Aggression, and Anxious-Withdrawn. The effect for Conduct Disorder but not for Socialized Aggression might suggest that the enrichment preferentially affects non-aggressive forms of antisocial behavior. In reality, the reverse is the case. Despite its name, the "Socialized Aggression" subscale of the RBPC assesses non-aggressive forms of antisocial behavior (steals, cheats, lies, loyal to delinquent friends) carried out in the company of others – in other words subcultural delinquency. In contrast, "Conduct Disorder" assesses the more serious aggressive forms of antisocial behavior (fight, cruel, bullies, attention-seeking) carried out independent of others.

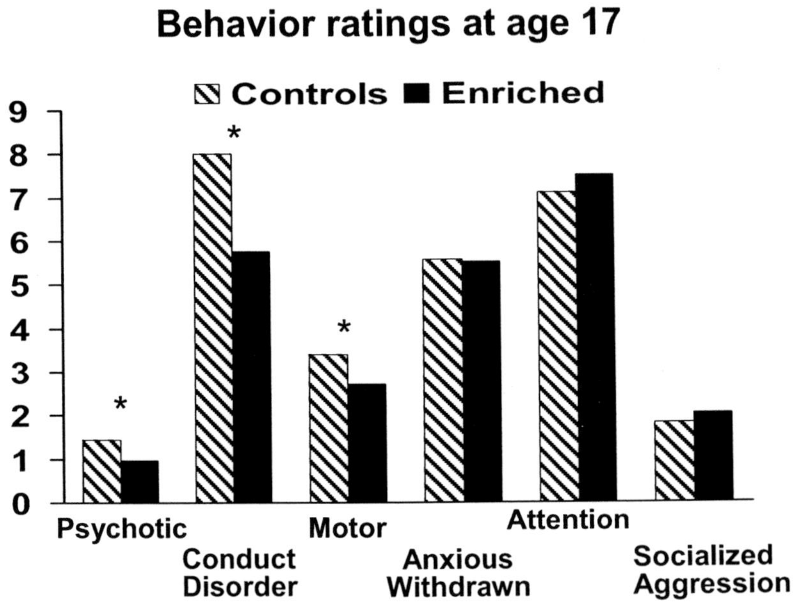

Figure 1. Statistically significant reductions in conduct disorder, psychotic behavior, and motor excess (marked with an asterisk) at age 17 years in those who experienced environmental enrichment from ages 3-5 years

The enrichment was also successful in reducing self-report schizotypal personality at age 17 years. At this age, schizotypal personality was assessed using a self-report questionnaire that yielded two indicators of schizotypal personality: positive schizotypal features (including unusual perceptual experiences and magical thinking - Venables, 1990; Venables, Wilkins, Mitchell, and Raine, 1990) and cognitive disorganization (Venables and Bailes, 1994; Venables et al., 1990).

In addition to these self-report items, behavioral ratings were available on the Psychoticism sub-scale from the RBPC. Again, the enrichment was effective in significantly reducing psychoticism scores. Items on this 6-item rating scale consist of two main sets of psychotic traits: odd beliefs / magical thinking (strange, far-fetched ideas, expresses beliefs that are clearly untrue, unable to tell real from imaginary) and odd speech (incoherent speech, repetitive speech, parrots other's speech). The former reflects cognitive-perceptual schizotypal features while the latter reflects more the disorganization factor of schizotypal personality (Raine et al., 1994b). Consequently, the objective ratings broadly parallel the self-report factors of magical thinking / unusual perceptual experiences and cognitive disorganization.

At age 23 years, schizotypal personality was assessed using the Schizotypal Personality Questionnaire (Raine, 1991). This instrument yields a total score of schizotypal personality together with three sub-factors measuring cognitive-perceptual, interpersonal, and disorganized features (Raine et al., 1994a). Subjects were interviewed on their histories of criminal offending using a structured interview consisting of an adult extension of the self-report delinquency measure used in the National Youth Survey (Elliott, Ageton, Huizinga, Knowles, and Canter, 1983) and which included 41 criminal offences that covered a wide-range of property, drug, violent, and white-collar crimes perpetrated by the subject over the past 5 years. The 33.6% who admitted to a criminal offense were categorized as an offender. In addition, court records were searched for registrations of offenses that included property, drug, violence, and serious driving offenses (e.g. driving while drunk, dangerous driving), but excluded petty offenses (e.g. parking fines, lack of vehicle registration). Those with a record were categorized as criminal.

There was no main effect of the enrichment on total schizotypal personality scores, but groups did differ on criminal behavior at this age (see Figure 2). There was a significantly lower rate of self-report offending in the enriched group (23.6%) compared to the control group (36.1%). For official offending (court convictions), the enriched group tended to have a reduced rate of offending (3.6%) compared to the control group (9.9%), but the difference was not quite statistically significant ($p = .07$).

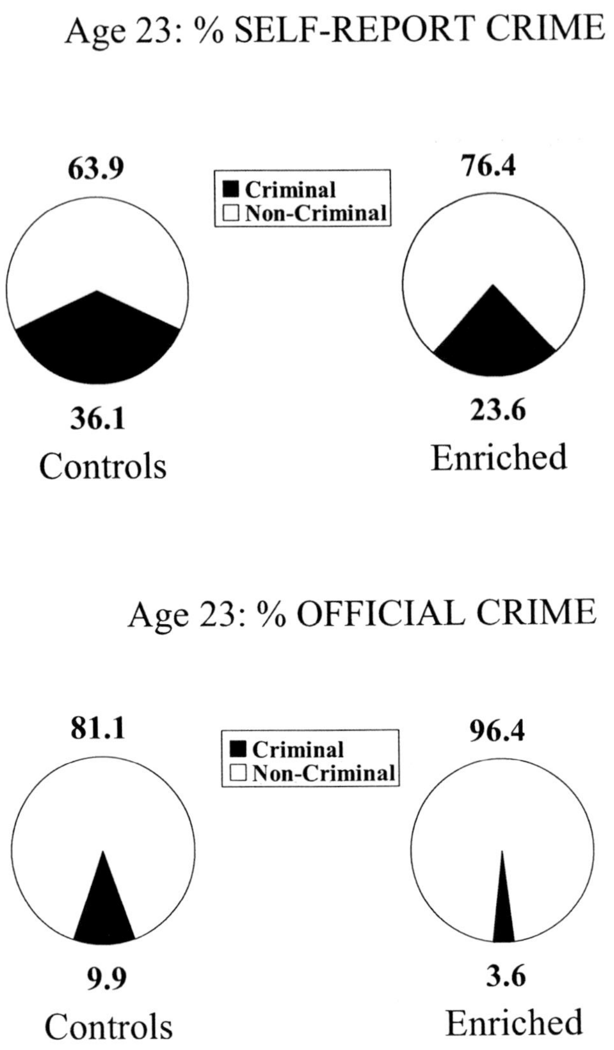

Figure 2. Reductions in self-report and court record indicators of criminal behavior at age 23 in the enriched group

The Moderating Effect of Early Malnutrition

An important result from our study concerned the effect of early nutritional status in moderating the relationship between early environmental enrichment and later behavior. Seven indicators of malnutrition were assessed in a pediatric examination of the child at age 3 years conducted by pediatricians as follows: *stunting* (reduced height for age) was based on the standing height of the child and expressed as observed height as a percentage of expected height at the same age, with expected height based on Mauritian norms from the entire birth cohort; *wasting* (reduced weight for height) was based on weight of the child in light clothes without shoes, and was expressed as the ratio of observed weight to expected weight based on

Mauritian norms of expected weight for height; *hemoglobin levels* were assessed from blood samples taken from the child; *angular stomatitis* (cracking in the lips and corners of the mouth) predominantly reflects riboflavin deficiency (vitamin B2) but also reflects niacin deficiency (Wong and Hess, 2000); *hair dyspigmentation* is one of the signs of kwashiorkor as indicated by red hair and reflects protein malnutrition, zinc, and copper deficiency (Subotzky et al., 1992); *sparse, thin hair* is a sign of protein-energy, zinc, and iron deficiency (Friedman and Orraca-Tetteh, 1978) as well as a sign of general malnutrition; *hair easily pulled out* similarly reflects protein energy malnutrition (Spencer and Callen, 1987). A confirmatory factor analysis of these seven variables established a one-factor (malnutrition) model with significant fit indices of 0.99 for the goodness-of-fit index, 0.98 for adjusted goodness-of-fit index, and 0.049 for the root-mean-square error of approximation. A median split on standardized factor scores designated subjects as either high or low on nutritional status.

For behavior ratings, at age 17 there was a significant enrichment x nutrition interaction for Conduct Disorder and Motor Excess. These interactions are illustrated in Figure 3 (upper and middle), and indicate that the malnourished group was especially likely to show lower conduct disorder and motor excess problems as a result of the enrichment as compared to malnourished controls. With respect to self-report schizotypy at age 17, there was similarly a significant Enrichment x Nutrition interaction for Disorganization (see Figure 3, lower part). The malnourished group were especially likely to show lower disorganization as a result of the enrichment as compared to malnourished controls. Although the interaction for the behavioral measure of Psychoticism was not statistically significant, there was a trend ($p = .09$) for the enrichment to selectively lower Psychoticism scores by 43% in malnourished children only ($d = .37$).

At age 23, for self-report schizotypy (the SPQ) there was a significant enrichment x nutrition interaction. This interaction is illustrated in Figure 4 (upper) where it can be seen that the malnourished group were more likely to show lower total SPQ scores as a result of the enrichment as compared to controls. Analysis of sub-factors of the SPQ indicated a significant Enrichment x Nutrition interaction for Interpersonal Deficits. This interaction is illustrated in Figure 4 (lower half) where it can be seen that the malnourished group were especially likely to shower lower interpersonal deficits as a result of the enrichment as compared to controls. The interaction between Disorganization scores and malnutrition was marginally significant ($p = .053$) and was in the same direction as for other schizotypy measures. That is, the enrichment specifically reduced disorganization scores in malnourished children. For cognitive-perceptual scores, the interaction effect was non-significant but again the same direction of effects was observed. For crime at age 23 years, unlike the data at age 17 years, there was no evidence that nutrition interacted with the enrichment with respect to criminal outcome.

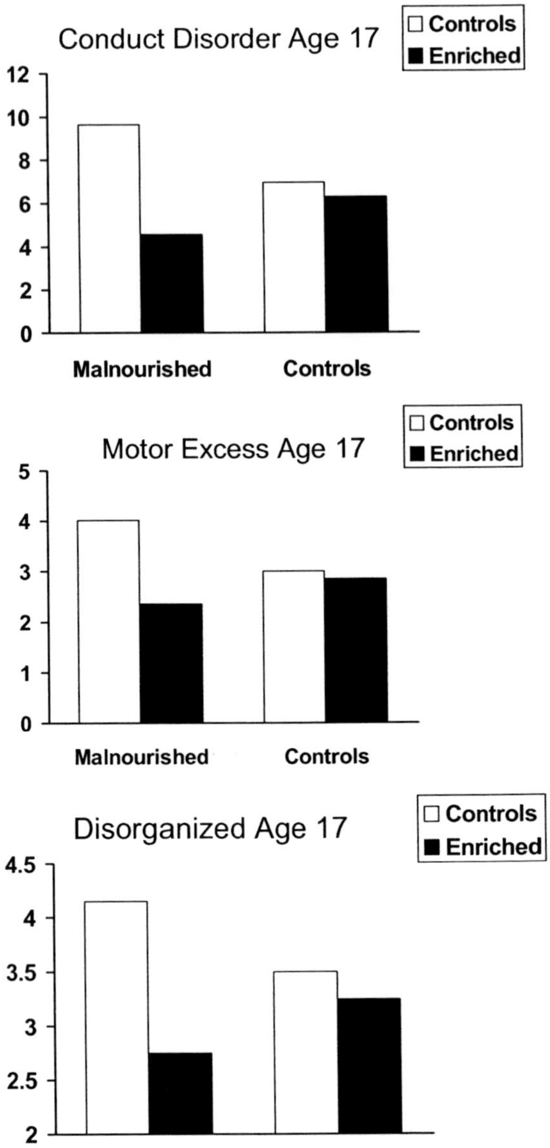

Figure 3. Interactions between enrichment and nutritional status for Conduct Disorder (age 17), Motor Excess (age 17) and Disorganization (age 17), illustrating the potentiating effect of the enrichment in malnourished children

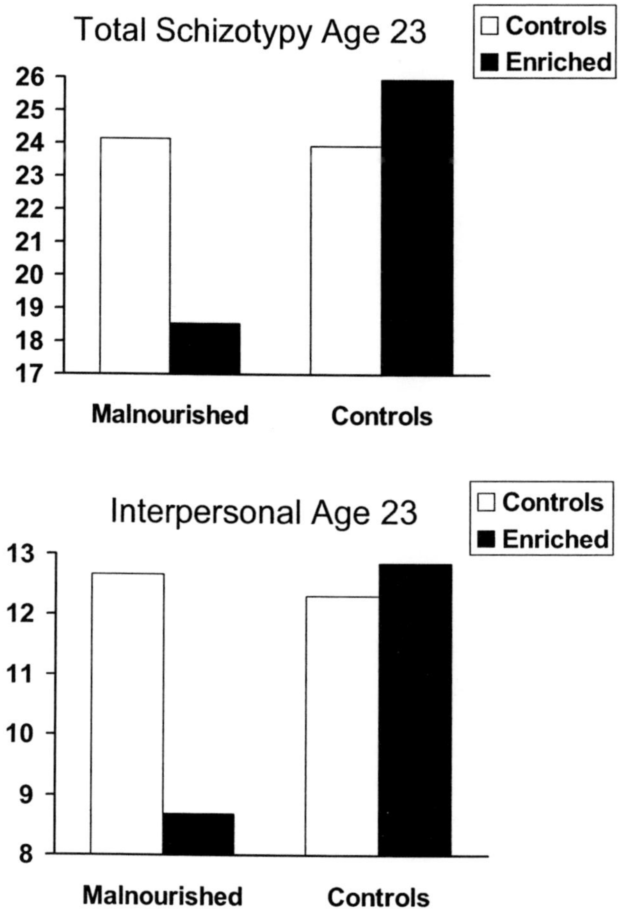

Figure 4. Lower total and interpersonal schizotypal personality at age 23 in enriched children with poor early nutritional status

The Role of Psychosocial Adversity

One important question concerns whether the beneficial effects of the enrichment was moderated by early psychosocial adversity. We tested this using a psychosocial adversity scale based on father uneducated, mother uneducated, semi-skilled or unskilled occupation, teenage mother, single parent status, separation from parents, large family size, poor health of mother, and overcrowded home. All analyses indicated however that psychosocial adversity did not interact with enrichment status in any analysis, indicating that the effects of enrichment were not stronger (or weaker) for those from more adverse home backgrounds.

Interpreting the Effects of Early Environmental Enrichment on Later Crime and Schizotypy

The results of our study indicated that a nutritional, educational, and physical exercise enrichment at ages 3-5 years reduces schizotypal personality and antisocial behavior 14-20 years later. Taking into account early nutritional status, the enrichment resulted in a 53% reduction in conduct disorder (age 17), a 41% reduction in motor excess (age 17), a 43.2% reduction in psychotic behavior (age 17), a 32.4% reduction in cognitive disorganization (age 17), a 34.6% reduction in self-report crime (age 23), a 63.6% reduction in official crime (age 23), a 23% reduction in total schizotypy (age 23) and a 31.6% reduction in interpersonal deficits (age 23). Clearly, the early enrichment could in no way eradicate conduct disorder, crime, and schizotypal personality, but at the same time the effects were statistically significant and not trivial, suggesting some role of the early environment in reducing crime and schizotypy.

The beneficial effects of the intervention tended to be greater for children who were malnourished at age 3, particularly with respect to schizotypy at ages 17 and 23, and with conduct disorder at age 17. The facts that the prevention program affected two different forms of psychopathology at two different, widely-spaced ages extending over 20 years and using two different measures of outcome (self-report and objective measures) indicates the robustness of the effects. Results could not be attributed to pre-prevention group differences in temperament, cognitive ability, nutritional status, autonomic reactivity, or demographic variables (Raine et al., 2003). To our knowledge, this is the first attempt at primary prevention of schizotypal personality. Findings are consistent with an increasing body of knowledge that implicate an enriched, stimulating environment in beneficial psychological and behavioral outcome (Farrington, 1992; Gorey, 2001; Schweinhart and Weikart, 1997), and have potential implications for the prevention of crime and schizotypal personality, particularly in populations at risk for malnutrition.

One limitation of our study is the inability to determine which component(s) of the intervention (nutrition, exercise, or education) accounted for the later beneficial effects. Nevertheless, malnourished children at age 3 years were significantly more likely to benefit from the program. Nutritional deficits have been linked to both schizophrenia and schizoid personality (Hoek et al., 1996; Dalman, Allebeck, Cullberg, Grunewald, and Koster, 1999; Tsuang, 2000) and also to antisocial behavior (Fishbein et al., 1994). In particular, a double-blind, placebo-controlled, randomized trial has shown the effectiveness of nutritional supplements in reducing antisocial and violent behavior in prisoners (Gesch, Hammond, Hampson, Eves, and Crowder, 2002). It is conceivable that aspects of the nutritional intervention such as fish supplementation could benefit brain function because omega-3 fatty acids have been reported by some to have beneficial effects on both schizophrenia (Mahadik, Evans, and Lal, 2001; Post, 1999; Warner, Laugharne, Peet, Brown, and Rogers, 1999; Mellor, Laugharne, and Peet, 1995) and externalizing behavior problems (Stevens, Zentall, Abate, and Kuczek, 1996; Arnold, Kleykamp, Votolato, and Gibson, 1994; Corrigan et al., 1994). Taken together with other successful early prevention programs that have manipulated nutrition (Olds et al., 1998), findings suggest, but do not prove, that the nutrition component in the enrichment may account for some of the benefits.

Alternative hypotheses must also be considered. For example, the prevention program included 2.5 hours each day devoted to physical exercise and outdoor play, and it is conceivable that exercise by itself could account for a significant proportion of the observed effects. Exercise in animals is known to increase mRNA in the hippocampus and to have other beneficial effects on brain structure and function (Gomez-Pinilla, Dao, and So, 1997). Furthermore, the effect of environmental enrichment in producing neurogenesis in mice has been attributed to the sole effects of running, independent of other components of enrichment such as maze training (van Praag, Kempermann, and Gage, 1999). As such, physical exercise could benefit brain functioning and protect individuals from both schizotypal and antisocial behavior which have both been linked to structural and functional brain deficits (Andreasen, 1999).

Another hypothesis that also needs to be considered is that the increased social interaction with positive, educated preschool teachers in the experimental enrichment may in part account for the beneficial effects of the prevention program. Alternatively, it may be unreasonable to focus on any single component of the intervention. Instead, the multi-modal nature of the prevention program which incorporated social and cognitive components alongside nutrition and exercise components may have facilitated interactions between these components which critically impacted later development. Follow-up studies which both replicate the multi-modal enrichment as well as tease apart the individual components could usefully address this issue.

One prior study has shown that the effects of educational enrichment have long-term effects in reducing antisocial and criminal behavior (Weikart, 1998). As such, it is possible that the educational component of the prevention program could account for the long-term reduction in crime. This prior program was conducted on children from poor homes, and it has been argued that enrichment may particularly benefit children suffering from social adversity (Weikart, 1998). No support was found for this argument in the current study as social adversity did not moderate the effects of the enrichment. Instead, children suffering specifically from malnutrition were more likely to benefit from the enrichment. Consequently nutritional status in particular, rather than social adversity in general, may be a particular factor to consider in future prevention programs aimed at schizotypy and antisocial behavior.

Implications for Schizophrenia Prevention

Because schizotypal personality, not schizophrenia, constituted the outcome measure, we cannot make any claim to have prevented schizophrenia itself. Nevertheless, the fact that the prevention program was associated with reduced levels of schizotypal personality in late adolescence and in early adulthood in the malnourished group may help intervention efforts aimed at preventing or delaying the onset of schizophrenia (McGorry, 2000; Tsuang et al., 2000). Schizotypal personality is a disorder that shares in common with schizophrenia a range of neurocognitive, neurophysiological, genetic, psychophysiological, and symptom characteristics (Siever et al., 2002; Raine, Lencz, and Mednick, 1995), and has much in common with the prodromal, pre-psychotic stage of schizophrenia. If features of schizotypal personality can be attenuated by early environmental enrichment, it is possible that the development of prodromal features of schizophrenia may also be reduced, in turn delaying or preventing the onset of schizophrenia itself (Tsuang, Stone, and Faraone, 2001; McGorry, 2000).

The fact that one of the strongest effect sizes in this study was obtained for interpersonal deficits in the malnourished group at age 23 years (d = .67) is of particular relevance as these negative schizotypal traits feature strongly in the schizophrenia prodrome (American Psychiatric Association, 1994; McGorry and Edwards, 1998; Tsuang, Stone, Tarbox, and Faraone, 2002). This notwithstanding, it must be re-emphasized that this study only shows reductions in levels of schizotypal features in a non-selected group, and it remains to be seen whether such prevention efforts can achieve results of clinical significance to schizophrenia itself as has been the case with secondary prevention efforts (McGorry et al., 1998).

Implications for Crime Prevention

Although the prevention program was associated with a significant reduction in conduct disorder at age 17 (d = .44), we caution that the effect size for the intervention up to age 23 years was smaller in size (d = 0.26 for self-report offending, d = 0.22 for official offending). While there was a statistically significant reduction in self-report criminal offending (p = .045), and while there was a 63.6% reduction in official offending at age 23 that equals or exceeds effects found in more short-term intervention studies (Surgeon General, 2001), this latter difference failed to reach statistical significance (p = .069). On the other hand, base-rates for official offending were lower than for self-report offending and the possibility that floor effects precluded statistical significance in this case must also be considered.

A recent review of prevention programs of crime show that even the very few model prevention programs that have shown success rarely if ever show effects beyond the teenage years (Surgeon General, 2001). The large majority of prevention programs do not start early in life when it is believed the pathway to antisocial behavior begins to be laid down (Moffitt, 1993; Tremblay, 2000). On the other hand, it may be questioned why there was *any* effect 20 years later from a prevention program that only lasted 2 years early in life. While stronger long-term effects may be expected of a longer environmental enrichment, it has been found that early withdrawal from an environmental enrichment doubles the number of new cells in mice compared to a more sustained enrichment (Kempermann and Gage, 1999). As such, some long-term beneficial effect of the two-year enrichment is not inconceivable. Future studies may assess whether a booster enrichment session later in childhood leads to stronger effect sizes for criminal behavior in adulthood.

Conclusions

In conclusion, these initial finding suggest that early environmental enrichment is associated with reduced levels of antisocial behavior and schizotypal personality in adulthood, and that benefits are greatest in children with poor nutrition. We caution that findings from a country that was still developing when the prevention program was conducted cannot be directly extrapolated to more developed countries such as the U.S.. Nevertheless, findings may be particularly relevant to poor rural areas of the U.S. such as the Mississippi delta region and also U.S. inner-cites where rates of both malnutrition and behavioral problems in children are relatively high (Murphy et al., 1998; Smith et al., 1999).

Inevitably, these initial findings raise more questions than they answer. It would be invaluable to conduct a replication study in Western counties where the main components of the enrichment – nutrition, exercise, and cognitive stimulation – are broken down into separate experimental conditions in order to tease out the active ingredient in the enrichment. Furthermore, it would be of great value to uncover specific processes or mechanisms that mediate the relationship between early enrichment and later psychiatric and behavioral change. For example, we suspect that the early enrichment altered brain structure / function in a way that protected otherwise vulnerable individuals from expressing schizotypal personality and conduct disorder / criminal behavior, but the nature of this brain mechanism is not known. Prefrontal structural and functional impairments have been found to be common to both schizotypal personality (Raine et al., 2002) and antisocial / violent behavior (Raine et al., 1997; Raine et al., 2000). Similarly, structural hippocampal impairments have been found in antisocial / psychopathic offenders (Raine et al., 2004) as well as in schizophrenia patients (Keshavan et al., 2002), and because environmental enrichment in animals increases the size of the dentate gyrus by approximately 15%, this could in theory account for better behavioral and personality outcome. Detailed neurocognitive and brain imaging assessments in future studies could test these neurocognitive mediation hypotheses further.

Acknowledgements

This paper was written with the support of an Independent Scientist Award from NIMH (K02 MH01114-01) to the first author.

References

American Psychiatric Association. (1994). *Diagnostic and statistical manual of mental disorders.* (4th ed.). Washington, D.C.: American Psychiatric Association.

Andreasen, N. C. (1999). A unitary model of schizophrenia: Bleuler's "fragmented phrene" as schizencephaly. *Archives of General Psychiatry, 56*, 781-787.

Arnold, L. E., Kleykamp, D, Votolato, N, and Gibson, R A. (1994). Potential link between dietary intake of fatty acids and behavior: Pilot exploration of serum lipids in attention-deficit hyperactivity disorder. *Journal of Child and Adolescent Psychopharmacology, 4*, 171-182.

Buchsbaum, M. S., and Hazlett, E A. (1998). Positron emission tomography studies of abnormal glucose metabolism in schizophrenia. *Schizophrenia Bulletin, 24*, 343-364.

Buchsbaum, M. S., Trestman, R L, Hazlett, E, Siegel, B V J, Schacfer, C H, Luu-Hsia, C, Tang, C, Herrera, S, Solimando, A C, Losonczy, M, Serby, M, Silverman, J, and Siever, L J. (1997). Regional cerebral blood flow during the Wisconsin Card Sort Test in schizotypal personality disorder. *Schizophrenia Research, 27*, 21-28.

Cannon, T. D., van Erp, T G M, and Glahn, D C. (2002). Differential metabolic rates in prefrontal and temporal Brodmann areas in schizophrenia and schizotypal personality disorder. *Schizophrenia Research, 54*, 141-150.

Cornblatt, B., Lencz, T, and Obuchowski, M. (2002). The schizophrenia prodrome: treatment and high-risk perspectives. *Schizophrenia Research, 54*, 177-186.

Corrigan, F., Gray, R, Strathdee, A, Skinner, R, Van Rhijn, A, and Horrobin, D. (1994). Fatty acid analysis of blood from violent offenders. *Journal of Forensic Psychiatry, 5*, 83-92.

Dalman, C., Allebeck, P, Cullberg, J, Grunewald, C, and Koster, M. (1999). Obstetric complications and the risk of schizophrenia: a longitudinal study of a national birth cohort. *Archives of General Psychiatry, 56*, 234-240.

Elliott, D. S., Ageton, S, Huizinga, D, Knowles, B, and Canter, R. (1983). The prevalence and incidence of delinquent behavior: 1976-1980. In Anonymous, *National Youth Survey, Report No. 26*. Boulder Colorado: Behavior Research Institute.

Farrington, D. P. (1992). Criminal career research: Lessons for crime prevention. *Studies on Crime and Crime Prevention, 1*, 7-29.

Fishbein, D. (2001). *Biobehavioral perspectives in criminology*. Belmont, CA: Wadsworth.

Fishbein, D H. (1999). *The science, treatment, and prevention of antisocial behavior: Applications to the criminal justice system*. New York: Civic Research Institute.

Fishbein, D. H., and Pease, S E. (1994). Diet, nutrition, and aggression. *Journal of Offender Rehabilitation, 21*, 117-144.

Friedman, M., and Orraca-Tetteh, R. (1978). Hair as an index of protein malnutrition. *Advances in Experimental Medicine and Biology, 105*, 131-154.

Gesch, C. B., Hammond, S M, Hampson, S E, Eves, A, and Crowder, M J. (2002). Influence of supplementary vitamins, minerals and essential fatty acids on the antisocial behaviour of young adult prisoners: Randomised, placebo- controlled trial. *British Journal of Psychiatry, 181*, 22-28.

Gomez-Pinilla, F., Dao, L, and So, V. (1997). Physical exercise induces FGF-2 and its mRNA in the hippocampus. *Brain Research, 764*, 1-8.

Gorey, K. M. (2001). Early childhood education: A meta-analytic affirmation of the short- and long-term benefits of educational opportunity. *School Psychology Quarterly, 16*, 9-30.

Guerra, N. G., Tolan, P H, and Hammond, W R. (1994). Prevention and treatment of adolescent violence. *Reason to hope: A psychosocial perspective on violence and youth.*, 383-403.

Gur, R. E., Cowell, P E, Latshaw, A, Turetsky, B I, Grossman, R I, Arnold, S E, Bilker, W B, and Gur, R C. (2000). Reduced dorsal and orbital prefrontal gray matter volumes in schizophrenia. *Archives of General Psychiatry, 57*, 761-768.

Hoek, H. W., Susser, E, Buck, K A, Lumey, L H, Lin, S P, and Gorman, J M. (1996). Schizoid personality disorder after prenatal exposure to famine. *American Journal of Psychiatry, 153*, 1637-1639.

Kempermann, G., and Gage, F H. (1999). Experience-dependent regulation of adult hippocampal neurogenesis: effects of long-term stimulation and stimulus withdrawal. *Hippocampus, 9*, 321-332.

Kempermann, G., Kuhn, H G, and Gage, F H. (1997). More hippocampal neurons in adult mice living in an enriched environment. *Nature, 386*, 493-495.

Keshavan, M. S., Dick, E, Mankowski, I, Harenski, K, Montrose, D M, Diwadkar, V, and DeBellis, M. (2002). Decreased left amygdala and hippocampal volumes in young offspring at risk for schizophrenia. *Schizophrenia Research, 58*, 173-183.

Lim, S., and Suzuki, H. (2001). Changes in maze behavior of mice occur after sufficient accumulation of docosahexaenoic acid in brain. *Journal of Nutrition, 131*, 319-324.

Mahadik, S. P., Evans, D, and Lal, H. (2001). Oxidative stress and role of antioxidant and omega-3 essential fatty acid supplementation in schizophrenia. *Progress in Neuro-Psychopharmacology and Biological Psychiatry, 25*, 463-493.

McGorry, P. D. (2000). The nature of schizophrenia: Signposts to prevention. *Australian and New Zealand Journal of Psychiatry, 34*, S14-S21

McGorry, P. D., and Edwards, J. (1998). The feasibility and effectiveness of early intervention in psychotic disorders: The Australian experience. *International Clinical Psychopharmacology, 13*, S47-S52

Mellor, J. E., Laugharne, J D E, and Peet, M. (1995). Schizophrenic symptoms and dietary intake of n-3 fatty acids. *Schizophrenia Research, 18*, 85-86.

Mercy, J. A., and Hammond, W R. (1999). Combining action and analysis to prevent homicide: A public health perspective. *Homicide: A sourcebook of social research.*, 297-310.

Moffitt, T. E. (1993). Adolescence-limited and life-course-persistent antisocial behavior: A developmental taxonomy. *Psychological Review, 100*, 674-701.

Murphy, J. M., Wehler, C A, Pagano, M E, Little, M, Kleinman, R E, and Jellinek, M S. (1998). Relationship between hunger and psychosocial functioning in low-income American children. *Journal of the American Academy of Child and Adolescent Psychiatry, 37*, 163-170.

Olds, D., Henderson, C R J, Cole, R, Eckenrode, J, Kitzman, H, Luckey, D, Pettitt, L, Sidora, K, Morris, P, and Powers, J. (1998). Long-term effects of nurse home visitation on children's criminal and antisocial behavior: 15-year follow-up of a randomized controlled trial. *JAMA: Journal of the American Medical Association, 280*, 1238-1244.

Pham, T. M., Soderstrom, S, Winblad, B, and Mohammed, A H. (1999). Effects of environmental enrichment on cognitive function and hippocampal NGF in the non-handled rats. *Behavioural Brain Research, 103*, 63-70.

Post, R. M. (1999). Comparative pharmacology of bipolar disorder and schizophrenia. *Schizophrenia Research, 39*, 153-158.

Quay, H C, and Peterson, D R. *Manual for the Revised Behavior Problem Checklist.* (un pub)

Raesaenen, P., Tiihonen, J, Isohanni, M, Rantakallio, P, Lehtonen, J, and Moring, J. (1998). Schizophrenia, alcohol abuse, and violent behavior: A 26-year followup study of an unselected birth cohort. *Schizophrenia Bulletin, 24*, 437-441.

Raine, A., Ishikawa, S.S., Arce, E, Lencz, T, Knuth, K H, Bihrle, S, LaCasse, L, and Colletti, P. (2004). Hippocampal structural asymmetry in unsuccessful psychopaths. *Biological Psychiatry, 55*, 185-191.

Raine, A., Lencz, T, Yaralian, P, Bihrle, S, LaCasse, L, Ventura, J, and Colletti, P. (2002). Prefrontal structural and functional deficits in schizotypal personality disorder. *Schizophrenia Bulletin, 28*, 501-513.

Raine, A., Mellingen, K, Liu, J H, Venables, P H, and Mednick, S A. (2003). Effects of environmental enrichment at 3-5 years on schizotypal personality and antisocial behavior at ages 17 and 23 years. *American Journal of Psychiatry, 160*, 1627-1635.

Raine, A. (1991). The SPQ: A scale for the assessment of schizotypal personality based on DSM-III--R criteria. *Schizophrenia Bulletin, 17*, 555-564.

Raine, A. (1993). *The psychopathology of crime: Criminal behavior as a clinical disorder*. San Diego: Academic Press.

Raine, A., Buchsbaum, M, and LaCasse, L. (1997). Brain abnormalities in murderers indicated by positron emission tomography. *Biological Psychiatry, 42*, 495-508.

Raine, A., Lencz, T, and Mednick, S A. (1995). *Schizotypal personality*. New York: Cambridge University Press.

Raine, A., Lencz, T, Bihrle, S, LaCasse, L, and Colletti, P. (2000). Reduced prefrontal gray matter volume and reduced autonomic activity in antisocial personality disorder. *Archives of General Psychiatry, 57*, 119-127.

Raine, A., Reynolds, C, Lencz, T, Scerbo, A, Triphon, N, and Kim, D. (1994b). Cognitive-perceptual, interpersonal, and disorganized features of schizotypal personality. *Schizophrenia Bulletin, 20*, 191-201.

Raine, A., Venables, P H, Dalais, C, Mellingen, K, Reynolds, C, and Mednick, S A. (2001). Early educational and health enrichment at age 3-5 years is associated with increased autonomic and central nervous system arousal and orienting at age 11 years: Evidence from the Mauritius Child Health Project. *Psychophysiology, 38*, 254-266.

Salvati, S., Attorri, L, Avellino, C, Di Biase, A, and Sanchez, M. (2000). Diet, lipids and brain development. *Developmental Neuroscience, 22*, 481-487.

Schweinhart, L. J., and Weikart, D P. (1997). The High/Scope Preschool Curriculum Comparison study through age 23. *Early Childhood Research Quarterly, 12*, 117-143.

Siever, L. J., Koenigsberg, H W, Harvey, P, Mitropoulou, V, Laruelle, M, Abi-Dargham, A, Goodman, M, and Buchsbaum, M. (2002). Cognitive and brain function in schizotypal personality disorder. *Schizophrenia Research, 54*, 157-167.

Smith, J., Lensing, S, Horton, J A, Lovejoy, J, Zaghloul, S, Forrester, I, McGee, B.B., and Bogle, M L. (1999). Prevalence of self-reported nutrition-related health problems in the Lower Mississippi Delta. *American Journal of Public Health, 89*, 1418-1421.

Spencer, L. V., and Callen, J P. (1987). Hair loss in systemic disease. *Dermatologic Clinics, 5*, 565-570.

Stevens, L. J., Zentall, S.S., Abate, M L, and Kuczek, T. (1996). Omega-3 fatty acids in boys with behavior, learning, and health problems. *Physiology and Behavior, 59*, 915-920.

Subotzky, E. F., Heese, H D, Sive, A.A., Dempster, W S, Sacks, R, and Malan, H. (1992). Plasma zinc, copper, selenium, ferritin and whole blood manganese concentrations in children with kwashiorkor in the acute stage and during refeeding. *Annals of Tropical Paediatrics, 12*, 13-22.

Surgeon General. *Youth violence: A report of the Surgeon General*. (2001). Washington, D.C.: DHHS.

Tremblay, R. E. (2000). The development of aggressive behaviour during childhood: What have we learned in the past century? *International Journal of Behavioral Development, 24*, 129-141.

Tsuang, M. (2000). Schizophrenia: genes and environment. *Biological Psychiatry, 47*, 210-220.

Tsuang, M. T., Stone, W S, Tarbox, S I, and Faraone, S V. (2002). Elucidating continuities and discontinuities between schizotypy and schizophrenia in the nervous system. *Schizophrenia Research, 54*, 151-156.

Tsuang, M. T., Stone, W S, and Faraone, S V. (2000). Towards the prevention of schizophrenia. *Biological Psychiatry, 48*, 349-356.

Tsuang, M. T., Stone, W S, and Faraone, S V. (2001). Genes, environment and schizophrenia. *British Journal of Psychiatry, 178*, s18-s24

van Praag, H., Kempermann, G, and Gage, F H. (1999). Running increases cell proliferation and neurogenesis in the adult mouse dentate gyrus. *Nature Neuroscience, 2*, 266-270.

Venables, P. H. (1990). The measurement of schizotypy in Mauritius. *Personality and Individual Differences, 11*, 965-971.

Venables, P. H., and Bailes, K. (1994). The structure of schizotypy, its relation to subdiagnoses of schizophrenia and to sex and age. *British Journal of Clinical Psychology, 33*, 277-294.

Venables, P. H. (1978). Psychophysiology and psychometrics. *Psychophysiology, 15*, 302-315.

Venables, P. H., Wilkins, S, Mitchell, D A, and Raine, A. (1990). A scale for the measurement of schizotypy. *Personality and Individual Differences, 11*, 481-495.

Volavka, J. (1999). The neurobiology of violence: An update. *Journal of Neuropsychiatry and Clinical Neurosciences, 11*, 307-314.

Volavka, J., Laska, E, Baker, S, and Meisner, M. (1997). History of violent behaviour and schizophrenia in different cultures. Analyses based on the WHO study on Determinants of Outcome of Severe Mental Disorders. *British Journal of Psychiatry, 171*, 9-14.

Warner, R., Laugharne, J, Peet, M, Brown, L, and Rogers, N. (1999). Retinal function as a marker for cell membrane omega-3 fatty acid depletion in schizophrenia: A pilot study. *Biological Psychiatry, 45*, 1138-1142.

Weikart, D. P. (1998). Changing early childhood development through educational intervention. *Preventive Medicine: An International Journal Devoted to Practice and Theory, 27*, 233-237.

Wong, D L, and Hess, C S. (2000). *Clinical Manual of Pediatric Nursing*. St. Louis: Mosby.

In: Crime and Schizophrenia: Causes and Cures
Editor: Adrian Raine, pp. 267-286
ISBN 1-59454-609-6

Chapter 14

PREVENTION OF CHRONIC PHYSICAL AGGRESSION: AN EPIGENETIC PERSPECTIVE

Richard E. Tremblay
University of Montréal

From an evolutionary perspective aggression is a solution to a problem. From a historical, social, and moral perspective, humans decide at different places and times which solutions are acceptable. The general aim of this chapter is to discuss the scientific evidence which can help prevent the development of chronic physical aggression by humans living in the wealthiest countries of the 21st century. To put this discussion in perspective let us go back in time 400 years to one of the wealthiest families in the world, and briefly examine the use of physical aggression in the socialization process of children.

The Borchard Foundation Conference, on the causes and cures of crime and schizophrenia, was held in a room of Le Chateau de la Bretesche decorated with Louis XIII (1601-1643) furniture. From the conference table we could see in the adjoining room a large painting of Henri IV (1553-1610), the protestant king of Navarre who converted to Catholicism to become king of France. Henri was Louis' father; his mother was Italian, Marie of Medicis (1573-1642), a daughter of the Grand Duke of Florence. Immediately after his birth, Louis was assigned a private doctor, Jean Hérouard, to insure the health of the heir to the throne. Henri and Marie were extremely busy running the country, so they hired a Governess, Mme de Monglat, who had the responsibility of Louis' royal education. Hérouard made daily notes on the precious child's health and behavior. He also noted events that could affect his health and his royal up-bringing. For example, he noted every time he saw his mother and father. An analysis of this information indicates that between his first and eight birthday, Louis' mother spent 573 days with him, while his father spent 606 days. Hérouard describes Louis as irritable and bent on temper tantrums. He notes that his father first threatened him with a whip when he was 18 months old. Mme de Monglat was given permission by King Henri to use the whip, and apparently first used it when he was 26 months old. Henri was assassinated when Louis was 9 years old. Marie ruled with the help of an Italian friend, apparently her lover. Louis officially became king at 15, and one year later had his domineering mother imprisoned and her lover killed. Louis went on to marry Anne of Austria, and their son became Louis XIV, the Sun King.

Physical aggression in the 17th century was not a behavior learned from television. It was a way of life for Kings and commons, essentially from birth to death. To dominate, wits were not enough; you needed to be prepared to physically attack and defend yourself at all times. This chapter summarizes recent findings from three different strains of research on the development and prevention of chronic physical aggression which will highlight to what extent 400 years after the birth of Louis XIII, physical aggression is still very much part of young children's lives. The aim of the chapter is to highlight how the three strains of research lead to the conclusion that prevention of chronic physical aggression should target early childhood. The first strain of research involves longitudinal studies on the development of physical aggression from birth to adulthood. The second refers to genetic studies, including twin and molecular genetics, on the causes of physical aggression and violence. Finally, experimental and natural prevention studies of aggression and violence comprise the third strain of research. The chapter ends with the conclusion that we need to create studies which combine these three methodological approaches during the first four or five years of life to identify key gene-environment effects on the development of chronic physical aggression, and to also identify the best early prevention interventions for children with different genetic and environmental profiles.

Longitudinal Studies on the Development of Physical Aggression

The recent longitudinal analyses of official criminal data for 500 juvenile delinquents followed from ages 7 to 70 (Sampson and Laub, 2003) replicate the age-crime curve, and age-violent crime curve results which have been observed in 20th century cross-sectional studies based on official crimes (e.g. Blumstein, Cohen and Farrington, 1988). Violent offenses appear in pre-adolescence, increase sharply during adolescence, and then decrease slowly up to old age. If, as hypothesized by learning theories (Bandura, 1973; Reiss and Roth, 1993; US Human Capital Initiative Coordinating Committee on Reducing Violence, 1997), young humans learn to physically aggress by imitation of aggressions observed in the home, in the neighborhood, and in the media, the increase in physical violence during adolescence makes sense. The older they are, the more they have observed acts of physical aggression, and the more likely they are bound to imitate what they have seen. The beauty of these data is not only that they confirm the prevalent psychological theory, but they replicate the data that Adolphe Quetelet, the Belgian astronomer-statistician, started collecting in the late 1820s (Quetelet, 1833). They also replicate data on homicides in the 17th, 18th, and 19th centuries which were recently analyzed by Manuel Eisner (2003).

The age-crime curve is probably the most robust criminological observation. However, there is a major problem with that robust finding: the age-violent crime curve studies limited their focus on adolescents and adults (Tremblay, 2003). The age-violent crime curve figures give the impression that physical aggressions appear with the legal age for criminal responsibility - as if lawmakers had chosen the age for criminal responsibility after detailed studies of child development. Those who decided to study elementary school children to understand the precursors of adolescent delinquency discovered that elementary school children used physical aggression before they had accumulated 12 or 13 years of social learning.

The Columbia County Study, initiated in the State of New York in 1960, was one of the rare longitudinal studies of elementary-school children specifically focused on aggression. More than 800 third grade school children rated each other on different behavioral dimensions, including aggression, to test the social-learning hypothesis. Following the analysis of the first wave of data when the children were 8 years old, the investigators gave the following summary of their findings: "It is fair to say that all the major findings of that analysis were consistent with the hypothesis that aggression may be learned by a child from his interactions with his environment" (Lefkowitz, Eron, Walder, and Huesmann, 1977, p. 37). Note that this was a conclusion from cross-sectional data. Later analyses of data collected at ages 8, 19, and 30 revealed relatively high correlations between aggression assessments at these different points in time (Huesmann, Eron, Lefkowitz, and Walder, 1984).

These results led Eron (1990), in his presidential address to the International Society for Research on Aggression in 1990, to conclude that aggression crystallizes at 8 years of age. Thus the social learning of aggression would occur much earlier than the start of the agecrime curve. But there were two important limitations with the Columbia County Study. First, the aggression scale used at age 8 should have been labeled a "disruptive behavior" scale (e.g. who does not obey the teacher, who gives dirty looks, who does things that bothers others, who is always getting in trouble). Only 2 of the 10 items referred specifically to physical aggressions (who starts a fight over nothing; who pushes and shoves children). The second limitation is that the data collection points had 10-year gaps, making it impossible to study developmental trajectories.

Fortunately, a similar US study, was initiated 20 years later and collected annual data on physical aggression. The Carolina Longitudinal Study followed 220 boys and girls from 4th to 12th grade and obtained assessments of physical aggression from the students and the teachers (Cairns and Cairns, 1994). Analyses of these data painted an unexpected picture with regard to the "social-learning" hypotheses. The information from teachers as well as from students was showing a clear mean decrease in the frequency of physical aggression from 10 to 18 years of age, and this was true for males as well as for females (Cairns, Cairns, Neckerman, Ferguson, and Gariépy, 1989). How could longitudinal data from a population sample of American adolescents, living in a southern state, show a physical aggression curve exactly the reverse of the age-crime curve?

One explanation could be that, although the majority of youth reduce the frequency of physical aggressions as they grow older, a minority are increasing their frequency of physical violence and are being processed through the legal system which generates the statistics for the age-crime curve. To test this hypothesis we needed to go beyond a description of the mean developmental trajectories of a given sample, and identify the different types of developmental trajectories that children are following. Nagin and Tremblay (1999) used a semi-parametric mixture model with a longitudinal sample of more than 1,000 kindergarten boys in schools from low-socioeconomic areas of Montreal to describe these different trajectories. Why use males from low-socio-economic areas to study the development of physical aggression? The answer can be found in the report "Reducing Violence" from the Human Capital Coordinating Committee (1997, p. 11): "Certain environmental conditions not only trigger violence, they can also seem to teach aggressive or violent behavior patterns. For example, poverty is associated with both sudden violent outbursts and long-term, habitual aggression."

Results (Figure 1) from teacher ratings confirmed the North Carolina data. The large majority of boys from the poorest inner city areas of Canada were using physical aggression less frequently as they grew older. Only a very small group of boys (4%) did not show the declining trend; these were the boys who had the highest level of physical aggression in kindergarten and remained at the highest level until adolescence. When interviewed at ages 15 and 17, they were the boys who reported the highest frequency of physical violence, and they were the ones most frequently found guilty of infractions before 18 years of age. Thus, the increase in the age-crime curve during adolescence for physical aggression would be produced by the fact that, during this period, the police and judicial system start arresting and convicting individuals who have been physically aggressing others at least since kindergarten. An international team of investigators replicated these finding using 5 other longitudinal studies in Canada, New Zealand, and the USA (Broidy et al., 2003).

Figure 1 clearly shows that all the boys tended to be at their peak level in frequency of physical aggression at 6 years of age, when they were at the end of their kindergarten year. If this is the case, when do they start to use physical aggression? There is a long history of case studies of physical aggression in young children. One of the first publication of a "developmental origins of aggression" study was published by Augustine of Thagaste (AD 397/1960, p. 49), later known as Saint Augustine. One millenium and a half later, in the "rage" section of the "The expression of the emotions in man and animals", Darwin (1872, p. 243) writes: "Every one who has had much to do with young children must have seen how naturally they take to biting, when in a passion. It seems as instinctive in them as in young crocodiles, who snap their little jaws as soon as they emerge from the egg."

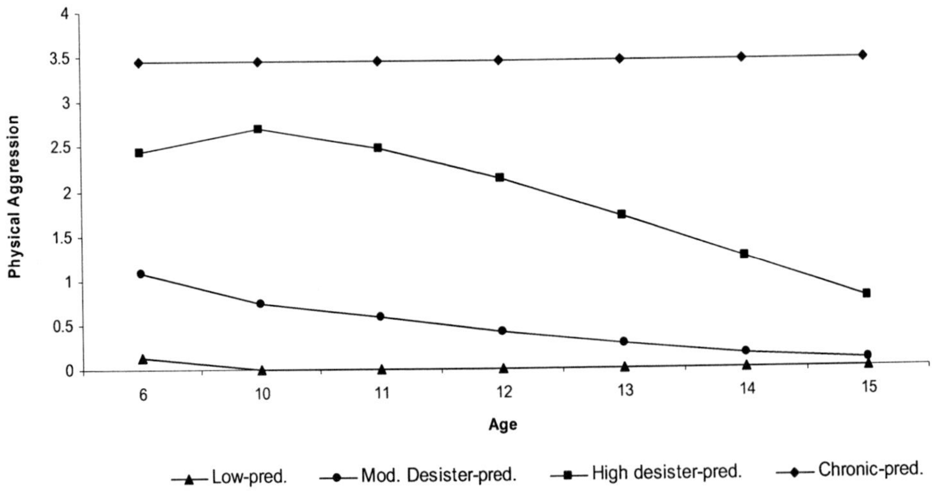

Figure 1. Physical aggression trajectories (Nagin & Tremblay, 1999)

More than half a century after Darwin, Bridges (1931) concluded from daily observations of 2- to 5-year-olds in Montreal day care centers that children, more than adults, were susceptible to anger expressed by physical aggression. Interestingly, two years later, she introduced a paper on the observation of 62 children, between 3 weeks to 2 years of age, by writing that "the trends of development" between 2 and 5 years of age described in her previous book "must have had their beginnings in early infancy" (Bridges, 1933, p. 36). Her three month cross-sectional observation of infant interactions led her to the conclusion that by 1 year of age children start "to struggle slightly for possession" of objects, and by fifteen months "aggressive attacks are indulged in at this stage for their own sake and are not out-grown till well after two years of age" (p. 48).

At the same time in Minnesota, Florence Goodenough (1931), was studying anger in children (7 to 94 months) by asking "intelligent parents", mostly college graduates, to keep records of their child's anger outbursts during a one-month period. One thousand eight hundred and seventy eight anger outbursts were recorded, for a mean of approximately 1 outburst per 10 hours of observation. The 17- to 23-month-olds had the highest mean with 1.3 outbursts per 10 hours. Data from a longitudinal study of temper tantrums reported by the mothers of a sample of 126 Belgian children at the end of the 1950s led to very similar results (Sand, 1966). An observational study of French children's social interactions in day care during the 1970s reported on the frequency of physical aggressions, compared to other forms of social interactions, for children of different age groups (Restoin et al., 1985). Results from 30 hours of filmed interactions showed that the relative frequency of physical aggression increases from the first year after birth to the second and then decreases (Figuer 2). Holmberg (1977) also found that physical attacks increased from 12 to 30 months and then decreased from 30 to 42 months when she observed 16 boys and girls interacting with peers in the US.

Recently, similar results were obtained in large Canadian cross-sectional and longitudinal epidemiological studies using parent reports. From 9 months to 30 months of age the proportion of children who are reported to use physical aggressions increases substantially (Tremblay, 2004); also, the frequency of use appears to increase up to nearly the end of the third year after birth (Tremblay et al., 2004) (Figure 3). This remarkable increase is then followed by a continuous decline in frequency (Côté et al., submitted; Tremblay et al., 1996).

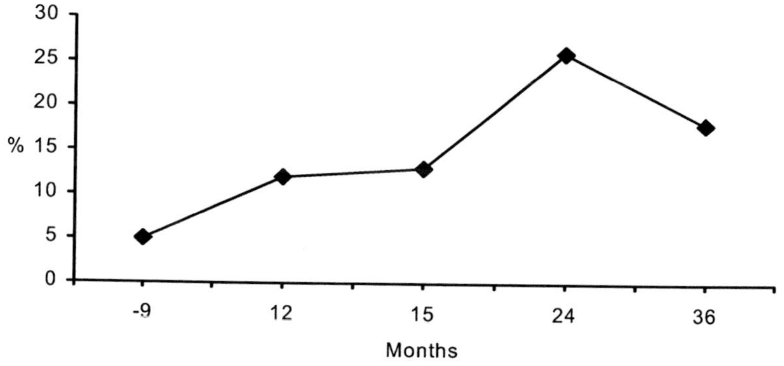

Figure 2. Relative frequency of aggressive behavior between peers from age 6 to 36 months in day care centers (Restoin et al., 1985)

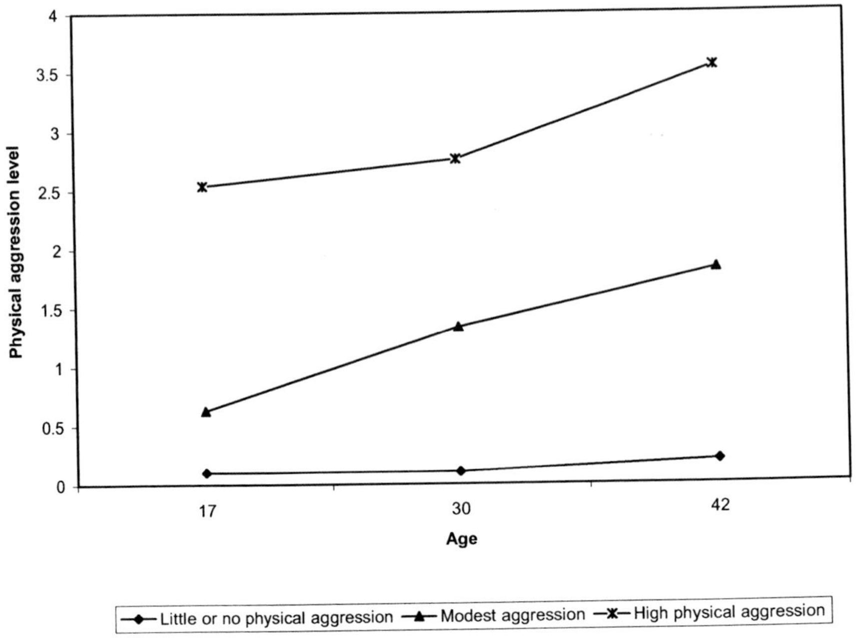

Figure 3. Trajectories of physical aggression from 17 to 42 months of age (Tremblay et al., 2004)

Clearly, the same general developmental picture is drawn whether we use data from different times (1920s, 1970s or 1990s), data from different countries (Belgium, Canada, France or the US), data from different reporting sources (filmed interactions in day care, parents' detailed records, or parents' recall of behavior in the past months), or data from different methodologies (cross-sectional or longitudinal, calculated as an absolute frequency over a given period of time, a relative percentage of social behaviors, a percentage of individuals using the behavior, or a general estimate of the frequency of the behavior). Frequency of anger outbursts and physical aggression increase rapidly from the first year after birth to approximately the third, and then the frequency decreases. Unfortunately, none of the longitudinal studies which started in early childhood have yet reported on physical aggression up to the end of adolescence. From the Restoin et al. (1985) data it appears that, at the peak frequency of physical aggression in a day care environment, physical aggression represents one in four social interactions. This is certainly a high frequency of aggressions, but, even at the worst of times, there are more prosocial or neutral social interactions than there are physically aggressive ones. This can probably be said for any social group, whether they are non human primates (see de Waal, 2000) or Hells' Angels. Social life would probably be impossible within a group where physical aggression is the most frequent form of social interaction. However, it does appear clear that most humans have used physical aggression before they reach 36 months of age, that humans use physical aggression most often between 18 and 42 months after birth, and that if humans are learning to physically aggress through imitation, this learning is happening in the first two years after birth, not by watching television and playing video games in middle childhood or adolescence. After many decades of training chimpanzees to use "language" David and Ann Premack (2003, p. 72) write: "Biting, hitting, kicking, scratching, pushing are natural reactions to the offensive behavior of another individual. These require no training." Figure 4 is an attempt to illustrate the life-span developmental trajectories of physical aggression in humans, using the available pieces of longitudinal studies.

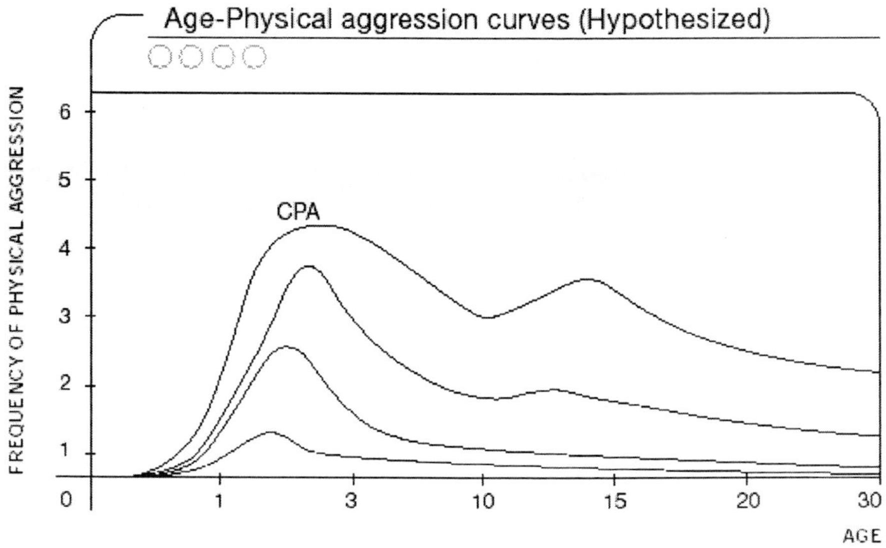

Figure 4. Age-physical aggression curves (Tremblay, 2003)

Genetically Informative Studies on the Development of Physical Aggression

There has been much research over the past two decades on the "onset" of children's disruptive behaviors, such as physical aggression, opposition and hyperactivity. Most of that work focused on school-age children (e.g. Lahey, Moffitt, and Caspi, 2003; Loeber and Farrington, 2001; McCord, Widom, and Crowell, 2001; Tremblay, Hartup, and Archer, in press). The longitudinal data on physical aggression from infancy onwards, summarized in the previous section, leads to the conclusion that physical aggression is not a behavior children learn like reading or writing, nor an illness children "catch" like poliomyelitis or smallpox. It is rather a behavior like crying, eating, grasping, throwing, and running, which young humans do when the physiological structure is in place, but then learn to regulate with experience. The learning to control process implies regulating your needs to adjust to those of others, and this process is generally labeled "socialization".

It is not hard to understand why the evolutionary process would have given humans a genetic program coding for all the basic mechanisms in order to react to hunger and to threat. Young children's muscles are activated to run, push, kick, grab, hit, throw, and yell with extreme force when hungry, when angry, or when they are strongly attracted by something. Stating that humans are genetically programmed to be able to physically aggress when needed, is different from stating that the frequency of physical aggression they use is genetically programmed. Thus, although all 18-month-olds who have developed normally can, and possibly, do physically aggress, not all do so at the same frequency and with the same vigor.

The trajectories shown in Figure 2 clearly indicate that these individual differences exist at any given point, starting in early childhood; but the most interesting phenotype is the development over time. There is obviously intra-individual change over time. Most children learn to reduce the frequency of the use of a behavior which they apparently did not need to learn. However, relatively stable differences among individuals remain. What are the gene-environment mechanisms which explain the change and stability? They are possibly very similar to the mechanisms which explain the developmental trajectories of growth in height. Genes code for the growth mechanisms, but there are individual differences in this coding, as well as environmental differences (e.g. access to food) which lead to stable individual differences. Thus the individual differences in the frequency of physical aggression at one point in time, and over time, can be due to a large number of "causes", e.g. to individual differences in the genetic coding for serotonin (see Pihl and Benkelfat, in press), or testosterone (see van Goozen, in press), or language development (see Dionne, in press), or cognitive development (see Séguin and Zelazo, in press), or to environmental differences such as mother's tobacco use during pregnancy (see Wakschlag, Pickett, Cook, Benowitz, and Leventhal, 2002), birth complications (see Arseneault, Tremblay, Boulerice, and Saucier, 2002), parental care (see Gatti and Tremblay, in press; Raine, Brennan, and Mednick, 1997; Zoccolillo et al., in press), and peer characteristics (see Boivin, Vitaro, and Poulin,in press). However, the individual differences that we observe are very likely to be due to interactions between many of these mechanisms, hence to epigenetic mechanisms (Francis, Diorio, Plotsky, and Meaney, 2002; Francis, Szegda, Campbell, Martin, and Insel, 2003; Weaver et al., 2004).

Knowledge on gene-environment interactions which could explain the development of chronic physical aggression is perilously close to zero. The first reason is that gene-environment interaction studies are recent. The second reason is that there are very few longitudinal studies that have included repeated assessments of physical aggression from early childhood to adulthood (see Rhee and Waldman, 2002). However, the most important problem is that molecular genetic studies and twin studies have concentrated on global antisocial behavior phenotypes, generally assessed at one point in time. This is an old problem in the antisocial behavior literature (e.g. see Blumstein et al., 1988; Gottfredson and Hirschi, 1990; Tremblay, 2000, 2003; Tremblay et al., 1991). Genetic studies have simply followed the main trend which tends to rely on measurement scales constructed by lumping items that are shown to correlate at one point in time. The problem is well illustrated in an extensive meta-analysis of gene and environment influences on antisocial behavior (Rhee and Waldman, 2002). The authors state: "The validity of the measures used in the studies considered for the meta-analysis was an important issue in deciding whether to include or exclude a study. Only studies examining antisocial behavior were included, and those examining related constructs such as anger and hostility were excluded. A study was included if it was clearly evident that it examined ASPD, CD, criminality, or aggression" (p. 497). Indeed, this statement gives the impression that the authors went out of their way to study a phenotype which is very clearly defined. However, at the end of the section on construct validity they add that they decided to include another construct: antisocial behavior (sic). They give as an example the "externalizing" scale of the CBCL (Achenbach and Edelbrock,

1983) which sums scales labeled "sex problems", "delinquency", "hyperactivity", "aggression", and "cruel". Note that although the ASPD (Antisocial personality disorder) and CD (conduct disorder) diagnoses appear to be relatively clearly defined in the DSM manuals (e.g. APA, 1987; 1994), they are a mix of very different behaviors (e.g., physical aggression, rule breaking, fraud, vandalism), and each new edition of the manual has a different set of symptoms and rules. The other category they included, "criminality", is in principle well defined by each jurisdiction, but it varies among jurisdictions, and a criminal who commits a homicide must generally be a different phenotype from a prostitute. The "aggression" criterion seems more specific. The authors state: "A study examining aggression was included if it examined behavioral aggression (e.g., physical fighting, cruelty to animals, bullying)" (p. 497). Note here that the three examples given relate to some form of physical aggression. However, the authors then go on to include a number of studies using the well known "aggression" scale of the CBCL (parent or teacher version; Achenbach and Edelbrock, 1983, 1986) which includes only 3 physical aggression items out of its 25 item scale (Achenback and Edelbrock, 1983). The other items include: jealous, cries much, whining, excess talk, sulks, shows off, demands attention, teases, loud. How this scale became known as an aggression scale rather than an "obnoxious" or "disruptive" scale, and why it continues to be considered a gold standard for assessing aggression in children is a puzzlement. The problems with this "aggression" scale are the same as with the "aggression" scale used in the Columbia County longitudinal study of aggression described above (see also Huesmann and Eron, 1986). The way these scale have been used to create a large body of scientific work on aggression clearly shows that there is magic in titles, and some magic in genetic analyses.

A strong heritability of the aggression (read disruptive or obnoxious) score of the CBCL was shown with British, Swedish and USA pre-adolescent samples (Edelbrock, Rende, Plomin, and Thompson, 1995; Eley, Lichenstein, and Stevenson, 1999). In fact the heritability for the aggressive behavior scale was stronger than for the delinquency scale. Ely et al. (1999) went on to compare the pre-adolescent sample to an adolescent sample. They observed high heritability for both groups on the aggressive scale, and observed higher shared environmental effects for the delinquency scale, especially for the adolescent group. These results led them to conclude: a) that aggressive antisocial behavior (CBCL aggression scale) is highly heritable, and that this confirms that life-course persistent antisocial behavior is highly heritable (Moffitt, 1993); b) that nonaggressive antisocial behavior (CBCL delinquency measure: e.g., bad friends, truant, alcohol, drugs, run away, prefers older kids) is more influenced by the shared environment, confirming that adolescent-limited antisocial behavior is caused by environmental factors (Moffitt, 1993). Note that these conclusions concerning a life-course developmental model were drawn from a cross-sectional study with an aggression scale that looks like an extraversion personality scale, and a delinquency scale which focuses on behavior that tends to start when children have become adolescents (drugs, alcohol, truant, run away). The phenotypes which are being assessed are not the developmental trajectories hypothesized by the theory. They are assessments at one point in time.

Lyons et al. (1995) addressed a similar issue with retrospective data on a large sample of twins (N = 3,226) who had served in the US military during the Vietnam war. They were interviewed between ages 36 and 55 with the computerized Diagnostic Interview Schedule. This interview provided information on conduct disorder (CD) symptoms before age 15, and antisocial personality (APD) symptoms since age 15. This is one of the rare studies that performed genetic analyses on items. Four of the ten behavioral items before age 15 (with a prevalence of at least 1%) included physical aggression: initiates fights, used weapons, cruel to people, cruel to animals. Only one of the ten APD items referred to some physical aggression: repeated physical fights or assaults. Percent of variance explained by the genetic component was 50% for repeated physical fights or assaults after age 15; for physical aggression before 15 years of age it varied from 0% for cruel to people, to 21% for cruel to animals, 37% for initiates fights, and 40% for using a weapon. The results with the physical aggression items are similar to the analysis in which they entered all the items in the diagnostic criteria: a stronger genetic influence was observed for adult symptoms compared to adolescent symptoms. These results led the researchers to conclude that "Genetic causal factors are much more prominent for adult than for juvenile traits" (p. 906). A similar conclusion could be reached for the physical aggression symptoms; however it must be noted that the physical aggression symptoms during adolescence, compared to other "antisocial" symptoms) had the highest genetic influence. There are many limitations to using retrospective data on behaviors which occurred 20 to 30 years earlier. For example, the percentage of individuals who answered positively to initiating fights during adolescence was only 5%, compared to 38.5% who reported using physical aggression during adulthood. Using age 15 years as a cut-off to determine juvenile and adult genetic influence is also a problem. The highest frequency of violent criminality are usually observed between 15 and 25, not after 30 (see Tremblay, 2004). However, the major problem with such studies is comparing behavior at two points in time during the life course to determine the strength of genetic and environmental effects on development. To test developmental theories of antisocial behavior we need prospective developmental trajectories. Lyons et al. (1995) could have created trajectories with the retrospective data, however they followed the tradition of taking a cross-sectional approach to longitudinal data.

The genetic study on physical aggression which starts at the earliest point during development is a twin study. Dionne, Tremblay, Boivin, Laplante, and Pérusse (2003) showed, with a large sample of 19-month-old female and male twins, that variance in mother reports of physical aggression was explained about equally by genetic and environmental factors. These results, coupled with the Lyons (1995) study of Vietnam veterans described above, would suggest that there are strong genetic effects on physical aggression during early childhood, that these diminish as children learn to regulate physical aggression, and that they reappear at least during late adolescence and early adulthood. One could speculate that this reappearance is due to the mating pressures at that age. However we need better prospective data, and we need to identify the developmental trajectories from early childhood to adulthood to test to what extent these trajectories are under the influence of genetic and environmental effects. The Dionne et al. study (2003) shows that both the genetic and environmental causes of a very specific socially disruptive behavior, physical aggressions, are in place by 19 months of age, long before the violent video games, the delinquent peers, and the effects of a Vietnam war.

Many molecular genetic studies have attempted to identify polymorphisms related to aggressive behavior, mainly with animal and human adult samples (see for example Pihl and Benkelfat, in press). Caspi et al. (2002) used a longitudinal study to specifically address gene-environment interactions. They observed that the most maltreated males were at higher risk of being convicted of a violent crime before 27 years of age only if they had the short version of the functional polymorphism in the gene coding for monoamine oxidase A (MAOA) activity.

The MAOA enzyme metabolizes neurotransmitters linked in previous studies to behavior problems (e.g. dopamine, norepinephrine, and serotonin), and the short version of the allele leads to low activity. Effects were similar for conduct disorder assessed between 10 and 18 years of age, antisocial personality symptoms, and disposition to violence measured at 26 years of age. Individuals with a history of chronic physical aggression may be the driving force in these associations, since they are the most likely to be found in each of the assessed categories. This study is a good illustration of gene-environment issues related to prevention which need to address. First, although the study was a longitudinal study from birth to 26 years of age, the analyses did not provide information on the developmental impact of the gene-environment interaction. Was the effect of the gene-environment interaction on physical aggression present in early childhood? Did it appear later during elementary school, adolescence, and even adulthood? These are important questions for preventive interventions. From the developmental data presented in the preceding section, one would expect that the effect was present early, and may have grown with time. A second question concerns the intervention strategies. Lets assume that the gene-environment interaction effects appear in early childhood and will increase with time if there are no early interventions. Which type of intervention should we use? For example, we could screen pregnant women soon after conception to identify those at risk of maltreating their child and offer a support program to help prevent the family from abusing the child (e.g. Olds et al., 1998). An alternative strategy would be to give the child a chemical treatment which would correct or compensate for the low MAOA activity (Caspi et al., 2002; Weaver et al., 2004). Both strategies could also be used with some cases. Thus, much research is needed to understand the gene-environment impact on the development of physical aggression, but research is also needed on the use of that knowledge to prevent the *development* of chronic physical aggression.

Prevention Experiments, Causal Explanations and Reduction of Physical Aggression

Twin studies and molecular genetic studies can address the gene-environment interaction issue. However, concerning causal mechanisms leading to chronic physical aggression, they are still limited to a correlational analysis. To address causal issues we need to be able to manipulate putative causal variables. Cross-fostering experiments like those done with rats, mice and monkeys (e.g. Francis et al., 2003; Suomi, in press; Weaver et al., 2004) would give better insights into causal mechanisms than studies which are limited to correlational analyses. Obviously, it is hard to conduct such studies with humans. However, prevention experiments aimed at helping high risk families give better care during early childhood could be used to understand the mechanisms that prevent children from behaving as if physical aggression was the best option for adjusting to their environment.

For example, Olds et al. (1998) randomly allocated a nurse home visitation program to young underprivileged pregnant women at high risk of child abuse and neglect. The children of these women were also at high risk of chronic physical aggression. The long term follow-up of the children from the intervention group showed that they were less frequently abused and neglected, and were also less likely to exhibit delinquent behaviors during adolescence. Unfortunately, the development of physical aggression does not appear to have been included in the follow-up assessments. One would expect that the intervention group learned more rapidly to regulate physical aggression and was less frequently involved in physical aggression during childhood and adolescence. Schweinhart and Weikart (1993, 1997) also published a long-term follow-up of a randomised controlled trial targeting preschool children. In this case the intervention started more than three years after birth and targeted the children's executive functions. Follow-up data well into adulthood showed that the males who received the intervention were much less likely to be arrested and put in prison. Again, there is apparently no information on the development of physical aggression in this study. Can an intervention starting three years after birth and targeting cognitive development have as much an impact on developmental trajectories of physical aggression as an intervention which started during pregnancy and which could affect the developing brain? These are important questions for assessing the cost and benefits of interventions during the developmental cycle, but they are also important questions for understanding the mechanisms which lead to or prevent chronic physical aggression. To what extent are the control mechanisms plastic, and over what period of time? Preventive studies with disruptive children after school entry indicated that there is still some plasticity, but it appears extremely limited (Ialongo and al., 1999; Lacourse et al., 2002; Tremblay, 2003).

Drug companies are developing a new research field which has been labelled Pharmacogenomics. Its aim is to create the knowledge which will enable the creation of pharmaceutical products which will specifically match the genetic makeup of an individual. It is easy to imagine that we can do the same with psychosocial interventions: match the intervention to the genetic profile of the client. Weaver et al. (2004) recently showed how an environmental event during early childhood (rat pups licked by their mothers) activated gene expression which influenced the development of the HPA axis and increased life expectancy. This phenomenon is a good illustration of the complex epigenetic mechanisms which are involved in gene-environment interactions. Psychosocial interventions can offer programs which will help activate the right genes at the right time. They can also compensate for defective genes, as is often done with nutrition (e.g. Scriver and Kaufman, 2001).

The ultimate prevention experiment to test early interventions and gene-environment interactions are adoption studies. Instead of trying to change an individual's environment by trying to change the behaviour of his or her parents, adoption simply changes the parents. One would expect that the environment provided by good adoptive parents would be much better than the environment created by at-risk parents who are being supported by a nurse or a social worker. Thus, adoption studies should give a good indication of the maximum effect one could obtain with the best psychosocial interventions targeting biological parents. Van Dusen, Mednick, and Gabrielli (1983) provided data from a Danish adoption study which can illustrate how an adoption study can help understand the maximum effect one can expect from an intervention with parents. Criminal convictions of adopted females (N = 6,374) and males (N = 5,649) were identified and reported with reference to the biological and adoptive parents' socioeconomic status (SES). Results are presented in Table 1.

Table 1. Percent Adopted Children with Criminal Convictions as a Function of Adoptive and Biological Parents' SES (From Van Dusen et al., 1983)

	Male adoptees biological parents' SES				Female adoptees biological parents' SES			
	High	Middle	Low	Total	High	Middle	Low	Total
Adoptive parent SES								
High	9.30 (441)	11.52 (903)	12.98 (775)	11.58 (2,099)	0.64 (467)	2.56 (1,056)	2.09 (861)	2.01 (2,384)
Middle	13.44 (320)	15.29 (870)	16.86 (795)	15.62 (1,985)	0.61 (330)	1.84 (980)	3.67 (954)	2.43 (2,264)
Low	13.81 (210)	17.25 (568)	18.04 (787)	17.19 (1,565)	2.38 (210)	3.66 (655)	3.02 (861)	3.19 (1,726)
Total	11.64 (971)	14.31 (2,341)	16.00 (2,337)	14.55 (5,649)	0.99 (1,067)	2.56 (2,691)	2.95 (2,676)	2.48 (6,374)

Note: Tabled values are percent adoptees with criminal convictions. Numbers in parentheses are cell total Ns

We can see from that table that the probability of a criminal conviction increases with the decrease in the socioeconomic status of both biological and adoptive parents, especially for males. The level of criminal convictions for males is close to six times that of females. We also see that males with High SES biological parents were less likely to have a criminal conviction if they were adopted into a High SES family (9.3%) than if they were adopted into a Low SES family (13.8%). Similarly, males with Low SES biological parents were less likely to have a criminal record if they were adopted into a High SES family (12.98%) than if they were adopted in a family with the Low SES of his biological parents (18.04%). Note that the former (Low SES biological-High SES adoptive) were as likely to have a criminal record as the High SES biological-Low SES adoptive (12.98% vs 13.8%). The largest differences between groups of males that we can observe is between the High SES biological-High SES adoptive (9.3%) and the Low SES biological-Low SES adoptive (18.04%). The latter are close to two times more likely to have a criminal conviction. If we were successful in changing the behaviour of high risk Low SES parents it would be surprising that we would achieve better results than placing a High SES biological parent male into a High SES adoptive family. The data also indicate that the interventions with females may have proportionally more impact (0.64% vs 3.02%), although the number, and probably the severity, of convictions are substantially lower for females.

CONCLUSION

The aim of the chapter was to highlight how three strains of research on physical aggression lead to the conclusion that prevention of chronic physical aggression should target early childhood. The first strain of research comprises longitudinal studies on the development of physical aggression from birth to adulthood. Although we are still missing the complete intra-individual developmental picture from birth to late adulthood, there is good evidence that frequency of physical aggression is at its peak in early childhood when children are learning alternatives to the use of physical force. The second strain of research on genetic effects is still far from having taken a developmental approach. However, the available evidence suggests strong genetic effects on frequency of physical aggression in early childhood, and important gene-environment interactions in the development of chronic physical aggression. Finally, there is a serious lack of experimental and natural prevention studies specifically targeting early causes of chronic physical aggression. The existing evidence suggests that pregnancy and early childhood interventions should have the greatest impact on the long term prevention of chronic physical aggression. However this needs to be demonstrated.

It seems obvious that the next generation of studies on the development and prevention of chronic physical aggression should use designs where longitudinal, genetic, and experimental preventions are integrated. From this perspective, the Mauritius study, initiated by Sarnoff Mednick and Peter Venables (Mednick, Sarnoff, Schulsinger, and Cudeck, 1982), was at least 30 years in advance of its time. To understand the development of behavior problems in humans we have to start at the beginning, and the beginning is at conception, not during childhood or adolescence. Onset of behavior problems in humans starts with the genes we inherit and the in-utero environment. To understand the development of behavior problems we need to take into account genes and environment, but we also need to experiment. Correlational evidence is useful, but insufficient to understand causal effects. The best approach to experimentally study causal effects of behavior problems in humans is to manipulate putative causal factors. If causal factors of chronic physical aggression are in the genetic information and the early environment, we need to manipulate epigenetic mechanisms. The work on early epigenetic programming of the HPA axis by maternal licking of rat pups is probably the best model we have for future studies with humans (Weaver et al., 2004). This work shows not only that early maternal behavior establishes an epigenomic state of a gene, but also that it is potentially reversible. Genetically informative prevention experiments with pregnant women and infants with long term follow-ups will provide the information needed to understand the development of chronic physical aggression, but more importantly will provide the information needed to prevent that development.

However, this work must be done with an eye on a broad context concerning human aggression. Most social scientists investigating human aggression, and indeed, most humans, forget that physical aggression is not in itself a "bad" "destructive" behavior. It is a solution for securing resources and surviving in a given environment. Humans have inherited the ability to use that solution, but they have also inherited the ability to use many other strategies, including cooperation and conflict resolution not based on physical force (see Peterson and Flanders, in press; de Waal, 2000). We are slowly creating a social environment where the physical aggression solution generally becomes a much less adaptive strategy than its alternatives. Young children will spontaneously cooperate and fight, but they need to learn which of the alternatives is the most effective in which situation. Some, because of their genetic makeup, will more easily learn some solutions than others. Similarly, some environments will tend to facilitate some solutions more than others. The gene-environment interactions will favor different developmental trajectories. The simple law that Darwin put forward was that those who will thrive are those who will be most able to learn to use the solutions which are most appropriate for the problems they face. In a social group that does not tolerate physical aggression, it is better to use a form of aggression which is less sanctioned. This does not mean that a punch in the nose is more harmful than an indirect aggression to your reputation. It simply means that a group of humans have decided that conflicts should not be solved by physical force.

The fact that physical aggression peaks in early childhood when limbs are weak, and when the brain is at its peak flexibility for learning, leads to two important conclusions concerning research and action during early childhood. First, it is clear that we need to better understand the mechanisms that underlie the rapid increase in frequency of physical aggression in infancy, and the mechanisms which lead to the large differences among infants. Second, this knowledge will need to be used by taking into account the social context in which individuals are living. For example, 40% of the male sample in the Caspi et al. (2002) study had the low activity version of the gene coding for MAOA activity and 34% of the sample was classified as having been maltreated. These distributions indicate that low MAOA activity and child maltreatment are relatively frequent occurrences in our societies. By all our standards, Louis XIII would have been classified as maltreated and a physically violent child, and adolescent. He may have become a good king, and the father of a great king because he inherited and transmitted the polymorphism coding for high MAOA activity. But he may also have had the low activity form which enabled him to keep on fighting in an environment where he could have been dominated by his mother and all others who were competing for control over attractive resources.

REFERENCES

Achenbach, T. M., and Edelbrock, C. (1983). *Manual for the child behavior checklist and revised child behavior profile.* Burlington, VT: University of Vermont, Department of Psychiatry.

Achenbach, T. M., and Edelbrock, C. (1986). *Manual for the teacher's report form and teacher version of the child behavior profile.* Burlington, VT: University of Vermont, Department of Psychiatry.

American Heritage Dictionary. (1985). (Second College Edition). Boston: Houghton Mifflin Company.

American Psychiatric Association. (1987). *Diagnostic and statistical manual of mental disorders: DSM-III-R.* Washington, DC: American Psychiatric Association.

American Psychiatric Association. (1994). *Diagnostic and Statistical Manual of Mental Disorders* (4th edition). Washington, DC: Author.

Arseneault, L., Tremblay, R. E., Boulerice, B., and Saucier, J.-F. (2002). Obstetrical complications and violent delinquency: Testing two developmental pathways. *Child Development, 73*(2), 496-508.

Bandura, A. (1973). *Aggression: A social learning analysis*. New York: Holt.

Blumstein, A., Cohen, J., and Farrington, D. P. (1988). Criminal career research: Its value for criminology. *Criminology, 26,* 11.

Boivin, M., Vitaro, F., and Poulin, F. (in press). Peer relationships and the development of aggressive behavior in early childhood. In R. E. Tremblay, W. W. Hartup, and J. Archer (Eds.), *Developmental origins of aggression*. New York: Guilford.

Bridges, K. M. B. (1931). *The social and emotional development of the pre-school child.* London: Kegan Paul.

Bridges, K. M. B. (1933). A study of social development in early infancy. *Child Development, 4,* 36-49.

Broidy, L. M., Nagin, D. S., Tremblay, R. E., Brame, B., Dodge, K., Fergusson, D., Horwood, J., Loeber, R., Laird, R., Lynam, D., Moffitt, T., Bates, J. E., Pettit, G. S., and Vitaro, F. (2003). Developmental trajectories of childhood disruptive behaviors and adolescent delinquency: A six site, cross national study. *Developmental Psychology, 39*(2), 222-245.

Cairns, R. B., and Cairns, B. D. (1994). *Life lines and risks: Pathways of youth in our time.* New York: Cambridge University Press.

Cairns, R. B., Cairns, B. D., Neckerman, H. J., Ferguson, L. L., and Gariépy, J. L. (1989). Growth and aggression: 1. Childhood to early adolescence. *Developmental Psychology, 25*(2), 320-330.

Caspi, A., McClay, J., Moffitt, T., Mill, J., Martin, J., Craig, I. W., Taylor, A., and Poulton, R. (2002). Role of genotype in the cycle of violence in maltreated children. *Science, 297,* 851-854.

Côté, S., Vaillancourt, T., Farhat, A., LeBlanc, J., Nagin, D. S., and Tremblay, R. E. (submitted). The development of physical aggression during childhood.

Darwin, C. (1872). *The expression of the emotions in man and animals*. London: John Murray, reprinted by Gryphon Editions 1989.

de Waal, F. B. (2000). Primates - a natural heritage of conflict resolution. *Science, 289,* 586-590.

Dionne, G. (in press). Language development and aggressive behavior. In R. E. Tremblay, W. W. Hartup, and J. Archer (Eds.), *Developmental origins of aggression*. New York: Guilford.

Dionne, G., Tremblay, R. E., Boivin, M., Laplante, D., and Pérusse, D. (2003). Physical aggression and expressive vocabulary in 19 month-old twins. *Developmental Psychology, 39*(2), 261-273.

Edelbrock, C., Rende, R., Plomin, R., and Thompson, L. A. (1995). A twin study of competence and problem behavior in childhood and early adolescence. *Journal of Child Psychology and Psychiatry, 36*(5), 775-785.

Eisner, M. (2003). Long-term historical trends in violent crime. *Crime and Justice: A review of research, 30,* 83-142.

Eisner, M. (in press). Secular trends of violent crime: Evidence and theoretical interpretations. *Crime and Justice: An Annual Review.*

Eley, T. C., Lichenstein, P., and Stevenson, J. (1999). Sex differences in the etiology of aggressive and nonaggressive antisocial behavior: Results from two twin studies. *Child Development, 70*(1), 155-168.

Eron, L. D. (1990). Understanding aggression. *Bulletin of the International Society for Research on Aggression, 12,* 5-9.

Francis, D. D., Diorio, J., Plotsky, P. M., and Meaney, M. J. (2002). Environmental enrichment reverses the effects of maternal separation on stress reactivity. *Journal of Neuroscience, 22,* 7840-7843.

Francis, D. D., Szegda, K., Campbell, G., Martin, W. D., and Insel, T. (2003). Epigenetic sources of behavioral differences in mice. *Nature Neuroscience, 6,* 445-446.

Gatti, U., and Tremblay, R. E. (in press). Social capital and physical violence. In R. E. Tremblay, W. W. Hartup, and J. Archer (Eds.), *Developmental origins of aggression.* New York: Guilford.

Goodenough, F. L. (1931). *Anger in young children.* Westport, CT: Greenwood Press.

Gottfredson, M. R., and Hirschi, T. (1990). *A general theory of crime.* Stanford, CA: Stanford University Press.

Holmberg, M. C. (1977). *The development of social interchange patterns from 12 to 42 months: cross-sectional and short-term longitudinal analyses* [Ph.D. Thesis]. The University of North Carolina at Chapel Hill: Microfilms International 78-7137.

Huesmann, L. R., and Eron, L. D. (1986). *Television and the aggressive child: A cross-national comparison.* Hillsdale, NJ: L. Erlbaum Associates.

Huesmann, L. R., Eron, L. D., Lefkowitz, M. M., and Walder, L. O. (1984). Stability of aggression over time and generations. *Developmental Psychology, 20*(6), 1120-1134.

Human Capital Initiative Coordinating Committee. (1997). Reducing violence: A research agenda. *APS Observer, Special issue*_(November).

Ialongo, N. S., Werthamer, L., Kellam, S. G., Brown, C. H., Wang, S., and Lin, Y. (1999). Proximal impact of two first-grade preventive interventions on the early risk behaviors for later substance abuse, depression, and antisocial behavior. *American Journal of Community Psychology, 27*(5), 599-641.

Lacourse, E., Côté, S., Nagin, D. S., Vitaro, F., Brendgen, M., and Tremblay, R. E. (2002). A longitudinal-experimental approach to testing theories of antisocial behavior development. *Development and Psychopathology, 14,* 909-924.

Lahey, B. B., Moffit, T. E., and Caspi, A. (2003*). Causes of conduct disorder and juvenile delinquency.* New York: Guilford Press.

Lefkowitz, M. M., Eron, L. D., Walder, L. O., and Huesmann, L. R. (1977). *Growing up to be violent. A longitudinal study of the development of aggression.* New York: Pergamon Press.

Loeber, R., and Farrington, D. P. (2001). *Child delinquents: Development, interventions and service needs.* Thousand Oaks, CA: Sage Publications.

Lyons, J. J., True, W. R., Eisen, S. A., Goldberg, J., Meyer, J. M., Faraone, S. V., Eaves, L. J., and Tsuang, M. T. (1995). Differential heritability of adult and juvenile antisocial traits. *Archives of General Psychiatry, 52,* 906-915.

McCord, J., Widom, C. S., and Crowell, N. E. (2001). *Juvenile crime, juvenile justice.* Washington: National Academy Press.

Mednick, S. A., Venables, P. H., Schulsinger, F., and Cudeck, R. (1982). The Mauritius Project: An experiment in primary prevention. In M. J. Goldstein (Ed.), *Preventive intervention in Schizophrenia: Are we ready* (pp. 287-296). Washington, DC: NIMH Primary Prevention Series, Government Printing Office.

Moffitt, T. E. (1993). Adolescence-limited and life-course persistent antisocial behavior: A developmental taxonomy. *Psychological Review, 100*(4), 674-701.

Nagin, D., and Tremblay, R. E. (1999). Trajectories of boys' physical aggression, opposition, and hyperactivity on the path to physically violent and non violent juvenile delinquency. *Child Development, 70*(5), 1181-1196.

Olds, D., Henderson, C. R., Cole, R., Eckenrode, J., Kitzman, H., Luckey, D., Pettitt, L., Sidora, K., Morris, P., and Powers, J. (1998). Long-term effects of nurse home visitation on children's criminal and antisocial behavior: Fifteen-year follow-up of a randomized controlled trial. *Journal of the American Medical Association, 280*(14), 1238-1244.

Peterson, J. B., and Flanders, J. L. (in press). Play and the regulation of aggression. In R. E. Tremblay, W. W. Hartup, and J. Archer (Eds.), *Developmental origins of aggression*. New York: Guilford.

Pihl, R. O., and Benkelfat, C. (in press). Neuromodulators in the development and expression of inhibition and aggression. In R. E. Tremblay, W. W. Hartup, and J. Archer (Eds.), *Developmental origins of aggression*. New York: Guilford.

Premack, D., and Premack, A. (2003). *Original intelligence*. New York: McGraw-Hill.

Quetelet, A. (1833). *Research on the propensity for crime at different ages*. Brussels: M. Hayez, Printer to the Royal Academy.

Raine, A., Brennan, P., and Mednick, S. A. (1997). Interaction between birth complications and early maternal rejection in predisposing individuals to adult violence: Specificity to serious, early-onset violence. *American Journal of Psychiatry, 154*, 1265-1271.

Rhee, S. H., and Waldman, I. D. (2002). Genetic and environmental influences on antisocial behavior: A meta-analysis of twin and adoption studies. *Psychological Bulletin, 128*(3), 490-529.

Reiss, A. J., and Roth, J. A. (Eds.) (1993). *Understanding and preventing violence*. Washington, DC: National Academy Press.

Restoin, A., Montagner, H., Rodriguez, D., Girardot, J. J., Laurent, D., Kontar, F., Ullmann, V., Casagrande, C., and Talpain, B. (1985). Chronologie des comportements de communication et profils de comportement chez le jeune enfant. In R. E. Tremblay, M. A. Provost, and F. F. Strayer (Eds.), *Ethologie et développement de l'enfant* (pp. 93-130). Paris: Editions Stock/Laurence Pernoud.

Rhee, S. H., and Waldman, I. D. (2002). Genetic and environmental influences on antisocial behavior: A meta-analysis of twin and adoption studies. *Psychological Bulletin, 128*(3), 490-529.

Sampson, R. J., and Laub, J. H. (2003). Life-course desisters? Trajectories of crime among delinquent boys followed to age 70. *Criminology, 41*, 301-339.

Sand, E. A. (1966). *Contribution à l'étude du développement de l'enfant. Aspects médico-sociaux et psychologiques*. Bruxelles: Éditions de l'Institut de sociologie de l'Université libre de Bruxelles.

Schweinhart, L. J., and Weikart, D. P. (1993). Success by Empowerment: The High/Scope Perry Preschool Study through age 27, Public Policy Report. *Young Children, 49*(1), 54-58.

Schweinhart, L. J., and Weikart, D. P. (1997). The High/Scope Preschool Curriculum Comparison study through age 23. *Early Childhood Research Quarterly, 12*(2), 117-143.

Scriver, C. R., and Kaufman, S. (2001). Hyperphenylalaninemia: Phenylalanine hydroxylase deficiency. In C. R. Scriver, A. L. Beaudet, W. S. Sly, and D. Valle (Eds.), *The metabolic and molecular bases of inherited disease* (pp. 1667-1724). New York: McGraw-Hill.

Séguin, J. R., and Zelazo, P. (in press). Executive function in early physical aggression. In R. E. Tremblay, W. W. Hartup, and J. Archer (Eds.), *Developmental origins of aggression.* New York: Guilford.

St. Augustine. (A.D.397/1960). *Confessions.* New York: Doubleday.

Suomi, S. J. (in press). Genetic and environmental factors influencing the expression of impulsive aggression and serotonergic functioning in rhesus monkeys. In R. E. Tremblay, W. W. Hartup, and J. Archer (Eds.), *Developmental origins of aggression.* New York: Guilford.

Tremblay, R. E. (2000). The development of aggressive behaviour during childhood: What have we learned in the past century? *International Journal of Behavioral development, 24*(2), 129-141.

Tremblay, R. E. (2003). Why socialization fails?: The case of chronic physical aggression. In B. B. Lahey, T. E. Moffitt, and A. Caspi (Eds.), *Causes of conduct disorder and juvenile delinquency* (pp. 182-224). New York: Guilford Publications.

Tremblay, R. E. (2003, November 20). *Presidential plenary. Age, crime, and human development: Looking for the highest peaks with our backs to the Rocky Mountains.* Paper presented at the American Society of Criminology 55th Annual Meeting: Age, crime, and human development. The future of life-course criminology, Denver, Colorado.

Tremblay, R. E. (2004). The development of human physical aggression: How important is early childhood? In L. A. Leavitt, and D. M. B. Hall (Eds.), *Social and moral development: Emerging evidence on the toddler years* (pp. 221-238). New Brunswick, NJ: Johnson and Johnson Pediatric Institute.

Tremblay, R. E., and Nagin, D. S. (in press). The developmental origins of physical aggression in humans. In R. E. Tremblay, W. W. Hartup, and J. Archer (Eds.), *Developmental origins of aggression.* New York: Guilford Press.

Tremblay, R. E., Boulerice, B., Harden, P. W., McDuff, P., Pérusse, D., Pihl, R. O., and Zoccolillo, M. (1996). Do children in Canada become more aggressive as they approach adolescence? In Human Resources Development Canada and Statistics Canada (Eds.), *Growing up in Canada: National Longitudinal Survey of Children and Youth* (pp. 127-137). Ottawa: Statistics Canada.

Tremblay, R. E., Loeber, R., Gagnon, C., Charlebois, P., Larivée, S., and LeBlanc, M. (1991). Disruptive boys with stable and unstable high fighting behavior patterns during junior elementary school. *Journal of Abnormal Child Psychology, 19,* 285-300.

Tremblay, R. E., Nagin, D. S., Séguin, J. R., Zoccolillo, M., Zelazo, P., Boivin, M., Pérusse, D., and Japel, C. (2004). Physical aggression during early childhood: Trajectories and predictors. *Pediatrics, 114*(1), e43-e50.

US Human Capital Initiative Coordinating Committee (1997). Reducing violence: A research agenda. *Observer, Special issue* (November).

Van Dusen, K. T., Mednick, S. A., and Gabrielli, W. (1983). Social class and crime in an adoption cohort. In K. T. Van Dusen and S. A. Mednick (eds), *Prospective studies of crime and delinquency* (pp. 57-71).Hingham, MA: Kluwer.

van Goozen, S. H. M. (in press). Hormones and the developmental origin of aggression. In R. E. Tremblay, W. W. Hartup, and J. Archer (Eds.), *Developmental origins of aggression.* New York: Guilford.

Wakschlag, L., Pickett, K. E., Cook, E., Benowitz, N. L., and Leventhal, B. (2002). Maternal smoking during pregnancy and sever antisocial behavior in offspring: A review. *American Journal of Public Health, 92*(6), 966-974.

Weaver, I. C. G., Cervoni, N., Champagne, F. A., D'Alessio, A. C., Sharma, S., Seckl, J. R., Dymov, S., Szyf, M., and Meaney, M. J. (2004). Epigenetic programming by maternal behavior. *Nature Neuroscience, 7*(8), 847-854.

Zoccolillo, M., Romano, E., Joubert, D., Mazzarello, T., Côté, S., Boivin, M., Pérusse, D., and Tremblay, R. E. (in press). The intergenerational transmission of aggression and antisocial behavior. In R. E. Tremblay, W. W. Hartup, and J. Archer (Eds.), *Developmental origins of aggression.* New York: Guilford.

In: Crime and Schizophrenia: Causes and Cures
Editor: Adrian Raine, pp. 287-299

ISBN 1-59454-609-6

Chapter 15

Sexual Hormones and Aggressive Behavior: Are They Relevant to Schizophrenia?

Florence Thibaut
University Hospital Ch. Nicolle, INSERM U 614,
University of Medicine, Rouen, France

Animal and human studies have revealed an association between androgens and aggressive behavior. Schizophrenic patients show aggressive behavior but little is known about sexual offending in schizophrenia. There are few data about the relationship between testosterone levels and schizophrenia. One study has reported a positive correlation between testosterone levels and paranoid schizophrenia while two studies have found normal testosterone levels in schizophrenic subjects. Moreover chronic neuroleptic treatment may decrease testosterone levels (for review see Räsänen et al., 1999). We will present epidemiological data concerning deviant sexual behaviour in schizophrenic patients and we will review the relationships between sex hormones and sexual behaviour and aggressive behavior.

I. Schizophrenia and Deviant Sexual Behavior

More than 10% of schizophrenic patients show aggressive symptoms, varying from threatening behavior and agitation, to assault. Cheung and Schweitzer (1998) have reviewed the clinical correlates of non specific aggressive behavior in schizophrenia. Comorbid substance misuse, a history of violence, neurological/neuropsychological deficits, medication noncompliance, active psychotic symptoms have been proposed as putative risk factors for violence (Jones et al., 1992 ; Craissati and Hodes, 1992 ; Phillips et al., 1999). In Walsh' study (2004), similar proportions of men and women committed assaults. In the UK, approximately 10% of all restricted in-patients detained under the legal category of mental illness have been convicted of an index sex offence (Home Office, 1997). Very little is known about individuals who commit sex offences in the context of active psychosis. Although reviews of sexual offending rarely offer comments on how many sex offenders may be psychotic, it is likely that the vast majority of contact sex offences are committed by men without major mental illness. Moreover, sexual dysfunction has been described in schizophrenic patients. It is also a well-known complication of antipsychotic treatment. By contrast, some authors have reported an increase in sexual drive in some schizophrenic patients (Cournos et al., 1994). The maintenance of sexual drive and interest in the context of impaired sexual and social functioning may be relevant in relation to sexual offending (Phillips et al., 1999).

Some anecdotal cases reporting paraphilic behaviors in schizophrenic patients have been published (transvestism, fetishism) (Ponikiewska and Szczesna, 1973 ; Vish et al., 1996). Few case reports of autocastration of young male paranoid schizophrenic patients (because of religious delusions and sexual guilt) have been published (Waugh, 1986 ; Linn, 2001 ; Myers and Nguyen, 2001 ; Gossler et al., 2002 ; Novak-Grubic and Tavcar, 2002). It has also been suggested that the administration of androgens to paranoid schizophrenics who castrated themselves might exacerbate the psychosis and increase the risk of further self-mutilation. Barbenel et al. (2000) described mania in a patient receiving testosterone after orchidectomy, but this was not confirmed by Cooper et Swany (1994) and Novak-Grubic et Tavcar (2002). Dirksen and Monikes (1995) have reported the case of a 48 year-old patient with a diagnosis of hebephrenic schizophrenia. He was under suspicion of having sexually abused his two children. The hebephrenic symptoms were in fact the expression of an XYY chromosome abnormality. Lee (1996) has published a rare case of XXYY associated with chronic paranoid schizophrenia and impulsive aggression. Cooper and colleagues (1990) have reported the case of a 25 year-old schizophrenic patient with conduct disorder who has been treated for 10 years for anomalous aggressive and sexual behavior (he was preoccupied with rape and sexual assault themes). His IQ was in the borderline range. Previously, phenothiazines, behavior therapy have failed and the patient was treated with medroxyprogesterone acetate for 12 weeks. As compared with pre and post MPA treatment periods, clinical evaluation and the patient self-report questionnaire have suggested much reduced sexual activities and preoccupation during MPA treatment. He was also quieter. Nocturnal penile tumescence and tumescence responses to provocative audiotapes during wakefulness in the laboratory were decreased during MPA treatment. The effects of MPA on nocturnal penile tumescence and laboratory arousal were still partially in evidence two months after the drug had been stopped, although testosterone levels had returned to predrug levels. In contrast, Thibaut et al (1992) have reported the case of a 40-year-old schizophrenic male patient whose hallucinations and delusions worsened while treated with cyproterone acetate for severe and uncontrolled aggressive behavior.

Smith and colleagues have carried out a study of records of 80 male psychotic patients (without mental impairment or organic brain disease) with an index conviction for a contact sex offence against a woman committed while psychotic (rape, attempted rape or indecent assault of a female 16 years old and above) (Smith and Taylor, 1999 ; Smith 2000). These patients were resident in any hospital in England and the Wales during May 1997. The median age was 28 years. 54% were Black Afro Caribbean and 46% were Caucasian. 94 and 78% of patients still had respectively delusions or auditive or tactile hallucinations at the time of the index sex offence which does not mean that their deviant behavior was necessarily driven by them. However, in 50% of cases, these hallucinations or delusions were directly or, indirectly, related to the offence. Exclusive sex offending was uncommon. 55% of men had previously served at least one prison sentence for sex offending or non sexual violence after the onset of illness. In 23 men, there was clinical evidence that they had sexually offended prior to onset of schizophrenia. Concerning the type of offences, they involved strangers in 61% of the cases. In these cases, they were more likely to occur outdoors and without any preceding social interaction with the victim, compared to those involving assailants known to their victims. 38% of patients had consumed either alcohol or illicit substances prior to their offences. Offence sexual behaviors were: breast/genital fondling (79%), vaginal intercourse (52%), fellatio (10%), anal intercourse (9%) and cunnilingus (8%). These proportions are in keeping with those reported in studies of not mentally ill sex offenders. Excessive violence or bizarre behavior occurred in a minority of offences. These data do not support popular images that most psychotic sex offenders behave in an exceptionally violent or bizarre manner. Phillips and colleagues (1999) have described a group of 150 schizophrenic patients who had committed sexual offences (rape or indecent assault) or shown antisocial sexual behavior. They have compared them with a group of schizophrenic patients with a history of non sexual violent behavior. In the vast majority of cases, the sexual offending behavior occurred in the context of psychotic symptoms but there was no difference between those with sexual offences and those with non sexual violent offending behaviour, in terms of severity of psychotic symptoms. Most of these patients were not receiving adequate care or supervision at the time of the offence. They reported unimpaired sexual interest as compared with schizophrenic patients showing violent non sexual behavior. Their victims were all females and predominantly strangers. There was no difference as regards IQ or Stroop color task between schizophrenics who committed sexual offences and those who did not.

Drake and Pathe (2004) have proposed that schizophrenic patients who engage in sex offensive activities fall into four groups : those with a pre-existing paraphilia ; those whose deviant sexuality arises in the context of illness and or its treatment, those whose deviant sexuality is one manifestation of more generalized antisocial behavior ; and factors other than those previously mentioned.

II. Testosterone and Sexual Behavior

II.1. Testosterone and Dihydrotestosterone

Approximately 95% of the testosterone is produced in the testes, the other 5% by the adrenal glands. The secretion of testosterone is regulated by a feedback mechanism in the hypothalamus-pituitary-testis axis. The hypothalamus produces gonadotrophin hormone-releasing hormone (GnRH), which stimulates the pituitary gland to produce luteinizing hormone (LH). LH stimulates the release of testosterone from the testes. Testosterone has an inhibiting effect on the hypothalamus and the pituitary. Testosterone entering the cell from the circulation is converted to dihydrotestosterone (by 5α-reductase 1 or 2) which acts through binding to the androgen receptor. The physiological effects of testosterone (and of its reduced metabolite (5α-dihydrotestosterone) are mediated through their actions on the intracellular androgen receptor. In humans, testosterone plays a major role not only in the development and maintenance of male sexual characteristics but also in sexuality and aggression (for review, see Rubinow and Schmidt, 1996 ; Thibaut, 2003). Testosterone has been shown to restore nocturnal penile tumescence responses in hypogonadal men with impaired nocturnal penile tumescence. A certain level of testosterone is necessary for sexual desire in males, above which testosterone levels does not seem to be correlated with levels of sexual drive. However, the threshold remains questionable. Doses of testosterone up to five times physiologic dose appear to have minimal risk of adverse psychosexual effect in the majority of normal men. However, at around 500 mg per week of testosterone cypionate, a minority of normal men may experience significant adverse psychological effects (Yates et al., 1999). Although rigidity and detumescence seem to be androgen dependent to a certain degree, erections in response to visual erotic stimuli are not dependent on androgens, but erections in response to auditory stimuli possibly are (Carani et al., 1992). Whether, or to what extent, erections, as a result of fantasies and tactile stimulation, are androgen dependent remains controversial. In women, a relationship between high levels of testosterone and increased sexual motivations has been suggested (De Jonge and Van de Poll, 1984). Two important phases have been identified in the effects of testosterone on brain structures and consequently on behavior in males. During foetal and neonatal life, relatively high concentrations of testosterone are thought to influence brain development by organizing the undifferentiated brain in a sex specific manner. It has been shown, in animal models, that the hypothalamus, the hippocampus, the preoptic-septal region and the limbic system are important target areas for sex steroid action (for review, see Christiansen, 2001).

Although androgen-depleting agents are useful in controlling paraphilia, there is neither evidence that sex offenders have higher testosterone levels nor data indicating an increased androgen receptor activity (Thibaut et al., 1993 ; Aromaki et al., 2002). In Aromaki ' study, in the sexual offenders group (10 rapists and 10 child molesters) the presence of antisocial personality disorder was positively correlated with saliva testosterone. Sexual activity (self-reports of masturbation and sexual intercourse) was significantly related to testosterone levels in sex offenders only but the mean saliva testosterone levels did not differ between sex offenders and controls. Räsänen et al., (1999) have reported lower plasma testosterone levels among male criminals with schizophrenia (33% homicides) which may be due, according to them, to long-term use of neuroleptic treatment or to the mental illness itself (due to withdrawal from environmental challenges, which may increase testosterone levels). The expected benefit of decreasing testosterone activity (by lowering testosterone levels or by competing with testosterone at the receptor level) is probably derived from decreasing non-specifically sexual arousal and behavior. However, Gaffney and Berlin (1984) reported a marked hypersecretion of LH in response to GnRH in pedophiles, as compared to controls and other paraphilias, whereas baseline LH and testosterone values were in the normal range.

II.2. Testosterone and its Conversion to Estradiol

Testosterone is also converted to 17β-estradiol by the P450 aromatase (encoded by the CYP19 gene). P450 aromatase is a critical enzyme responsible for the last and irreversible step in estrogen synthesis from androgens. This enzyme is expressed in multiple tissues, including many regions of the CNS. Estradiol binds with similar affinity to either the alpha or the beta estrogen receptors (ERα or ERβ). Both receptors have been identified in numerous sites in the brain such as the hypothalamus (ERα is present in the ventromedial nucleus while

Erβ is present in the paraventricular nucleus); the amygdala and the hippocampus, where they may be involved in short term memory and emotion. Erβ has also been identified in the cerebellum and in cortical regions. However, estradiol is also synthesized from androgen precursors (mainly androstenedione, dehydroepiandrosterone and its sulfate) by the aromatase enzyme. Estrogen has an essential role in maintenance of bone mass (especially via ERα), pubertal growth and skeletal maturation in both males and females. It has also effects on the cardiovascular system and the lipid metabolism. The role of estrogens on psychosexual development in the human, in contrast to other mammals, is less understood.

The men with aromatase deficiency, owing to a mutation in CYP19 and the man with estrogen resistance, due to a homozygous mutation in the estrogen α receptor, had sex appropriate gender identities, but unfortunately their behavior is not described (for review, see Grumbach and Auchus, 1999). Estrogen treatment of one of the men with aromatase deficiency resulted in increased libido, frequency of intercourse, masturbation and erotic fantasies (Carani et al., 1999). Few cases of syndrome of nonadrenal female pseudohermaphrodism associated with missense mutation in the gene encoding aromatase were reported (Conte et al., 1994, Morishima et al., 1995). Various mouse models involving lack of estrogens have been used (failure of synthesis or insensivity of response). These include knock-outs of the Erα, Erβ genes as well as the double Erα and Erβ knock-out, and the aromatase knock-out mice (for review, see Simpson and Davis, 2000). Aromatase KO male mice showed severe deficits in male sexual behavior. A reduction of aggressive behavior against males was also observed. Studies in mice lacking the gene for either Erα or Erβ have shown that male sexual behavior is only partially disrupted or virtually normal. ER activation may be only partially responsible for the induction of male sexual behavior or either in these ErαKO or ErβKO mice, the missing ER gene is compensated for by the other (for review, Simpson and Davis, 2000). In αβERKO male mice, sexual behavior was completely disrupted.

Estrogen elicits masculine sexual behavior in male rodents via ERα in the brain and the establishment of estrogen responsiveness requires estrogen during the perinatal period (Simon and Whalen, 1987). ERα may be responsible for the regulation by testosterone of consummatory, but not motivational, aspects of male mice sexual behavior (Ogawa et al., 1998). In the brain, the conversion from androgen into estrogen is also an important process for the differentiation of the brain function in male rodents. In addition, estrogen plays an important role in neural differentiation and influences cell migration, cell survival, cell death, synaptic neuronal plasticity (Miranda et al., 1994). The midbrain dopaminergic and noradrenergic neurons, which are marked by tyrosine hydroxylase, are especially affected by perinatal estrogen with respect to functional and morphological maturation (Beyer, 1999). Stevens (2002) have reviewed the interactions between estrogen, testosterone and neuromediators that occur in the basal forebrain at the initiation of and throughout the reproductive period in Humans.

Neuropathological examination of two cases with a history consistent with DSM IV diagnosis of paraphilia revealed simple atrophy of pyramidal cells confined to different hippocampal subfields. Reactive astrocytosis was present. These changes resemble those reported after persistent stress or long term chronic glucocorticoid treatment (Casanova et al., 2002).

III. Testosterone and Aggression

III.1. Testosterone

In almost all mammals, including humans, levels of physical violence are greater in males than in females. The incidence of high level of violence follows the testosterone curve in a variety of cultures across the world and is worst in pubertal and post pubertal males. In animals, testosterone or its metabolites (dihydrotestosterone and estradiol) are a necessary prerequisite for offensive or defensive male aggressive behavior and social dominance (Rose et al., 1972 ; Mc Kenna, 1983). Testosterone administered to female rats may lead to a drastic increase of aggressive behavior and to an increase in sexual behavior (De Jonge et al., 1986). However, the role of testosterone and its influence on general aggression in humans remains unclear. The experience of winning and of a rise in status seemed to produce a rise in testosterone, or to maintain an already elevated level, sustaining the winner's activation and reinforcing assertiveness or aggression to enter subsequent competitions for higher status (Booth et al., 1989). Exposure of women to exogenous androgens has yielded conflicting results (for review, see Sanders and Bancroft, 1982). In humans, more aggressive acts are often associated with higher testosterone levels, but these levels remain in the normal range (Dabbs et al., 1987 ; Rubinow and Schmidt, 1996). There is consistent evidence from studies carried out in prison on different types of violent male offenders that they had higher testosterone levels than those found in samples of less violent prison inmates (for review, see Christiansen, 2001). Even in female prison inmates, testosterone exerts an influence on unprovoked violence (Dabbs et al., 1988). In a clinic for nervous diseases, males and females showing more destructive aggression had higher levels of testosterone (Kedenburg 1977, Ehlers, 1980). In male hockey players, the preplay testosterone levels correlated positively with reactive aggression during the tournament (Scamarella and Brown, 1978). However, in most studies, neither normal males and pubescent boys nor rapists exhibited a significantly positive testosterone – aggression relationship (Rada et al., 1983 ; Susman et al., 1987 ; Aromaki et al., 1999). In the same way, correlations between self-reports measures of aggressive behavior, irritability or hostility and androgen levels in men and women are generally low (Archer, 1991). However, Gladue et al (1991) found a significantly negative relationship between testosterone and aggressiveness in female college students. Even if there is a weak relationship between aggressive behavior and endogenous testosterone levels in men and women, there is no evidence for a causal relationship. In addition, we cannot predict future aggressive behavior for any individual subject. In some cases of anabolic-androgenic steroid abuse in men and women or in cases of testosterone replacement therapy for hypogonadal adolescent or adult males, in surgically menopausal females or, finally, in female to male transsexuals undergoing testosterone treatment, an increase in irritability and aggressiveness had been reported (Salamimies et al., 1982 ; for review, see Van Goozen et al, 1994 ; Bahrke et al., 1996 ; Hines, 1998 ; for review, see Christiansen, 2001). In dependent anabolic-androgenic steroid users, unexpected suicides or depressive symptoms may appear when the drug is withdrawn (Brower et al., 1989). One case of child sexual abuse associated with anabolic androgenic steroid use was reported by Driessen et al. (1996) (mean dose per week: 500 mg of methandienone methandrostenolone). Some studies showed a slight, but significant, effect of prenatal testosterone exposure : an increase in physical aggressiveness (e.g. vigorous play) but not in verbal aggression during childhood years for both boys and girls (for review, see Christiansen, 2001).

Thibaut et al (1991) have reported the case of a 30-year-old man with infantile psychosis whose aggressive behavior was improved by cyproterone acetate whereas GnRH analogue treatment failed to maintain the antiaggressive effect of cyproterone acetate (CPA). The beneficial effect of CPA treatment on aggressive behavior could be explained either by its antiandrogenic effects or rather by its progestational properties leading to antiestrogenic effets, while GnRH analogues is devoid of these latter effects. In contrast, the intracerebroventricular administration of GnRH suppresses aggression in male rats (Kadar et al., 1992).

Sex hormones have a direct and rapid effect on gender specific behaviors. During a course of three months of treatment, the administration of androgens to 35 female to male transsexuals resulted in an increase in anger and aggression proneness, in sexual motivation and arousability, and in visuospatial ability (map reading, mental rotation and manipulation), whereas verbal fluency performance deteriorated without any increase in overt aggressive behavior (Van Goozen et al., 1994 and 1995). By contrast, the administration of antiandrogens and estrogens to 15 male to female transexuals had the complete reverse effects: anger and aggression proneness, sexual interest and arousability, and visuospatial ability decreased, whereas verbal fluency showed notable improvement (Van Goozen et al, 1995). However, in controls, there is more variation within each sex than between sexes concerning cognitive abilities (Gouchie et Kimura, 1991).

III.2. Testosterone and its Conversion to Estradiol

The estrogen receptor ERα is required for high levels of offensive aggression in male mice. Interestingly, aggressive behavior was dramatically reduced and male-typical offensive attacks were rarely displayed by ERαKO or ER αβKO male mice (Ogawa et al., 1997). In contrast, mice bearing a knockout of the gene for Erβ are hyperaggressive, as compared with controls, especially if the test male is just postpubertal and socially inexperienced (Nomura et al., 2002). In addition, the lack of social recognition and memory in Erβ KO males (via the ocytocinergic projections to the amygdala) could contribute to the hyperaggressiveness displayed by these mice (Choleris, 2003). The effect of Erβ on aggression is exactly the opposite of Erα. Interestingly, a higher percentage of ERα knock out male mice (70%) showed infanticide compared with wild type mice (35%) (Ogawa et al., 1998). Aromatase KO male mice have been reported to show little aggressive behavior.

In summary, estrogen elicits aggressive behavior and masculine sexual behavior in male rodents via estrogen receptor alpha in the brain, and the establishment of estrogen responsiveness requires endogeneous estrogen during the perinatal period which depends on local aromatase activity (Simon and Wahlen, 1987). ERβ might be inhibitory of male aggressive behavior which is facilitated by the action of the androgen receptor, ERα or both.

III.3. Relationship between Testosterone, Estradiol and Serotonin

Besides testosterone and its metabolites, it is obvious that serotoninergic projections to the forebrain play an important role in the neurobiological control over aggression. Serotonin (5HT) exerts an inhibitory effect on aggressive or violent behaviour and especially on impulsivity (Soubrié, 1986). A decreased activity of the serotoninergic presynaptic neurons and an up regulation of post synaptic $5HT_{2a/c}$ receptors may be related to pedophilia (Maes et al, 2001) (direct aggression or inability to control deviant impulses). In the same way, Giotakos et al. (2004) have reported higher levels of testosterone and dihydrotestosterone and lower levels of 5-hydroxyindoleacetic acid (5HIAA, the major metabolite of serotonin) in rapists as compared with controls. Interestingly, self-injurious behavior was decreased by cyproterone acetate (CPA) (5 to 10 mg/kg/week) in adult male rhesus macaques (Eaton et al., 1999). Serum testosterone and cerebro-spinal fluid levels of 5HIAA and HVA (homovanillic acid) declined significantly during CPA treatment. The decrease in 5HIAA and HVA may be related to the decrease of the monoamine oxidase (MAO) activity by cyproterone acetate. The reduction of aggression may be related either to the decrease in testosterone or to an increase in the availability of active dopamine and serotonin in the central nervous system. In addition, the antiaggressive effect of cyproterone acetate was reported in several studies in humans (for review, see Thibaut, 2003). In animal studies, Sundblad and Eriksson (1997) have suggested that the effects of testosterone on sex-dependent behaviors such as aggression and sexual activity may be at least partly due to a reduction in amygdala serotonin function in androgenized female rats. Somehow, the action of testosterone on the $5HT_{2a}$ receptors and on the serotonin transporter in brain depends upon its conversion to estradiol (Fink et al., 1999). Estrogens increase the $5HT_2$ receptor concentration in brain areas. Both the $5HT_{2a}$ receptors and serotonin transporters are decreased after castration in males and their levels are restored by treatment with testosterone or estradiol but not by dihydrotestosterone (Fink et al., 1999). In addition, the patterns of expression of Erβ and aromatase in the brain, but not that of Erα follow closely the pattern of $5HT_{2a}$ receptors.

In addition to its effect on the serotoninergic system, estrogen also strongly influences the dopaminergic system and increases the dopamine-mediated activity. Dopamine-stimulated sexual behavior is testosterone dependent in mice (Szczypka, 1998).

CONCLUSION

Little is known about individuals who commit sex offences in the context of active psychosis, however, the data do not support the fact that most psychotic sex offenders behave in an exceptionally violent or bizarre manner, or that their deviant behavior is necessarily driven by the psychotic symptoms. However, in many cases, the hallucinations or delusions were directly or, indirectly, related to the offence. In addition, most of these patients were not receiving adequate care or supervision at the time of the offence. The increase in sexual drive that was reported in some schizophrenic patients and its relationships with deviant sexual behaviour need further investigation. The relationship between testosterone levels and schizophrenia is not clear. Some controversial data have been published. However, one study has observed low testosterone levels in male criminals schizophrenics, 30% of them were convicted of homicide but no deviant sexual behaviour was reported in this sample.

In humans, testosterone plays a major role not only in the development and maintenance of male sexual characteristics but also in sexuality and aggression. However, the exact role of testosterone and its influence on general aggression in humans remains unclear. Even if there is a weak relationship between aggressive behavior and endogenous testosterone levels in men and women, there is no evidence for a causal relationship. In addition, the relationship between sexual hormones and deviant sexual behavior is poorly understood. There is neither evidence that sex offenders have higher testosterone levels, nor data indicating an increased androgen receptor activity. In addition, low testosterone levels have been reported in male criminals with schizophrenia.

In animal studies, the role of testosterone is mediated at least in part by its conversion in the brain into estradiol. Abolition of estrogen (via ErαβKO or aromatase KO male mice) results in loss of male rodent sexual behavior. The induction of offensive aggressive behavior may be regulated predominantly, in a facilitating manner, by the activation of Erα in male rodents. In addition, estrogens strongly influence the serotoninergic system and to a lesser extent the dopaminergic system. Aggression may be related either to testosterone or to available active serotonin in the brain.

Antiandrogen treatments must be prescribed very carefully in sex offenders schizophrenic patients, since several authors have described a worsening of psychotic symptoms. Their efficacy in controlling deviant sexual behaviour is probably derived from decreasing non-specifically sexual arousal and behaviour. However, the antiestrogenic effect of CPA may contribute to the reduction of sexual and non sexual aggression observed with this treatment. In addition, the decrease of the MAO activity observed with CPA treatment may increase the availability of serotonin in the brain and consequently may reduce the level of aggression.

REFERENCES

Archer, J. (1991). The influence of testosterone on human aggression. *Br J Psychol,* 82, 1-28.

Aromaki, A.S., Lindman R.E., and Eriksson C.J. (1999). Testosterone, aggressiveness, and antisocial personality. *Aggressive Behavior* 25, 113-123.

Aromaki, A.S., Lindman, R.E., and Eriksson C.J. (2002). Testosterone, sexuality and antisocial personality in rapists and child molesters: a pilot study. *Psychiatry Res* 110(3), 239-47.

Bahrke, M.S., Yesalis, C.E., and Wright, J.E. (1996). Psychological and behavioural effects of endogenous testosterone and anabolic-androgenic steroids. An update. *Sports Med,* 22(6), 367-90.

Barbenel, D.M., Yusufi, B., O'Schea, D., and Bench, C.J. (2000). Mania in a patient receiving testosterone replacement postorchidectomy taking St John's wort and sertraline. *J Psychopharmacol,* 14(1), 84-6.

Beyer, C. (1999). Estrogen and the developing mammalian brain. *Anat Embryol,* 199(5), 379-90.

Booth, A., Shelly, G., Mazur, A., Tharp, G., and Kittok, R. (1989). Testosterone, and winning and loosing in human competition. *Hormones and Behavior*, 23, 556-71.

Brower, K.J., Blow, F.C., Beresford, T.P., and Fuelling, C. (1989). Anabolic-androgenic steroid dependence. *J Clin Psychiatry,* 50(1), 31-3.

Brower, K.J., Blow, F.C., Young, J.P., and Hill, E.M. (1991). Symptoms and correlates of anabolic-androgenic steroid dependence. *Br J Addict,* 86(6), 759-68.

Carani, C., Bancroft, J., Granata, A., Del Rio, G., and Marrama, P. (1992). Testosterone and erectile function, nocturnal penile tumescence and rigidity, and erectile response to visual erotic stimuli in hypogonadal and eugonadal men. *Psychoneuroendocrinology,* 17(6), 647-654.

Carani, C., Rochira, V., Faustini-Fustini, M., Balestrieri, A., and Granata, A. R. (1999). Role of estrogen in male sexual behavior : insights from the natural model of aromatase deficiency. *Clin. Endocrinol,* 51, 517-524.

Casanova. M.F., Mannheim, G., Kruesi, M. (2002). Hippocampal pathology in two mentally ill paraphiliacs. *Psychiatry Res,* 115(1-2), 79-89.

Choleris, E., Gustafsson J.A., Koracj, K.S., Muglia, L.G., Pfaff, D.W., Ogawa, S. (2003). An estrogen dependent four-gene micronet regulating social recognition : a study with ocytocin- and estrogen receptor alpha- and beta-knockout mice. *Proc Natl Acad Sci USA,* 100(10), 6192-7.

Christiansen, K. (2001). Behavioural effects of androgen in men and women. *J Endocrinol,* 170, 39-48.

Chueng, P., and Schweitzer, I. (1998). Correlates of aggressive behaviour in schizophrenia: an overview. *Aust N Z J Psychiatry,* 32(3),400-9.

Conte, F.A., Grumbach, M.M., Ito, Y., Fisher, C.R., and Simpson, E.R. (1994). A syndrome of female pseudohermaphrodism, hypergonadotropic, hypogonadism, and multicystic ovaries associated with missense mutation in the gene encoding aromatase (P450arom). *J Clin Endocrinol Metab,* 78(6), 1287-92.

Cooper, A.J., and Swamy, G.N. (1994). The effect of testosterone on psychopathology and sexual function in a paranoid schizophrenic self-castrate. *Can J Psychiatry,* 39(7), 436-8.

Cooper, A.J., Losztyn, S., Russell, N.C., and Cernovsky, Z. (1990). Medroxyprogesterone acetate, nocturnal penile tumescence, laboratory arousal, and sexual acting out in a male with schizophrenia. *Arch. Sex. Behav,* 19(4), 361-72.

Cournos, F., Guido, J.R., Coomaraswamy, S., Meyer-Bahlburg, H, Sugden, R, and Horwath, E. (1994). Sexual activity and risk of HIV infection among patients with schizophrenia. *Am J Psychiatry,* 151(2), 228-32.

Craissati, J., Hodes, P. (1992). Mentally ill sex offenders : the experience of a regional secure unit. *Br J Psychiatry.* 161, 846-9.

Dabbs, J.M Jr., Frady, R.L., Carr, R.S., and Besch, N.F. (1987) Saliva testosterone and criminal violence in young adult prison inmates. *Psychosom Med,* 49(2), 174-82.

Dabbs, J.M., Ruback, R.B., Frady, R., Hopper, C.H., and Sgoutas, D.S. (1988). Saliva testosterone and criminal violence among women. *Personality and Individual Differences,* 9, 269-75.

De Jonge, F.H., and Van de Poll, N.E. (1984). Relationships between sexual and aggressive behavior in male and female rats: effects of gonadal hormones. *Prog Brain Res,* 61, 283-302.

De Jonge, F.H., Eerland, E.M., and Van de Pool, N.E. (1986). The influence of estrogen, testosterone and progesterone on partner preference, receptivity and proceptivity. *Physiol Behav,* 37(6), 885-91.

Dirksen, T., and Monikes, E. (1995). Hebephrenic symptons as an expression of an XYY chromosome abnormality? Case report of a patient with suspected sexual abuse of his own 2 minor children. *Fortschr Neurol Psychiatr, 63*(6), 232-7.

Drake, C.R., and Pathe, M. (2004). Understanding sexual offending in schizophrenia. *Crim Behav Ment Health,* 14(2), 108-20.

Driessen, M., Muessigbrodt, H., Dilling, H., and Driessen, B. (1996). Child sexual abuse associated with anabolic androgenic steroid use. *Am J Psychiatry,* 153(10), 1369.

Eaton, G.G., Worlein, J.M., Kelley, S.T., Vijayaraghavan, S., Hess, D.L., Axthelm, M.K., & Betea, C.L. (1999). Self-injurious behavior is decreased by cyproterone acetate in adult male rhesus monkeys (Macaca Mulatta). *Horm Behav,* 35(2), 195-203.

Ehlers, C.L., Rickler, K.C., and Hovey. J.E. (1980). A possible relationship between plasma testosterone and aggressive behavior in a female outpatient population. In *Limbic Epilepsy and Dyscontrol Syndrome*, Eds M. Girgis and L.G. Kiloh, New York : Elsevier/North Holland Biomedical Press. pp 183-194.

Fink, G., Sumner, B., Rosie, R., Wilson, H., and Mc Queen, J. (1999). Androgen actions on central serotonin neurotransmission: relevance for mood, mental state and memory. *Behav Brain Res,* 105(14), 53-68.

Gaffney, G.R., Berlin, F.S. (1984). Is there hypothalamic-pituitary-gonadal dysfunction in paedophilia, *Br J Psychiatry*, 145, 657-60.

Giotakos, O., Markianos, M., Vaidakis, N., and Christodoulou, G.N. (2004). Sex hormones and biogenic amine turnover of sex offenders in relation to their temperament and character dimensions. *Psychiatry Res,* 127(3), 185-93.

Gladue, B.A. (1991). Aggressive behavioral characteristics, hormones, and sexual orientation in men and women. *Aggressive Behavior,* 17, 313-26.

Gossler, R., Vesely, C., and Friedrich, M.H. (2002). Autocastration of a young schizophrenic man. *Psychiatr Prax,* 29(4), 214-7.

Grumbach M.M., Auchus R.J. (1999). Estrogen: consequences and implications of human mutations in synthesis and action. *J Clin Endocrinol Metab,* 84, 4677-93.

Gouchie, C., Kimura, D. (1991). The relationship between testosterone levels and cognitive ability patterns. *Psychoneuroendocrinology*, 16, 323-46.

Hines, M. (1998). Abnormal sexual development and psychosexual issues. *Baillieres Clin Endocrinol Metabolism,* 12(1), 173-89.

Home Office (1997). Statistics of mentally disordered offenders in England and Wales 1996. *Home Office Statistical Bulletin*, 20/97. London : Home Office.

Jones, G., Huckle, P.N Tanaghow, A. (1992). Command hallucinations, schizophrenia and sexual assaults. *Ir J Psychol Med*, 9, 47-9.

Kadar, T., Telegdy, G., Schally A.V. (1992). Behavioral effects of centrally administered LH-RH agonist in rats. *Physiol Behav*, 50, 601-5.

Kedenburg, H.D. (1977). Androgens and aggressive behavior in man. *Ann Arbor (MI)*: University Microfilms International.

Lee, J.W. (1996). An XXYY male with schizophrenia. *Aust N Z J Psychiatry,* 30(4), 553-6.

Linn, L. (2001). Autocastration and psychosis. *Psychiatr Serv,* 52(9), 1258.

Maes, M., De Vos, H., Van Hunsel, F., Van West, D., Westenberg, H., Cosyns, P., & Neels, H. (2001). Pedophilia is accompanied by increased plasma concentrations of catecholamines, in particular epinephrine. *Psychiatry Res,* 103(1), 43-9.

Mc Kenna., J., J. (1983). Primate aggression and evolution : an overview of sociobiological and anthropological perspectives. *Bull Am Acad Psychiatry Law*, 2, 105-30.

Miranda, RC., Sohrabji, F., and Toran-Allerand, D. (1994). Interactions of estrogen with the neurotrophins and their receptors during neural development. *Horm Behav,* 28(4), 367-75.

Morishima A., Grumbach M.M., Simpson E.R., Fisher C., Qin K. (1995). Aromatase deficiency in male and female siblings caused by a novel mutation and the physiological role of estrogens. *J Clin Endocrinol Metab*, 80 (12), 3689-98.

Myers, W.C., and Nguyen, M. (2001). Autocastration as a presenting sign of incipient schizophrenia. *Psychiatr Serv,* 52(5), 685-6.

Nomura, M., Durbak, l., Chan, J., Smithies, O., Gustafsson, H.A., Korach, K.S., Pfaff, D.W., and Ogawa, S. (2002). Genotype/age interactions on aggressive behavior in gonadally intact estrogen receptor beta knockout (beta ERKO) male mice. *Horm Behav,* 41(3), 288-96.

Novak-Grubic, V., and Tavcar, R. (2002). Autocastration and schizophrenia. *Psychiatr Serv,* 53(4), 485-6.

Ogawa, S., Lubahan, D.B., Korach, K.S., and Pfaff, D.W. (1997). Behavioral effects of estrogen receptor gene disruption in male mice. *Proc Natl Acad Sci USA,* 94(4)1476-81.

Ogawa, S., Washburn, T.F., Taylor, J., Lubahn, D.B,, Korach, K.S., and Pfaff, D.W. (1998). Modifications of testosterone-dependent behaviors by estrogen receptor-alpha gene disruption in male mice. *Endocrinology,* 139(12), 5048-69.

Phillips, S.L. (1999). Sexual offending and antisocial sexual behavior among patients with schizophrenia. *J Clin Psychiatry* 60 (3), 170-5.

Ponikiewska, W., and Szczesna, H. (1973). Fetishism in the course of simple schizophrenia. *Psychiatr Pol,* 7(6), 645-7.

Rada, R.T., Laws, D.R., Kellner, R., Stivastava, L., and Peake, G. (1983). Plasma androgens in violent and non-violent sex offenders. *Bull Am Acad Psychiatry Law*, 11, 149-58.

Räsänen P., Hakko H., Visuri S., Paanila J., Kapanen P., Suomela T., Tiihonen J. (1999). Serum testosterone levels, mental disorders and criminal behaviour. *Acta Psychiatr Scand*, 99, 348-52.

Rose, R.M., Holaday, J.W., Bernstein, I.S. (1972). Plasma testosterone, dominance rank and aggressive behaviour in male rhesus monkeys. *Nature*, 231, 366-8.

Rubinow, D.R., Schmidt. M.J. (1996). Androgens, brain and behavior. *Am J Psychiatry*, 153, 974-984.

Salmimies, P., Kockott, G., Pirke, K.M., Bogt, H.J., and Schill, W.B. (1982). Effects of testosterone replacement on sexual behavior in hypogonadal men. *Arch Sex Behav,* 11(4), 345-53.

Sanders, D., Bancroft, J. (1982). Hormones and the sexuality of women – The menstrual cycle. *Clin Endocrinol Metabolism*, 11, 639-659.

Scamarella, T.J., Brown, W.A. (1978). Serum testosterone and aggressiveness in hockey players. *Psychosomatic Medicine*, 40, 262-265.

Simon, N.G., and Whalen, R.E. (1987). Sexual differentiation of androgen-sensitive and estrogen-sensitive regulatory systems for aggressive behavior. *Horm Behav,* 21(4), 493-500.

Simpson, E. R., and Davis, S. R. (2000). Another role highlighted for estrogens in the male: sexual behavior. *Proc Natl Acad Sci,* 97(26), 14038-40.

Smith, A.D., and Taylor, P.J. (1999). Serious sex offending against women by men with schizophrenia. Relationship of illness psychotic symptoms to offending. *Br J Psychiatry,* 174, 233-7.

Smith, A.D. (2000). Offence characteristics of psychotic men who sexually assault women. *Med Sci Law,* 40(3), 223-8.

Soubrie, P. (1986). Serotonergic neurons and behavior. *J Pharmacol,* 17(2), 107-12.

Stevens, J;R. (2002). Schizophrenia : reproductive hormones and the brain. *Am J Psychiatry,* 159 (5), 713-9.

Sundblad, C., and Eriksson, E. (1997). Reduced extracellular levels of serotonin in the amygdala of androgenized female rats. *Eur Neuropsychopharmacol,* 7(4), 253-9.

Susman, E.D., Inoff-Germain, G., Nottlemann, E.D., Loriaux, D.L., Cutler, G.B., Chrousos, G.P., (1987). Hormones, emotional dispositions, and aggressive attributes in young adolescents. *Child Dev*, 58, 1114-34.

Szczypka, M.S., Shou, Q.Y., and Palmiter, R.D. (1998). Dopamine-stimulated sexual behavior is testosterone dependent in mice. *Behav Neurosci,* 112(5), 1129-35.

Thibaut, F., Kuhn, J.M., Colonna, L., (1991). A possible antiaggressive effect of cyproterone acetate. *Br J Psychiatry*, 159, 298-9.

Thibaut, F., Colonna. L., (1992). Cyproterone acetate in the treatment of aggression. *Am J Psychiatry*, 143 (3), 411.

Thibaut, F., Cordier, B., Kuhn, J.M., (1993). Effect of a long-lasting gonodatrophin hormone-releasing hormone agonist in six cases of severe male paraphilia. *Acta Psychiatr Scand,* 87, 445-50.

Thibaut, F., (2003). Perspectives on treatment interventions in paraphilias. In : *Handbook of Medical Psychiatry*, Eds JC Soares and S Gershon. Marcel Dekker: New York Press, (*pp*.909-916).

Van Goozen,, S.H.M., Frijada, N.H., Van de Poo, N.E., (1994). Anger and aggression in women : Influence of sports choice and testosterone administration. *Aggressive Behav*, 20, 213-22.

Van Goozen, S.H., Cohen-Kettenis, P.T., Gooren, L.J., Frijda, N.H., and Van de Poll, N.E. (1995). Gender differences in behaviour: activating effects of cross-sex hormones. *Psychoneuroendocrinology,* 20(4), 343-63.

Vish, I.M., Shpizel, R.S., and Sviripa, E.V. (1996). Transvestism in a schizophrenic patient. *Zh Nevropatol Psikhiatr Im S S Korsakova,* 96(6), 77-8.

Walsh, E., Gilvarry, C., Samele, C., Harvey, K., Manley, C., Tattan, T., and Tyrer, P., (2004). Predicting violence in schizophrenia: a prospective study. *Schizophrenia Res,* 67, 247-52.

Waugh, A.C. (1986). Autocastration and biblical delusions in schizophrenia. *Br J Psychiatry,* 149, 656-8.

Yates, W.R., Perry, P.J., MacIndoe, H., Holman, T., and Ellingrod, V. (1999). Psychosexual effects of three doses of testosterone cycling in normal men. *Biol Psychiatry,* 45(3), 254-60.

In: Crime and Schizophrenia: Causes and Cures
Editor: Adrian Raine, pp. 301-314
ISBN 1-59454-609-6

Chapter 16

TREATMENT APPROACHES TO AGGRESSIVE BEHAVIOR IN SCHIZOPHRENIA

Jan Volavka *
Nathan Kline Institute and New York University

Treatment of psychiatric disorders is hampered by the fact that their causes are poorly understood. Our ignorance is even deeper when it comes to aggressive behavior in psychiatric patients. Clearly, without better understanding of underlying neuropsychobiology of aggression we cannot improve the existing treatments. This chapter therefore first reviews neurobiological and psychosocial factors affecting aggression in schizophrenia, and then proceeds to discuss their implications for treatment. Finally, the current state of the psychopharmacology of aggression in schizophrenia is briefly reviewed.

1. NEUROBIOLOGICAL AND PSYCHOSOCIAL FACTORS THAT AFFECT AGGRESSION IN SCHIZOPHRENIA

Modern studies of the neurobiological factors that modulate aggressive and criminal behavior in humans rest largely on the innovative approaches pioneered by Sarnoff A. Mednick (Mednick and Volavka, 1980; Mednick, Pollock, Volavka, and Gabrielli, Jr., 1982; Mednick, Gabrielli, Jr., and Hutchings, 1983; Mednick, Gabrielli, Jr., and Hutchings, 1984; Mednick and Kandel, 1988). His contributions to our understanding of the neurobiology of schizophrenia, discussed elsewhere in this volume, are enormous. The study of the aggressive behavior in schizophrenia, representing the confluence of these two lines of inquiry, has been heavily influenced by Mednick's thought, and many of the current outstanding researchers in the area had been his students.

Schizophrenia patients living in the community have an elevated risk for aggressive behavior in comparison with community residents who are not diagnosed with mental disorder (Swanson, Holzer, Ganju, and Jono, 1990). The elevated risk is present even if the patient has no comorbidity with other disorders (Swanson, 1994; Arseneault, Moffitt, Caspi, Taylor, and Silva, 2000; Brennan, Mednick, and Hodgins, 2000), and it is further elevated by comorbidities.

1.1. Comorbid Substance Use Disorders

The risk for aggressive behavior is increased, quite dramatically, with comorbid substance use disorders (Lindqvist and Allebeck, 1990; Swanson, 1994). Comorbidity of schizophrenia and substance use disorders is highly prevalent: almost 50% of schizophrenia patients have a comorbid substance use disorder, and schizophrenia patients are almost 5 times more likely to develop a substance use disorder than the rest of the population (the odds ratio was estimated at 4.6) (Regier et al., 1990). Therefore, the propensity of schizophrenia patients to abuse alcohol or drugs represents an important pathway towards the development of aggressive behavior. Furthermore, successful treatment of comorbid substance use disorders is expected to reduce aggressive behavior in schizophrenia patients.

1.2. Comorbid Personality Disorders

Personality disorders, particularly antisocial personality disorder (DSM-IV) or psychopathy (Hare, 1986) are associated with aggressive behavior in the general population (Volavka, 2002; Hart, Hare, and Forth, 1994). The relation between these two diagnoses is discussed elsewhere (Hare, 1996). Comorbidity of schizophrenia and personality disorders has not been studied with the same epidemiological rigor as the comorbidity with substance use disorders. However, limited data suggest that comorbidity of psychopathy and schizophrenia exists, and that it is higher among violent than among non-violent patients (Nolan, Volavka, Mohr, and Czobor, 1999). Comorbid psychopathy may thus be another risk factor for aggression in schizophrenia patients.

1.3. Treatment Non-Adherence

As we will see, antipsychotics possess varying degrees of antiaggressive effects in schizophrenia patients. It is therefore not surprising that the risk of aggressive behavior increases if the patient stops taking his medication. Thus, non-adherence to pharmacological treatment is another factor that elevates the risk of aggressive behavior (Swartz et al., 1998a; Swartz et al., 1998b). Non-adherence to recommended antipsychotic treatment in the community occurs in a majority of patients (Dolder, Lacro, Dunn, and Jeste, 2002).

Non-adherence to antipsychotic medication regimens has many causes. Some of these are *drug-related*: the side effects may be difficult to tolerate. Such intolerable side effects may include extrapyramidal symptoms (more common with typical antipsychotics), weight gain

* Email: janvolavka@gmail.com. Phone 406 995 2776. Mailing address: 55 Blue Spruce Road #E3, P.O. Box 160663, Big Sky, MT 59716-0663

(more common with atypicals, particularly clozapine and olanzapine) and sexual dysfunction related to prolactin elevation due to dopamine D2 receptor blocking (more common with typical antipsychotics and risperidone). Atypical antipsychotics appear to have a slightly better treatment adherence record than the typicals (Dolder et al., 2002), and clozapine has the best adherence overall. This may be due to the frequent mandatory blood tests; regular contacts with the treatment team maintain and strengthen treatment alliance; they also improve the monitoring of the patient. Slow-release injectable forms of antipsychotics are generally superior to the oral forms in terms of adherence (Swartz, Swanson, Wagner, Burns, and Hiday, 2001).

Other factors that may contribute to non-adherence involve *environmental influences, including treatment management.* The psychiatrist may not have established the appropriate treatment alliance with the patient, or may not have adequately explained the benefits of treatment and the risks of discontinuing it. The patient's family may not have been adequately informed about the treatment, or it chose not to be involved. Finally, non-adherence may be caused by *patient-related* factors. These include delusional beliefs about medication, inadequate insight or denial of mental illness, and cognitive problems that interfere with the patient's ability to understand and adhere to a treatment regimen. Non-adherence is frequently combined with comorbid substance abuse which may further impair patients' judgment and motivation.

1.4. Heterogeneity of Aggressive Behavior

Comorbid substance use disorders and non-adherence to treatment are important factors in the development of aggressive behavior in schizophrenia patients residing in the community. However, aggressive behavior occurs frequently even when substance use is precluded and treatment adherence is close to complete (Volavka, 2002). Such conditions can be created at psychiatric inpatient units. Overt physical aggression can be closely observed and studied prospectively at such units; the observations of individual aggressive incidents would not be feasible in the community.

It has long been assumed that aggression in psychiatric patients (and, more generally, in humans) is a heterogeneous phenomenon in terms of its causation and underlying neurobiology. Nevertheless, current research into the treatment of aggressive behavior tacitly assumes neurobiological and sociobiological homogeneity across all incidents of aggression: to assess treatment effect, the incidents are counted and their severity quantified, without any attempt at causative analysis. This shortcoming is understandable since empirical research addressing causative heterogeneity of aggressive incidents is sparse. Such research is important: if there are different causes, for example different neurobiological mechanisms, one would assume that the appropriate treatments might vary accordingly.

One of the ways to assess the heterogeneity of aggressive incidents is to observe them and to interview the participants and witnesses. We have installed a video camera system that is continuously recording the activity in the public areas of our research inpatient unit. The aggressive incidents that are captured are archived for further study. At a minimum, the video permits a reliable identification of the assailant and the victim. As soon as possible after the incident occurs, researchers interview the assailant, the victim, and any witnesses. A semi-structured interview was developed to assess the causal contributions of psychotic symptoms, disordered impulse control, and psychopathy to the observed aggressive incident. The data on 70 incidents were published (Nolan et al., 2003). The results indicated that approximately 20 percent of the assaults in this sample were directly related to positive psychotic symptoms. Factor analysis revealed two psychosis-related factors, one related to positive psychotic symptoms and the other to psychotic confusion and disorganization, as well as a third factor that differentiated impulsive from psychopathic assaults.

This information is potentially useful in the selection of rational antiaggressive treatment strategies: hypothetically, the psychosis-related assaults would respond to atypical antipsychotics, and impulse-control disorder assaults to adjunctive anticonvulsants. Psychopathy assaults might respond to an elaborate, long-term term cognitive-behavioral treatment that will be described below.

This study represents only a first step in the effort to understand the heterogeneity of aggressive behavior. We have collected additional data on aggressive incidents and replicated these results (Nolan et al., in preparation). However, we are still not sure that our classification of assaults will help to classify people. Such classification is of course important from the standpoint of treatment: we treat people, not assaults.

1.5. Genetics and Genomics

Genetics and genomics represent another approach to the analysis of aggressive behavior in schizophrenia that has potential therapeutic implications. Many neurotransmitter systems that are under partial genetic control play a role in the regulation of aggressive behavior; most research has focused on serotonin (Volavka, 2002). Recently, catecholamines such as dopamine and norepinephrine have been receiving increased attention. These substances enhance aggression in animals, and their antagonists (such as haloperidol and propranolol) are known to reduce certain types of aggressive behavior in humans (Volavka, 2002).

The major enzymes responsible for catecholamine catabolism are catechol-*O*-methyltransferase (COMT) and monoamine oxidase (MAO). A common biallelic single nucleotide polymorphism, involving a Met → Val substitution at codon 158 of the COMT gene has been identified at chromosome 22q11.1-q11.2 (Lachman et al., 1996). The methionine (Met) allele at this locus is associated with low enzymatic activity, whereas the valine (Val) allele is associated with high activity. Homozygosity for the Met allele yields a 3- to 4-fold reduction in COMT activity relative to Val homozygotes, with heterozygotes demonstrating intermediate activity.

If catecholamines enhance aggression and their antagonists suppress it, then the Met allele conferring low enzymatic activity of COMT should be associated with enhanced aggressive behavior because low catabolism of catecholamines leads to greater amounts of these compounds in the brain (and elsewhere). This prediction has been confirmed in some (Strous, Bark, Parsia, Volavka, and Lachman, 1997; Strous et al., 2003; Lachman, Nolan, Mohr, Saito, and Volavka, 1998; Kotler et al., 1999; Volavka et al., 2004b), but not all (Jones et al., 2001) studies of schizophrenia, schizoaffective disorder, and other disorders (Rujescu, Giegling, Gietl, Hartmann, and Moller, 2003).. Also consistent with the prediction, COMT knockout mice show elevated aggressive behavior (Gogos et al., 1998). Furthermore, when 8 inbred mouse strains were ranked by their aggressiveness, the ranking was inversely correlated with the expression of the COMT gene in the hippocampus: the lower the COMT expression, the higher the strain aggressiveness. (Fernandes et al., 2004).

Thus, the Met allele (and the attendant lowering of COMT activity) is associated with aggression. However, it is also associated with enhanced cognitive performance (Egan et al., 2001). This conjunction is counterintuitive, since elevated aggression is typically associated with low cognitive performance; higher intelligence is generally considered a protective factor against aggressive behavior (Volavka, 2002). Reconciling these findings is beyond the scope of this chapter; information can be found elsewhere (Bilder, Volavka, Lachman, and Grace, 2004).

2. Treatment Implications of the Neurobiological and Psychobiological Factors

2.1. Comorbid Substance Use Disorders

Schizophrenia patients with comorbid substance use disorders require services of integrated treatment teams that are equipped to approach both illnesses as primary targets of intervention. Since the comorbidity is so prevalent, the goal is to define all psychiatric programs as "dual diagnosis programs" and to make them capable to treat these difficult patients. Integrated philosophy of treatment is based on a disease and recovery model.

Continuing psychopharmacological treatment of schizophrenia is an integral part of the treatment.

There is some evidence suggesting that clozapine may reduce the drug and alcohol use in schizophrenia patients (Drake, Xie, McHugo, and Green, 2000). The mechanism of such effect is not clear. Perhaps clozapine treats a reward deficiency syndrome (Green, Zimmet, Strous, and Schildkraut, 1999), reduces craving (Buckley, McCarthy, Chapman, Richman, and Yamamoto, 2000), or its superior antipsychotic effect enables the patients to make more rational choices about their lifestyles. It is also possible the that the frequent blood tests required for the safety of clozapine treatment have the side benefit of keeping in touch with patients on a regular basis; this may improve the patients' engagement in treatment programs as well as enable closer monitoring and case management.

2.2. Comorbid Personality Disorders

Antisocial Personality Disorder and psychopathy are associated with criminal behavior, and schizophrenia patients with these comorbidities typically have a history of arrest and incarceration. When discharged into the community after a short stay in a psychiatric hospital, these patients are at a high risk for re-arrest or re-hospitalization. Their recidivistic criminal behavior results in a cycle of psychiatric admissions, discharges, arrests, and re-admissions or incarcerations.

Patients with these comorbid disorders are particularly difficult to treat. These personality disorders do not respond to any specific pharmacological interventions, and the usual psychiatric treatment programs are not effective. In response to the needs of this patient population, a specialized cognitive-behavioral treatment program has been developed (Kunz et al., 2004); (Yates et al., 2005). The program, called STAIR (System for Treatment and Abatement of Interpersonal Risk), aims to break the cycle of repeated hospitalization and incarceration. It is based at a State Hospital in New York City. The program teaches cognitive skills (problem solving, creative thinking, value enhancement, social skills, critical reasoning, and managing emotions). Skills are taught in group sessions; the program consists of 72 sessions. Furthermore, the STAIR incorporates a 12-step substance abuse program. Patients receive standard psychopharmacological treatment for their Axis I disorders (mostly psychosis). The first follow-up reports for 6-24 months after discharge are available for 85 patients; the results appear to support the effectiveness of the program (Kunz et al., 2004).

2.3. Treatment Non-Adherence

The cause or causes of non-adherence must be explored in individual patients. If the patient does not tolerate side effects, an effort must be made to reduce or eliminate them by adjusting the dose of antipsychotic, prescribing another medication to counteract the side effects (eg, an anticholinergic to reduce extrapyramidal symptoms), to switch to another antipsychotic, or to switch to a long-acting injectable antipsychotic. This has to be done in collaboration with the patient, and, if possible, with the patient's family. Therapeutic alliance based on mutual respect is conducive to psycho-education about acceptance of the illness, need to continue taking medication, and risks and benefits of treatments. Such psychosocial interventions are considered the first choice of treatment for patients demonstrating partial adherence to treatment (Kane, Leucht, Carpenter, and Docherty, 2003).

However, not all patients and their families are accessible to such efforts. The patients with comorbid substance abuse, those who have weak family and community support, the undomiciled, and the patients who simply refuse treatment are difficult to reach. Some of these patients have also comorbid personality disorders and a history of arrests and incarceration for violent crimes. Inpatient treatment for such patients was described in the preceding section. However, such treatment is not yet generally available. Thus, these patients are usually admitted or arrested after a violent incident, they are given antipsychotics, improve in several weeks, and they are discharged. Soon after the discharge, they discontinue their antipsychotic medication, do not keep their outpatient appointments, may start using drugs or alcohol, and become involved in violent incidents. Since such patients are repeatedly dangerous to others and themselves and are unable to break the cycle of violence, re-arrests and re-admissions, they may be subject to involuntary out-patient commitment (IOPC). Non-violent patients who are endangering only themselves may also qualify for IOPC.

IOPC is a legal intervention: a judge orders a patient residing in the community to adhere to recommended outpatient treatment. If the patient fails to do so, the responsible clinician may request the police to escort the patient to the treatment center. Once there, the clinicians try to persuade the patient to adhere to treatment, and evaluate him for inpatient commitment.

IOPC may have multiple positive effects beyond improving adherence to pharmacological treatments. It may also improve access to other treatments, result in better monitoring of patients' behavior and mental status, and thereby reduce the likelihood of a relapse. However, IOPC is coercive and may be seen as an infringement on the patients' civil liberties. Arguably, IOPC may not be necessary if appropriate voluntary treatment would be available in an adequately funded, well functioning mental health system. Such treatment might be expected to improve adherence through cooperation with the patient and his family. This libertarian argument has merit, but I think that there will always be patients who are just too difficult to reach on a voluntary basis even with an optimal mental health system. The question is, does IOPC yield better outcomes than voluntary outpatient treatment in difficult non-adherent patients?

A pilot study of IOPC in New York City suggested a negative answer to that question (Steadman et al., 2001). However, that study excluded patients with a history of violence, and the pick-up order procedures for non-adherent subjects were actually not implemented. A more definitive study was conducted in North Carolina (Swartz et al., 1999). Subjects who were hospitalized involuntarily were randomly assigned to IOPC or to voluntary outpatient treatment (control group) and followed up for 1 year. The control and IOPC groups did not differ significantly in readmission rates. However, a post-hoc analysis indicated that subjects with prolonged periods of IOPC (beyond that of the initial court order) had fewer readmissions and fewer hospital days than control subjects. (Swartz et al., 1999). The post-hoc nature of these analyses and various other methodological problems were criticized in subsequent correspondence (Segal, 2001; Szmukler and Hotopf, 2001). The North Carolina IOPC data were re-analyzed using violent behavior as the principal outcome variable. These analyses have demonstrated that IOPC of at least 6 months duration, combined with regular outpatient services, improved treatment adherence and reduced the risk of violent behavior and of substance abuse (Swanson et al., 2000). These important results await replication.

3. Psychopharmacology of Aggression in Schizophrenia

3.1. Current Treatmets

Recent reviews have addressed various aspects of this topic (Citrome, Nolan, and Volavka, 2004; Citrome and Volavka, 2003; Citrome and Volavka, 2002b; Citrome and Volavka, 2002a; Volavka, 2002). Therefore, there is no need for a detailed assessment of the field in this chapter.

Atypical Antipsychotics

Clozapine appeared to be the superior antipsychotic to treat hostility (Citrome et al., 2001) in 157 patients with schizophrenia or schizoaffective disorder participating in a randomized controlled trial comparing clozapine, olanzapine, riperidone, and haloperidol. Further analyses of measures of overt aggression in this trial (Volavka et al., 2004a) demonstrated that antipsychotic efficacy of clozapine was greatest in aggressive patients, whereas the opposite was true for risperidone and olanzapine. Importantly, a therapeutic dose of clozapine was necessary for the superior antiaggressive effect. This issue is particularly significant because it can take several weeks to titrate clozapine to a therapeutic dose. Therefore, it is important not to terminate a clozapine trial prematurely.

The results of that randomized controlled trial (Citrome et al., 2001; Volavka et al., 2004a)were consistent with a large number of preceding uncontrolled studies and case reports. The antiaggressive effect of clozapine appears to be independent of its sedative effect as well as of its general antipsychotic effect against positive symptoms of schizophrenia.

Risperidone demonstrated a selective effect on hostility that was superior to haloperidol (Czobor, Volavka, and Meibach, 1995). Similar antihostility/antiaggressive effects of risperidone were observed in a retrospective study of seclusion and restraint (Chengappa et al., 2000), but risperidone was not more effective than typical antipsychotics in other studies of aggression (Buckley et al., 1997; Beck et al., 1997). In a randomized double-blind trial, patients assigned to risperidone or olanzapine treatments were less likely to exhibit incidents of overt aggression than those on haloperidol (Volavka et al., 2004a). Effects of aripiprazole (Dillenschneider et al., 2004) and quetiapine (Chengappa, Goldstein, Greenwood, John, and Levine, 2003) on hostility and excitement were explored in post-hoc preliminary analyses and a case report (Citrome, Krakowski, Greenberg, Andrade, and Volavka, 2001).

Adjunctive Pharmacological Treatments

Adjunctive treatments that are added to an antipsychotic may have some antiaggressive effect. Adjunctive valproate was rated as the first-line treatment for aggressive behavior in schizophrenia patients in an expert consensus statement ((Kane et al., 2003), p.77). There is some evidence for the valproate efficacy in the first week of treatment treatment: In one study, 249 schizophrenia inpatients were randomly assigned to receive olanzapine plus placebo, olanzapine plus divalproex, risperidone plus placebo, or risperidone plus divalproex in a double-blind, 28-day trial. Adjunctive divalproex reduced hostility in the first week of treatment, but the efficacy was lost in the subsequent 3 weeks (Citrome et al., 2004). Efficacy in the initial stage of treatment is valuable since this is the time when much aggressive behavior occurs. However, as many as 30% of schizophrenia patients receive adjunctive valproate on a long-term basis, months beyond the initial stage of treatment (Citrome, Jaffe, and Levine, 2002). The antiaggressive or antihostility efficacy of such long-term valproate treatment has not been conclusively demonstrated in randomized clinical trials. Uncontrolled studies are reviewed elsewhere (Lindenmayer and Kotsaftis, 2000).

Adjunctive citalopram, a selective serotonin reuptake inhibitor, reduced aggressive behavior in chronic schizophrenia patients in a double-blind crossover study (Vartiainen et al., 1995).

Propranolol, a beta-adrenergic blocking agent, was first noted to reduce aggressive behavior in mice (Valzelli, Giacalone, and Garattini, 1967). Propranolol was then reported to reduce aggressive behavior following acute brain damage in humans (Elliott, 1977). It is possible (but not certain) that the antiaggressive effects of beta-blockers are mediated, at least in part, by adrenergic receptors. Propranolol has been used to control aggression primarily in patients with organic brain disease. However, there are some reports of propranolol added to antipsychotic regimens as an adjunctive treatment for schizophrenia (Yorkston et al., 1977; Sheppard, 1979); it reduced symptoms, including aggression. Case reports of successful treatment of aggression with propranolol in assaultive schizophrenic patients have been published (Sorgi, Ratey, and Polakoff, 1986; Whitman, Maier, and Eichelman, 1987). Reports of successful antiaggressive treatments with other beta-adrenergic blockers, such as nadolol, metoprolol, and pindolol, are summarized elsewhere (Volavka, 2002). The recent expert consensus guidelines list adjunctive beta blockers as a potential second line treatment for persistently aggressive schizophrenia patients ((Kane et al., 2003), p.77), but the treatment is not much used in clinical practice. Patients vary considerably in the degree to which they respond to beta blockers. Other adjunctive treatments tried as treatments of aggressive behavior in schizophrenia include lithium, carbamazepine, lamotrigine, and benzodiazepines.

Adjunctive Electroconvulsive Therapy (ECT)

Adjunctive ECT may be helpful in schizophrenia patients who are treatment-refractory, and in particular, in patients with persistent aggressive behavior. An open trial of ECT in combination with risperidone in male patients with schizophrenia and aggression resulted in a reduction in aggressive behavior for nine of the ten patients (Hirose, Ashby, Jr., and Mills, 2001). In that series of patients, bilateral ECT was administered five times a week, with a mean total number of 6.6 treatments. A large randomized clinical trial that will shed additional light on this issue is now in progress in the United States.

3.2. Future Directions

Tailoring treatments to fit individual aggressive patients is an important challenge for the future. Research into the phenotypic heterogeneity of assaults described in this chapter is a step towards this goal. The hypothesis that assaults (and perhaps patients) can be classified into aggression subtypes that respond to different treatments remains to be tested. The three subtypes that we isolated probably oversimplify and underestimate the real diversity of aggression.

The recently developed pharmacogenetic approaches to the treatments of mental illness can be expanded to address the problems of the heterogeneity of the aggressive behavior and its treatment. For example: As noted in the segment on beta-blockers above, there is a considerable variation in the patients' response to this treatment. Allelic variation of the COMT gene may underlie this variability. The Met allele of the COMT gene codes for the low activity form of this enzyme, resulting in an inadequate biotransformation of catecholamines. Theoretically, blocking beta-adrenergic transmission would partially correct for the relatively inadequate biotransformation of catecholamines. Therefore, one might test the hypothesis that the COMT allele coding for the low activity form of the enzyme will be associated with a greater antiaggressive effect of a beta-adrenergic blocking agent. If this is true, the patients most likely to benefit from beta-blocking agents would be the Met-Met homozygotes; the Val-Val homozygotes would be least likely to benefit. The observed interindividual variation of the response to beta-blockers would be explained, and the treatment could be tailored on the genetic basis.

There is a large group of persistently aggressive and criminal patients who are unlikely to benefit from any foreseeable biological treatment. Developing cognitive-behavioral or other similar programs for these patients is a major challenge for research and policy. Testing the effectiveness of such programs using established methods such as randomized clinical trials is usually not feasible due to political, ethical, and financial obstacles. It may be necessary to develop novel scientific methods for this important field. Somewhat similar obstacles are in the way of developing better methods for the reduction of comorbid substance abuse and improvement of treatment adherence.

References

Arseneault, L., Moffitt, T. E., Caspi, A., Taylor, P. J., and Silva, P. A. (2000). Mental disorders and violence in a total birth cohort: results from the Dunedin Study. *Arch.Gen.Psychiatry, 57,* 979-986.

Beck, N. C., Greenfield, S. R., Gotham, H., Menditto, A. A., Stuve, P., and Hemme, C. A. (1997). Risperidone in the management of violent, treatment-resistant schizophrenics hospitalized in a maximum security forensic facility. *Journal of the American Academy of Psychiatry and the Law, 25,* 461-468.

Bilder, R. M., Volavka, J., Lachman, H. M., and Grace, A. A. (2004). The Catechol-O-Methyltransferase Polymorphism: Relations to the Tonic-Phasic Dopamine Hypothesis and Neuropsychiatric Phenotypes. *Neuropsychopharmacology, In Press.*

Brennan, P. A., Mednick, S. A., and Hodgins, S. (2000). Major mental disorders and criminal violence in a Danish birth cohort. *Arch.Gen.Psychiatry, 57,* 494-500.

Buckley, P. F., Ibrahim, Z. Y., Singer, B., Orr, B., Donenwirth, K., and Brar, P. S. (1997). Aggression and schizophrenia: efficacy of risperidone. *J Am Psychiatry Law, 25,* 173-181.

Buckley, P. F., McCarthy, M., Chapman, P., Richman, C. G., and Yamamoto, B. (2000). Craving reduction and clozapine response in patients with comorbid substance abuse and schizophrenia. *Biological Psychiatry* 47, 18S-19S.

Chengappa, K. N., Goldstein, J. M., Greenwood, M., John, V., and Levine, J. (2003). A post hoc analysis of the impact on hostility and agitation of quetiapine and haloperidol among patients with schizophrenia. *Clin.Ther., 25,* 530-541.

Chengappa, K. N. R., Levine, J., Ulrich, R., Parepally, H., Brar, J., and Atzert, R. (2000). Impact of risperidone on seclusion and restraint at a state psychiatric hospital. 153rd Annual Meeting of the American Psychiatric Association. New Research Abstracts, Chicago, IL , 199.

Citrome, L., Nolan, K. A., and Volavka, J. (2004). Science-Based Treatment of Aggression and Agitation. In D.Fishbein (Ed.), *The Science, Treatment, and Prevention of Antisocial Behaviors: Evidence-Based Practice* (1 ed., pp. 11-1-11-31). Kingston, NJ: Civic Research Institute, Inc.

Citrome, L., Casey, D. E., Daniel, D. G., Wozniak, P., Kochan, L. D., and Tracy, K. A. (2004). Adjunctive divalproex and hostility among patients with schizophrenia receiving olanzapine or risperidone. *Psychiatr.Serv., 55,* 290-294.

Citrome, L., Jaffe, A., and Levine, J. (2002). Datapoints - mood stabilizers: Utilization trends in patients diagnosed with schizophrenia 1994-2001. *Psychiatric Services, 53,* 1212.

Citrome, L., Krakowski, M., Greenberg, W. M., Andrade, E., and Volavka, J. (2001). Antiaggressive effect of quetiapine in a patient with schizoaffective disorder. *Journal of Clinical Psychiatry, 62,* 901.

Citrome, L. and Volavka, J. (2002a). Clinical management of persistent aggressive behavior in schizophrenia, Part I: Definitions, epidemiology, assessment, and acute treatment. *Essential Psychopharmacology, 5,* 1-16.

Citrome, L. and Volavka, J. (2002b). Clinical management of persistent aggressive behavior in schizophrenia, Part II: Long-term pharmacotherapeutic strategies. *Essential Psychopharmacology, 5,* 17-30.

Citrome, L. and Volavka, J. (2003). Treatment of Violent Behavior. In A.Tasman, J. Kay, and J. A. Lieberman (Eds.), *Psychiatry* (2 ed., pp. 2136-2146). Chichester: John Wiley and Sons, Ltd.

Citrome, L., Volavka, J., Czobor, P., Sheitman, B., Lindenmayer, J.-P., McEvoy, J. et al. (2001). Effects of clozapine, olanzapine, risperidone, and haloperidol on hostility in treatment-resistant patients with schizophrenia and schizoaffective disorder. *Psychiatric Services, 52,* 1510-1514.

Czobor, P., Volavka, J., and Meibach, R. C. (1995). Effect of risperidone on hostility in schizophrenia. *Journal of Clinical Psychopharmacology, 15,* 243-249.

Dillenschneider, A., Marcus, R., Kostic, D., Stringfellow, J., Hardy, S., Carson, W. et al. (2004). Short- and long-term effects of aripiprazole treatment on the excitement/hostility symptoms of schizophrenia. *The International Journal of Neuropsychopharmacology* 7, 243.

Dolder, C. R., Lacro, J. P., Dunn, L. B., and Jeste, D. V. (2002). Antipsychotic medication adherence: is there a difference between typical and atypical agents? *American Journal of Psychiatry, 159,* 103-108.

Drake, R. E., Xie, H., McHugo, G. J., and Green, A. I. (2000). The effects of clozapine on alcohol and drug use disorders among patients with schizophrenia. *Schizophr.Bull., 26,* 441-449.

Egan, M. F., Goldberg, T. E., Kolachana, B. S., Callicott, J. H., Mazzanti, C. M., Straub, R. E. et al. (2001). Effect of COMT Val108/158 Met genotype on frontal lobe function and risk for schizophrenia. *Proc.Natl.Acad.Sci.U.S.A, 98,* 6917-6922.

Elliott, F. A. (1977). Propranolol for the control of belligerent behavior following acute brain damage. *Annals of Neurology, 1,* 489-491.

Fernandes, C., Paya-Cano, J. L., Sluyter, F., D'Souza, U., Plomin, R., and Schalkwyk, L. C. (2004). Hippocampal gene expression profiling across eight mouse inbred strains: towards understanding the molecular basis for behaviour. *Eur.J Neurosci., 19,* 2576-2582.

Gogos, J. A., Morgan, M., Luine, V., Santha, M., Ogawa, S., Pfaff, D. et al. (1998). Catechol-O-methyltransferase-deficient mice exhibit sexually dimorphic changes in catecholamine levels and behavior. *Proceedings of the National Academy of Sciences of the United States of America, 95,* 9991-9996.

Green, A. I., Zimmet, S. V., Strous, R. D., and Schildkraut, J. J. (1999). Clozapine for comorbid substance use disorder and schizophrenia: do patients with schizophrenia have a reward-deficiency syndrome that can be ameliorated by clozapine? *Harv.Rev.Psychiatry, 6,* 287-296.

Hare, R. D. (1986). Twenty years of experience with the Cleckley psychopath. In W. H. Reid, D. Dorr, J. I. Walker, and J. W. I. Bonner (Eds.), *Unmasking the Psychopath. Antisocial Personality and Related Syndromes.* (pp. 3-27). New York: W. W. Norton and Company.

Hare, R. D. (1996). Psychopathy and antisocial personality disorder: a case of diagnostic confusion. *Psychiatric Times, February,* 39-40.

Hart, S. D., Hare, R. D., and Forth, A. E. (1994). Psychopathy as a risk marker for violence: development and validation of a screening version of the revised psychopathy checklist. In J. Monahan and H. J. Steadman (Eds.), *Violence and Mental Disorder. Developments in Risk Assessment* (pp. 81-98). Chicago: The University of Chicago Press.

Hirose, S., Ashby, C. R., Jr., and Mills, M. J. (2001). Effectiveness of ECT combined with risperidone against aggression in schizophrenia. *J.ECT., 17,* 22-26.

Jones, G., Zammit, S., Norton, N., Hamshere, M. L., Jones, S. J., Milham, C. et al. (2001). Aggressive behaviour in patients with schizophrenia is associated with catechol-O-methyltransferase genotype. *British Journal of Psychiatry, 179,* 351-355.

Kane, J. M., Leucht, S., Carpenter, D., and Docherty, J. P. (2003). The expert consensus guideline series. Optimizing pharmacologic treatment of psychotic disorders. *The Journal of Clinical Psychiatry, 64, Suppl. 12,* 1-100.

Kotler, M., Barak, P., Cohen, H., Averbuch, I. E., Grinshpoon, A., Gritsenko, I. et al. (1999). Homicidal behavior in schizophrenia associated with a genetic polymorphism determining low catechol O-methyltransferase (COMT) activity. *Am.J.Med.Genet., 88,* 628-633.

Kunz, M., Yates, K. F., Czobor, P., Rabinowitz, S., Lindenmayer, J. P., and Volavka, J. (2004). Course of patients with histories of aggression and crime after discharge from a cognitive-behavioral program. *Psychiatr.Serv., 55,* 654-659.

Lachman, H. M., Nolan, K. A., Mohr, P., Saito, T., and Volavka, J. (1998). Association between catechol O-methyltransferase genotype and violence in schizophrenia and schizoaffective disorder. *American Journal of Psychiatry, 155,* 835-837.

Lachman, H. M., Papolos, D. F., Saito, T., Yu, Y.-M., Szumlanski, C. L., and Weinshilboum, R. M. (1996). Human catechol-O-methyltransferase pharmacogenetics: description of a functional polymorphism and its potential application to neuropsychiatric disorders. *Pharmacogenetics, 6,* 243-250.

Lindenmayer, J.-P. and Kotsaftis, A. (2000). Use of sodium valproate in violent and aggressive behaviors: a critical review. *Journal of Clinical Psychiatry, 61,* 123-128.

Lindqvist, P. and Allebeck, P. (1990). Schizophrenia and assaultive behaviour: the role of alcohol and drug abuse. *Acta Psychiatrica Scandinavica, 82,* 191-195.

Mednick, S. A., Gabrielli, W. F., Jr., and Hutchings, B. (1983). Genetic influence in criminal behavior: evidence from an adoption cohort. In K.T.Van Dusen and S. A. Mednick (Eds.), *Prospective Studies of Crime and Delinquency* (pp. 39-56). Boston: Kluwer-Nijhoff Publishing.

Mednick, S. A., Gabrielli, W. F., Jr., and Hutchings, B. (1984). Genetic influences in criminal convictions: evidence from an adoption cohort. *Science, 224,* 891-894.

Mednick, S. A. and Kandel, E. (1988). Genetic and perinatal factors in violence. In T.E.Moffitt and S. A. Mednick (Eds.), *Biological Contributions to Crime Causation* (pp. 121-131). Dordrecht: Martinus Nijhoff Publishers.

Mednick, S. A., Pollock, V. E., Volavka, J., and Gabrielli, W. F., Jr. (1982). Biology and violence. In M.E.Wolfgang and N. A. Weiner (Eds.), *Criminal Violence* (4 ed., pp. 21-80). Beverly Hills: Sage Publications.

Mednick, S. A. and Volavka, J. (1980). Biology of crime. In N.Morris and M. Tonry (Eds.), *Crime and Justice: An Annual Review of Research* (pp. 85-158). Chicago: The University of Chicago Press.

Nolan, K. A., Czobor, P., Roy, B. B., Platt, M. M., Shope, C. B., Citrome, L. L. et al. (2003). Characteristics of assaultive behavior among psychiatric inpatients. *Psychiatr.Serv., 54,* 1012-1016.

Nolan, K. A., Volavka, J., Mohr, P., and Czobor, P. (1999). Psychopathy and violent behavior among patients with schizophrenia or schizoaffective disorder. *Psychiatric Services, 50,* 787-792.

Regier, D. A., Farmer, M. E., Rae, D. S., Locke, B. Z., Keith, S. J., Judd, L. L. et al. (1990). Comorbidity of mental disorders with alcohol and other drug abuse. Results from the Epidemiologic Catchment Area (ECA) Study. *JAMA, 264,* 2511-2518.

Rujescu, D., Giegling, I., Gietl, A., Hartmann, A. M., and Moller, H. J. (2003). A functional single nucleotide polymorphism (V158M) in the COMT gene is associated with aggressive personality traits. *Biol.Psychiatry, 54,* 34-39.

Segal, S. P. (2001). Effectiveness of involuntary outpatient commitment. *American Journal of Psychiatry, 158,* 654-656.

Sheppard, G. P. (1979). High-dose propranolol in schizophrenia. *British Journal of Psychiatry, 134,* 470-476.

Sorgi, P. J., Ratey, J. J., and Polakoff, S. (1986). Beta-adrenergic blockers for the control of aggressive behaviors in patients with chronic schizophrenia. *American Journal of Psychiatry, 143,* 775-776.

Steadman, H. J., Gounis, K., Dennis, D., Hopper, K., Roche, B., Swartz, M. et al. (2001). Assessing the New York City involuntary outpatient commitment pilot program. *Psychiatr.Serv., 52,* 330-336.

Strous, R. D., Bark, N., Parsia, S. S., Volavka, J., and Lachman, H. M. (1997). Analysis of a functional catechol O-methyltransferase gene polymorphism in schizophrenia: evidence for association with aggressive and antisocial behavior. *Psychiatry Research, 69,* 71-77.

Strous, R. D., Nolan, K. A., Lapidus, R., Diaz, L., Saito, T., and Lachman, H. M. (2003). Aggressive behavior in schizophrenia is associated with the low enzyme activity COMT polymorphism: A replication study. *Am.J.Med.Genet., 120B,* 29-34.

Swanson, J. W. (1994). Mental disorder, substance abuse, and community violence: an epidemiological approach. In J.Monahan and H. J. Steadman (Eds.), *Violence and Mental Disorder. Developments in Risk Assessment* (pp. 101-136). Chicago: The University of Chicago Press.

Swanson, J. W., Holzer, C. E., Ganju, V. K., and Jono, R. T. (1990). Violence and psychiatric disorder in the community: evidence from the Epidemiologic Catchment Area surveys. *Hospital and Community Psychiatry, 41,* 761-770.

Swanson, J. W., Swartz, M. S., Borum, R., Hiday, V. A., Wagner, H. R., and Burns, B. J. (2000). Involuntary out-patient commitment and reduction of violent behaviour in persons with severe mental illness . *Br.J.Psychiatry, 176,* 324-331.

Swartz, M. S., Swanson, J. W., Hiday, V. A., Borum, R., Wagner, H. R., and Burns, B. J. (1998a). Violence and severe mental illness: the effects of substance abuse and nonadherence to medication. *American Journal of Psychiatry, 155,* 226-231.

Swartz, M. S., Swanson, J. W., Hiday, V. A., Borum, R., Wagner, R., and Burns, B. J. (1998b). Taking the wrong drugs: the role of substance abuse and medication noncompliance in violence among severely mentally ill individuals. *Soc Psychiatry Psychiatr Epidemiol, 33 Suppl 1,* S75-S80.

Swartz, M. S., Swanson, J. W., Wagner, H. R., Burns, B. J., and Hiday, V. A. (2001). Effects of involuntary outpatient commitment and depot antipsychotics on treatment adherence in persons with severe mental illness. *J Nerv.Ment.Dis., 189,* 583-592.

Swartz, M. S., Swanson, J. W., Wagner, H. R., Burns, B. J., Hiday, V. A., and Borum, R. (1999). Can involuntary outpatient commitment reduce hospital recidivism?: Findings from a randomized trial with severely mentally ill individuals. *American Journal of Psychiatry, 156,* 1968-1975.

Szmukler, G. and Hotopf, M. (2001). Effectiveness of involuntary outpatient commitment. *American Journal of Psychiatry, 158,* 653-654.

Valzelli, L., Giacalone, E., and Garattini, S. (1967). Pharmacological control of aggressive behavior in mice. *European Journal of Pharmacology, 2,* 144-146.

Vartiainen, H., Tiihonen, J., Putkonen, A., Koponen, H., Virkkunen, M., Hakola, P. et al. (1995). Citalopram, a selective serotonin reuptake inhibitor, in the treatment of aggression in schizophrenia. *Acta Psychiatrica Scandinavica, 91,* 348-351.

Volavka, J. (2002). *Neurobiology of Violence.* (2 ed.) Washington, DC: American Psychiatric Publishing, Inc.

Volavka, J., Czobor, P., Nolan, K., Sheitman, B., Lindenmayer, J. P., Citrome, L. et al. (2004a). Overt aggression and psychotic symptoms in patients with schizophrenia treated with clozapine, olanzapine, risperidone, or haloperidol. *J Clin.Psychopharmacol., 24,* 225-228.

Volavka, J., Kennedy, J. L., Ni, X., Czobor, P., Nolan, K., Sheitman, B. et al. (2004b). COMT158 polymorphism and hostility. *Am J Med.Genet., 127B,* 28-29.

Whitman, J. R., Maier, G. J., and Eichelman, B. (1987). Beta-adrenergic blockers for aggressive behavior in schizophrenia [letter]. *American Journal of Psychiatry, 144,* 538-539.

Yates, K., Kunz, M., Czobor, P., Rabinowitz, S., Lindenmayer, J.P., Volavka, J. (2005) A cognitive, behaviorally based program for patients with persistent mental illness and a history of aggression, crime, or both: Structure and correlates of completers of the program. *J Am Acad Psychiatry Law,33:214-222.*

Yorkston, N. J., Zaki, S. A., Pitcher, D. R., Gruzelier, J. H., Hollander, D., and Sergeant, H. G. (1977). Propranolol as an adjunct to the treatment of schizophrenia. *Lancet, 2,* 575-578.

In: Crime and Schizophrenia: Causes and Cures
Editor: Adrian Raine, pp. 315-334

ISBN 1-59454-609-6

Appendix

THE MAURITIUS CHILD HEALTH PROJECT: ITS ORIGINS, PROCEDURES, ETHICAL ISSUES, AND OUTCOME

P. H. Venables[1], A. Raine [2], S. A. Mednick[3], F. Schulsinger[4] and C. Dalais[5]

[1]Department of Psychology, University of York, Heslington, York YO10 5DD, UK.
[2]Department of Psychology, University of Southern California, Los Angeles, USA
[3]Social Science Research Institute, University of Southern California, Los Angeles USA
[4]Psykologisk Institut Kommunehospitalet Copenhagen
[5] Joint Child Health Project, Mauritius

INTRODUCTION

The aim of this appendix is to provide a description of the Mauritius Child Health Project[1] which was started in 1972. The project is described here as it is a study which exemplifies some of the difficulties in conducting longitudinal studies where aspects of investigation which are thought to be important change over time and also where the opportunities for conducting such studies have been changed from almost complete lack of laboratory computer facilities to the present where much of the work relies directly on their presence. Also of importance are the ethical issues which arise in carrying out a longitudinal project, which are unique to this kind of work and have changed since its inception.

[1] Known locally and by the Mauritian Government as the Joint Child Health Project.

ORIGINS

The background for the Mauritius Project was Mednick and Schulsinger's study (Mednick and Schulsinger, 1968) on children at high risk for schizophrenia started in Copenhagen in 1962 which identified a high-risk group as the children of schizophrenic mothers. Following this study a WHO Scientific Group on Neurophysiological Research in Psychiatry (WHO, 1968) met in 1967 with the aim of seeing how far neurophysiological methods and results could be applied to further high risk studies. It was from the recommendations of this group that the Mauritius study was initiated. The WHO Group outlined the advantages of examining high risk individuals in early childhood. These were (a) the subjects would not have experienced exposure to psychotropic drugs, (b) researchers and informants would, with appropriate safeguards, not know who was at risk and (c) the information collected on social, familial and developmental aspects would not be retrospective. An important part of the report, as far as the Mauritius study is concerned stated (*p*. 23):

> Three-year old high risk subjects and controls could be brought together in nursery schools, drugs could be used to bring their autonomic functions within the normal range and learning techniques to help them in their social interactions. The efficacy of these measures could be evaluated in the nursery schools and by future performance at school

Later (*p*. 24) it was proposed that there should be experimental and control groups so that half the high-risk (and the low-risk) subjects should be exposed to the interventions outlined above and half should not, thereby giving the possibility of measuring the efficacy of the interventions. Following this (*p*. 27), the value of transcultural studies was introduced:

> The stresses imposed on an organism, for example by rapid economic changes as well as by poverty and by malnutrition can be studied best in the developing countries

It was also pointed out that by setting up such a study in a developing country its own services might be enhanced and that these might include provision of educational facilities as well as health services. Two difficulties were however recognized. One was whether, in a developing country, adequate records would exist to enable high risk subjects to be genetically identified and secondly whether there was application of established diagnostic tools which would allow standardised assessment both of parents to allow high risk determination, and of offspring for eventual evaluation of the research.

The Copenhagen study was based on a theory which suggested the existence of differences in Aarousal between low and high risk groups (Mednick, 1958). In consequence, putitative indices of Aarousal (skin conductance and heart rate) were included in the measurements made in the 1962 Copenhagen study. Most use has subsequently been made of skin conductanc (Mednick (1967) and Mednick and Schulsinger (1968) described how the high risk group could be differentiated from the control group (children of normal mothers) on indices derived from skin conductance measures. This evidence suggesting that persons at risk for schizophrenia could, in part, be differentiated from those not at risk by a relatively simple biological measure inspired the idea that the Mauritius study should be based, not as in former studies on genetic status, but on the basis of a biologically measured variable (see

Venables, (1993) for a review on the use of electrodermal indices as risk markers for schizophrenia). The difficulty of the availability of adequate psychiatric records in a developing country could thus be overcome.

In summary, therefore, the points arising out of the Scientific Group's 1968 report which were to form the basis for the Mauritian study were: (a) the conduct of the study in a developing country, (b) the initial investigation on 3-year-olds, (c) the establishment of nursery schools as settings for the study of the children, and (d) the use of psychophysiological methods as a possible means of identifying children at risk.

One particular issue which arises with this study is that in 1972 when the project started, common practice concerning ethical issues was significantly different from that to-day. Curran(1977) for instance identifies 1973 as the time in the United States when ethical means of regulating the use of human subjects in medical and psychological investigation were replaced by legal controls. It is thus particularly important to describe the ethical principles under which various stages of the study were undertaken. When the study was commenced in 1972 in the context of the ethical principles set down by the Nuremberg Code (Nuremberg, 1949) and the Declaration of Helsinki (World Medical Association, 1964). One basic requirement of the Helsinki Declaration of 1964 is that the research should be carried out by Ascientifically qualified persons and under the supervision of a qualified medical man (*sic*) (Basic principle 2). The project was supervised by two psychiatrists; Schulsinger from Copenhagen and Raman from Mauritius and carried out by psychologists. It was continued until 1988 in accordance with the revisions of the Declaration of Helsinki (World Medical Association, 1975 and 1983).

The initial priming grant to assess the feasibility of the study was made by WHO in 1969. In a reply to Schulsinger from Lebedev (the then Chief of Mental Health in Geneva) welcoming the proposals for the study (and which were those which eventually the project followed closely), no mention was made of the application of any ethical principles. The study was welcomed because *inter alia* it would lead to the improvement of care of the children and education in Mauritius (Lebedev, 1969). From 1972 to 1988 the project was supported by a series of UK grants to Venables, for which there were no additional specific ethical requirements. However two research components were supported by U.S. funds, one on the study of cognitive status of the 3-year-old subjects with a grant (in 1972) to Sutton Smith from the National Association of Mental Health, again for which no special ethical requirements were laid down. The second component was neuropsychological work conducted in 1986/7 with a grant to Venables from the Schizophrenia Research Program of Scottish Rite (U.S.). For approval of this work, an Ethical Committee had to be set up and this committee duly approved the research. After 1988, when the study was supported by U.S. funds granted to Raine, it was conducted in accordance with the ethical requirements of the Belmont report (Belmont 1979). By this time the Arising tide of legal and ethical concerns (Curran, 1977, p. 65) had changed the ethical climate from that prevailing in 1972.

A part of the suggestion made by the WHO Scientific Group (p. 23) was that by bringing 3-year-old children together in a nursery school, procedures (medication and biofeedback) could be used as primary prevention of schizophrenia. The use of medication was dropped at an early stage in planning the study as it was thought that insufficient was known about the efficacy of drugs to modify autonomic status on a long term basis or their possible detrimental side effects. It is noteworthy that no mention was made in the WHO Scientific

Group report (1968) of any objection to the use of drugs in the research design which had been proposed. In 1972 the issue of the control of autonomic activity by instrumental conditioning was itself the concern of workers in the field (see for instance Dworkin and Miller, 1974) and it seemed unwise to base a long-term study on such methods. Hence, the proposal to attempt to control autonomic status was also dropped. However, apart from technical considerations, both procedures were thought to be contrary to Basic Principle 5 (World Medical Association 1964) which stated that: "Special caution should be exercised by the doctor in performing clinical research in which the personality of the subject is liable to be altered by drugs or experimental procedures" and which was the international ethical standard current at the time.

However, it is still important to note that the initial aim of the study, which would distinguish it from the Copenhagen and other high risk studies, was that it was conceptualized as an investigation of the possibility of primary prevention of schizophrenia and not merely as another high risk study. However, a WHO working group (WHO, 1977) which met to consider the possibility of primary prevention in high risk groups reached the conclusion (*p*. 87) that there are no data from controlled intervention studies that would provide an indication of which interventions, if any, are helpful to either the children at risk or their parents. The proposal to place some of the children in the study in nursery schools was therefore left as only a possibly prophylactic intervention. The purpose of placing children in the nursery schools was thus two-fold. First, to enable their behaviour to be observed and second, that location in special nursery schools in contrast to that normally available in Mauritius might act as a primary preventative agent against later psychiatric breakdown (Mednick, Venables, Schulsinger, Dalais, and Van Dusen, 1984, *p*. 74). The nature of this possible intervention was not unitary as it involved betterment in education, enhanced physical activity and better nutrition. These factors were not capable of separation. The nursery schools were set up on the best Scandinavian educational practice and the nature of the experiment was exposure of the children to the whole nursery experience and not to specific aspects of it. Nevertheless, in that there was a control group, matched to the nursery school group and not exposed to the experimental group's experience, the study can be considered experimentally interventive.

It is here that the ethical issues concerned in such intervention need to be considered. If the placement of the children in the nursery schools was indeed to be considered as intervention based on scientifically established facts, (World Medical Association 1964, Basic principles (1)), then the intervention might not be considered as in accord with the ethical code because technically its efficacy in reducing the prevalence of schizotypy or schizophrenia was not a scientific fact at that time. However, the 3rd and 4th basic principles also state that research cannot be carried out unless the importance of the objective is in proportion to the inherent risk to the subject and that there should be careful assessment of the inherent risks in comparison to the foreseeable benefits to the subjects and to others. In this instance it was considered that there was no risk but only potential benefit in placing the subjects in the nursery schools. It is perhaps also noteworthy that at this time "head start" programmes of special education were taking place and these were not the subject of ethical objection. Furthermore, there would be benefit to others in that the Project's nursery school might be an example to education in Mauritius stimulating the setting up of further similar schools. This was in accordance with the statement of the WHO scientific group (WHO, 1968) (*p*. 30) : "the inclusion of suitable centres in the developing countries in collaborative research programmes would provide an important contribution to general knowledge as well as to local facilities". The training of 14 Mauritians as nursery school teachers as part of the programme did in fact lead to the expansion of pre-school facilities in Mauritius.

Setting

The project took place in Mauritius because Dr. Raman, the then Medical Director of the Brown Sequard Hospital in Mauritius, had contacted WHO and suggested that Mauritius might be a suitable place in which to conduct the proposed work. It appeared to offer a better chance of success than India which had been suggested in the WHO report (WHO, 1968, p.33) because the island's limited area would permit subjects to be contacted more readily than in the less restricted context of India. Mauritius is an island nation which gained independence from British rule in 1968. In 1972 it had a population of approximately 0.75 million which has increased to1.2 million by 2000. It lies in the Indian Ocean just inside the tropic of Capricorn and extends 38 miles (61 km) from north to south and 29 miles (47 km) from east to west. Mauritius has a multi-racial society and its ethnic distribution was in 1970; 68.7% of Indian origin, 25.7% of 'General Population', 1.8% Chinese, 0.1% English, 0.1% French, and 3.6% other. The Indian group is comprised largely of descendants of indented labour brought to the island by the British after the abolition of slavery in 1835 (Bowman, 1991). The term 'General Population' is a term used officially to represent those known locally as creoles who are largely descendants of slaves brought to the island by the French between 1670 and 1810 from Madagascar, the East African Coast, West Africa and India (Barker, 1996; Filliot, 1974). The majority of the population speak kreol or patois créole, a francophone creole language. However, at the time of the initiation of the project (and largely still today), teaching in the schools was mainly in French and English, with tests and examinations being in English. The official government language was and remains English. Many of the Indian origin population in addition to kreol speak a variety of creole derivatives of Indian languages.

Preparation for the Project

Schulsinger travelled to Mauritius in 1969 and laid the foundation of the study. In a report of the meetings which were held it was suggested that approximately 2000, 3-year-old children should be studied. Every child in Mauritius is vaccinated at 14 months and it was established that the Vaccination Register held the names, birth places and birth dates of children together with their father's profession and mother's name. Thus there was the possibility of creating a sample of children representative of the population. The sample of children studied was to be drawn from two adjacent large towns each with 40,000 to 50,000 inhabitants, where it was proposed to set up the nursery schools. The ethnic distribution in these towns was representative of the total island. A laboratory was set up close to the schools.

It was also decided to collect birth records and it was established that this was possible in a reasonable number of cases. This proposal was included because work in Copenhagen had shown that obstetric complications were a potentially important predictor of later mental health and also criminality (Mednick, 1970).

In May 1969 Mednick, Schulsinger and Raman made an application for a grant to WHO elaborating on the suggestions made above. They stated to WHO that in planning the research design:

1. While maintaining a goal of cross-cultural research compatibility, the research plan should make use of information gathered in the Danish study and other recent research.
2. The research plan should reflect awareness of the cultural diversity of the people of Mauritius. In the light of this awareness, culture bound techniques of research (particularly those which are heavily verbal) should be eschewed in favour of more culture free methods of investigation e.g., psychophysiology.

At the outset it was, of course, difficult to predict the outcome of the study starting at age 3 and with an anticipated completion at age 25. This period was foreseen as the minimum in which it would be possible to have access to at least the peak of those succumbing with schizophrenia. There was a necessity to examine about 2,000 children in one year so as to start the study with a constrained age range but with the aim of obtaining a workable sample of patients to examine at completion. With an incidence of 1% of schizophrenic breakdowns in the general population (Rosenthal, 1967, *p*. 19) only 20 patients might be expected and this would be attenuated with an anticipated completion of the study at age 25 given that continued breakdowns would be anticipated in further years. Furthermore, differences might be expected in the incidence and course of the disease in Mauritius as a developing country (Murphy and Raman, 1971; Murphy, 1994) which might further attenuate the numbers of breakdowns expected. Even if autonomic indicators were successful in identifying at risk subjects, these would be drawn from the anticipated 20 in the overall sample. The hope was that successful identification would mean that these subjects would be confined to the experimental group to be allocated to the nursery schools and to their matched controls. Because of the anticipation of this limited outcome and the cost both in finance and in effort of running such a long term project, it became appropriate that other outcomes with higher base rates be investigated during the course of the project, although this was not included in the original proposals. One, close to the originally anticipated outcome of schizophrenia, was the identification of participants with high levels of schizotypy. Larger numbers of subjects with characteristics analogous to those of schizophrenia might thus be expected. A schizotypy scale suitable for use in the Mauritian context was therefore developed (Venables, 1990; Venables, Wilkins, Mitchell, Raine, and Bailes, 1990). Later, the scale developed to measure DSM Schizotypal Personality Disorder, SPQ (Raine, 1991) which was shown to be appropriate in Mauritius (Reynolds, Raine, Mellingen, Venables, and Mednick, 2000) was used. Other outcomes with higher base rates investigated subsequently were antisocial behaviour, criminality, alcoholism and drug abuse.

In August 1969 WHO agreed that the proposal was an important one but was able to allocate only $4,000 towards the project. In a report to WHO in 1970, Schulsinger stated that an application had been made to the Danish State Department for Technical Collaboration with Developing Counties for a grant to establish and run two nursery schools and in April 1970 this had been granted.

At this time Mednick and Schulsinger contacted Venables at the University of London about the possibility of his cooperation in the project and with the proposal that he might apply for British funds to support the work. In 1971 Venables was granted funds by the British Medical Research Council (MRC) to undertake the psychophysiological examination of 2,000 three-year-old-children. Funds for converting a building for a laboratory were made available from Danish sources and much support was provided by the Ministry of Health in Mauritius by the secondment of a civil servant who with an assistant looked after the recruitment of the children. The Government also provided transport for the children. The Project was joined by Sutton-Smith, a developmental psychologist from New York who was funded by the Ford Foundation and the National Association for Mental Health (U.S.), to carry out cognitive tests on the children. The measurement of some indices which might be related to malnutrition was also implemented by asking local doctors to assess the health status of the children.

START OF THE PROJECT

The project started in July 1972 with the establishment of a permanent laboratory with Brian Bell as Research Officer. The first few weeks of work threw up problems, not all of which were anticipated. One was working with psychophysiological procedures in a tropical location and with three-year-old children, when there was little background experience with subjects of that age to call on. A review of the then available data on developmental psychophysiology which was subsequently published in 1980 (Venables, 1980) stated in its conclusion that Athere are probably more lacunae in the data than fully satisfactory coverage.

The first pilot trials on the data collection procedures using adults and older children showed that very little electrodermal activity could be elicited using stimuli which had been used in standard procedures in the UK and the U.S. and thus there appeared to be an excess of non-responders. Previous work had shown that electrodermal activity was suppressed when skin temperature was low (Venables and Christie, 1980, *p*. 45) and raising the temperature of the laboratory resulted in the responsivity in adults becoming normal (see Venables, 1978). However, even at that temperature, only 44% of three-year-old children showed responsivity and thus there was a possible confounding of pathological non-responsivity with what might be called developmental non-responsivity. Subsequent work in Mauritius, in a cross sectional study, showed that there was indeed a developmental increase in responsivity (74%, 87%, 95%, 90% and 88% in age groups 5, 10, 15, 20 and 25 years) using exactly identical recording techniques (Venables, 1978; Venables, 1996), thus suggesting that although age 3 had been chosen by the WHO working group (WHO, 1968) as the age with which to start such a study, the technical difficulties to be encountered had not been anticipated. However, by August 1973 psychophysiological data were recorded from 1,795 of the 2,000 children brought to the laboratory and thus a unique set of data were obtained, probably the largest of its type worldwide. A full description of the psychophysiological data are given in (Venables, 1978). Other data collected at the same time included measures of IQ, demographic, obstetric and paediatric information.

The psychophysiological data were all measured by hand from polygraph records and coded on data sheets. The coded data together with those from the other aspects of data collection were sent to London.

SELECTION OF SUBJECTS

The psychophysiological data were punched onto cards and entered into a database on a mainframe computer so that at the end of the testing period in August 1973 selection of subjects could be made. One of the early findings of the work in Denmark, on which the Mauritian study was based, was that children at risk for schizophrenia tended to show electrodermal hyper-responsivity in comparison to low risk children (Mednick and Schulsinger, 1968). In addition it had been shown by the start of the project that among schizophrenic patients, there were in addition to the electrodermal hyper-responders, those who were designated as non-responders who showed no electrodermal responsivity whatsoever (Gruzelier and Venables, 1972). It was therefore decided that in addition to the children who appeared to be at risk due to hyper-responsivity, a further group might be established who had the characteristics of being electrodermal non-responders. It is noteworthy that a later finding from the Danish High-risk study showed that later negative symptom schizophrenia was predicted, in part, by electrodermal hypo-responsivity (Cannon et al., 1990).

A control group was made up of children whose electrodermal responses had median values. Because, eventually it was not possible to fill all the places available in the nursery school and comparison groups with participants from the hyper-responder, median and non-responder categories, a small group of subjects was created whose characteristic was that they had long electrodermal recovery time response patterns. Data were available at the time to show that a long electrodermal recovery time was a characteristic of subjects with criminal attributes (see Siddle, Mednick, Nicol, and Foggitt, 1976, for a later study and review of this area). The criteria to establish groups of electrodermal hyper-responders, non-responders, long recoverers and median responders are provided in Venables (1978).

Stratified random sampling was conducted to select which 100 children drawn from the autonomically defined groups (also chosen to be equally representative of gender and ethnic status) would enter the two nursery schools and which 100 matched to them would remain as community controls continuing through the usual schooling of three-year-olds. The sampling was conducted using random number tables.Telegrams between London and Mauritius proposed subjects to be selected. The parents of those selected on this basis to enter nursery schools were approached and if willing their children were allocated to the nursery schools. In the end the actual numbers in groups was not completely balanced due to recruitment difficulties; the numbers of electrodermally selected children in each school and control group are given in Venables, et al., (1978, table 5, *p*. 287). At no stage were parents of the matched 100 control children or those from the 1,600 remaining approached to indicate that their children were not selected. It was therefore hoped that the potentially negative aspect of not being selected for a potential benefit was minimized.

Longitudinal research of the type we have conducted raises several interesting and important ethical issues that potentially impact many developmental research programs.

Issues include whether to intervene on risk factors assessed, the restriction of beneficial procedures to one group and not others, and the retrospective application of current ethical requirements to past research.

Regarding the first issue, it is perhaps particularly important to introduce the assessment of malnutrition in that recent findings from the Mauritius study have shown that the benefits of exposure to nursery school experience are greatest in those subjects who were showing signs of malnutrition at the time of the original age 3 testing (Raine, Mellingen, Liu, Venables, and Mednick, 2003), and that malnutrition increases the risk for later externalizing behaviour (Liu et al., 2004). It could be argued that it is not ethical to assess a risk factor for later pathology such as malnutrition, and not act to remediate it. Such an argument has its basis in the 1932-1974 Tuskegee study in which African-Americans with syphilis went untreated in order to learn more about the natural course of this disease.

In the case of our assessment of malnutrition, a number of important considerations need to be taken into account. First, selection for the nursery school was not made on the basis of signs of malnutrition. Second, at the inception of the study the investigators were in fact informed by the Mauritian Ministry of Health that there was no malnutrition on the island and that all that might be observed was mild hypoprotenaemia. Because of this, the local doctors who examined the children at age 3 were not asked to code cases of malnutrition but were instead asked to rate certain features such as condition of hair and skin. Together with measures of height and weight, these variables were used to provide measures of nutritional status on which the findings of Raine, Mellingen, Liu, Venables, and Mednick, (2003), Liu et al. (2004), and Venables et al. (this volume), were based. Consequently, these analyses essentially made use of retrospectively collected incidental data to create a construct of "malnutrition" that was not formally assessed as a clinical construct at the time.

Third, it is important to emphasise that unlike the Tuskegee study, treatment for malnutrition was not withheld from one group or another. The nursery school children did not receive any specific or special treatment to alleviate their malnutrition but in this respect are no different from both the matched control group, or indeed the remainder of the project's population and the general population of Mauritius at that time. The better nutrition which the nursery school children did receive happened to be an integral part of the good practice adopted in those schools.

Fourth and importantly, any child in the total sample of 1,795 who was found in the pediatric examination to have significant clinical problems of any kind, was referred to appropriate agencies (Bell, 1977). In the specific case of malnutrition, the child was also referred to programmes which were operated at the time, including the Save the Children Fund. Medical aid was also given for scabies and parasitic worm infections for which referrals were made to the appropriate hospital department (see Bell, 1977, *p.* 26). Consequently, there were significant benefits from the study not only to the participants, but also to a larger population of children that were never included in the experimental and control groups. Given these contextual factors, assessment of indicators of malnutrition in this study was ethically appropriate.

Nevertheless, this issue raises intriguing ethical issues. Are researchers who collect data on putative risk factors for psychopathology ethically obliged to remediate these factors as soon as they are uncovered? For example, are they duty-bound to correct for low intelligence, poor parenting, social adversity, smoking during pregnancy, and birth complications given knowledge from past studies that they are at least linked to later psychopathology? To attempt to do so might, in practice, be impossible and certainly impossible in the short term. However, even if they were to do so successfully, would this not undermine the whole purpose of the study (to assess whether or not a specific early condition increases the probability of a specific later psychopathology) and thus make null and void the scientific benefits of the study to society? Furthermore, it would become in theory impossible to research risk factors for later psychopathology as they would all be remediated. Would funding agencies be required to provide coverage of the significant cost of such remediative efforts?

The second issue concerns the selection of one group, but not others, to benefit from a given treatment. Is it ethical to withhold the putative beneficial treatment to all groups? It was after all only tentatively felt at the time that environmental enrichment might be effective in reducing psychopathology. In addition, funding limitations restricted the number of children who could received the early environmental enrichment. Certainly, providing the enrichment to all children would result in no control group and the inability to assess the effectiveness of the prevention program. More importantly, at that point in time no research study had demonstrated the effectiveness of this type of prevention program for the long-term reduction in crime or schizotypal personality. It is important to distinguish studies which attempt intervention on the basis of tenable theory, on the basis of preliminary findings or for the definite establishment of preliminary practice. The extent to which proposed research falls under one or other of these categories, not only influences the extent to which it is valuable but also the extent to which different treatment of experimental and control groups might be thought desirable or not. It is also important to differentiate this community study from clinical drug trials in which a patient with a specific clinical condition is assigned to one of a number of treatment regimens. In the case of the Mauritius study, pathological behaviour was neither assessed nor used to assign subjects to groups. The stratified random sampling was instead based on psychophysiological functioning, and in 1972 there was very limited scientific knowledge on the significance of these putative risk factors for early detection and prevention, particularly in non-Western cultures.

The third issue concerns the retrospective application of current ethical requirements to past research. Ethical research standards have changed significantly in the past 30 years, and what was acceptable 30 years ago would not always be acceptable today. More concretely, in 1972 informed consent from the parents of the children was obtained verbally, whereas today written informed consent would be expected except under certain circumstances. In fact, in the context of the research started in Mauritius in 1972 less than half the parents in the study were literate and able to give written consent. The question must arise as to whether it would be permissible to carry out research in 2005 on a population who were unable, because they were illiterate, to give written consent to take part in an otherwise acceptable study although it would have been possible in a population who were literate.

Continuation of the Project (1973-1978)

After the initial assessment and selection of subjects, the project was joined by Cyril Dalais, a Mauritian educational psychologist. During the next two years grants were obtained from the MRC which allowed the psychophysiological retesting of the 100 selected subjects and their 100 matched controls on 4 occasions, and observation of the nursery school children at play using standardised instruments. The grant also allowed the psychophysiological testing of a factorially balanced sample of 640 subjects at ages 5, 10, 15, 20 and 25 years using exactly the same techniques as those used earlier so as to provide a cross-sectional view of the development of skin conductance and heart rate. This provided a set of data to compare with the longitudinal data which would be collected from the prime population as they developed. The results of this cross-sectional study are provided in Venables and Mitchell, (1996).

Further data on the main group of subjects was collected when they were aged 8 in 1978/9. The Rutter's Childrens Behaviour Questionnaire (Rutter 1967) was completed by the childrens' Primary School Teachers. In 1976, Dr. R. Q. Bell of the University of Virginia visited the project for one month as a WHO Consultant. Among other things Dr. Bell recommended that there should be few follow-ups of the children in order to minimize the biasing effect of repeated contact and to permit concentration of efforts on crucial phases of psychosocial development. One such phase is the pre-adolescent period. If that phase is selected, it is recommended that the children be studied in special vacation camps.

Continuation of the Project (1979-1987)

In the light of Dr. Bell's comments, at age 11 a major follow-up study was planned and carried out by Venables and Dalais. This study was timed to take place when according to local data almost all the subjects would still be pre-pubertal and to be just after a major qualifying examination had been taken which would allow some children to enter the best secondary schools. It was decided that the setting of the study should be an Educational Camp. This allowed the children to take part in educational projects and thus permitted them to be absent from their schools for a week during term time with the consent of their parents and the school authorities. As per Dr. Bell's suggestion, this gave the opportunity for psychosocial development to be assessed, cognitive testing conducted and for further psychophysiological data to be collected. Children attended the Camp in a large bungalow at the seaside for a week in groups of 16. Five members of staff were appointed to look after the children and to prepare food for them. Psychophysiological data collected at this time included skin conductance, EKG, EEG, cortical evoked potentials and smooth pursuit eye movement. Cognitive measures included WISC indices, the Holborn Reading test and the Trail Making test.

This work was supported by the Mauritian government and also grants from both the Wellcome Foundation and the Leverhulme Trust (U.K.). Psychophysiological data were collected on 1,150 subjects. The children were transported back to the original laboratory in groups of four for psychophysiological testing, thus ensuring that psychophysiological assessment was undertaken in an environment which was familiar to them. During this time, mothers were visited by a social worker who recorded ratings of their children's behaviour using the Achenbach Child Behavior Checklist (Achenbach and Edelbrock, 1983) and also supplied up-to-date demographic data. If the parent expressed any worry about the child's health at that time, he/she was referred to the appropriate agency. The fact that data were not collected on all the 1,795 original subjects was largely due to two factors. The first was that a major cyclone had dispersed some of the original families and tracing them was difficult, while the second was that at the end of the grant support period, when not all testing had been completed, it was no longer possible to continue to use the building housing the educational camp and to fund research staff.

During this phase of the project consent was obtained from parents for their children to live away from home for a week in a mixed sex situation. Parents were invited to come to the camp with their children and to see the facilities available and to meet the teaching, domestic and research staff running the camp. They only were invited to allow their children to participate if they were completely satisfied with the conditions at the Camp.They were informed that we were continuing to study the health of their children. In this instance permission was also sought from the education authorities to take the children out of their normal schools and was obtained because the Camp was considered educational.

The psychophysiological data collected during this period were recorded on magnetic tape and sent to U.K. for analysis. One of the lessons learned here was that although programs for the analysis of skin conductance were available, the process of analysis took much longer than anticipated. Programs were not then readily available for the analysis of the remainder of the psychophysiological data and had to be written specially. Thus usable data were not available until several years after data collection. As a result of this experience it was decided that there should be no further major collection of psychophysiological data until it could be analysed on the spot and sent to the U.K. or U.S. in a form ready to incorporate directly into databases.

With this in mind, the next major collection of data was carried out in 1986/7 when the subjects had a mean age of 17.2 years. In addition to a schizotypy questionnaire (Venables, 1990; Venables, Wilkins, Mitchell, Raine, and Bailes, 1990) and the Revised Behaviour Problem Checklist (Quay and Peterson, 1987), the assessment included a battery of neuropsychological tests (Bartfai, Levander, Nyback, Berggren, and Schalling, 1985; Levander, 1987) collected using the Apple II computer. This choice was made because a series of tests was then available for this computer and had not yet been implemented on IBM Personal Computers which had only just become available. The output of the Apple computer could not be entered directly into the Project's database without conversion to MSDOS which was then becoming the standard in the field and thus involved time consuming transcription. The tests used were the Span of Apprehension (Asarnow, Nuechterlein, and Marder, 1983) and the Continuous Performance Tests (Cornblatt, Lenzenweger, and Erlenmeyer-Kimling, 1989). Support for this work was provided by the Mental Health Foundation (UK) and the Schizophrenia Research Program of Scottish Rite (U.S.). For approval of this work an Ethical Committee had to be set up, which duly approved the research.

At this point Venables reached retirement age and the running of the project was taken over by Raine working from Los Angeles. However, in order that this handover be conducted successfully, Venables spent the first year of retirement writing a full documentation of the database with support of a Leverhulme Emeritus Fellowship.

CONTINUATION OF STUDY 1988 - PRESENT

With Raine's involvement in the study from 1987, its scope widened from an emphasis on the development of schizophrenia and schizotypy to cover factors involved in the development of alcoholism and drug abuse and crime and delinquency. This conceptual shift was made possible by the fact that many of the earlier etiological processes that are of relevance to understanding schizophrenia and assessed in the early phases of the project, e.g. electrodermal activity, birth complications, malnutrition, IQ, neuropsychological test data, have also been found to relate to antisocial and violent behaviour (Raine and Venables, 1984; Raine, Brennan, and Mednick, 1994; Moffitt, 1990; Raine, 1993). A grant from the National Institute of Mental Health (NIMH) from 1990-1993 made possible the collection of data on self-report crime, schizotypal personality, depression, alcohol use, and demographic/ psychosocial variables from over 1,300 of the original subjects, together with official crime data on all 1,795 subjects. The main goal of this study was to assess early factors that predispose to later crime and violence.

Work was also conducted on drug and alcohol abuse. A grant from the National Institute of Alcoholism and Alcohol Abuse (NIAAA) has resulted in diagnostic assessment for alcohol and drug abuse, again with the aim of understanding the etiology of alcoholism. Recent funding from both the National Institute of Child Health and Development (NICHD) and NIMH is also allowing for a study on the intergenerational transmission of antisocial behaviour. In this study, the three-year-old offspring of the original subjects who were tested in 1972/3 are being brought back to the laboratory. Measures of parenting are also taken in addition to the assessment of marital conflict.

To capitalise on the work already done, considerable effort was now been made to derive measures from the data that had been gathered previously to enable hypotheses to be answered more easily. The data from the Boehm test of Basic Concepts (Boehm, 1986) which had been collected at age 3 were reanalysed and it was shown that reliable measures of verbal and spatial IQ could be derived. The child's behaviour during psychophysiological and cognitive testing was used to produce measures of stimulus seeking, fearlessness, and inhibited – disinhibited temperament. The measures of health and nutritional status made by local doctors were used to provide a scale of malnutrition and demographic measures collected when the children at age 3 were used to construct indices of social economic status and social adversity. The Rutter's Children's Behaviour Questionnaire (Rutter, 1967) which had been completed by teachers when the children were age 8 years was used to provide measures of aggression. Data had been collected at age 11 using the Child Behavior Checklist (CBCL) (Achenbach and Edelbrock, 1983) and this was used to construct indices of aggressive and non-aggressive forms of antisocial behaviour. With the use of these indices together with the psychophysiological data collected at age 3 and at age 11, it was possible to conduct a series of analyses which used age 3 status to predict to behaviour at age 11. Later data from the Revised Behavior Problem Checklist (Quay and Peterson, 1987) were used to provide scales of conduct disorder and psychotic behaviour at age 17.

SUMMARY OF FINDINGS

It will be remembered that the original intention of the study was to examine the possibility of prevention of disorder. However, the elimination due to ethical considerations of intervention by medication or biofeedback modification of autonomic nervous system status left only exposure to nursery school experience as a possible prophylactic measure. Some doubt was felt that this might have a positive effect because experience with the Head Start programmes had (with a few exceptions) shown few lasting positive changes.

One of the first studies to examine the effect of exposure to the nursery school experience and its differential effect in biologically selected groups of children (see *Selection of Subjects* above) is reported in Venables, et al., (1978). When the children reached the age of 6 years aspects of their behaviour in a play situation were assessed by trained observers. Time spent watching and not interacting with other children was greatest in the skin conductance of non-responders. This aspect play behaviour was not affected by nursery school experience and was reduced in the other groups. The effect of school experience on constructive play was greatest in the control group but it had non-significant effects on the other groups. The rate of positive interaction with other children or with a teacher was greatly increased in the long recovery group who had been exposed to the school experience. The importance of these findings lay in the demonstration that school exposure was having an interventive effect. That this lasts longer than 3 years is shown in later studies.

The first of these studies (Raine, et al., 2001) showed that those children who had experienced the nursery school environment of cognitive, physical, and nutritional enrichment showed increased autonomic and central nervous system arousal and orienting at age 11. A further study (Raine, Mellingen, Liu, Venables, and Mednick, 2003) showed that the effect of this enrichment was to lower levels of schizotypal and antisocial behaviour at ages 17 and 23. As this early environmental enrichment involved multiple factors (cognitive stimulation, physical exercise, nutrition) it is difficult to isolate which of these factors was responsible for the long-term effects observed. However, the fact that it was greater in those children who originally showed signs of malnutrition suggests that improved nutrition might be the active ingredient in the prevention program.

Other findings show that features of the children at age 3 are predictive of later behaviour. The well supported finding that low heart rate in children was associated with later aggression (Ortiz and Raine, 2004) was extended by showing that low heart rate at age 3 was predictive of aggression at age 11, and that this relationship held when several possible confounds such as body size, health and socioeconomic conditions were taken into account (Raine, Venables, and Mednick, 1997). This work was important in that it showed that the heart rate-aggression association holds even when starting from age 3. The earliest age at which this association had been shown previously was 11 years (Wadsworth, 1976).

One set of findings deals with early temperament. It was demonstrated that there was relative stability of disinhibited/inhibited temperament from age 3 to 8 to 11 years (Scerbo et al., 1995), and furthermore that disinhibited children at age 3 years showed lower resting heart rates, lower skin conductance levels, and shorter latency of the skin conductance orienting response relative to inhibited children (Scarpa et al. 1997). These finding confirm and extend similar findings in Western cultures. Another study (Raine, Reynolds, Venables, Mednick, and Farrington, 1998) showed that childhood aggression at age 11 was related to fearlessness, stimulation-seeking and large body size at age 3. Using the index of stimulation-seeking at age 3, another study showed that age 3 stimulation seekers scored 12.6 points higher on total IQ than low stimulation seekers (Raine, Reynolds, Venables, and Mednick, 2002). This latter finding suggest that early stimulation-seekers create for themselves an enriched environment over a sustained period of time which in turn enhances cognitive ability.

Moffitt (1993) has developed the concept of persistent (or life-course) versus non-persistent (or adolescent-limited) antisocial behaviour. This idea was used in the Mauritius project to isolate a group of individuals who showed persistent antisocial behaviour between 8 and 17 years. Whereas previous studies have shown verbal intelligence defects in adolescent antisocial individuals, it has not been known whether such a relationship would hold between intelligence measured at preschool level and later antisocial behaviour. Analysis of the data has shown that in contrast to expectations, persistently antisocial individuals had a lower *spatial* but not *verbal* IQ at age 3 (Raine, Yaralian, Reynolds, Venables, and Mednick, 2002).

The idea of persistent deviant behaviour used in the previous study was applied in another where high scores on schizotypy scales at both 17 and 23 years were used to isolate a group of subjects. It was found that these subjects exhibited at both age 3 and at age 11 increased arousal and orienting in comparison to a control group (Raine, Venables, Mednick, and Mellingen, 2002).

Another precursor of antisocial/aggressive behaviour at ages 8, 11 and 17 years was found to be the nutritional state of the subject at age 3. A dose-response relationship was shown between the degree of malnutrition and degree of externalizing (aggression and conduct disorder) behaviour at ages 8 and 17 (Liu et al., 2004). Malnutrition at this age was also found to result in poorer cognitive functioning at ages 3 and 11 years (Liu et al., 2003), and low IQ was found to moderate the malnutrition–antisocial behaviour relationship. This finding supports a model that malnutrition results in low IQ which in turn results in externalizing behaviour problems.

By chance, some of the participants in the study were in utero at the time of the 1968-72 Hong Kong/A2 influenza virus epidemic when it reached Mauritius in January 1970. The opportunity was taken to examine, in a non-Western context, the association that had been shown between maternal exposure to the influenza virus and the development of schizophrenia in the offspring (McGrath and Castle, 1995). It was shown (Venables, 1996; Venables, 1997) that those children whose mothers were exposed to the virus in the second trimester of pregnancy had elevated positive schizotypy scores and also showed electrodermal hyper-responsivity. This latter finding was replicated (Venables, 1998) in another sample of Mauritian subjects (Venables and Mitchell, 1996) whose mothers were exposed in the second trimester to the 1957 A2/Singapore influenza virus.

CONCLUSIONS

This series of studies indicates that conditions around the time of birth or in infancy influence the extent of disorder later in childhood or young adulthood. It is evident that there are too few schizophrenics in the sample to provide statistically viable evidence that the incidence of schizophrenia was modified by early exposure to nursery school. To that extent, the original aim of the study may not be forthcoming and that may be because the incidence of schizophrenia is lower in Mauritius than in Western societies (Murphy and Raman, 1971). However, the use of schizotypy as a substitute for clinical schizophrenia suggests that the findings are in accord with others in the current literature. The findings on antisocial behaviour do seem to be capable of being generalised elsewhere. One aspect that does require care in interpretation are findings which depend on assessment of verbal ability in what is a bilingual and in some instances a quadrilingual society.

Methodological lessons which can be learnt from the study are that data collection methods which take a great time in preliminary processing before producing numbers for use in analyses need to be minimized. The psychophysiological data now being collected (2001-present) involve the use of advanced computer programs enabling the data obtained to be immediately usable, thus obviating the difficulties occurring in the earlier phases of the project. Even so, a study such as this yields much more data than can be analyzed in the course of one cycle of grant support. Thus it is suggested that grant-giving organizations give thought to the funding of analyses of data already collected in longitudinal studies such as this in order that the value of linking data collected over time is not lost. There is certainly sufficient data available from this project to provide material for many more analyses than are likely to be conducted using currently available resources.

FUTURE GOALS

It is important to capitalise on the fact that the study has generated a very large database covering over 30 years of material. In particular, this enables work on intergenerational transfer of characteristics to be mounted. The recent introduction of an MRI facility in Mauritius, to which the project may have access, could enable us to study whether the improvements in behaviour brought about by nursery school exposure are accompanied by alterations in brain structure, and whether such changes are associated with reductions in psychopathology. We also hope that it will be possible to conduct a study to isolate which elements of nursery school exposure (improved nutrition, physical activity, or cognitive enrichment) are responsible for the results which have been obtained to date.

REFERENCES

Achenbach, T.M., and Edelbrock, C.S. (1983). *Manual for the Child Behavior Checklist and Revised Behavior Profile*. Burlington, VT: University of Vermont , Department of Psychiatry.

Asarnow, R.F., Nuechterlein, K.H., and Marder, S.R. (1983). Span of apprehension performance, neuropsychological functioning, and indices of psychosis-proneness. *Journal of Nervous and Mental Disorders*, *171*(11), 662-9.

Barker, A.J. (1996). *Slavery and anti-slavery in Mauritius*. Basingstoke: Macmillan Press Ltd.

Bartfai, A., Levander, S.E., Nyback, H., Berggren, B.-M., and Schalling, D. (1985). Smooth pursuit eye tracking, neuropsychological test performance and computed tomography in schizophrenia. *Psychiatry Research, 15*, 49-62.

Belmont, R. (1979). *The Belmont Report: Ethical Principles and Guidelines for the Protection of Human Subjects of Biomedical and Behavioral Research.* US Dept of Health and Human Services.

Boehm, A. (1986). Boehm Test of Basic Concepts-Preschool version. San Antonio: Psychological Corporation.

Bowman, L.W. (1991). *Mauritius: Democracy and development in the Indian Ocean.* London: Westview Press.

Cannon, T.D., Mednick, S.A., and Parnas, J. (1990). Antecedents of predominantly negative- and predominantly positive- symptom schizophrenia in a high -risk population. *Archives of General Psychiatry, 47*, 622-632.

Cornblatt, B.A., Lenzenweger, M.F., and Erlenmeyer-Kimling, L. (1989). The Continuous Performance Test, Identical Pairs Version: II. Contrasting attentional profiles in schizophrenic and depressed patients. *Psychiatry Research, 29*, 65-85.

Curran, W.J. (1974). Ethical and legal considerations in high risk studies of schizophrenia. *Schizophrenia Bulletin*(10), 74-92.

Curran, W.J. (1977). Civil-liberties-activated controls in psychiatric research. *Primary prevention of schizophrenia in high-risk groups: Report of a working group: Copenhagen June 1975.* (pp. 64-69). Copenhagen: WHO regional office for Europe.

Dworkin, B.R., and Miller, N.E. (1974). Visceral learning: recent difficulties with curarized rats and significant problems for human research. In P.A. Obrist, A.H. Black, J. Brener, and L.V. DiCara (Eds.), *Cardiovascular psychophysiology* (pp. 312-331). Chicago: Aldine.

Filliot, J.M. (1974). *La traite des esclaves vers mascareignes au XVIII siecle.* Paris: ORSTOM.

Gruzelier, J.H., and Venables, P.H. (1972). Skin conductance orienting activity in a heterogenous sample of schizophrenics. *Journal of Nervous and Mental Disease, 155*, 277-287.

Lebedev, B.A. (1969). Letter informing Dr Schulsinger of award of $4000 for the start of the Mauritius Project. Geneva: WHO.

Levander, S. (1987). Evaluation of cogntive impairment using a computerised neuropsychological test battery. *Nordic Journal of Psychology, 41*, 417-422.

Liu, J., Raine, A., Venables, P.H., Dalais, C. and Mednick, S.A. (2003). Malnutrition at age 3 years and lower cognitive ability at age 11: Independence from social adversity. *Archives of Pediatric and Adolescent Medicine 157* 593-600.

Liu, J., Raine, A., Venables, P.H., Dalais, C., and Mednick, S.A. (2004). Malnutrition at age 3 predisposes externalizing behavior problems at ages 8, 11 and 17. *American Journal of Psychiatry 161* 2005-2013.

McGrath, J., and Castle, D. (1995). Does influenza cause schizophrenia? - A 5 Year Review. *Australian and New Zealand Journal of Psychiatry, 29*(1), 23-31.

Mednick, S.A. (1958). A learning theory approach to research in schizophrenia. *Psychological Bulletin, 55*, 316-327.

Mednick, S.A. (1967). The children of schizophrenics: Serious difficulties in current research methodologies which suggest the use of the "High-risk-group" method. In J. Romano (Ed.), *Origins of schizophrenia* (pp. 179-200). Amsterdam: Excerpta Medica.

Mednick, S.A. (1970). Breakdown in individuals at high risk for schizophrenia: possible predispositional perinatal factors. *Mental Hygiene, 54*, 50-63.

Mednick, S.A., and Schulsinger, F. (1968). Some pre-morbid characteristics related to breakdown in children with schizophrenic mothers. In D. Rosenthal and S.S. Kety (Eds.), *The transmission of schizophrenia* (pp. 267-291). New York: Pergamon Press.

Mednick, S.A., Venables, P.H., Schulsinger, F., Dalais, C., and Van Dusen, K. (1984). A controlled study of primary prevention: the Mauritius Project. In N.F. Watt, E.J. Anthony, L.C. Wynne, and J.E. Rolf (Eds.), *Children at risk for schizophrenia: A longitudinal perspective.* (pp. 71-78). Cambridge: Cambridge University Press.

Moffitt, T.E. (1990). The neuropsychology of delinquency: A critical review. In M. Tonry and M. Morris (Eds.), *Crime and Justice: A review of research* (pp. 99-169). Chicago: University of Chicage Press.

Moffitt, T.E. (1993). Adolescence limited and life course persistent antisocial behavior: A developmental taxonomy. *Psychological Review, 100*, 674-701.

Murphy, H.M.B., and Raman, A.C. (1971). The chronicity of schizophrenia in indigenous tropical peoples: Results of a twelve-year follow-up survey in Mauritius. *British Journal of Psychiatry, 118*, 489-97.

Murphy, J.M. (1994). Anthropology and psychiatric epidemiology. *Acta Psychiatrica Scandinavica, 90* (Suppl. 385), 48-57.

Nuremberg, (1949). *Directives for Human Experimentation. Trials of War Criminals before the Nuremberg Military Tribunals under Control Council Law.* US Goverment Printing Office.

Ortiz, J. and Raine, A. (2004) Heart rate level and antisocial behavior in children and adolescents: A meta-analysis. *Journal of the American Academy of Child and Adolescent Psychiatry, 43,* 154-162

Quay, H.C., and Peterson, D.R. (1987). *Manual for the Revised Behavior Problem Checklist.* Coral Gables, Miami: H. C. Quay and D.R.Peterson.

Raine, A. (1991). The SPQ: A scale for the assessment of Schizotypal Personality Disorder based on DSM-III-R criteria. *Schizophrenia Bulletin, 17*, 555-564.

Raine, A. (1993). *The Psychopathology of Crime*. San Diego: Academic Press.

Raine, A., Brennan, P., and Mednick, S.A. (1994). Birth complications combined with early maternal rejection at age 1 year predispose to violent crime at age 18 years. *Archives of General Psychiatry, 51*, 984-988.

Raine, A., Venables, P.H., and Mednick, S.A. (1997). Low resting heart rate at age 3 years predisposes to aggression at age 11 years: Evidence from the Mauritius Child Health Project. *Journal of the Academy of Child and Adolescent Psychiatry, 36*, 1457-1464.

Raine, A., Reynolds, C., Venables, P.H., Mednick, S.A., and Farrington, D.P. (1998). Fearlessness, stimulation-seeking and large body size at age 3 years as early predispositions to childhood aggression at age 11 years. *Archives of General Psychiatry, 55*, 745-751.

Raine, A., Mellingen, K., Liu, J., Venables, P., and Mednick, S.A. (2003). Effects of environmental enrichment at ages 3-5 years on schizotypal personality and antisocial behavior at ages 17 and 23 years. *Am J Psychiatry, 160*, 1627-35.

Raine, A., Reynolds, C., Venables, P.H., and Mednick, S.A. (2002). Stimulation seeking and intelligence: A prospective longitudinal study. *Journal of Personality and Social Psychology*, *82*, 663-674.

Raine, A., Yaralian, P.S., Reynolds, C., Venables, P.H., and Mednick, S.A. (2002). Spatial but not verbal cognitive defects at age 3 in persistently antisocial individuals. *Developmental Psychopathology*, *14*, 25-44.

Raine, A., and Venables, P.H. (1984). Electrodermal non-responding, antisocial behaviour and schizoid tendencies in adolescents. *Psychophysiology*, *21*, 424-433.

Raine, A., Venables, P.H., Dalais, C., Mellingen, K., Reynolds, C., and Mednick, S.A. (2001). Early educational and health enrichment at age 3-5 years is associated with increased autonomic and central nervous system arousal and orienting at age 11 years: Evidence from the Mauritius Child Health Project. *Psychophysiology*, *38*, 254-266.

Raine, A., Venables, P.H., and Mednick, S.A. (1997). Low resting heart rate at age 3 years predisposes to aggression at age 11 years: Evidence from the Mauritius Child Health Project. *Journal of the Academy of Child and Adolescent Psychiatry*, *36*, 1457-1464.

Raine, A., Venables, P.H., Mednick, S.A., and Mellingen, K. (2002). Increased psychophysiological arousal and orienting at ages 3 and 11 years in persistently schizotypal adults. *Schizophrenia Research*, *38*, 254-266.

Reynolds, C.A., Raine, A., Mellingen, K., Venables, P.H., and Mednick, S.A. (2000). Three factor model of schizoptypal personality: Invariance across culture, gender, religious affiliation, family adversity and psychpathology. *Schizophrenia Bulletin*, *26*, 603-618.

Rosenthal, D. (1967). An historical and methodological review of genetic studies of schizophrenia. In J. Romano (Ed.), *The Origins of Schizophrenia* (pp. 15-16). Amsterdam: Excerpta Medica Foundation.

Rutter, M. (1967). A children's behaviour questionnaire for completion by teachers, preliminary findings. *Journal of Child Psychology and Psychiatry*, *8*, 1-11.

Scarpa, A., Raine, A, Venables, P.H. and Mednick, S.A. (1997). Heart rate and skin conductance in behaviorally inhibited Mauritian children. *Journal of Abnormal Psychology, 106,* 182-190.

Scerbo, A, Raine, A., Venables, P.H, and Mednick, S.A. (1995). The stability of inhibited / uninhibited temperament from ages 3 to 11 years in Mauritian children. Journal of Abnormal Child Psychology, 23, 607-618.

Siddle, D.A.T., Mednick, S.A., Nicol, A.R., and Foggitt, R.H. (1976). Skin conductance recovery in antisocial adolescents. *British Journal of Social and Clinical Psychology*, *15*, 425-428.

Venables, P.H. (1978). Psychophysiology and psychometrics. *Psychophysiology*, *15*(4), 302-315.

Venables, P.H. (1980). Autonomic reactivity. In M. Rutter (Ed.), *Scientific foundations of developmental psychiatry* (pp. 165-176). London: Heinemann.

Venables, P.H. (1990). The measurement of schizotypy in Mauritius. *Personality and Individual Differences*, *11*(9), 965-971.

Venables, P.H. (1993). Electrodermal indices as markers for the development of schizophrenia. In J. C. Roy, W. Boucsein, D. C. Fowles, and J. H. Gruzelier (Eds.), *Progress in electrodermal research* (pp. 187-205). New York: Plenum Press.

Venables, P.H. (1996). Schizotypy and maternal exposure to influenza and to cold temperature: The Mauritius study. *Journal of Abnormal Psychology*, *105*, 53-60.

Venables, P.H. (1997). Maternal exposure to influenza and cold in pregnancy, and electrodermal activity in offspring: The Mauritius study. *Psychophysiology*, *34*, 427-435.

Venables, P.H. (1998). Maternal exposure to influenza in pregnancy and electrodermal activity in offspring: A further study from Mauritius. *Psychophysiology*, *35*, 438-442.

Venables, P.H., and Christie, M.J. (1980). Electrodermal activity. In I. Martin and P.H. Venables (Eds.), *Techniques in Psychophysiology* (pp. 3-67). Chichester: John Wiley and Sons.

Venables, P.H., Mednick, S.A., Schulsinger, F., Raman, A.C., Bell, B., Dalais, J.C., and Fletcher, R.P. (1978). Screening for risk of mental illness. In G. Serban (Ed.), *Cognitive defects in the development of mental illness* (pp. 273-303). New York: Brunner/Mazel.

Venables, P.H., and Mitchell, D.A. (1996). The effect of age, sex and time of testing on skin conductance activity. *Biological Psychology*, *43*, 87-101.

Venables, P.H., Wilkins, S., Mitchell, D.A., Raine, A., and Bailes, K. (1990). A scale for the measurement of schizotypy. *Personality and Individual Differences*, *11*, 481-495.

Wadsworth, M.E.J. (1976). Delinquency, pulse rates and early emotional deprivation. *British Journal of Criminology*, *16*, 245-256.

WHO (1968). *Neurophysiological and Behavioural Research in Psychiatry* (381). World Health Organisation.

WHO (1977). *Primary prevention of schizophrenia in high-risk groups Report of a working group 9-12 June 1975*. Copenhagen: WHO Regional Office for Europe.

World, Medical Association. (1964). *Declaration of Helsinki, Recommendations guiding doctors in clinical research Adopted by the 18th World Medical Assembly. Helsinki, Finland.*

World, Medical Association. (1975). *Declaration of Helsinki, Recommendations guiding medical doctors in biomedical research involving human subjects. Adopted by the 18th World Medical Assembly. Helsinki, Finland and as revised by the 29th World Medical Assembly, Tokyo, Japan, October 1975.*

World, Medical Association (1983). *Declaration of Helsinki, Recommendations guiding physicians in biomedical research involving human subjects. Adopted by the 18th World Medical Assembly. Helsinki, Finland. and amended by the 29th World Medical Assembly Tokyo, Japan, October 1975 and the 35th World Medical Assembly, Venice, Italy, October 1983.*

INDEX

A

B

C

D

E

F

G

H

I

O

P

R

S

T